Cognition, Computation, and Consciousness

Cognition, Computation, and Consciousness

Edited by

Masao Ito,
Institute of Physical and Chemical Research,
Wako, Saitama, Japan

Yasushi Miyashita,
Department of Physiology,
Medical School,
The University of Tokyo, Japan

and

Edmund T. Rolls
Department of Experimental Psychology,
University of Oxford

Oxford   New York   Tokyo
OXFORD UNIVERSITY PRESS
1997

Oxford University Press, Great Clarendon Street, Oxford OX2 6DP
Oxford New York
Athens Auckland Bangkok Bogota Bombay Buenos Aires
Calcutta Cape Town Dar es Salaam Delhi Florence Hong Kong
Istanbul Karachi Kuala Lumpur Madras Madrid Melbourne
Mexico City Nairobi Paris Singapore Taipei Tokyo Toronto
and associated companies in
Berlin Ibadan

Oxford is a trade mark of Oxford University Press

Published in the United States
by Oxford University Press Inc., New York

A catalogue record for this book is available from the British Library

Library of Congress Cataloging in Publication Data
*Cognition, computation, and consciousness / edited by Masao Ito,
Yasushi Miyashita, Edmund T. Rolls.*
Includes index.
*1. Consciousness. 2. Philosophy of mind. 3. Cognitive
neuroscience 4. Human information processing. I. Itō, Masao,
1928– . II. Miyashita, Y. (Yasushi), 1949– . III. Rolls,
Edmund T.*
BF311.C54872 1997   153–dc21   96-40441
ISBN 0 19 852414 5 (Hbk)

Typeset by Advance Typesetting Ltd, Oxfordshire

*Printed in Great Britain by Bookcraft (Bath) Ltd,
Midsomer Norton, Avon.*

Preface

The issue of consciousness has long been a major problem of philosophy and has been set apart from the mainstream of science. However, recent remarkable advances in three lines of studies, namely, **neuroscience, cognitive science**, and **computational science**, give us hope that consciousness will eventually be related to brain mechanisms by joint efforts of these three disciplines.

Neuroscience is primarily aimed at localizing brain structures responsible for mental activity and at investigating neural events going on in them. **Cognitive science** is concerned with principles governing mental activity, and **computational science** at computational capabilities of artificial networks and systems. These three disciplines have been developed individually by separate groups of researchers, but recently these are often combined to form new fields such as cognitive neuroscience and computational neuroscience. Considerable progress has already been noted in these fields in clarifying brain mechanisms underlying visual perception, motor control, learning and memory, and emotion.

However, we are still far from the goal of understanding brain mechanisms of awareness, volition, affect, language, thought, and consciousness, which characterize us humans. In order to advance our endeavour towards this goal, further integration of cognitive and computational neuroscience is necessary. This book describes such efforts originally presented in the Symposium on Cognition, Computation, and Consciousness held in the International Institute of Advanced Studies, Kyoto, Japan, in 1994, and specially updated for this book.

The first section is concerned with philosophical approaches to consciousness. Many such approaches so far tried are surveyed, and the functionalism on which current cognitive and computational neuroscience are based is critically examined. One of the fundamental issues is that of subjective feeling or qualia—why it feels like something to be conscious.

The second section focuses on approaches to consciousness from cognitive neuroscience. One rich set of findings which helps to tease out different aspects of consciousness, and helps us to understand where these fit into brain functions, comes from patients with various types of neurological problems. Another set of findings comes from analysing brain activity in relation to such processes as imagery, and during conscious as compared to unconscious mental states, to help to define which brain processes are related to consciousness.

The third section deals with computational approaches to consciousness, for example how network processes such as coherence or attractor states are related to experienced phenomenology, and whether there is a certain type of computational processing that is especially difficult for the brain and that is related to explicit, conscious, control processing.

By showing how current cognitive and computational neurosciences converge towards the understanding of brain mechanisms of consciousness, this book will stand as a milestone in our everlasting efforts to reveal what we ourselves are.

The editors wish to record their appreciation to the International Institute for Advanced Studies, Kyoto, Japan for support for a scientific meeting on Cognition, Computation, and Consciousness, held in Kyoto. Those initial papers led to this book being written.

July 1996   M.I.
                                                                                                      Y.M.
                                                                                                   E.T.R.

Contents

Contributors

Masao Ito, Director-General, Frontier Research Program, Institute of Physical and Chemical Research (RIKEN), Wako, Saitama 351-01, JAPAN

Yasushi Miyashita, Department of Physiology, School of Medicine, University of Tokyo, 7-3-1, Hongo, Bunkyo-ku, Tokyo 113, JAPAN

Edmund T. Rolls, Department of Experimental Psychology, University of Oxford, South Parks Road, Oxford OX1 3UD, UK

Horace Barlow, The Physiological Laboratory, University of Cambridge, Downing Street, Cambridge CB2 3EG, UK

Ursula Bellugi, Director, Laboratory for Cognitive Neuroscience, The Salk Institute for Biological Studies, 10010 N. Torrey Pines Road, La Jolla, CA 92037, USA

Jack D. Cowan, Department of Mathematics, 5734 S University Avenue, University of Chicago, Chicago, IL 60637, USA

Daniel C. Dennett, Center for Cognitive Studies, Tufts University, Medford, MA, USA

Owen Flanagan, Department of Philosophy, West Duke Building, Duke University, Durham, NC 27708, USA

Michael S. Gazzaniga, Program in Cognitive Neuroscience, 6162 Silsby Hall, Dartmouth College, Hanover, New Hampshire 03755-3547, USA

R. Lauro-Grotto, SISSA-Biofisica, Via Beirut, 2–4, 34013 Trieste, ITALY

Güven Güzeldere, Department of Philosophy, West Duke Building, Duke University, Durham, NC 27708, USA

Mitsuo Kawato, ATR Human Information Processing, Research Laboratories, Hikaridai 2-2, Seika-cho, Soraku-gun, Kyoto 619-02, JAPAN

Edward S. Klima, Laboratory for Cognitive Neuroscience, The Salk Institute for Biological Studies, 10010 N. Torrey Pines Road, La Jolla, CA 92037, USA

Christoph von der Malsburg, Institut für Neuroinformatik, Ruhr-Universität Bochum, Bochum, GERMANY

Junichi Murata, Department of History and Philosophy of Science, University of Tokyo, 3-8-1 Komaba, Meguro-ku, Tokyo 153, JAPAN

Marcus E. Raichle, Washington University School of Medicine, Departments of Neurology and Radiology, Campus Box 8225, 4525 Scott Avenue East Building, St Louis, MO 63110, USA

S. Reich, Depto de Fisica, Lab. Tandar, Cnea, Buenos Aires, ARGENTINA

Hirotaka Tanabe, Department of Neuropsychiatry, Ehime University School of Medicine, Shitsukawa, Shigenobu-cho, Onsen-gun, Ehime 791-02, JAPAN

Miguel A. Virasoro, International Centre for Theoretical Physics, PO Box 586, 34100 Trieste, Italy [formerly Dipartimento di Fisica, Università di Roma 'La Sapienza', INFN Sezione di Roma 1, Roma, ITALY]

Atsushi Yamadori, Tohoku University, Graduate School of Medicine, Division of Disability Science, 2-1 Seiryo-machi, Aoba-ku, Sendai 980-77, JAPAN

Part I
Philosophical approaches

1

Consciousness: a philosophical tour

OWEN FLANAGAN AND GÜVEN GÜZELDERE

Introduction

The aim of this chapter is to provide an overview of the main philosophical positions on consciousness. The main focus will be on the ontological question. Ontology is the study of the way things are, the study of the nature of things. With respect to consciousness the ontological questions are what is its nature and how does it fit into the overall fabric of the universe. Answers to questions such as these are philosophical, but they do not come only from philosophers. Philosophy is continuous with science in two senses. Philosophical questions about the nature of things have been best addressed by thinkers, both philosophers and scientists, who pay attention to what the most relevant sciences say about the phenomena in question. Furthermore, scientific theories inevitably assume certain broad philosophical positions. Some world-class neuroscientists in the twentieth century have thought that the mind is the brain and thus that neuroscience holds the key to understanding mental life, while others have embraced dualism, the view that the conscious mind is a phenomenon of an altogether different kind than that countenanced by brain science.

Naturalism and non-naturalism

The most fundamental ontological question is this: why is there something rather than nothing? This almost everyone will admit is a perplexing question. Once we admit that there is something rather than nothing, even if we cannot explain why, other, potentially more tractable, questions arise: given that there is something rather than nothing, what is it that there is? What in the most general terms comprises reality? Why is some of the stuff that exists alive, and why is some of the live stuff conscious? These are among the basic ontological questions.

Naturalism is the view that what there is, and all there is, is natural, or physical, or material stuff. This, of course, is more of a motto or slogan than an analysis, since it is silent about what counts as natural, or physical, or material. The standard move here is to say that what is natural is whatever the physical sciences end up telling us exists, whatever the physical sciences end up being ontologically committed to as they proceed in the project of understanding the nature of things. For such reasons, naturalism is also sometimes called physicalism or materialism.

Non-naturalism comes in several versions. The version relevant for present purposes says that in addition to the material world there is an immaterial world. Physical science will suffice to teach us about the nature of the material world. But metaphysics (that which goes beyond physics) will be required to explain the nature of the immaterial world.

With respect to the nature of persons, the naturalist says that we are material beings living in a material world. The mind is the brain; mental events are brain events. The non-naturalist says that persons have an immaterial part, typically their souls or minds. The mind is not the brain, mental events are not brain events. Again, these are slogans. But they serve to capture the spirit of the position.

Consciousness and mind

Some philosophers equate the concept of mind with the concept of consciousness. Others, mostly contemporary thinkers, think that consciousness is one among many faculties of mind or, more plausibly, that the set of mental events is larger than and includes the set of conscious mental events.

According to the first view, a mind is necessarily a conscious mind. All mental events necessarily have the property of being conscious. It is fair to credit Descartes, the great seventeenth century philosopher, mathematician, and scientist, with the view that mental events are necessarily conscious and thus that there are no non-conscious mental events. 'As to the fact that there can be nothing in the mind, in so far as it is a thinking thing, of which it is not aware, this seems to me to be self-evident.' (Descartes 1993, p. 171 (fourth set of replies to Arnaud).)

John Locke, despite being engaged in a controversy with the Cartesians over innate knowledge, nonetheless agreed with Descartes and his followers that all mental events were conscious. In 1690 Locke wrote: 'thinking consists in being conscious that one thinks', and 'the idea of thinking in the absence of consciousness is as unintelligible as the idea of a body which is extended without having parts' (Locke 1959, Book 2, Chapter 1, p. 138).

According to the second view, there are non-conscious mental events. Freud canonized this idea. Indeed, until the time of Freud there was no widely shared theoretical framework in which to reject the Cartesian idea of equating the mind with whatever lay within the scope of one's consciousness. But the basic insight that mental events need not necessarily be conscious is available in the writings of Leibniz. Leibniz, in a series of responses to Locke written between 1703 and 1705, anticipated some important developments in psychology two centuries ahead of their time, especially those with regard to the nature and role of the unconscious:

[T]here are a thousand indications which lead us to think that there are at every moment numberless *perceptions* in us, but without apperception and without reflection.... In a word, *insensible* [unconscious] *perceptions* are of as great use in psychology as insensible corpuscles are in physics, and it is equally as unreasonable to reject the one as the other under the pretext that they are beyond the reach of our senses. (Leibniz 1951, pp. 374–8.)

Now we have not only the dynamic unconscious of Freud but also the information-processing unconscious of cognitive psychology and even the neurobiological unconscious. If one thinks that any of these systems exists, are mental, and are non-conscious, then the concept of mind includes as a subset the conscious mind but is not equivalent to it. In this way questions about mind and consciousness come apart. The relationship of the conscious mind and the body may require a different analysis than the relationship of the non-conscious mind and the body. And the relationship between non-conscious mental events and conscious mental events may require yet a third analysis.

Some distinguished contemporary philosophers reject the picture of mental activity as including both conscious and non-conscious events. John Searle (1992) and Galen Strawson (1994) argue that all mental events are conscious (or potentially conscious). According to both Searle and Strawson it is a misleading linguistic courtesy to extend the tribute of 'mental' to non-conscious information-processing states or to neural events that lack the property of being conscious.

Consciousness and intelligence

So far we have seen that according to many but not all contemporary philosophers, the concepts of 'mind' and 'consciousness' are not equivalent. The same is true for the concepts of 'consciousness' and 'intelligence'. Without defining either term— 'consciousness' or 'intelligence'—we can see some reasons for keeping the problem of the nature of consciousness separate from the problem of the nature of intelligence. This is true even though the normal use of our conscious minds may be to guide our actions rationally and intelligently. The reason is this: there are computational systems that display signs of intelligence—they play world-class chess and prove theorems in mathematics, for example. No one thinks that such systems are conscious. But they display flexible, novel, unpredictable behaviour just as humans faced by similar problems do.

Alan Turing, in a famous paper written in 1950, suggested interpreting the question: 'can machines think?' as equivalent to the question 'can a machine successfully mimic human behaviour?' (Turing 1964). If it can, we should say it thinks, that it is intelligent.

Is such a machine a *conscious* thinking thing? The answer has only become obvious recently, and the answer is 'no'. The question of consciousness was dropped by the wayside by the Turing test, the test designed to answer the question: can a machine think? Turing's insight, one might say, was to see that intelligent systems and conscious systems—smart or dumb—need not be equated.

To get a grip on Turing's insight one might imagine someone observing a world-class chess-playing computer asking the questions: how can it play so well?; how can a computer be so smart?; how can a mere machine display such intelligence? The answer would come from within a naturalistic ontology: the complex interplay between the software and hardware explains the intelligent behaviour displayed by the computer.

Complex adaptive systems such as computers, missiles, and robots perform all sorts of functions similar to those humans perform. Intelligence, reasoning according to the canons of deductive logic and probability theory, performing chemical assays, even 'visual' discrimination of objects and locomotion are capacities that most people can understand in naturalistic terms. What has historically been found puzzling is how *conscious* intelligence, *conscious* reasoning, *conscious* perception, *consciously* deciding to walk from home to the office can be explained in natural terms.

In 1898, physicist John Tyndall wrote: 'The passage from physics of the brain to the corresponding facts of consciousness is unthinkable.' (Tyndall 1898, p. 420.)

The difficulty of conceptualizing how physical brains can give rise to experience, how certain features of the objective world can give rise to subjectivity is the problem of 'the explanatory gap' (Levine 1983).

In his famous paper '*What is it like to be a bat?*' (1974), Thomas Nagel writes that 'Consciousness is what makes the mind–body problem really intractable.... Without consciousness the mind–body problem would be much less interesting. With consciousness it seems hopeless' (Nagel 1979, pp. 165–6).

One interpretation of Nagel's remark is this: if the mind–body problem is simply the problem of how physical systems such as ants, bats, and humans can intelligently get around, behave socially, and the like, then the resources of physics, neuroscience, and evolutionary biology can make visible the shape of a naturalistic solution. When consciousness, subjectivity, experience, qualia are added to the mix, confidence in the explanatory power of naturalism can easily wane. As Colin McGinn puts it: 'How can technicolour phenomenology arise from the soggy grey matter of brains?' (McGinn 1989).

The point is that problems of intelligence or rationality can, in principle, be prised apart from questions of conscious experience. David Chalmers calls the problems associated with intelligent information processing and action guidance 'the easy problems' in the sense that we can picture how the natural sciences can solve them. Consciousness is 'the hard problem'.

[E]ven when we have explained the performance of all the cognitive and behavioural functions in the vicinity of experience—perceptual discrimination, categorization, internal access, verbal report—there may still remain a further unanswered question: *Why is the performance of these functions accompanied by experience?* [...] This further question is the key question in the problem of consciousness. Why doesn't all this information-processing go on 'in the dark', free of any inner feel? (Chalmers 1995, p. 203.)

The official doctrine of the ghost in the machine

In the opening chapter of *The concept of mind*, entitled 'Descartes' Myth', Gilbert Ryle writes:

There is a doctrine about the nature and place of minds which is so prevalent among theorists and even among laymen that it deserves to be described as the official theory ... [T]he official doctrine, which hails chiefly from Descartes, is something like this ... every human being has both a body and a mind ... His body and his mind are ordinarily harnessed together, but after the death of the body his mind may continue to exist and function. (Ryle 1949, p. 11.)

This is the doctrine of 'the ghost in the machine'. My non-physical mind is harnessed to my body during my lifetime, but being non-physical it is of a different ontological kind than my body and can exist without it.

What could be at the basis of this powerful intuition that mind and body are ontologically different? For Descartes the intuition expressed a self-evident truth. Bodies are extended in space. Atoms, rocks, tables and chairs, and human bodies are extended in space. These are paradigm case physical objects. Thoughts are, or so it seemed to Descartes, unextended—paradigm case non-physical objects. Thoughts still *seem* this way to most people. Whether they *are* this way is a different question.

The official doctrine, despite its intuitive appeal, has some problems. How a non-physical mind which occupies no space can be 'in' anything is left unsolved, as is the problem of how the world can get information to the mind and how the mind can move the body. Descartes located the point of commerce between mind and body, between the ghost and the machine, in the pineal gland. But this tells us only where immaterial and material forces meet, it tells us nothing about *how* causation in either direction is possible (see Popper and Eccles (1977) for a recent attempt to spell out the details of a dualistic theory).

Parallelism and worries about interaction

The official doctrine of the ghost in the machine remains the most popular version of non-naturalism. Philosophers, among them Descartes' contemporaries and their followers, saw that the interaction problem among different ontological kinds was a *big problem.*

One strategy was to take the theological background theory available to all the modern philosophers working on the mind–body problem and have God more involved in making the mind–body relation intelligible. This Cartesian picture assumes an ontological continuum with God as pure mind, pure *res cogitans*, rocks as pure matter, pure *res extensa*, and humans, while embodied, as mixtures of thinking stuff and extended stuff. Once an omniscient God is part of the background, the Cartesian can say that God somehow solves the interaction problem. We may not understand how God solves the problem, but he, being God, does solve the problem.

Some other ontological non-naturalists or dualists seem to have thought that there were better ways for God to solve the mind–body problem than by allowing interaction among different ontological kinds. Leibniz' and Malebranche's different kinds of *parallelism* were similar ways of retaining dualism without the interaction problem, but at no small cost.

According to Leibniz, God (possibly at the creation of the universe) set a pre-established harmony between mind(s) and body(ies). When I decide to move my arm it moves, but not *because* my decision causes my arm to move but because God has willed that minds and bodies stay in synchrony. Malebranche's view (1638–1715) differed only in having God involved on each and every occasion in which a mental act and a bodily event needed to co-occur. While both views solve the interaction problem by denying that there is any interaction, they cause trouble for the concept of free will. According to Descartes, writing in 1649, one advantage of the official doctrine is the place it leaves for free will: 'But the will is so free in its nature, that it can never be constrained ... And the whole action of the soul consists in this, that solely because it desires something, it causes a little gland to which it is closely united to move in a way requisite to produce the effect which relates to this desire.' (Descartes 1968, p. 350.)

The Leibnizean has trouble with free will since he has us picture a world in which God sets all the clocks at creation. Malebranche's view has resources to avoid this problem (although these are not discussed by him). Since God is at all times involved in every life, he can wait until I make a decision and then (being God) simultaneously get my body to fall into line.

Without getting into unnecessary intricacies we can get a feel for parallelism from this quotation:

If we knew thoroughly the nervous system of Shakespeare, and as thoroughly all his environing conditions, we should be able to show why at a certain period of his life his hand came to trace on certain sheets of paper those crabbed little marks which we for shortness' sake call the manuscript of *Hamlet*. We should understand ... all this without in the slightest degree acknowledging the existence of thoughts in Shakespeare's mind. [B]ut, on the other hand, nothing in all this could prevent us from giving an equally complete account of ... Shakespeare's spiritual history, an account in which gleam of thought and emotion should find its place. The mind history would run alongside the body-history of each man, and each point in the one would correspond to, but not react upon, a point in the other. (James 1976, p. 136–7 quoting Clifford.)

Three points about parallelism. First, it might seem like a solution to the interaction problem, but it isn't since it still requires God, either at creation (Leibniz) or on each occasion (Malebranche), to get body and mind to be or appear to be coordinated. This is no less byzantine than Descartes' solution which just has God figure out how to make different ontological kinds interact.

Second, and on a different trajectory, the position contains an important insight which has contemporary relevance. Even today, philosophers, psychologists, neuroscientists, and laypeople will remind us that what we always and only seem to have when it comes to the consciousness–brain problem are correlations. A positron emission tomography (PET) scan shows Shakespeare's brain lighting up and he claims that he is thinking about writing a play called 'Hamlet'. What are we to say? That the lighted area *is* the thought of writing the play or that it is *correlated* with the thought (and the subsequent taking of pen in hand). The move from correlations to identities is a live ontological and methodological issue in contemporary mind science. We will return to this issue shortly.

Third, parallelism is instructive when thinking about reductionism or, more generally, the issue of levels of explanation. One might think that both stories, the mental story of Shakespeare's life and the bodily story of his life—or just take the Hamlet segment of both stories—are equally explanatory. But this is not obvious: the bodily story explains all his bodily movements but it does not explain the production of the meaningful play we call 'Hamlet', and this despite the fact that it does explain how certain marks on paper came to be. Nor, on the other side, does the mental story explain the bodily movements even though it explains the ideas behind the play.

Many contemporary naturalists, known as identity theorists, have taken the correlations identified by dualists of the parallelist persuasion and suggested that what we really have are identities. That is, Shakespeare's thoughts and intentions about the play are in fact identical to a certain set of events taking place in his nervous system. Just as water is H_2O and just as salt is NaCl, so too Shakespeare's plan to write Hamlet is some set $\{n_1, n_2...n_n\}$ of neural events. From a logical point of view, when we have strict identities we have synonyms, and synonyms can replace synonyms without any loss of meaning. Thus we should be able to tell the mental story of Shakespeare's writing of Hamlet in terms of the neural states which constitute the activity, which are, as it were, *the* very activity. This is reduction. But again, many baulk, since something seems to get lost in the reductive translation, namely, the *meaningful, intentional* properties of the activity.

Epiphenomenalism: Darwin, Freud, and cognitive science

If the Cartesian tradition inflates the importance of the conscious mind, the epiphenomenalist deflates its importance. Epiphenomenalism says that conscious events are 'mere' side-effects of the locus of the really interesting action. Epiphenomenalism comes in both a non-naturalist and naturalist version. The non-naturalist thinks that the conscious side-effects of bodily processes are non-physical; but they needn't worry those who are trying to develop a science of human behaviour since these non-physical side-effects do no significant causal work. The epiphenomenalist who is also a naturalist says that the side-effects are physical but causally inconsequential. William James quotes Thomas Huxley's startling version of epiphenomenalism.

The consciousness of brutes would appear to be related to the mechanism of their body simply as a collateral product of its working, and to be completely without any power of modifying that working, as the steam-whistle which accompanies the work of a locomotive engine is without influence upon its machinery. Their volition, if they have any, is an emotion *indicative* of physical changes, not a *cause* of such changes.... The soul stands to the body as the bell of a clock to the works, and consciousness answers to the sound which the bell gives out when it is struck ... to the best of my judgment, the argumentation which applies to brutes holds equally good of men.... We are conscious automata. (James 1976, p. 135.)

Why would anyone think that consciousness was a mere epiphenomenon, a side-effect of what the system is really doing? Part of the reason comes from evolutionary considerations. Nature abounds with creatures that are reproductively successful but are not conscious. The social insects are fantastically fit as measured by the criteria of evolutionary biology, but most philosophers and scientists do not attribute consciousness to the social insects. If consciousness is not necessary for reproductive success, then perhaps it is just an accidental and unnecessary appendage in creatures like us that are conscious.

Although James called epiphenomenalism 'an unwarrantable impertinence', claiming that '[i]t is inconceivable that consciousness should have *nothing to do* with a business which it so faithfully attends' (James 1976, pp. 140–1), epiphenomenalism has been taken more seriously in the twentieth century than at any previous time. One reason for the enhanced status of epiphenomenalism comes from the rejection of the Cartesian equation of mind with consciousness. Psychoanalysis, cognitive information-processing psychology, and neuroscience all attribute significant causal power to non-conscious mental events. This convergence of opinion about the causal efficacy of the non-conscious mind has reduced confidence in the causal powers of consciousness. Consciousness *seems* as if it runs the show, but then again conscious mental states are the only mental states that *seem* any way at all. This could easily have led us to overestimate dramatically the causal role of consciousness.

This issue of the causal role of conscious mental events in the overall economy of mental life remains very much a live issue.

Contemporary non-naturalists and agnostics

All the traditional views discussed so far continue to have advocates within the philosophical and scientific communities. Despite what many see as the ascendency of naturalistic or scientific views over more traditional theological views, *non-naturalism* continues to have articulate advocates. Some contemporary non-naturalists think, just as Descartes did, that consciousness can be made intelligible only if it is understood as a power of a non-physical substance or as composed of non-physical properties (Popper and Eccles 1977). Others think that we need to invoke a supernatural cause to explain why phenomenal qualia, the sensation of red or the scent of a rose, are correlated with specific types of brain states (Adams 1987; Swinburne 1984). Still others think that consciousness is miraculous. Like transubstantiation and the Trinity, it is not for us to fathom.

Thomas Nagel, more than anyone else, has articulated a certain uneasiness with both major ontological options. Call his position *principled agnosticism* (Nagel 1979, 1986). Naturalism is a position we do not understand, because we do not understand (at least at present) how the relation of consciousness and the brain can be made intelligible in naturalistic terms. We do not understand what it would mean to give an objective account of subjectivity. Since one should not believe a theory one does not even understand, agnosticism is the best policy.

One could add a further consideration in favour of agnosticism to which we alluded at the start. Namely, naturalism follows the lead of the physical sciences in determining what counts as natural. But the more science develops, the wilder and woollier the natural world seems. The science of Descartes' time took extension in space as definitive of matter. But today we countenance electrons as part of the material world and our best theories ask us to think of electrons as point-particles without extension. Developments such as these make the boundary between what is natural and what is non-natural increasingly obscure. Again, on the principle that one should not commit oneself to a position one does not understand, agnosticism is a position one might take for reasons of intellectual integrity.

New mysterianism

A somewhat different position is *anticonstructive naturalism*, noumenal naturalism, or *new mysterianism* (McGinn 1991). This is the view that naturalism is true. There are, in fact, properties of the brain that account naturalistically for consciousness. But we cannot grasp these properties or explain how consciousness depends on them. Consciousness is terminally mysterious to our minds but possibly not to minds of greater intelligence. It is terminally mysterious not because it is a non-natural phenomenon, and not because it is a miracle, but because an understanding of its nature is 'cognitively closed' to us. The problem of consciousness is a case where we know how to ask the question but lack the mental powers to find the answer.

To get a feel for this position imagine that the most intelligent creatures in the universe are the social insects. They cannot do science. Nonetheless, the laws of gravity, electromagnetism, relativity theory, quantum physics, and so on, hold in the world they live in. They are simply incapable of asking the questions that would lead them to discover the answers about the world that the world, as it were, exemplifies.

According to McGinn we are in a slightly better position: we can ask certain questions about how consciousness works, what it is, and so on. The social insects cannot even ask the questions. But, for this reason, our situation is considerably more frustrating. Since one doesn't miss what one doesn't want, the social insects are not frustrated by not understanding the nature of things. They have no desire to know. We can ask the questions and we want the answers, but at least with respect to the problem of consciousness we are simply not up to the task of answering the questions we ask—or so the new mysterians say.

Non-naturalists have their own reasons for thinking that the problem of consciousness will not yield to science. Anticonstructive naturalism, or new mysterianism, is the surprising view that consciousness, despite being a natural phenomenon, will *never* be understood. Whether its causal role is significant or not, it will not be understand. The 'old mysterians' were dualists who thought that consciousness cannot be understood scientifically because it operates according to non-natural principles and possesses non-natural properties. Consciousness might be understood in other ways, for example, by way of an elaborate metaphysical view about the nature of non-physical things and the ways in which they can interact with physical things, or by invoking supernatural phenomena (for some sophisticated contemporary defences of supernaturalism, see Swinburne 1984 and Adams 1987). Because it is somewhat counterintuitive it needs to be repeated that unlike the old mysterianism or contemporary supernaturalism, new mysterianism is a naturalistic position. Mind and consciousness exist, and they operate in accordance with natural principles and possess natural properties. But new mysterianism is a postmodern position designed to drive a railroad spike through the heart of scientism, the view that science will eventually explain whatever is natural.

Colin McGinn thinks that naturalism must be true. There is no other credible way to think about the relation of consciousness and the brain than as a natural relation. Nonetheless, he thinks, we will never be able to set out a credible constructive theory of that relation.

McGinn (1989, p. 349) writes, 'We have been trying for a long time to solve the mind–body problem. It has stubbornly resisted our best efforts. The mystery persists. I think the time has come to admit candidly that we cannot resolve the mystery'. McGinn (1989, p. 350) thinks that 'we know that brains are the *de facto* causal basis of consciousness', but 'we are cut off by our very cognitive constitution from achieving a conception of that natural property of the brain (or of consciousness) that accounts for the psychophysical link'.

Although the doctrine is mischievous, coming from a naturalist, it is a coherent position. There are limitative results in physics and mathematics, for example Heisenberg's Uncertainty Principle and Gödel's Incompleteness Theorem, that tell us of in-principle impossibilities faced by the physicist and mathematician. It is conceivable that just as we cannot know the position and momentum of an electron at one and the same time, or just as we can know that a certain sentence in arithmetic is true though it is in principle impossible for us to prove it within arithmetic, so we can know that consciousness is a natural phenomenon though it is in principle closed to us to know what sort of natural phenomenon it is.

It is important to see that new mysterianism is different from principled agnosticism. The agnostic thinks that we do not understand what form a naturalistic solution to the consciousness–brain problem would take, so we ought not to confidently claim that naturalism is true. What makes the principled agnostic position *agnostic* is that naturalism, materialism, and physicalism are not embraced because they are too poorly understood as ontological positions to commit oneself to; but neither is non-naturalism embraced nor is physicalism declared to be false. Nagel (1979, p. 176) writes: 'It would be a mistake to conclude that physicalism is false.... It would be truer to say physicalism is a position we cannot understand because we do not at present have any conception of how it might be true'.

In his book *The view from nowhere*, Nagel (1986, p. 47) puts it this way: 'We have at present no conception of how a single event or thing could have both physical and phenomenological aspects, or how if it did they might be related'. Because we do not understand what form a constructive naturalistic solution to the problem of consciousness would take, we cannot assign credibility to the claim that physicalism is true or to the claim that it is false. Intellectual honesty requires that we be agnostics.

Constructive naturalism

Finally, there is *constructive naturalism*. Against the anticonstructivist and principled agnostic, the constructive naturalist thinks that there is reason for optimism about our ability to understand that relation between consciousness and the brain—reason for hopefulness that we can make intelligible the existence of consciousness in the natural world. Constructive naturalists resist principled agnosticism because they think that the concept of 'the natural' can be filled out in a coherent way, and they resist anticonstructivist naturalism because they do not see the cognitive closure or epistemic impossibility that the new mysterian sees. After all, the main argument for the impossibility of solving the consciousness–brain problem comes from the failure to do so thus far. There is nothing like a formal Gödel-like result which proves that certain obstacles to knowledge in the domain of consciousness exist.

Recent work by David Chalmers (1996), Patricia S. Churchland (1986), Paul M. Churchland (1989, 1995), Daniel Dennett (1991), Fred Dretske (1995), Owen Flanagan (1991, 1992), Valerie Hardcastle (1995), William Lycan (1996), John Searle (1992), Galen Strawson (1994), and Michael Tye (1995) is in the constructive naturalist mode. All these philosophers take conscious experience seriously as a phenomenon or set of phenomena to be explained. And they all are optimistic that philosophy and science can build a credible theory of the nature and function of consciousness. There are many disagreements among these philosophers about a wide variety of issues. Where the views converge is on the ontological commitment to naturalism and optimism that consciousness can at least in principle be understood within such a framework.

The following three principles are not shared by all constructive naturalists but they provide a sense of the sort of commitments that might engender confidence that the problem of consciousness can be made to yield.

1. Principle of supervenience
(a) There exist emergent properties such as liquidity or solidity. Consciousness is in all likelihood an emergent property of complex states of the nervous system.
(b) A microlevel change need not produce a macrolevel change; for example, two H_2O molecules do not produce liquidity.
(c) But if there is a macrolevel change—if it gets wet in this vicinity—then there is (must have been) a microlevel change, that is, a sufficient number of H_2O molecules must have accumulated.
(d) Emergent, macrolevel properties, can causally interact with other emergent, macrolevel events or processes, as well as with (often because of) interactions with microlevel events and processes. So too can emergent conscious events and processes causally interact with conscious and non-conscious mental events (understood now as emergent neural events).

2. Principle of organismic integrity

That consciousness exists is amazing. But 'given that consciousness exists at all, there is no mystery in its being connected with what it is connected with' (Dewey 1922, p. 62). The basic idea behind this principle is to soothe, and then remove, certain troublesome intuitions about subjectivity. Given that emergent properties are possible, and that consciousness is probably such a property, then there should be no surprise in the fact that each person has their own and only their own experiences. It is because of the design of the nervous system. We are uniquely hooked up to ourselves. Given that there are experiences at all, it makes perfect evolutionary and physiological sense that I have my experiences and that you have yours.

3. Principle of biological naturalism

Consciousness … is a biological feature of human and certain animal brains. It is caused by neurobiological processes and is as much a part of the natural biological order as any other biological features such as photosynthesis, digestion, or mitosis. (Searle 1992, p. 90.)

Stated this way, the principle does not deny that consciousness could conceivably occur in systems with alternative biologies (non-carbon based ones, for example) or even in robots made of inorganic parts. It simply proposes that if you want to understand consciousness, study the systems that exist in our vicinity that are known to be conscious.

Conclusion

The aim of this chapter has been to provide an overview of the main ontological positions concerning the nature of consciousness, to provide a quick tour of the main live philosophical positions on the problem of consciousness. Although almost all philosophers and mind scientists are committed to one of the broad ontological positions discussed here, it would be premature to say that anyone knows which picture is 'the right one'. It is possible that the best ontological position has not yet been thought of. Happily, the area of consciousness research is at present engaging more good minds than at any point in human history. There is reason to be hopeful that philosophy and science will illuminate each other and take us in the direction of getting a better hold on the nature and function of consciousness. Time will tell.

References

Adams, R.M. (1987). Flavors, colors, and God. In *The virtue of faith and other essays in philosophical theology*. Oxford University Press, New York.

Chalmers, D. (1995). Facing up to the problem of consciousness. *Journal of Consciousness Studies*, **2**, 200–19.

Chalmers, D. (1996). *The conscious mind*. Oxford University Press, New York.

Churchland, P.M. (1989). *A neurocomputational perspective: the nature of mind and the structure of science*. MIT Press, Cambridge, MA.

Churchland, P.M. (1995). *The engine of reason: the seat of the soul*. MIT Press, Cambridge, MA.

Churchland, P.S. (1983). Consciousness: the transmutation of a concept. *Pacific Philosophical Quarterly*, **64**, 80–93.

Churchland, P.S. (1986). *Neurophilosophy*. MIT Press, Cambridge, MA.

Dennett, D. (1991). *Consciousness explained*. Little Brown, New York.

Descartes, R. (1968). *Passions of the soul*. In *The philosophical works of Descartes*, Vols 1 and 2 (ed. E. Haldane and G. Ross). Cambridge University Press.

Descartes, R. (1992). *The philosophical writings of Descartes*, Vol. 1 (trans. J. Cottingham, R. Stoothoff, and D. Murdoch). Cambridge University Press.

Descartes, R. (1993). *The philosophical writings of Descartes*, Vol. 2 (trans. J. Cottingham, R. Stoothoff, and D. Murdoch). Cambridge University Press.

Dewey, J. (1957). *Human nature and conduct*. Henry Hoet, New York.

Dretske, F. (1995). *Naturalizing the mind*. MIT Press, Cambridge, MA.

Flanagan, O. (1991). *The science of the mind*. MIT Press, Cambridge, MA.

Flanagan, O. (1992). *Consciousness reconsidered*. MIT Press, Cambridge, MA.

Hardcastle, V.G. (1989). *Locating consciousness*. Benjamins, Amsterdam.

James, W. (1976). *The principles of psychology*, Vols 1–3, written in 1890. Harvard University Press, Cambridge.

Leibniz, G.W. (1951). *Selections*. Charles Scribner's Sons, New York.

Levine, J. (1983). Materialism and qualia: the explanatory gap. *Pacific Philosophical Quarterly*, **64**, 257–72.

Locke, J. (1959). *An essay concerning human understanding*. Originally published in 1690, annotated by A.C. Fraser. Dover Publications, New York.

Lycan, W. (1996). *Consciousness and experience*. MIT Press, Cambridge, MA.

McGinn, C. (1989). Can we solve the mind–body problem? *Mind*, **98**, 349–66. Reprinted in McGinn 1991.

McGinn, C. (1991). *The problem of consciousness*. Blackwell, Oxford.

Nagel, T. (1979). What is it like to be a bat? In *Mortal Questions*. Cambridge University Press, Cambridge.

Nagel, T. (1986). *The view from nowhere*. Oxford University Press, New York.

Popper, K. and Eccles J. (1977). *The self and its brain*. Springer-Verlag, New York.

Ryle, G. (1949). *The concept of mind*. Hutchinson, London.

Searle, J. (1992). *The rediscovery of mind*. MIT, Cambridge.

Strawson, G. (1994). *Mental reality*. MIT, Cambridge.

Swinburne, R. (1984). Personal identity: the dualist theory. In *Personal identity* (ed. S. Shoemaker and R. Swinburne). Blackwell, Oxford.

Turing, A.M. (1964). Computing machinery and intelligence. In *Minds and machines* (ed. A.R. Anderson). Englewood Cliffs, NJ.

Tye, M. (1995). *Ten problems of consciousness*. MIT, Cambridge.

Tyndall, (1898). *Fragments of science*. Appleton, New York.

Appendix

In addition to the texts cited in the article, the following sources can serve as pointers to state-of-the-art consciousness research.

Anthologies

Block, N., Flanagan, O., and Güzeldere, G. (1997). *The nature of consciousness: philosophical and scientific debates*. MIT Press, Cambridge, MA.

Hameroff, S.R., Kaszniak, A.W., and Scott, A.C. (1996). *Towards a science of consciousness: the first Tucson discussions and debates*. MIT Press, Cambridge, MA.

Metzinger, T. (1995). *Conscious experience*. Paderborn: Schöningh / Imprint Academic.

Revonsuo, A. and Kamppinen, M. (1994). *Consciousness in philosophy and cognitive neuroscience*. L. Erlbaum, Hillsdale, NJ.

Davies, M. and Humphreys, G. (1993). *Consciousness: psychological and philosophical essays*. Basil Blackwell, Oxford, UK.

CIBA Foundation. (1993). *Experimental and theoretical studies of consciousness*. Wiley, Chichester, UK.

Journals

Journal of Consciousness Studies. Imprint Academic, Exeter, UK. [http://sol.zynet.co.uk/imprint/jcs.html]

Psyche: An Interdisciplinary Journal of Research on Consciousness. MIT Press, Cambridge, MA. [http://psyche.cs.monash.edu.au/]

Consciousness and Cognition. Academic Press, Orlando, FL.

Organizations and conferences

Association for the Scientific Study of Consciousness (ASSC). [http://www.phil.vt.edu/ASSC/]

Towards a Science of Consciousness (Tucson Conferences). [http://www/eu.arizona.edu/~uaextend/conferen/consc.html]

2

Consciousness in human and robot minds

DANIEL C. DENNETT

Good and bad grounds for scepticism

The best reason for believing that robots might some day become conscious is that we human beings are conscious, and we are a *sort* of robot ourselves. That is, we are extraordinarily complex, self-controlling, self-sustaining physical mechanisms, designed over the eons by natural selection, and operating according to the same well-understood principles that govern all the other physical processes in living things: digestive and metabolic processes, self-repair and reproductive processes, for instance. It may be wildly overambitious to suppose that human artificers can repeat Nature's triumph, with variations in material, form, and design process, but this is not a deep objection. It is not as if a conscious machine contradicted any fundamental laws of nature, the way a perpetual motion machine does. Still, many sceptics believe—or in any event want to believe—that it will never be done. I wouldn't wager against them, but my reasons for scepticism are mundane, economic reasons, not theoretical reasons.

Conscious robots probably will always simply cost too much to make. Nobody will ever synthesize a gall bladder out of atoms of the requisite elements, but I think it is uncontroversial that a gall bladder is nevertheless 'just' a stupendous assembly of such atoms. Might a conscious robot be 'just' a stupendous assembly of more elementary artefacts—silicon chips, wires, tiny motors, and cameras—or would any such assembly, of whatever size and sophistication, have to leave out some special ingredient that is requisite for consciousness?

Let us briefly survey a nested series of reasons someone might advance for the impossibility of a conscious robot:

1. Robots are purely material things, and consciousness requires immaterial mind-stuff. (Old-fashioned dualism.)

It continues to amaze me how attractive this position still is to many people. I would have thought a historical perspective alone would make this view seem ludicrous: over the centuries, every *other* phenomenon of initially 'supernatural' mysteriousness has succumbed to an uncontroversial explanation within the commodious folds of physical science. Thales, the pre-Socratic protoscientist, thought the loadstone had a soul, but we now know better; magnetism is one of the best understood of physical phenomena, strange though its manifestations are. The 'miracles' of life itself, and of reproduction, are now analysed into the well-known intricacies of molecular biology. Why should consciousness be any exception? Why should the brain be the only complex physical object in the universe to have an interface with another realm of being? Besides, the notorious problems with the supposed trans-actions at that dualistic interface are as good as a *reductio ad absurdum* of the view. The phenomena of consciousness are an admittedly dazzling lot, but I suspect that dualism would never be seriously considered if there was not such a strong under-current of desire to protect the mind from science, by supposing it composed of a stuff that is in principle uninvestigatable by the methods of the physical sciences.

But if you are willing to concede the hopelessness of dualism, and accept some version of materialism, you might still hold that:

2. Robots are inorganic (by definition), and consciousness can exist only in an organic brain.

Why might this be? Instead of just hooting this view off the stage as an embarrassing throwback to old-fashioned vitalism, we might pause to note that there is a respect-able, if not very interesting, way of defending this claim. Vitalism is deservedly dead; as biochemistry has shown in matchless detail, the powers of organic compounds are themselves all mechanistically reducible and hence mechanistically reproducible at one scale or another in alternative physical media. But it is conceivable, if unlikely, that the sheer speed and compactness of biochemically engineered processes in the brain are in fact unreproducible in other physical media (Dennett 1987). So there might be straightforward reasons of engineering that showed that any robot that could not make use of organic tissues of one sort or another within its fabric would be too ungainly to execute some task critical for consciousness. If making a con-scious robot were conceived of as a sort of sporting event—like the America's Cup —rather than a scientific endeavour, this could raise a curious conflict over the official rules. Team A wants to use artificially constructed organic polymer 'muscles' to move its robot's limbs, because otherwise the motor noise wreaks havoc with the robot's artificial ears. Should this be allowed? Is a robot with 'muscles' instead of motors a robot within the meaning of the act? If muscles are allowed, what about lining the robot's artificial retinas with genuine organic rods and cones instead of relying on relatively clumsy colour-TV technology?

I take it that no serious scientific or philosophical thesis links its fate to the fate of the proposition that a *protein-free* conscious robot can be made, for example. The standard understanding that a robot shall be made of metal, silicon chips, glass, plastic, rubber, and such, is an expression of the willingness of theorists to bet on a simplification of the issues: their conviction is that the crucial functions of intel-ligence can be achieved by one high-level simulation or another, so that it would be no undue hardship to restrict themselves to these materials, the readily available cost-effective ingredients in any case. But if somebody were to invent some sort of cheap artificial neural network fabric that could usefully be spliced into various tight corners in a robot's control system, the embarrassing fact that this fabric was made of organic molecules would not and should not dissuade serious robotics from using it—and simply taking on the burden of explaining to the uninitiated why this did not constitute 'cheating' in any important sense.

I have discovered that some people are attracted by a third reason for believing in the impossibility of conscious robots:

3. Robots are artefacts, and consciousness abhors an artefact; only something natural, born not manufactured, could exhibit genuine consciousness.

Once again, it is tempting to dismiss this claim with derision, and in some of its forms, derision is just what it deserves. Consider the general category of creed we might call *origin essentialism*: only wine made under the direction of the proprietors of Château Plonque counts as genuine Château Plonque; only a canvas every blotch on which was caused by the hand of Cezanne counts as a genuine Cezanne; only someone 'with Cherokee blood' can be a real Cherokee. There are perfectly respectable reasons, eminently defensible in a court of law, for maintaining such distinctions, so long as they are understood to be protections of rights growing out of historical processes. If they are interpreted, however, as indicators of 'intrinsic properties' that set their holders apart from their otherwise indistinguishable counterparts, they are pernicious nonsense. Let us dub *origin chauvinism* the category of view that holds out for some mystic difference (a difference of value, typically) due *simply* to such a fact about origin. Perfect imitation Château Plonque is exactly as good a wine as the real thing, counterfeit though it is, and the same holds for the fake Cezanne, if it is really indistinguishable by experts. And of course no person is intrinsically better or worse in any regard just for having or not having Cherokee (or Jewish, or African) 'blood'.

And to take a threadbare philosophical example, an atom-for-atom duplicate of a human being, an artefactual counterfeit of you, let us say, might not *legally* be you, and hence might not be entitled to your belongings, or deserve your punishments, but the suggestion that such a being would not be a feeling, conscious, alive *person* as genuine as any born of woman is preposterous nonsense, all the more deserving of our ridicule because if taken seriously it might seem to lend credibility to the racist drivel with which it shares a bogus 'intuition'.

If consciousness abhors an artefact, it cannot be because being born gives a complex of cells a property (aside from that historic property itself) that it could not otherwise have 'in principle'. There might, however, be a question of practicality. We have just seen how, as a matter of exigent practicality, it could turn out after all that organic materials were needed to make a conscious robot. For similar reasons, it could turn out that any conscious robot had to be, if not born, at least the beneficiary of a longish period of infancy. Making a fully-equipped conscious adult robot might just be too much work. It might be vastly easier to make an initially unconscious or non-conscious 'infant' robot and let it 'grow up' into consciousness, more or less the way we all do. This hunch is not the disreputable claim that a certain sort of historic process puts a mystic stamp of approval on its product, but the more interesting and plausible claim that a certain sort of process is the only practical way of designing all the things that need designing in a conscious being.

Such a claim is entirely reasonable. Compare it to the claim one might make about the creation of Steven Spielberg's film, *Schindler's List*: it could not have been created entirely by computer animation, without the filming of real live actors. This impossibility claim must be false 'in principle', since every frame of that film is nothing more than a matrix of grey-scale pixels of the sort that computer animation can manifestly create, at any level of detail or 'realism' you are willing to pay for. There is nothing mystical, however, about the claim that it would be practically impossible to render the nuances of that film by such a bizarre exercise of techno-logy. How much easier it is, practically, to put actors in the relevant circumstances, in a concrete simulation of the scenes one wishes to portray, and let them, via en-semble activity and re-activity, provide the information to the cameras that will then fill in all the pixels in each frame. This little exercise of the imagination helps to drive home just how much information there is in a 'realistic' film, but even a great film, such as *Schindler's List*, for all its complexity, is a simple, non-interactive artefact many orders of magnitude less complex than a conscious being.

When robot makers have claimed in the past that in principle they could construct 'by hand' a conscious robot, this was a hubristic overstatement analogous to what Walt Disney might once have proclaimed: that his studio of animators could create a film so realistic that no one would be able to tell that it was a cartoon, not a 'live action' film. What Disney couldn't do in fact, computer animators still cannot do, perhaps only for the time being. Robot makers, even with the latest high-tech inno-vations, also fall far short of their hubristic goals, now and for the foreseeable future. The comparison serves to expose the likely source of the outrage so many sceptics feel when they encounter the manifestos of the 'Artificial Intelligencia'. Anyone who seriously claimed that *Schindler's List* could in fact have been made by com-puter animation could be seen to betray an obscenely impoverished sense of what is conveyed in that film. An important element of the film's power is the fact that it *is* a film made by assembling human actors to portray those events, and that it is not actually the newsreel footage that its black-and-white format reminds you of. When one juxtaposes in one's imagination a sense of what the actors must have gone through to make the film with a sense of what the people who actually lived the events went through, this reflection sets up reverberations in one's thinking that draw attention to the deeper meanings of the film. Similarly, when robot enthusiasts proclaim the likelihood that they can simply *construct* a conscious robot, there is an understandable suspicion that they are simply betraying an infantile grasp of the subtleties of conscious life. (I hope I have put enough feeling into the condemnation to satisfy the sceptics.)

But however justified that might be in some instances as an *ad hominem* suspicion, it is simply irrelevant to the important theoretical issues. Perhaps no cartoon could be a great film, but they are certainly real films—and some are indeed good films; if the best the roboticists can hope for is the creation of some crude, cheesy, second-rate, artificial consciousness, they still win. Still, it is not a foregone conclusion that even this modest goal is reachable. If you want to have a defensible reason for claiming that no conscious robot will ever be created, you might want to settle for this:

4. Robots will always be much too simple to be conscious.

After all, a normal human being is composed of trillions of parts (if we descend to the level of the macromolecules), and many of these rival in complexity and design cunning the fanciest artefacts that have ever been created. We consist of billions of cells, and a single human cell contains within itself complex 'machinery' that is still well beyond the artefactual powers of engineers. We are composed of thousands of different kinds of cells, including thousands of different species of symbiont visitors, some of whom might be as important to our consciousness as others are to our ability to digest our food! If all that complexity was needed for consciousness to exist, then the task of making a single conscious robot would dwarf the entire scientific and engineering resources of the planet for millennia. And who would pay for it?

If no other reason can be found, this may do to ground your scepticism about conscious robots in your future, but one shortcoming of this last reason is that it is scientifically boring. If this is the only reason that there won't be conscious robots, then consciousness isn't that special, after all. Another shortcoming with this reason is that it is dubious on its face. Everywhere else we have looked, we have found higher-level commonalities of function that permit us to substitute relatively simple bits for fiendishly complicated bits. Artificial heart valves work really very well, but they are orders of magnitude simpler than organic heart valves, heart valves born of woman or sow, you might say. Artificial ears and eyes that will do a serviceable (if crude) job of substituting for lost perceptual organs are visible on the horizon, and anyone who doubts they are possible in principle is simply out of touch. Nobody ever said a prosthetic eye had to see as keenly, or focus as fast, or be as sensitive to colour gradations as a normal human (or other animal) eye in order to 'count' as an eye. If an eye, why not an optic nerve (or acceptable substitute thereof), and so forth, all the way in?

Some (Searle 1992; Mangan 1993) have supposed, most improbably, that this proposed regress would somewhere run into a non-fungible medium of conscious-ness, a part of the brain that could not be substituted on pain of death or zombiehood. Once the implications of that view are spelled out (Dennett 1993*a,b*), one can see that it is a non-starter. There is no reason at all to believe that any part of the brain is utterly irreplacable by a prosthesis, provided we allow that some crudity, some loss of function, is to be expected in most substitutions of the simple for the complex. An artificial brain is, on the face of it, as 'possible in principle' as an artificial heart, just much, much harder to make and hook up. Of course once we start letting crude forms of prosthetic consciousness—like crude forms of prosthetic vision or hearing—pass our litmus tests for consciousness (whichever tests we favour) the way is open for another boring debate, over whether the phenomena in question are too crude to count.

The Cog project: a humanoid robot

A much more interesting tack to explore, in my opinion, is simply to set out to make a robot that is theoretically interesting independent of the philosophical conundrum about whether it is conscious. Such a robot would have to perform a lot of the feats that we have typically associated with consciousness in the past, but we would not need to dwell on that issue from the outset. Maybe we could even learn something interesting about what the truly hard problems are without ever settling any of the issues about consciousness.

Such a project is now underway at MIT. Under the direction of Professors Rodney Brooks and Lynn Andrea Stein of the AI Lab, a group of bright, hard-working young graduate students are labouring as I write to create Cog, the most humanoid robot yet attempted, and I am happy to be a part of the Cog team. Cog is just about life-size—that is, about the size of a human adult. Cog has no legs, but lives bolted at the hips, you might say, to its stand. It has two human-length arms, however, with somewhat simple hands on the wrists. It can bend at the waist and swing its torso, and its head moves with three degrees of freedom just about the way yours does. It has two eyes, each equipped with both a foveal high-resolution vision area and a low-resolution wide-angle parafoveal vision area, and these eyes saccade at almost human speed. That is, the two eyes can complete approximately three fixations a second, while you and I can manage four or five. Your foveas are at the centre of your retinas, surrounded by the grainier low-resolution parafoveal areas; for reasons of engineering simplicity, Cog's eyes have their foveas mounted above their wide-angle vision areas.

This is typical of the sort of compromise that the Cog team is willing to make. It amounts to a wager that a vision system with the foveas moved out of the middle can still work well enough not to be debilitating, and the problems encountered will not be irrelevant to the problems encountered in normal human vision. After all, nature gives us examples of other eyes with different foveal arrangements. Eagles have three different foveas in each eye, for instance, and rabbit eyes are another story all together. Cog's eyes won't give it visual information exactly like that provided to human vision by human eyes (in fact, of course, it will be vastly degraded), but the wager is that this will be plenty to give Cog the opportunity to perform impressive feats of hand–eye co-ordination, identification, and search. At the outset, Cog will not have colour vision.

Since its eyes are video cameras mounted on delicate, fast-moving gimbals, it might be disastrous if Cog were inadvertently to punch itself in the eye, so part of the hard-wiring that must be provided in advance is an 'innate' if rudimentary 'pain' or 'alarm' system to serve roughly the same protective functions as the reflex eye-blink and pain-avoidance systems hard-wired into human infants.

Cog will not be an adult at first, in spite of its adult size. It is being designed to pass through an extended period of artificial infancy, during which it will have to learn from experience, experience it will gain in the rough-and-tumble environment of the real world. Like a human infant, however, it will need a great deal of protection at the outset, in spite of the fact that it will be equipped with many of the most crucial safety systems of a living being. It has limit switches, heat sensors, current sensors, strain gauges, and alarm signals in all the right places to prevent it from destroying its many motors and joints. It has enormous 'funny bones'—motors sticking out from its elbows in a risky way. These will be protected from harm not by being shielded in heavy armour, but by being equipped with patches of exquisitely sensitive piezoelectric membrane 'skin' which will trigger alarms when they make contact with anything. The goal is that Cog will quickly 'learn' to keep its funny bones from being bumped—if Cog cannot learn this in short order, it will have to have this high-priority policy hard-wired in. The same sensitive membranes will be used on its fingertips and elsewhere, and, like human tactile nerves, the 'meaning' of the signals sent along the attached wires will depend more on what the central control system 'makes of them' than on their 'intrinsic' characteristics. A gentle touch, signalling sought-for contact with an object to be grasped, will not differ, as an information packet, from a sharp pain, signalling a need for rapid countermeasures. It all depends on what the central system is designed to do with the packet, and this design is itself indefinitely revisable—something that can be adjusted either by Cog's own experience or by the tinkering of Cog's artificers.

One of its most interesting 'innate' endowments will be software for visual face recognition. Faces will 'pop out' from the background of other objects as items of special interest to Cog. It will further be innately designed to 'want' to keep its 'mother's' face in view, and to work hard to keep 'mother' from turning away. The role of mother has not yet been cast, but several of the graduate students have been tentatively tapped for this role. Unlike a human infant, of course, there is no reason why Cog can't have a whole team of mothers, each of whom is innately distinguished by Cog as a face to please if possible. Clearly, even if Cog really does have a *Lebenswelt*, it will not be the same as *ours*.

Decisions have not yet been reached about many of the candidates for hard-wiring or innate features. Anything that can learn must be initially equipped with a great deal of unlearned design. That is no longer an issue; no *tabula rasa* could ever be impressed with knowledge from experience. But it is also not much of an issue which features ought to be innately fixed, for there is a convenient trade-off. I haven't mentioned yet that Cog will actually be a multigenerational series of ever-improved models (if all goes well), but of course that is the way any complex artefact gets designed. Any feature that is not innately fixed at the outset, but does get itself designed into Cog's control system through learning, can then be lifted whole into Cog-II, as a new bit of innate endowment designed by Cog itself, or rather by Cog's history of interactions with its environment. So even in cases in which we have the best of reasons for thinking that human infants actually come innately equipped with pre-designed gear, we may choose to try to get Cog to learn the design in question, rather than be born with it. In some instances, this is laziness or opportunism—we don't really know what might work well, but maybe Cog can train itself up. This insouciance about the putative nature/nurture boundary is already a familiar attitude among neural net modellers, of course. Although Cog is not specifically intended to demonstrate any particular neural net thesis, it should come as no surprise that Cog's nervous system is a massively parallel architecture capable of simultaneously training up an indefinite number of special-purpose networks or circuits, under various regimes.

How plausible is the hope that Cog can retrace the steps of millions of years of evolution in a few months or years of laboratory exploration? Note first that what I have just described is a variety of Lamarckian inheritance that no organic lineage has been able to avail itself of. The acquired design innovations of Cog-I can be immediately transferred to Cog-II, a speed-up of evolution of tremendous, if incalculable, magnitude. Moreover, if you bear in mind that, unlike the natural case, there will be a team of overseers ready to make patches whenever obvious shortcomings reveal themselves, and to jog the systems out of ruts whenever they enter them, it is not so outrageous a hope, in our opinion. But then, we are all rather outrageous people.

One talent that we have hopes of teaching to Cog is a rudimentary capacity for human language. And here we run into the fabled innate language organ or Language Acquisition Device (LAD) made famous by Noam Chomsky. Is there going to be an attempt to build an innate LAD for our Cog? No. We are going to try to get Cog to build language the hard way, the way our ancestors must have done, over thousands of generations. Cog has ears (four, because it's easier to get good localization with four microphones than with carefully shaped ears like ours) and some special-purpose signal-analysing software is being developed to give Cog a fairly good chance of discriminating human speech sounds, and probably the capacity to distinguish different human voices. Cog must also have speech synthesis hardware and software, of course, but decisions have not yet been reached about the details. It is important to have Cog as well-equipped as possible for rich and natural interactions with human beings, for the team intends to take advantage of as much free labour as it can. Untrained people ought to be able to spend time—hours if they like, and we rather hope they do—trying to get Cog to learn this or that. Growing into an adult is a long, time-consuming business, and Cog—and the team that is building Cog—will need all the help it can get.

Obviously this will not work unless the team manages somehow to give Cog a motivational structure that can be at least dimly recognized, responded to, and exploited by naive observers. In short, Cog should be as human as possible in its wants and fears, likes and dislikes. If those anthropomorphic terms strike you as unwarranted, put them in scare-quotes or drop them altogether and replace them with tedious neologisms of your own choosing: Cog, you may prefer to say, must have *goal-registrations* and *preference-functions* that map in rough isomorphism to human desires. This is so for many reasons, of course. Cog won't work at all unless it has its act together in a daunting number of different regards. It must somehow delight in learning, abhor error, strive for novelty, recognize progress. It must be vigilant in some regards, curious in others, and deeply unwilling to engage in self-destructive activity. While we are at it, we might as well try to make it crave human praise and company, and even exhibit a sense of humour.

Let me switch abruptly from this heavily anthropomorphic language to a brief description of Cog's initial endowment of information-processing hardware. The computer-complex that has been built to serve as a development platform for Cog's artificial nervous system consists of four backplanes, each with 16 nodes; each node is basically a Mac-II computer—a 68332 processor with a megabyte of RAM. In other words, you can think of Cog's brain as roughly equivalent to 64 Mac-IIs yoked in a custom parallel architecture. Each node is itself a multiprocessor, and they all run a special version of parallel Lisp developed by Rodney Brooks, and called, simply, L. Each node has an interpreter for L in its ROM, so it can execute L files independently of every other node.

Each node has six assignable input–output (i–o) ports, in addition to the possibility of separate i–o to the motor boards directly controlling the various joints, as well as the all-important i–o to the experimenters' monitoring and control system, the Front End Processor or FEP (via another unit known as the Interfep). On a bank of separate monitors, one can see the current image in each camera (two foveas, two parafoveas), the activity in each of the many different visual processing areas, or the activities of any other nodes. Cog is thus equipped at birth with the equivalent of chronically implanted electrodes for each of its neurons; all its activities can be monitored in real time, recorded, and debugged. The FEP is itself a Macintosh computer in more conventional packaging. At startup, each node is awakened by an FEP call that commands it to load its appropriate files of L from a file server. These files configure it for whatever tasks it has currently been designed to execute. Thus the underlying hardware machine can be turned into any of a host of different virtual machines, thanks to the capacity of each node to run its current program. The nodes do not make further use of disk memory, however, during normal operation. They keep their transient memories locally, in their individual megabytes of RAM. In other words, Cog stores both its genetic endowment (the virtual machine) and its long-term memory on disk when it is shut down, but when it is powered on, it first configures itself and then stores all its short-term memory distributed one way or another among its 64 nodes.

The space of possible virtual machines made available and readily explorable by this underlying architecture is huge, of course, and it covers a volume in the space of all computations that has not yet been seriously explored by artificial intelligence researchers. Moreover, the space of possibilities it represents is manifestly much more realistic as a space to build brains in than is the space heretofore explored, either by the largely serial architectures of GOFAI ('Good Old Fashioned AI', Haugeland 1985), or by parallel architectures simulated by serial machines. Nevertheless, it is arguable that every one of the possible virtual machines executable by Cog is minute in comparison to a real human brain. In short, Cog has a tiny brain. There is a big wager being made: the parallelism made possible by this arrangement will be sufficient to provide real-time control of importantly humanoid activities occurring on a human time scale. If this proves to be too optimistic by as little as an order of magnitude, the whole project will be forlorn, and the motivating insight for the project is that by confronting and solving *actual, real time* problems of self-protection, hand–eye coordination, and interaction with other animate beings, Cog's artificers will discover the *sufficient* conditions for higher cognitive functions in general—and maybe even for a variety of consciousness that would satisfy the sceptics.

It is important to recognize that although the theoretical importance of having a body has been appreciated ever since Alan Turing (1950) drew specific attention to it in his classic paper, 'Computing machines and intelligence', within the field of Artificial Intelligence there has long been a contrary opinion that robotics is largely a waste of time, money, and effort. According to this view, whatever deep principles of organization make cognition possible can be as readily discovered in the more abstract realm of pure simulation, at a fraction of the cost. In many fields, this thrifty attitude has proven to be uncontroversial wisdom. No economists have asked for the funds to implement their computer models of markets and industries in tiny robotic Wall Streets or Detroits, and civil engineers have largely replaced their scale models of bridges and tunnels with computer models that can do a better job of simulating all the relevant conditions of load, stress, and strain. Closer to home, simulations of ingeniously oversimplified imaginary organisms foraging in imaginary environments, avoiding imaginary predators, and differentially produc- ing imaginary offspring are yielding important insights into the mechanisms of evolution and ecology in the new field of Artificial Life. So it is something of a surprise to find this AI group conceding, in effect, that there is indeed something to the sceptics' claim (e.g. Dreyfus and Dreyfus 1986) that genuine embodiment in a real world is crucial to consciousness. Not, I hasten to add, because genuine embodiment provides some special vital juice that mere virtual-world simulations cannot secrete, but for the more practical reason—or hunch—that unless you saddle yourself with all the problems of making a concrete agent take care of itself in the real world, you will tend to overlook, underestimate, or misconstrue the deepest problems of design.

Besides, as I have already noted, there is the hope that Cog will be able to design itself in large measure, learning from infancy, and building its own representation of its world in the terms that it innately understands. Nobody doubts that any agent capable of interacting intelligently with a human being on human terms must have access to literally millions if not billions of logically independent items of world knowledge. Either these must be hand-coded individually by human programmers— a tactic being pursued, notoriously, by Douglas Lenat and his CYC team in Dallas— or some way must be found for the artificial agent to learn its world knowledge from (real) interactions with the (real) world. The potential virtues of this shortcut have long been recognized within AI circles (e.g. Waltz 1988). The unanswered question is whether taking on the task of solving the grubby details of real-world robotics will actually permit one to finesse the task of hand-coding the world knowledge. Brooks, Stein and their team—myself included—are gambling that it will.

At this stage of the project, most of the problems being addressed would never arise in the realm of pure, disembodied AI. How many separate motors might be used for controlling each hand? They will have to be mounted somehow on the forearms.

Will there then be room to mount the motor boards directly on the arms, close to the joints they control, or would they get in the way? How much cabling can each arm carry before weariness or clumsiness overcome it? The arm joints have been built to be compliant—springy, like your own joints. This means that if Cog wants to do some fine-fingered manipulation, it will have to learn to 'burn' some of the degrees of freedom in its arm motion by temporarily bracing its elbows or wrists on a table or other convenient landmark, just as you would do. Such compliance is typical of the mixed bag of opportunities and problems created by real robotics. Another is the need for self-calibration or re-calibration in the eyes. If Cog's eyes jiggle away from their preset aim, thanks to the wear and tear of all that sudden saccading, there must be ways for Cog to compensate, short of trying continually to adjust its camera-eyes with its fingers. Software designed to tolerate this probable sloppiness in the first place may well be more robust and versatile in many other ways than software designed to work in a more 'perfect' world.

Earlier I mentioned a reason for using artificial muscles, not motors, to control a robot's joints, and the example was not imaginary. Brooks is concerned that the sheer noise of Cog's skeletal activities may seriously interfere with the attempt to give Cog humanoid hearing. There is research underway at the AI Lab to develop synthetic electromechanical muscle tissues, which would operate silently as well as being more compact, but this would not be available for early incarnations of Cog. For an entirely different reason, thought is being given to the option of designing Cog's visual control software *as if* its eyes were moved by muscles, not motors, building in a software interface that amounts to giving Cog a set of *virtual* eye-muscles. Why might this extra complication in the interface be wise? Because the 'opponent-process' control system exemplified by eye-muscle controls is apparently a deep and ubiquitous feature of nervous systems, involved in control of attention generally and disrupted in such pathologies as unilateral neglect. If we are going to have such competitive systems at higher levels of control, it might be wise to build them in 'all the way down', concealing the final translation into electric-motor-talk as part of the backstage implementation, not the model.

Other practicalities are more obvious, or at least more immediately evocative to the uninitiated. Three huge red 'emergency kill' buttons have already been provided in Cog's environment, to ensure that if Cog happens to engage in some activity that could injure or endanger a human interactor (or itself), there is a way of getting it to stop. But what is the appropriate response for Cog to make to the KILL button? If power to Cog's motors is suddenly shut off, Cog will slump, and its arms will crash down on whatever is below them. Is this what we want to happen? Do we want Cog to drop whatever it is holding? What should 'Stop!' *mean* to Cog? This is a real issue about which there is not yet any consensus.

There are many more details of the current and anticipated design of Cog that are of more than passing interest to those in the field, but I want to use the remaining space to address some overriding questions that have been much debated by philosophers, and that receive a ready treatment in the environment of thought made possible by Cog. In other words, let's consider Cog merely as a prosthetic aid to philosophical thought-experiments, a modest but by no means negligible role for Cog to play.

Some philosophical considerations

A recent criticism of 'strong AI' that has received quite a bit of attention is the so-called problem of 'symbol grounding' (Harnad 1990). It is all very well for large AI programs to have data structures that *purport* to refer to Chicago, milk, or the person to whom I am now talking, but such imaginary reference is not the same as real reference, according to this line of criticism. These internal 'symbols' are not properly 'grounded' in the world, and the problems thereby eschewed by pure, non-robotic, AI are not trivial or peripheral. As one who discussed, and ultimately dismissed, a version of this problem many years ago (Dennett 1969, p. 182ff), I would not want to be interpreted as now abandoning my earlier view. I submit that Cog moots the problem of symbol grounding, without having to settle its status as a criticism of 'strong AI'. Anything in Cog that might be a candidate for symbolhood will automatically be 'grounded' in Cog's real predicament, as surely as its counterpart in any child, so the issue doesn't arise, except as a practical problem for the Cog team, to be solved or not, as fortune dictates. If the day ever comes for Cog to comment to anybody about Chicago, the question of whether Cog is in any position to do so will arise for exactly the same reasons, and be resolvable on the same considerations, as the parallel question about the reference of the word 'Chicago' in the idiolect of a young child.

Another claim that has often been advanced, most carefully by Haugeland (1985), is that nothing could properly 'matter' to an artificial intelligence, and mattering (it is claimed) is crucial to consciousness. Haugeland restricted his claim to traditional GOFAI systems, and left robots out of consideration. Would he concede that something could matter to Cog? The question, presumably, is how seriously to weight the import of the quite deliberate decision by Cog's creators to make Cog as much as possible responsible for its own welfare. Cog will be equipped with some 'innate' but not at all arbitrary preferences, and hence provided of necessity with the concomitant capacity to be 'bothered' by the thwarting of those preferences, and 'pleased' by the furthering of the ends it was innately designed to seek. Some may want to retort: 'This is not *real* pleasure or pain, but merely a simulacrum.' Perhaps, but on what grounds will they defend this claim? Cog may be said to have quite crude, simplistic, one-dimensional pleasure and pain, cartoon pleasure and pain if you like, but then the same might also be said of the pleasure and pain of simpler organisms—clams or houseflies, for instance. Most, if not all, of the burden of proof is shifted by Cog, in my estimation. The reasons for saying that something *does* matter to Cog are not arbitrary; they are exactly parallel to the reasons we give for saying that things matter to us and to other creatures. Since we have cut off the dubious retreats to vitalism or origin chauvinism, it will be interesting to see if the sceptics have any good reasons for declaring Cog's pains and pleasures not to matter—at least to it, and for that very reason, to us as well. It will come as no surprise, I hope, that more than a few participants in the Cog project are already musing about what obligations they might come to have to Cog, over and above their obligations to the Cog team.

Finally, J.R. Lucas (1994) has raised the claim that if a robot were really conscious, we would have to be prepared to believe it about its own internal states. I would like to close by pointing out that this is a rather likely reality in the case of Cog. Although equipped with an optimal suite of monitoring devices that will reveal the details of its inner workings to the observing team, Cog's own pronouncements could very well come to be a more trustworthy and informative source of information on what was really going on inside it. The information visible on the banks of monitors, or gathered by the gigabyte on hard disks, will be at the outset almost as hard to interpret, even by Cog's own designers, as the information obtainable by such 'third-person' methods as MRI and CT scanning in the neurosciences. As the observers refine their models, and their understanding of their models, their authority as interpreters of the data may grow, but it may also suffer eclipse. Especially since Cog will be designed from the outset to redesign itself as much as possible, there is a high probability that the designers will simply lose the standard hegemony of the artificer ('I made it, so I know what it is supposed to do, and what it is doing now!'). Into this epistemological vacuum Cog may very well thrust itself. In fact, I would gladly defend the conditional prediction: *if* Cog develops to the point where it can conduct what appear to be robust and well-controlled conversations in something like a natural language, it will certainly be in a position to rival its own monitors (and the theorists who interpret them) as a source of knowledge about what it is doing and feeling, and why.[1]

References

Dennett, D.C. (1969). *Content and consciousness.* Routledge and Kegan Paul, London.

Dennett, D.C. (1987). Fast thinking. In *The Intentional Stance* (ed. D.C. Dennett), pp. 323–37. MIT Press, Cambridge, MA.

Dennett, D.C. (1993*a*). *The rediscovery of the mind.* Review of John Searle. *Journal of Philosophy,* **90**, 193–205.

Dennett, D.C. (1993*b*). Caveat Emptor. *Consciousness and Cognition,* **2**, 48–57.

Dreyfus, H. and Dreyfus, S. (1986). *Mind over machine.* MacMillan, New York.

Harnad, S. (1990). The symbol grounding problem. *Physica D,* **42**, 335–46.

Haugeland, J. (1985). *Artificial intelligence: the very idea.* MIT Press, Cambridge, MA.

Lucas, J.R. (1994). Presentation to the Royal Society, Conference on Artificial Intelligence, April 14, 1994.

Mangan, B. (1993). Dennett, consciousness, and the sorrows of functionalism. *Consciousness and Cognition,* **2**, 1–17.

Searle, J. (1992). *The rediscovery of the mind.* MIT Press, Cambridge, MA.

Turing, A. (1950). Computing machinery and intelligence. *Mind,* **59**, 433–60.

Waltz, D. (1988). The prospects for building truly intelligent machines. *Daedalus,* **117**, 191–222.

[1] An earlier version of this chapter was presented to the Royal Society, London, April 14, 1994.

3

Consciousness and the mind–body problem

JUNICHI MURATA

Introduction

After the long ascendancy of philosophical treatments of behaviour and language, the problem of consciousness has once again become one of the predominant themes in philosophy. At least so it seems in analytic philosophy. Over the last ten years, hundreds of papers and books related to the problems of consciousness have been published, and it seems that the philosophy of mind has now created a huge philosophical industry. Here I cannot and have no desire to survey all the literature on consciousness in the philosophy of mind. Instead, in the following I would like to concentrate on and describe the problems about phenomenal consciousness or the so-called qualia or subjective aspects of sensations and perceptions, which are now considered to constitute the core of the problems of consciousness. Because I think that the qualia consciousness cannot be treated separately from other features of consciousness, such as intentionality and self-consciousness, I will also touch on these phenomena as necessary.

Consciousness and qualia

The Ignorabimus-thesis

In 1872 at the 45th Assembly of Natural and Medical Scientists in Germany, Emil Du Bois-Reymond, one of the most famous physiologists of the nineteenth century, gave a lecture entitled 'About the limits of the knowledge of nature'. In this lecture, and subsequently in a lecture called 'Seven riddles of the world', Du Bois-Reymond tried to show that there are riddles which continue to be unsolvable, to whatever extent our knowledge of natural science develops, and that, in particular, the most difficult one in those riddles is the existence of consciousness.

The astronomical knowledge about the brain, the highest knowledge which we could attain about the brain, reveals to us nothing but matter in motion in the brain. Through whatever arrangement and movement, we could not build a bridge to the kingdom of consciousness. (Du Bois-Reymond 1874, p. 70.)

With this thesis, the Ignorabimus-thesis, Du Bois-Reymond came out against the materialistic trend in the nineteenth century, arguing that the mind–body problem remains forever beyond the reach of the materialistic conception of the world. But

Du Bois-Reymond was neither a naive dualist nor did he consider the existence of consciousness in general as an impediment to materialism. What he saw as difficult to explain within the scope of natural science was neither intentionality nor reflexive self-consciousness, but the sensory consciousness or consciousness of qualia.

The point is that the highest activity of mind is not more difficult to understand on the basis of the material conditions than the consciousness on the first level, i.e. sensation. With the first excitement of pleasure and pain, which the simplest creature received at the beginning phase of animal life on the earth, that is with the first perception of a quality, that unbridgable abyss was opened up, and the world became since then twice as difficult to understand. (Du Bois-Reymond 1874, p. 66.)

Du Bois-Reymond was not a dualist. On the contrary, he even admitted that any psychological phenomena, whatever they are, could be produced from physical conditions. Thus, it is not because the connection or interaction between mind and body is incomprehensible, as the dualists assert, that we cannot solve the riddle of the existence of consciousness. Instead, it is precisely because consciousness is nothing more than brain activity, which is to say an epiphenomenon within the scope of natural science, that the questions of how and why such a thing as consciousness exists remain fundamentally unanswerable.

Therefore the mind-processes, which go on in the brain beside material processes, lack 'sufficient reason' to our understanding. They are outside the causal laws, and for this reason alone they are already as incomprehensible as a Mobile perpetuum (perpetual motion). (Du Bois-Reymond 1874, p. 70.)

Consciousness in the contemporary philosophy of mind

Today, more than one hundred years after the Ignorabimus-thesis of Du Bois-Reymond, the question about the existence of consciousness seems once again to have become a central topic of philosophy. In contemporary discussions about consciousness, it seems to have become not less but more difficult to answer the questions how and why such a thing as consciousness exists. We now have in the philosophy of mind not only the old naive materialistic conception of mind but several new models of mind as well. The paradigmatic view of mind in contemporary cognitive science, AI research, and philosophy of mind, is called functionalism. But it is precisely this functionalistic view which makes the questions more complicated.

While there are many versions of what is termed functionalism, they maintain a core thesis, according to which a mental state is generally characterized as having a causal role which produces a certain output corresponding to a certain input. From this standpoint, there is no fundamental difference between the following relationships: the relationship between thought-activity and brain, computational activity and computer, digestion and stomach, and so on. Since any question inclusive of our riddle can and must be answered here from the functionalistic viewpoint, there is no difficulty in answering the questions of how and why such a thing as consciousness exists, if some determination of the functional or causal role of consciousness is given. Until now we have had several functionalistic answers; for example, consciousness is characterized as the ability to adapt oneself to the environment, or the ability to use a language, etc. But no functionalistic answer can escape from one fundamental difficulty.

If we are given any functionalistic answer, for example, the ability to use language, we could in principle make some computer or robot which realizes that ability. (The use and understanding of language is one of the main targets of AI research.) But even if we have some language usage programme in hand, we cannot say that our riddle has been solved with it, because our question can be repeated about the computer, which realizes this ability. Why must we say that the computer has consciousness, when it uses language as perfectly as possible? Can we not say instead that the computer need not and does not have consciousness, when it uses language perfectly? The point is not that we human beings need and have consciousness in using language while a computer does not. On the contrary, from the functionalistic view, it is exactly when we become 'unconscious' of how we must use language that we are considered to use it in a competent way. It is indeed when we cannot use language smoothly that we are conscious of it, just as it is when our stomach and brain do not function smoothly that we are conscious of the digestion and thinking processes, which means we suffer from a stomach ache or a headache.

Since the goal of AI research does not lie in making computers which cannot function well and suffer from adverse circumstances, the functionalistic view of consciousness makes the question about the existence of consciousness purposeless and in that sense fundamentally unanswerable. The question is whether this characterization of functionalism shows that its view of the existence of consciousness has already answered all the sensible questions, or whether it shows that functionalism has a fundamental defect.

Critics of functionalism use a strategy like that of Du Bois-Reymond and insist that a quale phenomenon such as the feeling of pain or the experience of a colour appearance is a fundamental stumbling block for functionalism because they have no function at all. Even if an intentional state such as belief or desire could be explained in a functional way, it seems to remain impossible to reduce qualia-experience to some function.

The main representative of this line of thought, Thomas Nagel, declares the following:

But no matter how the form may vary, the fact that an organism has conscious experience *at all* means, basically, that there is something it is like to *be* that organism ... We may call this the subjective character of experience. It is not captured by any of the familiar, recently devised reductive analyses of the mental, for all of them are logically compatible with its absence. It is not analysable in terms of any explanatory system of functional status, or intentional status, since these could be ascribed to robots or automata that behaved like people though they experienced nothing. (Nagel 1979, p. 166.)

But it is exactly the fact that the qualia experience cannot be reduced which boomerangs on the critics. Why should such things as qualia exist, if they have neither a causal nor a functional role at all? The proponent of the 'reductive' direction,

D. Dennett, insists that, after he has explained all conceivable functions of qualia, '... contrary to what seems obvious at first blush, there simply are no qualia at all' (Dennett 1990, p. 544).

In this way we now have in the philosophy of mind a spectrum of various positions concerning the status of consciousness, from the eliminatists, who want not only to explain but explain *away* consciousness with physiological and functional theory, in the same way scientists eliminated phlogiston from the theory of combustion, to 'principled agnostics' or 'new mysterialists' (Flanagan 1992, p. 1ff.), who see in consciousness a limit in principle to any scientific understanding. In the middle are located several 'liberal' positions, one representative of which is Flanagan's position of 'reflective equilibrium among the phenomenological, psychological, and neuroscientific levels' (Flanagan 1992).

If we search for the origin of this problem, we come back to the emergence phase of modern natural science in the seventeenth century, when scientists and philosophers thought that in the objective world which is the theme of natural science there exist only primary qualities, such as growth, form, number, movement, and that other secondary qualities such as colour and sound are subjective phenomena and can exist only in the mind.

Under this world picture, qualia such as pain, colour, and sound are excluded from the themes of natural science, and considered to be something which is very peculiar, for example, diaphanous or ineffable. If we presuppose this kind of interpretation of qualia, there is no room for compromise between friends and foes of qualia, and phenomenology and brain science remain incompatible. But it is just in the tradition of phenomenology itself that such a Cartesian interpretation of qualia and consciousness has long been called into question, and alternative ways of seeing qualia and consciousness have been proposed.

As is well known, the direction of bodily movement and muscle tension are greatly influenced by various colour experiences, especially in the case of patients with cerebellar injury. On the grounds of such phenomena, Merleau-Ponty (1945, p. 241ff) has emphasized that qualia experience is influenced by and influences various types of behaviour, and qualia are always experienced in connection with biological, psychological, and social meanings. This means that qualia cannot be seen as having some intrinsic feature but must be seen as having some 'relational' and 'intentional' feature (Harman 1990), or that qualia are not something diaphanous, but have 'depth and hidden structure' (Flanagan 1992, p. 62). In the next section I would like to follow this direction one step further.

Qualia and intentionality

A phenomenological model of qualia consciousness

Descartes, who is one of the founders of a dualistic world picture of the seventeenth century, wrote an interesting comment, which indicates the peculiar 'unity' of mind and body in the qualia experience.

Nature teaches through these sensations of pain, of hunger, of thirst, etc., that I am not only present in my body as a sailor is present in a ship, but that I am very tightly joined to it and as if mixed through so as to compose one thing with it. For otherwise, when the body is injured, I, who am nothing but a thinking thing, would not feel pain on that account, but would perceive this injury by the pure understanding, as a sailor perceives by sight if something in the ship is broken; and when the body needs food or drink, I would have an explicit understanding of this fact. (Descartes 1973, p. 81.)

For example, when I burn my hand, I do not become conscious of it in the same way that the sailor becomes conscious of the ship which is burning. In both cases an emergency occurs, life becomes endangered, and both I and the sailor cope with these accidents in a similar way, but the ways in which these affairs are conscious are fundamentally different. While the sailor knows the danger without feeling pain or some qualia, I not only know the danger but also feel it with pain. According to Descartes, having the 'qualia' of pain shows that I and my body are 'so tightly joined and mixed through as to compose one thing', and that this 'proximity' is not understandable in the domain of 'understanding'.

I would like to interpret this comment of Descartes phenomenologically instead of invoking his dualistic ontology. Then we could understand that through this thought-experiment Descartes has contrasted two modes of the intentional structure of experience concerning one's own body. On the one hand, we can examine the bodily state of the injury and give it some treatment. In this case the body is an object of cognition and action. We treat our own body just like another person's body, and in this dimension it is irrelevant whether we ourselves feel pain or not. On the other hand, while we feel pain, the body is not objectively experienced but, with the words of phenomenologists, it is 'preobjectively' experienced and 'lived'. In this sense, the essence of qualia lies not in the being in the mind separated from the body, but lies in this intimate, lived relationship to the body. Sometimes, it is thought that the phenomenological analysis of the 'lived body' and scientific analysis of the objective body can be carried out separately, as if there were two bodies. But it is the character of the body that can be considered neither purely subjective nor purely objective. Merleau-Ponty has called its way of being 'ambiguous'. It means not only that we take two attitudes towards our bodies, but that we also *experience* the process of the change of these two ways of being of our bodies.

Merleau-Ponty has given famous examples of the extension of the 'lived body' through artefacts, for example, the car of a skilled driver, a feather in the hat of a woman, or a blind man's stick, and describes the switch of aspects from objective being to the embodied being of these artefacts. These phenomena in 'the phenomenological garden' (Dennett 1991, p. 47) seem to have now become trivialities for philosophers, but I will quote a frequently cited passage from Merleau-Ponty:

The blind man's stick has ceased to be an object for him and is no longer perceived for itself; its point has become an area of sensitivity extending the scope and active radius of touch and providing a parallel to sight. In the exploration of things, the length of the stick does not enter expressly as a middle term: the blind man is rather aware of it through the position of objects than of the position of objects through it. The position of things is immediately given through the extent of the reach which carries him to it, which comprises, besides the arm's reach, the stick's range of action. (Merleau-Ponty 1945, p. 143.)

This is exactly a description of the transformation of intentionality, that is, the transformation from the 'sailor–ship' relation to the 'I–my body' relation. So long as the stick remains an object, the thing touched with the stick can be known only indirectly through inference or computation and cannot be felt with special qualia. In contrast, if the stick becomes a part of the extended body and 'lived through', the thing touched with the stick can be felt directly with some special qualia. Here is the remarkable structure of the appearance and disappearance of qualia concerning the thing touched through the stick. This change can be seen as a process of an emergence of new qualia, and in this sense as a quasi-model of the process from consciousness without qualia to consciousness with qualia.

So long as the physical status of the stick remains the same through the change from the objective being to the lived being, we could say that the change lies in its functional status. But this 'function' is, if we may use the word, a 'phenomeno-logical' function, by which something which was hidden is made to appear and vice versa: it is not simply a causal function, which plays the role within the domain of what is already present.

The more radical extension of the lived body and the emergence of new qualia can be found in the case of a so-called TVSS (tactile visual substitute system) or pros-thetic vision. A blind person equipped with a television camera on the side of the head and a device which converts the visual image produced by the camera into an isomorphic cutaneous display in the form of a pattern of vibration on the back or the stomach comes to be able to 'see' things after some training. 'After a brief training period, their awareness of the tingles on their skin dropped out; the pad of pixels became transparent, one might say, and the subjects' point of view shifted to the point of view of the camera, mounted to the side of the heads.' (Dennett 1991, p. 341; see also Guarniero 1974).

As is indicated by these phenomenological descriptions of the transformation of intentionality, this change is considered to be a change in the way of being of the 'lived body'. So if there is some scientific approach to the being and the 'pheno-menological' function of this 'lived body', it would give us some scientific descrip-tion of an essential character of qualia consciousness. Is it possible to formulate a scientific theory about a functional system which corresponds to the 'lived body'?

The lived body and the perceptual system

Probably the most promising candidate corresponding to the concept of a lived body is J.J. Gibson's concept of a 'perceptual system'. Gibson's perceptual systems are senses considered in a new way 'as active rather than passive, as systems rather than channels, and interrelated rather than mutually exclusive' (Gibson 1966, p. 47). In this perspective the brain is not a substitute for a Cartesian theatre in which every-thing mental and conscious is situated, but is simply one organ in the whole system.

Vision is a whole perceptual system, not a channel of sense.... One sees the environment not with the eyes but with the eye-in-the-head-on-the-body-resting-on-the-ground. Vision does not have a seat in the body in the way that the mind has been thought to be seated in the brain. (Gibson 1979, p.205.)

In this perspective the traditional concept of 'special sense' is criticized and the concept of attention, closely connected with the concept of intentional consciousness, is also liberated from the centre to the whole system.

In the case of a special sense the process of attention occurs at centers with the nervous system, whereas in the case of a perceptual system attention pervades the whole input–output loop. In the first case attention is a consciousness that can be focused; in the second case it is a skill that can be educated. (Gibson 1979, p. 246.)

More than ten years ago there was a lively controversy between cognitivists/computationalists and Gibsonians/ecologists concerning the central question about perceptual cognition: the question concerned whether perceptual cognition is to be considered as information processing or information pick-up (in other words, 'resonating' to information) (Fodor and Pylyshyn 1981; Turvey *et al.* 1981). Whatever the consequence of this controversy may be, it seems that the Gibsonian approach is not neglected but taken into consideration in some way or other (for example, in the designing of 'artificial creatures') in contemporary cognitive science.

In any case, we could say that there is the possibility of building a bridge between the phenomenological world of consciousness and the scientific world with the help of the concepts of the 'lived body' and 'perceptual system'. Indeed, this possibility remains very limited so long as the Gibsonian approach is regarded as unorthodox in contemporary cognitive science. But it shows at least that phenomenology and the science of mind and brain are not incompatible, and that a way is open for a critical dialogue between them.

Consequences of the phenomenological model

Several points should be noted here. First, when the blind person becomes accustomed to the stick and is able to touch the thing directly through it, we could say that the stick becomes 'transparent'. But the way the thing touched through the stick appears is not exactly the same as the way it appears without the stick, however accustomed one becomes. When we talk with someone through a telephone, we hear the voice of the other directly, but the extension of hearing corresponds to a change in the situation of a conversation, for example, with the loss of the face-to-face situation. In this sense the stick of the blind person does not become perfectly transparent, instead the using of the stick shows itself in the way the thing appears. In other words, the qualia we experience show not only how the thing appears, but also how it appears *through* a certain thing each time: through a normal body, through a body plus a stick, through a body plus a telephone, or through a body minus some part of the body (when paralysed). In the qualia we experience not only the object of experience but also at the same time *we experience how we experience*. That means that the qualia experience can be considered 'self-referential'. This self-referentiality is not an explicit, reflective self-consciousness, but can be seen as the most primitive 'self-consciousness' of our experience. The self in this case is not the thinking self but the 'bodily self' (Merleau-Ponty 1945) or the 'ecological self' (Neisser 1988). If we have intentionality and qualia, we have already reached the first step of 'self-consciousness' without the higher-order thinking process.

The Gibsonian concept of 'awareness' (Gibson 1979, p. 250) or 'egoreption' (Gibson 1979, p. 205) can also be reinterpreted and considered to belong to this level of 'self-consciousness'. Against the often-made criticism that the Gibsonian theory of perception neglects the dimension of experience in perception, this interpretation makes it possible to understand the Gibsonian theory of perceptual *cognition* as a theory of perceptual *consciousness*, supporting our interpretation of the relation between the lived body and the perceptual system presented above.

Second, when the problem of intentionality of consciousness is discussed in the philosophy classroom, it has become almost a formality for the teacher to ask the question 'what kind of experience is thinkable as an experience without intentionality?' The answer is 'pain'. Those who are accustomed to such a formality would find a fundamental defect in my above discussion which extends the examples of Descartes to Merleau-Ponty. For, while in the first example what matters is pain, thirst, and hunger, that is, typical bodily sensations without intentionality, in the second example what matters is touch, that is, an intentional tactile perception. But can we really regard a difference between pain sensation and tactile perception as being such a fundamental difference as that between experience without intentionality and that with intentionality?

When I put my finger on the desk and touch the surface, I feel several qualities of the surface. But if I push my finger on the desk a little more strongly, I feel not only a surface but also the pressure from the desk in my finger, and if I push even more strongly, I begin to feel pain. I can find in this process only a gradual difference. I don't know exactly how physiologists explain this process and there may be a 'phenomenological fallacy' in this experience, but it is hard to imagine that a tactile sensory system and a pain sensory system function indifferently (Iggo 1987). What is more interesting is that one of the proposers of a physiological hypothesis about pain emphasizes that the pain is essentially connected with many factors and has multidimensional qualities.

Recent evidence, however, shows that pain is not simply a function of the amount of bodily damage alone, but is influenced by attention, anxiety, suggestion, prior experience, and other psychological variables.... Pain is a complex perceptual and affective experience determined by the unique past history of the individual, by the meaning to him of the injurious agent or situation, and by his 'state of mind' at the moment, as well as by the sensory nerve patterns evoked by physical stimulation. (Melzack 1987, p. 574.)

If we take this into consideration, the discussion about pain by philosophers, for example the discussion about whether pain is identical with the firing of C-fibres or not, seems to be very naive and abstract. It is so naive that it seems to be almost a

(Rylian) category mistake, i.e. a mistake which one makes when, asked what the University is, one answers only by pointing to the library building, the college building, or anything else.

Third, if the pain experience is essentially intentional and at least in the phenomenological perspective only different from the tactile experience in degree, it must be possible that we feel pain not only in our body but also at the tip of the stick through the extension of the lived body. Is it possible to feel pain outside our body? Why not?

In the well-known phenomenon of phantom limb one feels pain outside of one's 'real' body. There is no more mystery or contradiction here than the stick in the water which appears to be bent visually. There is a contradiction between the pain experience of a phantom limb and the visual and the tactile experience. This makes the lived body and the felt pain abnormal, making the situation of the patient very complex and difficult, as many examples of patients with anosognosia show, but in the fact that the pain is experienced outside the 'real' body itself there is no contradiction.

If one still finds difficulty here, one must find greater difficulty in distal visual perception in general. According to the typical explanation of visual experience, the causal chain begins from the object which is seen, goes through reflected light, the eyes, finally ending in the visual cortex in the brain. Even though there is no additional backward causal chain from the brain to the object, we see objects neither in the brain nor in the 'mind' which is connected to the brain, but directly outside our bodies, where the object exists. Someone who sees here an explanatory gap may invoke the notorious 'projection' by the brain. But nowadays few people accept such an act of 'projection' (as does, for example, Velmans 1990).

The easiest way to show that projection is unnecessary, I think, is to imagine a situation in which I take my brain out of my head and look at it. My brain appears in the centre of my visual field: in this case there is no gap between the beginning and the end of the causal chain, and therefore my brain can be seen without a 'projection'. This is not so special a situation. Seeing my own brain is not so different from touching my own head or seeing other parts of my body. In any case, if we think we do not need a 'projection' to see something outside our body, neither need we find any special difficulty in having a pain outside our bodies.

Fourth, while pain as consciousness without intentionality has long been a cliché in classroom philosophy, intentionality without consciousness has become a new widespread concept, as the functionalistic view has become dominant in the philosophy of mind. The case of blind sight is sometimes considered to be a paradigmatic example.

The case of blind sight is sometimes interpreted as demonstrating the division between 'automatic unmonitored acts and those acts that are effectively monitored' (Weiskrantz 1987, p. 112). I am not in the position to say anything definitive here, but I think that it is not necessary to interpret the case as showing the difference between an act accompanied by monitoring and one not. For the case of blind sight could be interpreted as the case of an intentional act without qualia or with a very low degree of qualia. If we could interpret it in this way, the intentional structure of blind sight is not to be considered as remaining the same, but as becoming fundamentally modified. The modified intentionality without qualia could be compared with the 'empty' intentionality which we experience when we have 'a word on the tip of the tongue'. In this case we 'know' the object in a sense, but we can only 'guess' what it is. At any rate, we must be careful to characterize such pathological cases simply as cases of unconscious intentionality, as if the intentionality and consciousness can be separated without serious modification. The process from conscious state to unconscious state and vice versa is not such a simple process as, for example, something sinking into water and re-emerging. In this sense the cases of unconscious intentionality do not give direct evidence for the functionalistic view of consciousness but present problems for it, like the case of Freudian unconscious intentionality, which remains problematical to this day.

Intentionality and self-consciousness

When it comes to the essence of the conscious state, it was not the qualia experience but mainly reflexive self-consciousness that has been treated in traditional philosophy. Descartes located the essential feature of spirit in the self-consciousness of 'I think', and found the ability to think reflectively that I sense, I imagine, or I will, and so on to be the essence of the rational spirit. Kant maintained, as is well known, that '"that I think" must be able to accompany all my representations; for, if not, something that could not be thought at all would be represented in me, which means just as well as that the representation would be either impossible or at least nothing for me.' (Kant 1956, B 131f.)

It is exactly this concept of mind and self-consciousness that was reversed in the view of contemporary cognitivism. Not that mental states become possible by being the objects of self-consciousness, but that self-consciousness only becomes possible after much unconscious mental processing has been worked out. Now that the view of mind and self-consciousness is reversed, the concept of self-consciousness is itself brought into question. If many things and perhaps everything could be realized without it, what is its function?

One of the appropriate ways of thinking about this question is, I think, to imagine such a person who has 'conscious' states but completely lacks reflexive self-consciousness. Koffka called the consciousness of such a person 'consciousness without insight' and described it in the following way:

This person would be surrounded by objects and feel himself approaching one, avoiding another, having pleasure in one set of conditions and being angry in another. But that would be all. He would, let us say, feel thirsty and drink a glass of water, and then feel his thirst quenched, but he would not know that he drank the water *because* he was thirsty, nor that his thirst vanished *because* of the drink. He would see a beautiful woman, would approach her, hear himself make the most clever and alluring speeches, find himself in flower shops ordering bunches of long-stemmed red roses addressed to that lady, he might even hear himself propose, be accepted, become married, but in the words of the baron in Gorki's *Lower Depths*, 'Why? No notion?' (Koffka 1935, p. 383f.)

In contrast to such a person, we, who are considered to have self-consciousness, can understand and answer such 'why' questions, and thus the most obvious function of self-consciousness could be found in the ability to understand the 'why' of one's behaviour and mental states. But we must note that here the question 'why' has at least two meanings.

One meaning is related to causal explanation. Let's take a simple example: I drink water because I feel thirsty. In order to understand my behaviour, I must at least identify a motive which caused it. Perhaps at the same time I felt hungry, but thirst, not hunger, was the cause of my behaviour. I could be mistaken in identifying the cause of my behaviour. It is possible that the cause was not the thirst but some repressed 'unconscious' desire, or that my behaviour was only a 'slip'. We could begin scientific studies in search of the genuine cause and try to explain the detailed process of my behaviour and mental states with the help of psychological, functional, and physiological theories, and data. In this sense there is nothing special in the explanatory function of self-consciousness. But when I identify a motive for my behaviour, it is not only considered as a cause but also as a 'reason'. That means that the relation between motive and behaviour is considered not only as causal but also as rational and intentional. As its rationality is closely connected with its normativity, the behaviour is sometimes described in saying that I have done it but I should not have done it. A person without such a consciousness of rationality lacks a most important ability for living with others in a society. We could not, for example, make a promise to such a person. The function of self-consciousness in this sense, therefore, can be found in the ability to live together in a society. This kind of ability cannot be acquired through scientific studies, however detailed its causal analysis may be. One must learn to understand which behaviour is rational and which is not through various interactions and communications with others through one's life.

In this way we can find in the functions of self-consciousness the well-known contrast between explaining (Erklären) and understanding (Verstehen), which corresponds to the methodological contrast between natural and human science.

Sometimes these two 'functions' are considered to be mutually exclusive and therefore mutually irrelevant, but, as the above considerations have already indicated, the situation is to the contrary.

On the one hand, even if we try to explain behaviour causally, the possibility of understanding it in the rational sense must be presupposed. Without this presupposition from the beginning the object of research cannot be regarded as behaviour.

On the other hand, that our self-understanding of our own behaviour is sometimes mistaken has already been demonstrated in various ways (Nisbett and Wilson 1977). Introspection itself is, so to speak, 'theory laden'.

The traditional belief that introspection is transparent is itself perhaps a construct based on a 'folk psychological' theory. If our understanding of self and other is produced through ascribing this psychological theory to each other, it may be that our social life is not constituted by mutual understanding, but is full of 'misunderstanding'. Then the traditional belief concerning self-understanding and introspection itself must be explained and criticized scientifically. Explanation and understanding, methods of natural science and human science are, far from being mutually exclusive and irrelevant, instead complementary.

The traditional conception of self-consciousness as transparent or infallible has now been persuasively falsified. But this does not mean that the asymmetry of the first person and third person points of view will completely disappear and the most 'mysterious' characteristic (or function?) of self-consciousness will vanish. Instead, exactly at this level of self-consciousness, that is, at the level on which the self can be explained and understood objectively and intersubjectively, the asymmetry becomes clearly conscious and problematical.

In order to indicate this feature I would like to bring to mind the well-known discussion about consciousness and reflexivity in traditional philosophy. If we try to analyse consciousness with the reflexive act of the second level, by which the intentional state of the first level becomes conscious, then the problem repeats itself concerning the second level act, whether it is itself conscious or not. And so we must either presuppose consciousness itself from the beginning or we cannot but fall into an infinite regress. If the above-mentioned self-consciousness is really self-*consciousness*, not only the ability to understand but also the more immediate and primitive level of consciousness must be presupposed. And it is entirely possible to think that the qualia experience takes the role of this primitive consciousness, for all explanation and understanding are founded on perceptual experience, in which various qualia are experienced. Because of this connection between self-consciousness and qualia consciousness, the self is not only explained and understood but also *experienced* with various qualia on the background of the objectivity and intersubjectivity, which makes the first and third person perspective inevitably asymmetrical. And it is this asymmetry that sometimes makes of something objectively thoroughly understandable something totally incomprehensible, for example, my death. As a biological and social event nothing is more certain than that everyone dies. But what is it like to experience my death, that is outside my understanding.

References

Dennett, D. (1990). Quining qualia. In *Mind and cognition* (ed. W.G. Lycan), pp. 519–47. Basil Blackwell, Cambridge.

Dennett, D. (1991). *Consciousness explained*. Penguin Books, London.

Descartes, R. (1973). Meditationes de prima philosophia. In *Oeuvres de Descartes*, Vol. 7 (ed. C. Adams and P. Tannery) Vrin/CNRS, Paris.

Du Bois-Reymond, E. (1874). Über die Grenzen des Naturerkennens. In *Vorträge über Philosophie und Gesellschaft*, pp. 54–77. Felix Meiner, Hamburg.

Flanagan, O. (1992). *Consciousness reconsidered*. The MIT Press, Cambridge, MA.

Fodor, J.A. and Pylyshyn, Z.W. (1981). How direct is visual perception? Some reflections on Gibson's ecological approach. *Cognition*, **9**, 139–96.

Gibson, J.J. (1966). *The senses considered as perceptual systems*. Houghton Mifflin, Boston.

Gibson, J.J. (1979). *The ecological appraoch to visual perception*. Houghton Mifflin, Boston.

Guarniero, G. (1974). Experience of tactile vision. *Perception*, **3**, 101–4.

Harman, G. (1990). The intrinsic quality of experience. In *Philosophical perspectives,* Vol. 4, *Action theory and philosophy of mind* (ed. J.E. Tomberlin), pp. 31–52. Ridgeview, Atascadero, CA.

Iggo, A. (1987). Touch. In *The Oxford companion to the mind* (ed. R.L. Gregory), pp. 778–81. Oxford University Press.

Kant, I. (1956). *Kritik der reinen Vernunft*. Felix Meiner, Hamburg.

Koffka, K. (1935). *Principles of Gestalt psychology*. Routledge and Kegan Paul, London.

Melzack, R. (1987). Pain. In *The Oxford companion to the mind* (ed. R.L. Gregory), pp. 574–5. Oxford University Press.

Merleau-Ponty, M. (1945). *Phénomenologie de la perception*. Gallimar, Paris.

Nagel, T. (1979). What is it like to be a bat? In *Mortal questions*, pp. 165–80. Cambridge University Press.

Neisser, U. (1988). Five kinds of self-knowledge. *Philosophical Psychology*, **1**, 35–59.

Nisbett R.E. and Wilson, T.D. (1977). Telling more than we can know: verbal reports on mental processes. *Psychological Review*, **84**, 231–59.

Turvey, M.T., Shaw, R.E., Reed, E.S., and Mace, W.M. (1981). Ecological laws of perceiving and acting: in reply to Fodor and Pylyshyn. *Cognition*, **9**, 237–304.

Velmans, M. (1990). Consciousness, brain and the physical world. *Philosophical Psychology*, **3**, 77–99.

Weiskrantz, L. (1987). Brain function and awareness. In *The Oxford companion to the mind* (ed. R.L. Gregory), pp. 110–13. Oxford University Press.

4

Understanding consciousness: the case of sleep and dreams

OWEN FLANAGAN

Introduction

I have by now been to many conferences in which 'Consciousness' was the topic, and I have noticed an apology prefacing talks with surprising frequency. It goes like this: 'I am an expert on language (or memory, or PET, or fMRI, or vision, or audition, or anaesthesia, etc.). But I am quite unsure that what I have to say sheds any light on "consciousness".'

As I've listened to learned colleagues apologize in this way, I am almost invariably struck with how much what they go on to say is relevant to the problem of consciousness. My analysis is that they are not being excessively or falsely modest. The apologies are sincere and due to the fact that scholars think that unless the word 'consciousness' is on centre stage in a talk, consciousness isn't. There is a misconception, as it were, about what consciousness is and what a theory of consciousness would look like.

My view is this. Consciousness is one of those things about which we will learn by a certain indirection, by studying systems or mental state types that have consciousness as one of their properties, but not by feeling compelled to confront constantly the property itself. To put my main idea in the form of a familiar platitude: it is often said that one will not gain happiness if one directly seeks it. I am suggesting that something similar is true of consciousness. It is a feature of mind, or better, of some mental states. But we will understand it better when we understand better the mind, not the other way around.

Constructive naturalism

'What is consciousness?' is not a good question to ask since it pushes one in the direction of thinking that consciousness is a faculty or a mental organ. Better questions are these:

(1) What, if anything, do conscious mental states have in common in virtue of which they are conscious?
(2) Does it make sense to try to build a theory of conscious mental state types? And if so, what form should such a theory take?

Regarding (1), my view is that 'consciousness' is a superordinate term for multifarious mental state types that share what I'll call 'Nagel's-property'. What conscious mental states have in common in virtue of which they are conscious is that '*there is something that it is like* for the subject (the whole organism) to be in one of these states'. A conscious mental state is a state that *seems* a certain way to the subject of that state. A conscious mental state has certain *phenomenal* aspects or properties. 'Consciousness' is a superordinate term meant to cover all mental states, events, and processes that are *experienced*—all the states that there is *something it is like for the subject of them to be in*. So, for example, sensory experience is a kind in the domain of consciousness which branches out into the types of experience familiar in the five sensory modalities. Each of these branches further, so that, for example, visual experience branches off from sensory experience and colour experiences branch off from it. My experience of red, like yours, is a token colour experience—a token of the type red-sensation. So sensory experience divides into five kinds and then branches and branches again and again as our taxonomic needs require. But of course consciousness covers far more than sensory experience. There is, in the human case, linguistic consciousness, and there is conscious propositional attitude thought which *seems* heavily linguistic but may or may not be; there are sensory memories, episodic memories, various types of self-consciousness, moods, emotions, dreams, and much else besides (see Fig. 4.1).

Conscious mental states have more than phenomenal aspects or properties. Seeing red and hearing a cat's meow differ phenomenally—in how they seem. They also differ in how they are realized in the nervous system. We can express this idea by saying that conscious mental states are heterogeneous in phenomenal kind *and* in neural realization.

Because conscious mental states do not reveal their neural structure first personally, to the subject of experience, it follows that conscious mental states have hidden structure. Let us call this *dual-aspect* theory. Conscious mental states have first-person phenomenal surface structure and neural deep structure. Furthermore, different conscious mental state types have multiple functions (audition can work with the linguistic system or with an individual's musical competence); and conscious mental states, like mental states generally, have complex natural and social histories.

In broad strokes there are two ways one might imagine building a theory of consciousness. Gathering together whatever scientific truths there are about this set of phenomena will constitute *one way* of building a theory of consciousness. Especially in the early stages, building such a theory might amount to the gathering together of all the interesting truths about the class of phenomena that possess the shared feature of being experienced. A theory of consciousness built in this way, around the shared phenomenological feature where it *really* resides, would cross-cut our theories of perception, memory, and learning. Or, to put it differently, the theory of consciousness, such as it was, would contain generalizations that also show up within these special theories.

A second, related possibility is that we might forego altogether a specially demarcated space for *the* theory of consciousness, allowing instead all the true generalizations

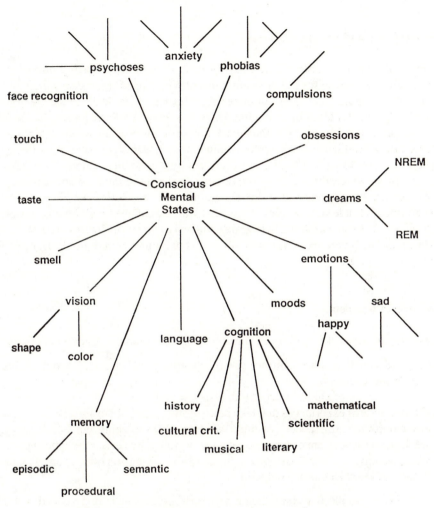

Fig. 4.1 The heterogeneity of conscious mental state types.

about conscious mental life to occur within the special theories. The idea is that the interesting facts and generalizations about consciousness might be gathered under the rubric of the special theories of perception, memory, learning, and so on. Presumably this would happen—and it is a very reasonable prospect—if the most interesting generalizations of the science of the mind weave together conscious and unconscious processes and their neural realizations in accordance with *what, from a functional point of view, the system is doing.* Since perceiving and remembering, and the like, are things we *do,* whereas consciousness may be *a way we are* or one of the *ways* we perceive, remember, and so on, it is easy to imagine embedding most of what needs to be said about consciousness into the special theories.

Neuroscience and meaninglessness

Many think that neuroscientific accounts of mental phenomena destroy meaning or significance. There are several different kinds of meaning or significance thought to be at stake, ranging from the meaning or significance of life itself to the meaning-fulness of particular kinds of mentation. Indeed, neuroscientific accounts change the way we understand mental phenomena; but there is no way in which the general charge that neuroscience is inherently eliminativist, reductive, or an enemy of mean-ing can be made to stick. I shall try to show this by way of an example—the case of dreaming—in which I think doing the science does require thinking about it differ-ently; but not so differently that dreams are not still self-expressive, interpretable, and meaningful, at least to a point. My remarks are part of an overall articulation and defence of J. Allan Hobson's activation–synthesis theory of dreams (see Hobson 1988). Hobson is read by some as thinking that dreaming is pure noise. But this is wrong. I'll explain.

Five dream problems

In two recent papers I've discussed four philosophical problems about dreams:

(1) How can I be sure I am not always dreaming? (Descartes's problem; also Plato's and Cicero's).

(2) Can I be immoral in dreams? (Augustine's problem).[1]

(3) Are dreams experiences that take place during sleep, or are so-called 'dreams' just reports of experiences we think we had while sleeping but which in fact are, in so far as they are experiences at all, constituted by certain thoughts we have while waking or experiences we have while giving reports upon waking? (Malcolm's and Dennett's problem).

The answers to the first three dream problems are these: (1) rest assured, you're not always dreaming; (2) you can be immoral while dreaming, but it is hard to pull off, requires planning, effort, and skill—roughly, it involves a complex project of character deformation through self-hypnosis; (3) dreams *are* experiences that take place during sleep.[2] But dreams are not a natural kind. The unity dreams possess consist in this alone: they comprise the set, or the dominant set, of experiences that take place while asleep.

Given that dreams are experiences that take place while sleeping, a fourth dream problem suggests itself:

(4) is dreaming functional? And if it is functional, in what sense is it so?

My answer to the fourth dream problem is this: although there are credible adapta-tionist accounts for sleep and the phases of the sleep cycle itself, there is reason to think that the mentation—the phenomenal mentation—that occurs during sleep is a bona fide example of a by-product of what the system was designed to do during sleep and sleep-cycling. If this is right then there is a sense in which dreaming, phenomenally speaking, is an automatic sequela (Gould 1984), a spandrel (Gould and Lewontin 1979), an exaptation (Gould and Vrba 1982).

In this paper, I shall first review my argument for this answer to the fourth dream problem and then go on to talk about the fifth dream problem:

(5) can dreams fail both to be a natural kind and fail to have an adaptationist evolutionary explanation but still make sense, still be identity expressive, and identity constituting?

My answer to (5) is 'yes'.

The answer has an air of paradox about it, and my job will be to explain away the air of paradox. Sleep and sleep-cycling have adaptationist evolutionary explanations, but mentation while asleep does not. It is a spandrel, an automatic sequela. Despite having no evolutionary proper function, dreams are self-expressive, and thus sometimes worth exploring, not simply noise.

Constructive naturalism and the natural method

'Consciousness' is a superordinate term for a heterogeneous array of mental state types. The types share the property of 'being experienced' or 'being experiences'. It is not the name of a faculty. And the phenomenal features, causal role, and evolutionary history of different types of 'consciousness' should not be assumed to possess some unified but heretofore hidden account. Consciousness in the sensory modalities differs across modalities, but, especially when it comes to selection pressures, sensory consciousness requires an utterly different story from both abstract problem solving and mentation while asleep.

From the first personal point of view consciousness only has *phenomenal-aspects*. So with respect to dreaming all we know about first personally is *phenomenal-dreaming*. The story of the brain side—of *brain-dreaming*—as it were, will need to be provided by the neuroscientists, and the functional–causal role(s) of dreaming (now taking both the phenomenal and brain sides together) will need to be nested in a general psychological-cum-evolutionary (both natural and cultural) account.

The idea here is to deploy what I call *the natural method* (see Flanagan 1992). Start by treating different types of analysis with equal respect. Give *phenomenology* its due. Listen carefully to what individuals have to say about how things seem. Also, let the psychologists and cognitive scientist have their say. Listen carefully to their descriptions about how mental life works, and what jobs if any consciousness has in its overall economy.[3] Third, listen carefully to what the neuroscientists say about how conscious mental events of different sorts are realized, and examine the fit between their stories and the phenomenological and psychological stories. Even the troika of phenomenology, psychology, and neuroscience is not enough. Evolutionary biology and cultural and psychological anthropology will also be crucial players as the case of dreams will make especially clear. Embedding the story of consciousness into theories of evolution (biological and cultural), thinking about different forms of consciousness in terms of their ecological niche, and in terms of the mechanisms of drift, adaptive selection, and free-riding will be an important part of understanding what consciousness is, how it works, and what, if anything, it is good for—again, taking as axiomatic that there will be no unified theory for all the kinds of conscious mental state types. Now *the natural method*, the tactic of 'collapsing flanks' will, I claim, yield success in understanding consciousness if anything will. The expectation that success is in store using this method is what makes my kind of naturalism *constructive* rather than *anti-constructive*, as is the naturalism of philosophers like Colin McGinn who thinks that although consciousness is a natural phenomena, we will *never* be able to understand it (see McGinn 1989).

Dreams: a double aspect model[4]

Phenomenal-dreaming (henceforth *p-dreaming*) is a good example of one of the heterogeneous kinds of conscious experience, and it is at the same time, given neuro-scientific evidence and evolutionary considerations, a likely candidate for being given epiphenomenalist status from an evolutionary point of view. *P-dreaming* is an interesting side-effect of what the brain is doing, the function(s) it is performing during sleep.[5]

To put it in slightly different terms: *p-dreams*, despite being experiences, have no interesting biological function—no evolutionary proper function. The claim is that *p-dreams* (and possibly even rapid eye movements after development of the visual system is secured) are likely candidates of epiphenomena. Since I think that all mental phenomena supervene on neural events I don't mean that *p-dreams* are non-physical side-effects of certain brain processes. I mean in the first instance that *p-dreaming* was probably not selected for, that *p-dreaming* is neither functional nor dysfunctional in and of itself, and thus that whether *p-dreaming* has a function depends not on Mother Nature's work as does, for example, the phenomenal side of sensation and perception. It depends entirely on what we as a matter of cultural inventiveness—*memetic selection* (see Dawkins 1976), one might say—do with *p-dreams*, and *p-dream reports*. We can, in effect, create or invent functions for dreams. Indeed, we have done this. But as temporally significant aspects of conscious mental life, they are a good example, the flip side say of awake perceptual consciousness which is neither an evolutionary adaptation nor ontogenetically functional or dysfunctional until we do certain things with 'our dreams'—for example use them as sources of information about 'what's on our mind', utilize dream mentation in artistic expression, and the like.

Despite being epiphenomena from an evolutionary perspective, the way the brain operates during sleep guarantees that the noise of *p-dreams* is revealing and potentially useful in the project of self-understanding. Thus many things stay the same on the view I am staking out. But there is a paradox: *p-dreams* are evolutionary epiphenomena, noise the system creates while it is doing what it was designed to do, but because the cerebral cortex is designed to make sense out of stimuli it tries half-successfully to put dreams into narrative structures already in place, structures which involve modes of self-representation, present concerns, and so on. But the cortex isn't designed to do this for sleep stimuli, it is designed to do it for stimuli *period* and it is ever vigilant. The idea is that it did us a lot of good to develop a cortex that makes sense out of experience while awake, and the design is such that there are no costs to this sense-maker always being ready to do its job. So it works during the chaotic neuronal cascades of part of the sleep-cycle that activate certain sensations and thoughts. So *p-dreams* despite their bizarreness, and epiphenomenal status, are meaningful and interpretable up to a point.

A problem with the concept of 'dreaming'

I have been using *p-dreaming* so far to refer to any mentation that occurs during sleep. But the term '*p-dreaming*', despite being useful for present purposes, ultimately won't carve things in a sufficiently fine-grained way. An example will help see why. Until I started working on dreams a few years ago, I often woke up remembering and reporting dreams like this: 'I dreamed about my budget meeting with the Dean. He explained that money was tight. I was rude, and the whole thing ended in a mess.'

Now to say that this is a dream is to use the term 'dream' as it is commonly used to refer to any mentation occurring during sleep. But research has shown that this sort of perserverative anxious rehearsal is most likely to occur during non-REM (NREM) sleep, the sleep standardly divided into four stages which occupies about 75% of the night. Night terrors, a common affliction of young children (my daughter had severe ones until she was ten or eleven, especially if she was feverish), are very puzzling since the child seems totally awake, eyes wide open, running about speaking alternately sense and nonsense, but almost impossible to comfort and wake up entirely and, on most every view, suffering terrifying hallucinations (which even if the child is finally awakened are remembered much less well than hallucinatory REM dreams). But, and here's the anomaly, the terrorized child is almost certainly in Stage III or IV NREM sleep. Sleepwalking, sleep-talking, and tooth-grinding are also NREM phenomena—and no one knows for certain whether we should say persons walking and talking in sleep are *phenomenally-conscious* or not. I'm inclined to say there are, and thus that the answer to William James's question: are we ever wholly unconscious, is 'no'—at least for sleep.

So the first point is that mentation occurs during NREM sleep as well as during REM sleep, and we report mentation occurring in both states as 'dreams'. Now since the discovery of REM sleep, and its close association with reports of vivid fantastic dreaming, many have simply identified dreaming with REMing or with mentation occurring during REM sleep.[6] But this goes against the grain of our folk psychological usages of the term 'dream'.

So much the worse for the folk psychological term one might say. But if one wants to regiment language in this way, the stipulation must be made explicitly and there are costs with the explicit stipulation. To the best of my knowledge, only one dream research team has made any explicit sort of definitional manoeuvre along these lines. Allan Hobson's group at Harvard (sometimes) defines 'dreams' as the bizarre fantastic, image-rich mentation that occurs during REM sleep. Hobson's group leaves the anxious perseveration about the meeting with the Dean, worries about having left the door unlocked, tomorrow's agenda, that the car needs gas first thing in the morning, and the like, on the side of *conscious but non-dreaming mentation* associated with NREM sleep (see Hobson and Stickgold 1994). This definitional manoeuvre cleans things up and helps in general to draw a distinction between different kinds of sleep-mentation. We can imagine people—I now do this—reporting as *real* dreams only the real weird sleep mentation, and thinking of the 'Dean dream', or the recurring thought of failing the exam as NREM mentation. But the definitional manoeuvre has costs for it does not deal well with the NREM states, like night terrors, that (probably) involve hallucinations and bizarre mentation. These will turn out to be *non-dreams* because they occur during NREM sleep, but, at the same time, *dreams* because they are bizarre and hallucinatory. So everything doesn't become neat and tidy once we use the natural method to make principled distinctions. One reason is that terms that have their roots in folk psychology, although often helpful, are not designed to specify scientific kinds or natural kinds, if there are such kinds in the science of the mind.

Having recognized the benefits and costs of the definitional manoeuvre, it will do no harm for present purposes if I continue to use *p-dreams* to refer to any mentation occurring during sleep, recognizing full well that since mentation occurs in all stages of NREM and REM sleep, *p-dreaming* isn't precise enough ultimately to type mentation during sleep from either a phenomenological or neuroscientific point of view.

Now some of the essential questions that any good theory of sleep and dreams will need to explain are these:

1. Why (and how) despite involving vivid experiences do *p-dreams* involve shut-downs of the attentional, motor, and memory systems, and insensitivity to disturbance by external stimuli?
2. Why do the phenomenology of NREM and REM mentation differ in the ways they do?
3. What function(s) does sleep serve and how does the clock-like cycling of NREM and REM sleep contribute to these functions?

The short answers to (1) and (2) are these: sleeping in general is controlled by a clock in the *suprachiasmatic nucleus of the hypothalamus*—the hypothalamus is an area importantly implicated in the manufacture of hormones and thermoregulation. This clock gets us into NREM sleep, a hypometabolic form of sleep, and moves us through its four stages. There is a second clock in the *pons* (the pontine brainstem) that sets off REM movements and its accompanying mentation.

In REM-sleep pulsing signals originate in the brain stem and reach the lateral geniculate body of the thalamus. When awake, this area (G) is a relay between the retina—on certain views part of the brain itself—and visual processing areas. Other pulses go to the occipital cortex, the main visual processing area of the brain. So *PGO waves* are the prime movers of REMing. This much accounts for the saliency of visual imagery in the dreams of sighted people. But the PGO noise is going to lots of different places and reverberating every which-way. This is why people who work at remembering dreams will report loads of auditory, olfactory, tactile kines-thetic, and motor imagery, as well as visual imagery and dreams in which linguistic exchanges occur.

Indeed, there is nice convergence of neuroscientific and phenomenological data here. Recent studies have shown that the parts of the brain that reveal robust activity on PETs, MRIs, or magneto-encephalographs indicate that 'mentation during dream-ing operates on the same anatomical substrate as does perception during the waking state' (Llinás and Paré 1991).[7] But the main point is that PGO waves are dominant during REM sleep and quiescent during NREM sleep and this explains (by inference to the best available explanation) a good deal about why the mentation of REM sleep involves vivid, bizarre, and multimodal imagery.[8]

The answer to another piece of the puzzle, namely, why don't we in fact get up and do or try to do the things we dream about doing, has to do with the fact that a certain area in the brain stem containing the bulbar reticular formation neurons sends hyperpolarizing signals to the spinal cord, blocking external sensory input and motor output. People with certain sorts of brain stem lesions do get up in the middle of the night and play linebacker to their dresser—presumably imagined to be an oncoming fullback.

Dreams and functional explanation

So far I have tried to answer questions (1) and (2) about the differences between REM sleep and NREM sleep and the accompanying mentation. The answer to (3), the question of the function(s) of sleep and sleep-cycling, is not as well understood as some of the matters just discussed. Based on my reading, I have a list of over 50 distinct functions that have been attributed to sleep and dreams in the last decade alone! Using the best theory in town principle: here is how things look to me regard-ing the function question.

First, some facts. (1) Fish and amphibia rest but do not sleep at all. The most ancient reptiles have only NREM sleep, while more recent reptiles and birds have robust NREM sleep and some REM sleep. All mammals save one, the egg-laying marsupial echidna of Australia, have REM sleep. (2) In creatures that REM, REM-ing is universally more frequent at the earliest stages of development. So for humans, newborns are REMing during half the sleep cycle, this drops to 33% at 3 months and at puberty REM sleep comprises about 25% of all sleep. It decreases in relative amounts as we age, as does Stage III and IV NREM sleep.

The fact that NREM is the oldest form of sleep and is hypometabolic suggests the following hypothesis: it was selected for to serve restorative and/or energy conservation and/or body-building functions. Now some people find this hypothesis empty—akin to saying sleep is for rest which, although true, is thought to be uninformative. But things are not so gloomy if we can specify some of the actual restorative/conservatory/building mechanisms and processes in detail. And we can. The endocrine system readjusts all its levels during sleep. For example, testosterone levels in males are depleted while awake regardless of whether any sexual or aggressive behaviour has occurred, and are restored during sleep; indeed, levels peak at dawn. Pituitary growth hormone does its work in NREM sleep. Growth hormone promotes protein synthesis throughout the body—new cell growth helps with tissue repair—for example, cell repair of the skin is well studied and known to be much greater while sleeping than awake. Protein synthesis in the cerebral cortex and the retina follow the same pattern of having a faster rate in sleep than while awake. And, of course, the amount of food needed for survival is lowered insofar as metabolic rate is. Indeed, much more needs to be said, and can be found in medical textbooks about the restorative/conservatory/building processes that are fitness enhancing and associated with NREM sleep (see Kryger *et al.* 1994).

Regarding REM-sleep, two functions suggest themselves. First, the much larger percentage of REMing in development across mammals suggests that it is important in helping build and strengthen brain connections, particularly ones in the visual system, that are not finished being built *in utero*. On the other side, the prominence of significantly greater time spent in REM sleep as an infant, where one doesn't know or care about right and wrong, than as an adolescent bubbling over with vivid and new socially unacceptable wishes, should go the other way, one would think, if anything like the orthodox Freudian view of dream function were true. What instinctual impulses, what sexual and aggressive fantasies are being released by a newborn, or even less credibly by 30-week-old-fetuses which, according to some experts, go through phases of REMing 24 hours a day?

Neurochemicals and NREM and REM

Now the biggest difference between waking and NREM sleep and REM sleep has to do with the ratios of different types of neurochemicals, modulators, and transmitters in the soup. In particular, the ratios of cholinergic and aminergic neurochemicals flip-flop. Neurons known to release serotonin and norepinephrine shut off in the brain stem during REM and neurons secreting acetylcholine are on.

What good could this do? Here's one possible answer. The best theory of attention, namely that of Posner and Petersen (1990) says that norepinephrine is crucial in getting the frontal and posterior cortical subsystems to do a good job of attending. Furthermore, both norepinephrine and serotonin are implicated in thermoregulation as well as in learning, memory, and attention; and dopamine has been shown to play an essential role in learning, at least in sea slugs. Now what happens in REM sleep that is distinctive, in addition to the dream-mentation part, is that there is a complete shift in the ratios of certain classes of neurochemicals. In particular, in waking serotonin is working hard as are dopamine and norepinephrine. The aminergic neurons that release these neurochemicals quiet down in NREM sleep and turn off during REM sleep; this helps to explain why memory for dreams is degraded. Meanwhile, cholinergic neurons, for example, those releasing acetylcholine, turn on. Here is a credible hypothesis for why this might be: by a massive reduction in firing during REM sleep the neurons releasing the neurochemicals most directly involved in attention, memory, and learning get a rest. While resting they can synthesize new neurotransmitters. The evidence points to a major function of REM sleep as involving 'stockpiling' the neurotransmitters that the brain will need in the morning for the day's work (see Hobson 1989).

Another hypothesized function of sleep and of REM sleep in particular, that I haven't yet mentioned, is that something like disk maintenance, compression, trash disposal, and memory consolidation take place (see, for example, Crick and Mitchison 1983; Hopfield *et al.* 1993; Steriade *et al.* 1993). These seem like good things for the system to do. But it's pie in the sky hypothesizing until some mechanism is postulated that could do the job. How could such memory consolidation or junkyard functions work? What sort of mechanism could govern such a process or processes. One idea is this: for memories to be retained they must be converted from storage in the halfway house of distributed electrical patterns into stable protein structures within neurons, in particular at the synapses. To get a feel for the need here: imagine your computer crashing and the different SAVES made. The idea is that memory reactivation involves the reactivation of the neural networks whose synaptic strengths have been altered. What happens during REM sleep is that the cholinergic neurons that are on and releasing acetylcholine interact with the temporary but connected electrical synaptic hot spots constituting a memory from the day, and change those hot spots to a more stable form, to some sort of protein structure (see Hobson 1989).

Natural functions

The hypothesis can be formulated somewhat more precisely given what has been written so far. It is that sleep and the phases of the sleep cycle—NREM and REM sleep—were selected for *and* are maintained by selective pressures. They are *adaptations* in the biological sense (see Burian 1992; West-Eberhard 1992; Kitcher 1993; Godfrey-Smith 1994). However, the mental aspects of sleep, the thoughts that occur during NREM sleep, as well as the dreams, and lucid dreams (dreams which contain the awareness that one is dreaming) that occur during REM sleep are probably epiphenomena in the sense that they are serendipitous accompaniments of what sleep is for.

Now some things that were originally selected for to serve a certain function, end up being able, with some engineering modifications, to serve another function.

Selection pressures then work as it were to select and maintain the adaptation because it serves both purposes, or to put it another way both the original phenotypic feature and the extended one serve to increase fitness. For example, feathers were almost certainly selected for thermoregulation, but now selective pressures work to maintain feathered wings because they enable flight.

It is standard in evolutionary biology to say of some 'automatic sequela', pleiotropic or secondary characteristic, that it is a *non-adaptation* only if it is a concomitant of a trait that was selected for and if, in addition, no concurrent positive selection or independent modification operates on the trait (West-Eberhard 1992). So the capacity to fly may have been a sequela of selection pressures to design efficient thermoregulation, but feathered wings are an adaptation because despite being a secondary characteristic they were (and are) subject to positive selection and modification pressures. But the colour of blood and the human chin are common examples of sequelae that are non-adaptations.

The biological notion of an *adaptation* and even a *non-adaptation* needs to be marked off from the concept of *adaptiveness* or *functionality*. The biological notion is tied to selection pressures which contribute to reproductive success in a particular environment or set of environments (Brandon 1990). But we also say of mechanical devices, intentional human acts or act-types, and of cultural institutions that they are *adaptive* or *functional*. Here we mean that the device, act, act-type, institution *does what it is designed to do*. Kitcher (1996) argues that this idea unifies attributions of *function* across biological and non-biological contexts.

We need to draw one further distinction within the nest of meanings of the terms 'function' and 'functional': this between (1) a causal contribution sense of function and (2) a functional versus dysfunctional sense. So to use Kitcher's example, mutant DNA causing tumour growth is functioning as it is supposed to; it is making the causal contribution we expect, but it is dysfunctional; bad biologically and psychologically for the organism in which the tumour is growing.

Now my argument is this: sleep and sleep-cycling are an adaptation for reasons given above—they restore, conserve, and build and we can specify some of the specific things they do and the mechanisms these are done by.[9] There is some reason to wonder whether REMing and NREMing, that is the moving or non-moving of eyes, is an adaptation. And there is very good reason to be positively dubious about the adaptive significance of the phenomenal experiences that supervene on REM and NREM-sleep. Dreaming, broadly construed, is pleiotropic, an automatic sequela, a spandrel. It is doubtful that dream-consciousness once in play as a sequela of causal processes originating in the brain stem which tickle the visual areas producing REMs was subjected to positive selection pressures and modification. Actually, I should put it this way: for reasons discussed earlier the brain stem is designed to activate the visual system to finish building it during the first year of life. Once the system is built the continuation of the activation of the visual system serves no obvious further developmental function. Furthermore, whereas the PGO waves of REM-sleep are implicated in the processes of stockpiling neurochemicals for the next day's work, for making what is learned more stable so it can be remembered, and possibly for trash disposal, there is no reason to believe that these jobs require mentation of any sort.

Assuming, tentatively, that the stabilizing idea is right, there is no phenomenological evidence that, as electrical patterns are transformed into protein structures, the associated mentation involves the activation of the thoughts worth remembering. People remember nonsense syllables better after sleep than if tested right after learning but before sleep. But, to the best of my knowledge, people never report *p-dreaming* about nonsense syllables. Nor do students of mathematics work through the proofs of the previous day in dreams. It may well be that the proof of the Pythagorean theorem would go in one ear and out the other if we didn't sleep in between. But I would place large bets that one will have trouble getting any phenomenological reports of sophomore geometry students dreaming through the steps of the theorem in REM sleep. The point is that PGO waves are causally implicated in the neurochemical stockpiling of amines (serotonin, norepinephrine, etc.) and in setting acetylcholine and its friends to the task of bringing stability to what has been learned. But there is no reason, so far as I can see, to think that the mentation caused by the PGO waves is causally relevant to these processes. The right circuits need to be worked on, but no mentation about the information that those circuits contain is needed, and typically such mentation does not occur. The visual, auditory, propositional, and sensory-motor mentation that occurs is mostly noise. One might be drawn to a different conclusion if the mentation was, as it were, about exactly those things one needs to stabilize for memory storage, but phenomenologically that seems not to be the case. It can't be the actual thoughts that occur during the bizarre mentation associated with REMing which the system is trying to stabilize, remember, or store—most of that is weird. Of course, some is not weird, and of course the so-called day's residue makes occasional appearances in dreams. It would be surprising if it didn't—it's on your mind. The incorporation of external stimuli is also easily explained; the system is designed to be relatively insensitive to outside noise, but it would be a pathetic survival design if it were completely oblivious to outside noise. Hence, dripping faucets, cars passing on the street outside, are being noticed but in a degraded way, they won't wake you, but a growling predator at your campsite will.

P-dreams are a special but by no means unique case where the epiphenomenalist suspicion has a basis. *P-dreaming* is to be contrasted with cases where phenomenal awareness was almost certainly selected for. Take normal vision, for example. It is, I think, a biological adaptation. Blind persons who have damage to area V1 in the visual cortex get visual information but report no phenomenal awareness of what is in the blindfield. They behave in degraded ways towards what is there if asked to guess what is there, or reach for it, which is why we say they are getting some information. One interpretation of these findings is that the damage to V1 is the cause of the problem with phenomenal visual awareness and it is the deficiency in phenomenal awareness which explains why the performance is degraded.[10] Such an interpretation lends support to the idea that the phenomenal side of vision is to be given an adaptationist account along with, and as part of, an adaptationist account of visual processing generally. This is not so with *p-dreaming*.

Do 40 Hz oscillations underwrite experiencing?

I insisted at the outset that we should not expect any unified theory of the hetero-geneous types of mental states that fall under the concept of 'consciousness'. This is compatible with there being a shared *brain-feature* which explains why certain mental events have *phenomenal properties* and others do not. Indeed, it has been suggested that subjective awareness is linked to oscillation patterns in the 40 Hz range in the relevant groups of neurons, that is, neurons involved in a certain decod-ing task 'synchronize their spike in 40Hz oscillations' (Crick and Koch 1990, p. 272). 40 Hz oscillations have been found in single neurons and neural nets in the retina, olfactory bulb, in the thalamus, and neocortex.

More recently, Rodolfo Llinás, Ribary, and Paré have produced strong evidence that such oscillation patterns characterize REM sleep. In a paper published in 1993, Llinás and Ribary report that 'during the period corresponding to REM sleep (in which a subject if awakened reports dreaming), 40Hz oscillation patterns similar in distribution phase and amplitude to that observed during wakefulness is observed.' The second finding of significance they express this way: 'during dreaming 40Hz oscillations are not reset by sensory input ... We may consider the dreaming condition a state of hyperattentiveness in which sensory input cannot address the machinery that generates conscious experience.'

The main point for present purposes is that the reason dreams *seem* like conscious experiences may be because they *are* conscious experiences and they are like awake conscious experiences in certain crucial aspects. Llinás and Ribary (1993, p. 2081) suggest this unifying hypothesis: 40 Hz activity in the non-specific system com-prised of the thalamo-cortical loop provides the temporal binding of contentful states that involve 40 Hz oscillations in the areas devoted to particular modalities. That is, the neural system subserving a sensory modality provides the *content* of an experi-ence and the non-specific system consisting of resonating activity in the thalamus and cortex provides 'the *temporal binding* of such content into a single cognitive experience evoked either by external stimuli or, intrinsically during dreaming'. Llinás and Paré (1991, p. 532) write '*it is the dialogue between the thalamus and the cortex that generates subjectivity*'.

These data and hypotheses, in the light of other data and theory, increase the credi-bility of the claim linking REM sleep with vivid experiences. Whether it is really true that the phenomenal properties of dreams are underwritten by a certain kind of oscillation, and whether the relevant oscillatory pattern underwrites *experiencing* generally, depends on whether 40 Hz oscillations turn out to be a marker, a constituent component, or a cause (which one it is, is, of course, very important) of conscious ex-periences. Are 40 Hz oscillations necessary or sufficient for experiencing? Or neither?

Given my line that mentation is ubiquitous during NREM sleep, for the 40 Hz 'necessity' idea to get off the ground, it will have to be the case that such oscillations show up in NREM sleep. For a time this looked like a non-starter, since EEGs just didn't turn up 40 Hz oscillations. One possibility is that 40 Hz oscillations may be a reliable marker of certain kinds of conscious mentation but are not necessary for all mentation (see Steriade *et al.* 1993). However, recent work indicates that when measured with MEG one does find 40 Hz oscillations during NREM sleep. The oscillations are much attenuated in amplitude and there is little amplitude modulation. Perhaps this will help explain something about the lack of vivacity, the relative qualitative dullness of NREM mentation. Perhaps not.

We also need to know why, despite involving vivid experience, dreams involve shut-downs of the attentional, motor, and memory systems, and insensitivity to disturbance by external stimuli. Here, as Allan Hobson has pointed out, under the rubric of (**M**)odulation (specifically de-modulation), ratios of neurochemicals of various sorts play the major role. Possibly 40 Hz oscillation (**A**)ctivation patterns might explain the similarity between dreams and waking states while input–output gating (**I**) and demodulation (**M**) explain the main differences.[11]

Invented functions

The phenomenal aspects associated with sleeping are non-adaptations in the biological sense. The question remains: does *p-dreaming* serve a function? If it does it is a derivative psychological function constructed via mechanisms of cultural imagination, and utilization of the fact that, despite not serving a direct biological or psychological function,[12] the content of dreams is not totally meaningless (this has to do with what the system is trying to do during sleep and sleep-cycling) and thus dreams can be used to shed light on mental life, on well-being, and on identity. What I mean by the last remark is this: *the cortex's job is to make sense out of experience and its doesn't turn off during sleep.* The logically perseverative thoughts that occur during NREM sleep are easy for the cortex to handle since they involve real, but possibly 'unrealistic' ideation about hopes, worries, and so on. Indeed, from both a phenomenological and neuroscientific perspective awake mentation and NREM sleep mentation differ more in degree than in kind: worrying and wondering and problem solving while awake are less likely than their NREM kin to get caught in perseverative ruts or involve running around in circles. The point remains: we express ourselves, what's on our minds when we wonder and worry and plan and rehearse. This is something we *learn* to do. Thinking comes in handy while awake, and apparently the costs of doing so while asleep do not exceed the benefits, unless of course perseveration is keeping us from sleep in which case we do need to learn how to prevent or control the thinking.

REM mentation is a different story. It differs in kind from ordinary thinking. Phenomenologically and brainwise it is a radically different state—closer to psychosis than to any other mental state type. Still the cortex takes what it gets during REM sleep and tries to fit it into the narrative, script-like structures it has in place about how my life goes and how situations, e.g. restaurant scenes, visits to amusement parks, to the beach, and so on, go.

Consider Sigmund Freud's famous dream of 'Irma's injection'. The dream I would argue makes sense, possibly the sense assigned by Freud to it, but it requires none of the psychoanalytic apparatus: no manifest, latent content distinction, no repressive dream working over, and certainly no symbols, requiring Lamarkian transmission. Here is Frank Sulloway's (1979) summary account of the dream of 'Irma's injection'.

The immediate circumstances associated with this famous dream were as follows. Irma, a young woman who was on very friendly terms with Freud and his family, had been receiving psychoanalytic treatment from Freud in the summer of 1895. After several months of therapy, the patient was only partially cured, and Freud had become unsure whether he should keep her on. He had therefore proposed a solution to her, but she was not inclined to accept it. The day before the dream, Freud was visited by his friend 'Otto' (Oskar Rie), who had been staying with the patient's family at a summer resort. Otto reproved Freud for his failure to cure Irma of all her symptoms. That evening Freud wrote out Irma's case history so that he might present it to 'Dr. M.' (Josef Breuer) in order to justify his treatment of the case. Later that night Freud dreamt that he met Irma at a large party and said to her, 'If you still get pains, it's really only your fault.' Irma looked 'pale and puffy', and Freud wondered if she might not have an organic disease after all. He therefore examined his patient and detected white patches and scabs in her mouth. Otto and Dr. M., who were also present in the dream, then examined the patient for themselves; it was agreed by all that Irma had contracted 'an infection': the three physicians further determined that the infection had originated from an injection previously given to the patient by Otto, who had apparently used a dirty syringe.

Upon interpretation the next morning, Freud's dream revealed the fulfillment of at least two unconscious wishes. First, the dream had excused him of responsibility for Irma's pains by blaming them on Otto (Oskar Rie). Simultaneously the dream had exercised revenge upon Otto for his annoying remarks about Freud's unsuccessful therapy (Origins, p. 403; Interpretation, 1900a, S.E., 4:106–21).

This dream I would argue involves the following: a life, an unfolding history, a sense of self, fairly normal insecurities about whether one is doing one's job well, various defensive strategies. What it does not seem to require is 'two unconscious wishes'. Certainly, the dream is not a simple read. What is? We think in scripts, prototypes, and stories; and metaphors and metynomic extension abound. We are story-telling animals and we think and say things before we know what they mean, or perhaps, more familiarly, we know what we think only once we have expressed ourselves. Freud's dream sounds more REM-like than NREM-like, but, that aside, it is no more hard to interpret than would a variation on my 'Dean dream' that involves the death of the fund-raiser who failed to raise the money for the new science centre causing fiscal misery and a thought about some (lesser) harm coming to my predecessor as Chair. In neither case is there any 'unconscious wish' in the sense Freud came to soon after the 'Irma dream'. This dream, as dreams go, is in need of interpretation. But it is hardly difficult to interpret.

Hobson's group is now studying the underlying *grammar of dream mentation* and the evidence is fascinating (see Stickgold *et al.* 1994*a,b*). *Settings* and scenes are fairly unconstrained, *plot* is intermediate, and *characters* and *objects* tend to be transformed in the most gradual ways. So one's true love might be in China one second and Brazil the next, there will be some work to make the plot coherent which will be hard, so what she's doing in China and Brazil might involve an odd plot shift but not a completely incoherent one. But you may also find that she has turned into an old true love, but probably not into a sofa, in the transcontinental scene shift.

Now mentation about one's current true love and one's old true love might be informative about what's on your mind, or it might be uninformative, just the best story-line the cortex can bring to the materials offered up, but this could be true and such a dream could still be a good place to start from in conversation with a psychiatrist if your love-life is going badly, or if you are suffering from any psychosocial malady. This may be because the content itself is revealing—remember there is a top-down/bottom-up struggle going on between the noise from below and the cortex which is trying to interpret the noise in terms of narrative structures, scripts, and self-models it utilizes in making sense of things while awake. It could be that the dream is uninterpretable, or is meaningless as an intentional narrative construct, or has nothing like the meaning we are inclined to assign, but is nonetheless a good conversation starter for someone trying to figure out the shape of their life. Obviously, from what I have said, the cortex is expressing what's on your mind, how you see things. Your dreams are expressions of the way you uniquely cast noise that someone else would cast differently. So things remain the same, *phenomenal-dreams* make a difference to your life. They may get you thinking in a certain way upon waking. You may find yourself in a hard to shrug-off mood despite learning that the imagined losses of loved-ones causing that mood were dreamed and didn't really happen.[13] You may be inspired to write a poem or a mystical text, and you may work at the project of interpretation. This is not silly. What you think while awake or while asleep is identity-expressive. The project of self-knowledge is important enough to us that we have learned to use the serendipitous mentation produced by a cortex working with the noise the system produces to further the project of self-knowledge and identity location. This is resourceful of us.

Another piece of evidence about dreams and self-expression involves the technique of *dream-splicing*. Hobson and his colleagues have tried two different techniques involving *third-party* judgments about the meaning, in particular the thematic integrity, of dream reports (mostly less than 80% REM-mentation reports). In one situation, subjects were given spliced dreams, that is, dreams cut at mid-point and connected to the dream of which they were a part *or* some other subject's report. Subjects correctly scored 82% of spliced and intact reports and over 50% were correctly scored by all five judges. In the second situation, subjects were provided with abridged but not spliced dreams. An abridged dream consisted of the first five and last five lines with a more than 50% missing mid-section. Abridged dreams are correctly identified as such in only 25% of the cases. This suggests to Hobson and his colleagues that dreams are self-expressive and have narrative structure. But the noise created, randomly enough, for the plot line is such that something like Seligman and Yellen's (1987) 'principle of adjacency' is deployed. That is, the rule for the dream narrator is to make sense in terms of what was just made sense of. This is hardly the Freudian line about night-long thematic continuity. But it allows for two things upon which I would insist at present: (1) that dreams be allowed meaning-fulness and significance, even if only prima facie meaningfulness; (2) that we keep alive the possibility that ordinary awake thought does not simply satisfy some principle of self-expression of who I *really* am—some principle much stronger than adjacency, for example. I am attracted to the idea that there is no way we really are until we engage in the project of self-narration. Once begun, a self-model is kept as a complex dispositional structure of the brain, and is involved (and updated) to some extent in subsequent thinking. So what I think is who I am, and what I think is made up as I go along. Dreams both reflect and participate in the project of self-creation. Perhaps they have less causal importance than awake thinking. We don't know at present how to perform this crucial experiment. But it is not trivial to be led to ordinary *thought*—'cognition', as we now say. For surely, ordinary thought is not self-expressive always. It is probably itself a spandrel. Exercising is a spandrel evolutionarily, but not biologically, psychologically speaking. It is functional. But thinking, dreaming, and exercising may all well be best viewed as *social* 'practices', as ways of being within a certain form of life. Sure, we couldn't do any of these if our biology didn't allow them. But none of these may be natural kinds; and what is permitted and what is required are as different as night and day. And there is a world, a natural and social environment, that antedates *this* organism. I'll express what is on *this* organism's mind, but as I go along—as I figure it out. Self-expression is ubiquitous. But you get the idea: the self is an *objet d'art*—the self is made not born. Dreams sometimes express aspects of you. But not always. When they do and when they don't, they can be used: grist for the interpretative mill or meaningless stimuli for further thought. Read your diary *or* look at a dot on the wall. It is by no means obvious which leads or would normally lead to better self-exploration or deeper self-knowledge. But surely, and this is perhaps the main point, *thinking* (awake, REM, NREM) is identity expressive. It is processed by and through me, this organism, this thinking thing.

Endnotes

[1] After his transformation from philandering pagan to an ascetic Christian, poor Augustine proposed a theory for how dreams might contain sinful content without being sins (see Pine-Coffin 1961). The proposal in modern terms was that dreams are happenings not actions. Augustine wrote,

> You commanded me not to commit fornication ... But when I dream [thoughts of fornication] not only give me pleasure but are very much like acquiescence to the act ... Yet the difference between waking and sleeping is so great [that] I return to a clear conscience when I wake and realize that, because of this difference, I am not responsible for the act, although I am sorry that by some means or other it happened in me.

[2] But Malcolm (1959) and Dennett (1978, 1979) are right to express the worry that dream reports are putrid evidence that this is so. We need a neuroscientific account to shore up the phenomenological confidence that dreams are experiences that take place while asleep. We now, I claim, have such a theory, although I won't set out the argument here (I have in Flanagan 1996; see also Hobson 1988, 1989 and Hobson and Stickgold 1994 for the theory

AIM that I depend on. Dreams turn out to be experiences on that theory and thus to belong to the heterogeneous set of experiences we call 'conscious'.

[3] When I say let the psychologists and cognitive scientists have their say I mean also to include amateurs—let folk wisdom be put out on the table along with everything else.

[4] Crick and Koch (1990) were the first to suggest that subjective awareness is linked to oscillation patterns in the 40 Hz range in the relevant groups of neurons. Recently, Llinás and Paré (1991) have produced strong evidence that such oscillation patterns characterize REM sleep. Within Hobson's theory, the 40 Hz oscillations pertain to (**A**) activation level, while the tuning out of external stimuli is explained by the mechanisms of input–output gating (**I**).

[5] See the exchange between Kathleen Emmett (1978) and Daniel C. Dennett (1979). Dreams are fodder for sceptics about the prospects for a theory of consciousness for a number of reasons. One route to scepticism is simple and straightforward. Common sense says that 'conscious' involves, among other things, being awake. But dreaming takes place during sleep, and, thus, by the distinguished deliverances of conceptual analysis, dreams cannot be conscious experiences. But common wisdom also says that dreams are experiences that take place during sleep, so our common sense taxonomy of 'consciousness' is worse than a hodgepodge; it is riddled with inconsistency from the start.

[6] The exciting work of Jouvet (1962), Aserinsky and Kleitman (1955), and Dement (1958) led to the identification of 'dream mentation' with REM sleep. But this, it appears, is a mistake: NREM sleep is also associated with reports of mentation, and although the phenomenological content of such mentation is mundane and fairly non-bizarre, involving such things as worries about something that needs to be done the next day, subjects do not say they were just thinking about what they needed to do the next day, but that they were '*dreaming*' about it (Foulkes 1985; Herman *et al.* 1978). Indeed, if one thinks that mentation is dreaming only if it occurs during REM sleep, then people are even more disastrously bad at giving dream reports than most have thought: for many reported dreams are of the 'I was supposed to do x, but didn't' sort and the evidence points to greater likelihood that such mentation occurs during NREM sleep than during REM sleep. It was Foulkes (1985) who led the credible movement, not yet won, to disassociate the virtually analytic connection that had been drawn and continues to be drawn by most researchers between REM and dreaming. Indeed, someone—I can't remember who it was—founded 'The Society for the prevention of cruelty to NREM sleep'. The idea was to let dreaming be, as a first pass, any mentation that takes place during sleep, and go from there. The frequency of NREM mentation casts doubt on the idea that dreaming is a natural kind, although we may well be able to discern differences between NREM mentation and REM mentation. Nonetheless, some researchers suggest that the conclusion to be gained from expanding the concept of dreaming is this: 'The hope that one stage of sleep, or a given physiological marker, will serve as the sole magic key for vivid dream mentation has all but faded from view.' (Herman *et al.* 1978, p. 92). The overall point is this: *p-dreams*, as we normally think of them, include both the perseverative, thoughtlike mentation of NREM sleep and the bizarre and fantastic mentation of REM sleep, but the foregoing scientific considerations suggest reasons for restricting the use of the term 'dreams' for certain scientific and philosophical purposes only to REM-mentation, but there are some reasons against doing this— for example, the hallucinatory night terrors of Stage III and IV NREM sleep. A further issue is this: since we are always in either NREM or REM sleep or awake it is possible that we are *never* unconscious. Alternatively, it is possible that there are times in both NREM and REM sleep when virtually nothing thoughtlike is happening—or perhaps we are informationally sensitive (this could explain how sleepwalking without awareness could be possible— similar to the way blindsight patients process some information about what's in the blind field without being *p-aware* of, or experientially sensitive to what's in that field). No one knows for sure.

[7] This helps explain why prosopagnosics don't report dreaming of faces and why people with right parietal lobe lesions who can't see the left side of the visual field report related deficits in their dream imagery (Llinás and Paré 1991, p. 524). On the other hand, it tells us something about memory that visual imagery sustains itself better in both the dreams and the awake experiences of people who develop various kinds of blindness in later life.

[8] Once such imagery is overrated, dreaming is equated with REMing and the sensorily dull but thought-like mentation of NREM sleep is ignored and the hasty inference is made that NREM sleep, especially Stage IV NREM sleep, is a period of unconsciousness.

[9] I haven't even mentioned some of the other systems that are being worked on in sleep, e.g. the immune system. People who are kept from sleeping die, not from lack of sleep as such, but from blood diseases. Without sleep the immune system appears to break down.

[10] See Block (1996) for an objection to this sort of reasoning; and see my response in Flanagan (1992, pp. 145–52).

[11] Hobson calls his theory **AIM**. It is a three component model: **A** = activation level; **I** = input–output gating; and **M** = what excitatory or inhibitory work neurochemicals are doing.

[12] I need to be clear here that the very same processes that produce *p-dreaming* as an effect produce the switch in neurotransmitter ratios which do serve an important psychological function. But *p-dreams* don't serve this function.

[13] I have talked very little about the activation of limbic areas during dreams. Hobson's group finds that emotions and moods are coherently coordinated with dream content. This, it seems to me, is good evidence of cortical domination of the plot line and of limbic cooperation.

References

Aserinsky, E. and Kleitman, N. (1958). Two types of ocular motility occurring in sleep. *Journal of Applied Physiology*, **8**, 1–10.

St Augustine. (trans. R.S. Pine-Coffin) (1961). St Augustine Confessions. Penguin, New York, pp. 233–4.

Block, N. (1995). On a confusion about a function of consciousness. *Brain and Behavioral Sciences*, **8**, 227–47.

Brandon, R. (1990). *Adaptation and environment*. Princeton University Press.

Burian, B. (1992). Adaptation: historical perspectives. In *Keywords in evolutionary biology* (ed. E.F. Keller and E. Lloyd), pp. 7–12. Harvard University Press, Cambridge.

Crick, F. and Koch, C. (1990). Towards a neurobiological theory of consciousness. *Seminars in the Neurosciences*, **2**, 263–75.

Crick, F. and Mitchison, G. (1983). The function of dream sleep. *Nature*, **304**, 111–14.

Dawkins, R. (1976). *The selfish gene*. Oxford University Press.

Dement, W. (1958). The occurrence of low voltage, fast, electroencephalogram patterns during behavioural sleep in the cat. *Electroencephalography and Clinical Neurophysiology*, **10**, 291–6.

Dennett, D. (1978). *Brainstorms*. MIT Press, Cambridge.

Dennett, D. (1979). The onus re experiences. *Philosophical Studies*, **35**, 315–18.

Emmett, K. (1978). Oneiric experiences. *Philosophical Studies*, **34**, 445–50.

Flanagan, O. (1992). *Consciousness reconsidered*. MIT Press, Cambridge.

Flanagan, O. (1997). Prospects for a unified theory of consciousness, or what dreams are made of. In *Scientific approaches to the question of consciousness*, 25th Carnegie Symposium on Cognition (ed. J. Cohen and J. Schooler). Erlbaum, Hillsdale.

Foulkes, D. (1985). *Dreaming: a cognitive-psychological analysis*. Erlbaum, Hillsdale.

Godfrey-Smith, P. (1994). A modern history theory of functions. *Nous*, **27**, 344–62.

Gould, S.J. (1984). Covariance sets and ordered geographic variation in *Cerion* from Aruba, Bonaire and Curacao: a way of studying nonadaptation. *Systematic Zoology*, **33**, 217–37.

Gould, S.J. and Lewontin, R.C. (1979). The spandrels of San Marco and the Panglossian paradigm. *Proceedings of the Royal Society of London, Series B*, **205**, 217–37.

Gould, S.J. and Vrba, E. (1982). Exaptation: a missing term in the science of form. *Paleobiology*, **8**, 4–15.

Herman, J.H., Ellman, S.J., and Roffwarg, H.P. (1978). The problem of NREM dream recall re-examined. In *The mind in sleep* (ed. A. Arkin, J. Antrobus, and S. Ellman). Erlbaum, Hillsdale, NJ.

Hobson, J.A. (1988). *The dreaming brain*. Basic Books, New York.

Hobson, J.A. (1989). *Sleep*. Scientific American Library, New York.

Hobson, J.A. and Stickgold, R. (1994). Dreaming: a neurocognitive approach. *Consciousness and Cognition*, **3**, 1–15.

Hopfield, J.J., Feinstein, D.I., and Palmer R.G. (1993). 'Unlearning' has a stabilizing effect on collective memories. *Nature*, **304**, 158–9.

Jouvet, M. (1962). Récherches sure les structures nerveuses et les mécanismes résponsables des différentes phases du sommeil physiologique. *Archives Italiennes de Biologie*, **100**, 125–206.

Kitcher, P. (1993). *Function and design. Midwest Studies in Philosophy*, XVIII, 379–97.

Kryger, M.H., Roth, T., and Dement, W. (1994). *Principles and practice of sleep medicine* (2nd edn). W.B. Saunders, London.

Llinás, R.R. and Paré, D. (1991). Of dreaming and wakefulness. *Neuroscience*, **44**, 521–35.

Llinás, R.R. and Ribary, U. (1993). Coherent 40-Hz oscillation characterizes dream state in humans. *Proceedings of the National Academy of Sciences of the United States of America*, **90**, 2078–81.

Malcolm, N. (1959). *Dreaming*. Routledge & Kegan Paul, London.

Marcel, A.J. and Bisiach, E. (ed.) (1988). *Consiousness in contemporary science*. Oxford University Press.

McGinn, C. (1989). Can we solve the mind-body problem? *Mind*, **98**, 349–66; reprinted (1991) in *The problem of consciousness*. Blackwell, Oxford.

Posner, M.I. and Petersen, S.E. (1990). The attention system of the human brain. *Annual Review of Neuroscience*, **13**, 25–42.

Seligman, M. and Yellen, A. (1987). What is a dream? *Behaviour Research and Therapy*, **25**, 1–24.

Steriade M., McCormick, D.A., and Sejnowski, T.J. (1993). Thalamocortical oscillations in the sleeping and aroused brain. *Science*, **262**, 679–85.

Stickgold, R., Rittenhouse, C.D., and Hobson, J.A. (1994*a*). Constraint on the transformation of characters, objects, and settings in dream reports. *Consciousness and Cognition*, **3**, 100–13.

Stickgold, R., Rittenhouse, C.D., and Hobson, J.A. (1994*b*). Dream splicing: a new technique for assessing thematic coherence in subjective reports of mental activity. *Consciousness and Cognition*, **3**, 114–28.

Sulloway, F. (1979). *Freud: biologist of the mind*. Basic Books, New York.

West-Eberhard, M.J. (1992). Adaptation: current usages. In *Keywords in evolutionary biology* (ed. E.F. Keller and E. Lloyd), pp. 13–18. Harvard University Press, Cambridge.

Part II
Approaches from cognitive neuroscience

5

Why can't I control my brain?
Aspects of conscious experience

MICHAEL S. GAZZANIGA

Introduction

It is really quite obvious and hilarious that our mind has a hard time of it when it tries to control our brain. Remember last night when you woke up at 3 a.m., full of concerns about this and that, concerns that always look black in the middle of the night? Remember how you tried to put them aside and get back to sleep? Remember how bad you were at it?

We have also all had the experience of having our interest sparked by an attractive stranger in the street. A struggle ensues as we try to override the deeply-wired brain circuitry that has been provided by evolution to maintain our desire to reproduce. Allaying possible embarrassment, the mind gets around the brain's assertion this time and manages to maintain control. All of the culture we are immersed in does have an effect, and so we are not completely at the mercy of our brains' desires. At least we like to maintain that belief.

And why is it that some of us like going to work so much? There goes that brain again. It has circuits that need attention, that want to work on certain problems. And then comes the weekly lunch, done right with wine and good food and good conversation. Mr Brain, there you go again. I suppose you will want to sleep after lunch too.

Nowhere is the issue of consciousness more apparent than when we see how ineffectual the mind is at trying to control the brain. In those terms, the conscious self is like a harried playground monitor, a hapless entity charged with the responsibility to keep track of multitudinous brain impulses running in all directions at once like impulsive children. Cognitive neuroscientists, in turn, attempt to understand the methods and strategies of that conscious self, and it is not an easy task.

There seems to be a private narrative taking place inside of each of us all the time, and it consists, in part, of the effort to tie together into a coherent whole the diverse activities of thousands of specialized systems we have inherited to deal with specific challenges. The great American writer John Updike (1989) muses upon the subject:

'Consciousness is a disease,' Unamuno says. Religion would relieve the symptoms. Religion construed, of course, broadly, not only in the form of the world's barbaric and even atrocious religious orthodoxies but in the form of any private system, be it adoration of Elvis Presley or hatred of nuclear weapons, be it a fetishism of politics or popular culture, that submerges in a transcendent concern the grimly finite facts of our individual human case. How remarkably fertile the religious imagination is, how fervid the appetite for significance; it sets gods to growing on every bush and rock. Astrology, UFOs, resurrections, mental metal-bending, visions in space, and voodoo flourish in the weekly tabloids we buy at the cash register along with our groceries. Falling in love—its mythologization of the beloved and everything that touches her or him is an invented religion, and religious also is our persistence, against all the powerful post-Copernican, post-Darwinian evidence that we are insignificant accidents within a vast uncaused churning, in feeling that our life is a story, with a pattern and a moral and an inevitability—that as Emerson said, 'a thread runs through all things: all worlds are strung on it, as beads: and men, and events, and life come to us, only because of that thread.' That our subjectivity, in other words, dominates, though secret channels, outer reality, and the universe has a personal structure.

Indeed. And what is it in our brains that provides for that thread? What is the system that takes the vast output of our thousands upon thousands of specialized systems and ties them into our subjectivity through secret channels to render a personal story for each of us?

It turns out that we humans have a specialized system to carry out this interpretive synthesis, and it is located in the brain's left hemisphere. I have called it the 'interpreter': a system that seeks explanations for both internal and external events in order to produce appropriate behaviours in response. For reasons I shall elaborate on below, we know that it resides in the left hemisphere, and it seems to be tied to the general capacity to see how contiguous events relate to one another. But before describing our research on these matters, it is valuable to sketch out a view of how the human mind has been built through natural selection. Assuming that this view is correct, it will make understanding the nature of conscious experience more tractable. It will review evidence that the interpreter, a built-in specialization in its own right, operates on the activities of the other specialized adaptations that are built into our brains. These adaptations are most probably cortically based, but they work largely outside of conscious awareness, as do the majority of our mental activities. It is the consequences of their activity that are interpreted, and that provide the thread that gives each of us our personal story.

Biological perspective

The powerful theory of natural selection confines how we should view the evolved brain and its functions. Accepting this simple fact immediately separates our discussion from the traditional behaviouristic views of formal psychology, which dictate that somehow our minds are built up from simple conditioning and associations. While that behaviouristic view has fallen pretty much into disrepute amongst psychologists, it always seems to lurk about in some context. Currently, the ideas of association networks have popped up again and are pushed by connectionist theorists. Although people want to believe that things work that way, biology is not obliging. It must be realized that the evolutionary engine of natural selection builds beautifully-crafted devices in bizarre ways, creating ever-more perfect machines from multitudinous random events. As a result, nature tends to use any trick that comes along to make things work. As George Miller recently put it when explaining why the cognitive revolution in psychology took place, 'during the 50s it became increasingly clear that behavior is simply the evidence, not the subject matter, of psychology.' I am sure that we are going to find some simple principles that describe our mental activity, and those principles are the goal of the mind sciences. But I am also sure they will be discovered to be instantiated into complex and often bizarre neural devices.

Niels Jerne (1967), the brilliant immunologist, played a primary role in alerting neuroscientists to the importance of basic biological mechanisms such as selection theory in trying to understand how the brain enables mind. When I minored in immunology in graduate school, conventional wisdom held that the body could make antibodies to any antigen. This was part of a prevalent view that many things in biology could be formed by instruction, that the biological organism took information from the environment and incorporated that information into its function. This idea indicated that globulin molecules would form around any antigen, generating an immune response.

By the mid-1960s, the revolution in biology had demonstrated that nothing could be further from the truth. It became clear that organisms, from mice to humans, were born with all of the antibodies they will ever have. Instead of the body being responsive to instruction from the environment, the invading antigen selects a group of antibodies that already exist in the body. These antibodies are amplified and result in the classical immune response. The complexity of the immune system is thus built into the body.

Despite the long history of belief that biological processes are subject to instruction, as Jerne pointed out, every time a biological process becomes understood, it is seen that selection mechanisms are at work, not instruction. For instance, the finches in the Galapagos Islands were subjected to a drought in 1977. Those individuals that had large beaks were able to make use of a more varied food supply, and so, after a generation or two, the smaller-beaked individuals had died off, and large beaks became a dominant feature among the finch population of the islands. It was not the case, clearly, that the finches learned to grow larger beaks to deal with the nature of the new food supply, but rather that the genetic characteristic of large-beakedness was rapidly selected for. And, of course, the same thinking applies to the well-known mutation of micro-organisms into resistant strains due to inappropriate use of antibiotics. Although it may appear that instruction is at work, as if somehow the environment were 'telling' organisms to change, in fact selection is at work.

Jerne made the suggestion in 1967 that perhaps the nervous system was built in a similar manner. Perhaps much of what appeared to be learning (and therefore the body receiving instruction from the environment) was in fact more akin to a selection process. The idea was that an organism has a variety of genetically-determined neural networks that are specialized for particular kinds of learning. When learning takes place, the system is in fact sorting through a vast array of built-in responses and seeking the one that is appropriate to use in response to the environmental challenge at hand.

This is a bold idea, and yet, so much of what we know about the brain, and about animal behaviour, psychological development, evolution, and human neuropsychology is consistent with some form of this idea. I have reviewed much of my thinking in this area elsewhere (see for example Gazzaniga 1992), but in brief it goes like this. Our modern brains are a collection of specialized systems that are designed to perform particular functions that contribute to the primary goal of every brain, that is, to enhance reproductive success. As Paul Rozin pointed out many years ago, just as one can view intelligence as a phenotype and look at the multitude of subprogrammes that contribute to that property, I believe that consciousness can be viewed as a phenotype, and one can identify subprogrammes that make up this feature of human brain activity. It is the accumulation of specialized circuits that accounts for the unique human experience.

The split-brain work I have been involved in has highlighted how the left and right hemispheres of the brain each possesses its own specialized functions. The left hemisphere is specialized for not only language and speech, but also for intelligent behaviour. Following disconnection of the human cerebral hemispheres, the verbal IQ of the patient remains intact (Nass and Gazzaniga 1987; Zaidel 1990), and problem-solving capacity, such as is seen in hypothesis formation tasks, remains unchanged for the left hemisphere (LeDoux *et al.* 1977). The left hemisphere thus remains unchanged from its pre-operative capacity, while the largely-disconnected, same-size right hemisphere is seriously impoverished on a variety of cognitive tasks. While the largely-isolated right hemisphere remains superior to the isolated left hemisphere for some activities, such as the recognition of upright faces, some attentional skills, and perhaps also emotional processes, it is poor at problem solving and many other mental activities.

Visuo-spatial function is generally superior in the right hemisphere, but left-hemisphere integration may be required for certain higher-order tasks. Likewise, superior use of visual imagery has been demonstrated in the left hemisphere when the stimuli being tested lend themselves to verbal naming (Gazzaniga and Smylie 1986). While the use of tactile information to build spatial representations of abstract shapes appears to be better developed in the right hemisphere, tasks such as the Block Design test from the WAIS, which are typically associated with the right parietal lobe, appear to require integration between the hemispheres in some patients (LeDoux *et al.* 1977). Furthermore, while the right hemisphere is better able to analyse unfamiliar facial information than the left hemisphere (Weiskrantz *et al.* 1974; Gazzaniga and Smylie 1983), and the left is better able to generate voluntary facial expressions (Gazzaniga and Smylie 1990), both hemispheres share in the management of facial expression when spontaneous emotions are expressed.

It is also evident that what we mean when we talk about consciousness is the feelings, the interpretations, and the memories we have about these specialized capacities. We have feelings about objects we see, hear, and feel. We have feelings about our capacity to think, to use language, and to apprehend faces. In other words, consciousness is not another system. It is the elusive thread that runs through the story enabled in each of us by the interpreter as the result of its coordinating the behaviour of all the specialized systems that have evolved to enable human cognitive processes. The discovery of the interpreter and its central role in our conscious experience is the subject of this paper, and the interpreter is responsible for generating the story that narrates the process of our brain doing its thing.

Early studies

Case W.J. was the first human split-brain case studied in modern times. Following callosal section in order to control intractable epilepsy, like all subsequent right-handed cases of relevance, he normally named and described information presented to his left speaking hemisphere (Gazzaniga *et al.* 1962). What was surprising was his seeming lack of response to stimuli presented to his surgically-isolated right hemisphere. It was as if he was blind to visual stimuli presented to his left visual field. Yet, with a series of tests I devised, it became obvious that while the left, talking hemisphere could not report on these stimuli, the right hemisphere, with its ability to control the manual responses of the left hand, could normally react to a simple visual stimulus.

An early conclusion about these phenomena was that dividing the hemispheres resulted in each half-brain behaving independently of the other. Information experienced by one side is unavailable to the other. Moreover, each half-brain seems to be specialized for particular kinds of mental activity. The left is superior for language, while the right is more able to carry out visual-spatial tasks. We had separated structures with specific and complex functions.

The capacities that were demonstrated from the left hemisphere were no surprise. However, when the first patients were able to read from the right hemisphere and were able to take that information and choose between alternatives, the case for a double conscious system seemed strong indeed. We could even provoke the right hemisphere in the sphere of emotions. I carried out dozens upon dozens of studies over five years on these patients, and all of them pointed to this dramatic state of affairs. After separating the human cerebral hemispheres, each half-brain seemed to work and function outside the conscious realm of the other. Each could learn, remember, emote, and carry out planned activities.

Although the observations were dramatic, we were still not close to capturing the essential nature of the dual consciousness in these patients. We had not tested the limits of mental capacities of the right hemisphere. We also had not seen many patients and did not have the opportunity to see the rich variation in right hemisphere capacity that has since been discovered by studying a larger group of split-brain patients. But most importantly, we really had not addressed the question of what consciousness actually is. After all, observing that a seemingly bilateral symmetrical brain can be divided, thereby producing two conscious systems, merely produces two systems that one does not understand instead of just one! In sum, these early findings provoked the curiosity that would lead to questioning of and insight into what is meant by the experience of being conscious.

By the mid 1970s, a new view of brain organization was proposed (Gazzaniga and LeDoux 1978; see also Gazzaniga 1985). A modular view of the brain was argued for, with multiple subsystems active at all levels of the nervous system and each subsystem processing data outside the realm of conscious awareness. These modular systems were hypothesized to be fully capable of producing behaviour, mood changes, and cognitive functions. These activities were, in turn, monitored and synthesized by the special system in the left hemisphere that I call the 'interpreter'.

The left-brain interpreter: initial studies

We first revealed the interpreter using a simultaneous concept test. In this type of test, the patient is shown two pictures, one exclusively to the left hemisphere and one exclusively to the right, and is asked to choose from an array of pictures placed in full view in front of him the ones associated with the pictures lateralized to the left and right brain. In one example of this kind of test, a picture of a chicken claw was flashed to the left hemisphere and a picture of a snow scene to the right hemisphere. Of the array of pictures placed in front of the subject, the obviously correct association is a chicken for the chicken claw and a snow shovel for the snow scene. Split-brain subject P.S. responded by choosing the shovel with his left hand and the chicken with his right. When asked why he chose those items, his left hemisphere replied, 'Oh, that's simple. The chicken claw goes with the chicken, and you need a shovel to clean out the chicken shed.' Here, the left brain, observing the left-hand's response, interprets that response in a context consistent with its sphere of knowledge —one that does not include information about the left hemifield snow scene. The result is absurd at first glance, but wholly logical in terms of the limited information available to the left hemisphere.

There are many ways to influence the left-brain interpreter. As I have mentioned in the foregoing, we wanted to know whether or not the emotional response to stimuli presented to one half-brain would have an effect on the affective tone of the other half-brain. But before going into these experiments, meet Case V.P. She is a patient of Dr Mark Rayport of the Medical College of Ohio. When we first tested her, she was a dazzling 28-year-old with a keen sense of life. She is introspective about her medical history and able to relate her feelings articulately. She, like P.S., has developed speech bilaterally, and like his, her initial right-hemisphere skills were limited to simple writing of answers along with the capacity to carry out verbal commands. If we flashed the command 'smile' to her right hemisphere, V.P. could do it. When we asked her why she was smiling, her left hemisphere, which could talk to the outside world, would concoct an answer. Two years later, V.P.'s right hemisphere would simply *tell* us why, since it had newly developed the capacity to talk.

For many purposes, however, it is more interesting to consider the kinds of studies that can be carried out when only one half-brain can talk. This scenario allows the experimenter to set up mood states in the non-talking hemisphere and to study whether or not the talking hemisphere is aware of the induced mood and, if so, how it reacts. From all of the other studies, of course, it is clear that the left brain is not directly knowledgeable about the actual visual images in a movie that has been presented to the right brain. The question we wanted to ask at this point, however, was whether the brain would react to the emotional content of those pictures. In other words, could we induce a mood in the left hemisphere based on visual stimuli of which it is not consciously aware?

Using a very elaborate optical–computer system that detects the slightest movement of the eyes, we were able to project a movie exclusively to V.P.'s right hemisphere. If she tried to cheat and move her eyes so that her left hemisphere could see it as well, the projector was automatically shut off. The movie her right hemisphere saw was about a vicious man pushing another man off a balcony and then throwing a fire bomb on top of him. It then showed other men trying to put the fire out. When V.P. was first tested on this task, she could not access speech from her right hemisphere. When asked about what she had seen, she said, 'I don't really know what I saw. I think just a white flash.' I asked her, 'Were there people in it?' She replied, 'I don't think so. Maybe just some trees, red trees like in the fall.' I asked, 'Did it make you feel any emotion?' She answered, 'I don't really know why, but I'm kind of scared. I feel jumpy. I think maybe I don't like this room, or maybe it's you, you're getting me nervous.' Then V.P. turned to one of the research assistants and said, 'I know I like Dr Gazzaniga, but right now I'm scared of him for some reason.'

That result represents an extreme case of an event that commonly occurs to all of us. A mental system sets up a mood that alters the general physiology of the brain. The verbal system notes the mood and immediately attributes cause to the feeling. It is a powerful mechanism and once so clearly seen, it makes you wonder how often we are victims of spurious emotional/cognitive correlations.

The interpreter: recent studies

Recent studies have further examined the properties of the interpreter and how its presence influences other mental capacities. There are, for example, hemisphere-specific changes in the accuracy of memory processes following callosotomy (Phelps and Gazzaniga 1992). The predilection of the left hemisphere to interpret events has an impact on the accuracy of memory. When subjects were presented with a series of pictures that represented common events (i.e. getting up in the morning or making cookies) and then asked several hours later to identify whether pictures in another series had appeared in the first, both hemispheres were equally accurate in recognizing the previously-viewed pictures and rejecting unrelated ones. Only the right hemisphere, however, correctly rejected pictures in the second set that were not previously viewed but were semantically congruent with pictures from the first set. The left hemisphere incorrectly 'recalled' significantly more of these pictures as having occurred in the first set, presumably because they fit into the schema it had constructed regarding the event. This finding is consistent with the idea of a left-hemisphere interpreter that constructs theories to assimilate perceived information into a comprehensible whole. In doing so, however, the elaborative processing involved has a deleterious effect on the accuracy of perceptual recognition. This result has been confirmed by Metcalfe *et al.* (1995) and extended to include verbal material.

A more recent example of the interpreter in action comes from studies documenting that Case J.W. can now speak out of his right hemisphere as well as his left. In brief, naming of left-field stimuli appears to be increasing at a rapid rate (Baynes *et al.* 1995; Gazzaniga *et al.*, in press). An interesting phenomenon that occurred during these naming tasks was J.W.'s tendency to sometimes report that he saw a stimulus in his right visual field that was actually presented to his left visual field. Although there is no convincing evidence of any genuine visual transfer between the hemispheres, on trials where he was certain of the name of the stimulus, he maintained that he saw the stimulus well. On trials where he was not certain of the name of the stimulus, he maintained that he did not see it well. This is consistent with the view that the left hemisphere's interpreter actively constructs a mental portrait of past experience, even though the experience in question did not directly occur in that hemisphere. We speculate that this experience was caused by the left-hemisphere interpreter giving meaning to right-hemisphere spoken responses, possibly by activating the left hemisphere's mental imagery systems.

A related phenomenon is seen in patients with cochlear implants. Implant surgery can enable patients who have become deaf after experiencing normal development of language to regain their capacity to hear (Schindler and Kessler 1987). The cochlear implant transduces auditory information into discrete patterns of stimulation on an eight-electrode array that is implanted on the cochlear nerve. After about three months of practice, subjects begin to be able to decode the implant's output as speech. As they become adept at this decoding task, they report that the speech they hear sounds normal. Since it is unlikely that the eight electrodes stimulate the cochlear nerve in the way that it was naturally activated prior to the hearing loss, the new auditory code must undergo a transformation such that the patients feel they are hearing undistorted speech. In other words, a new kind of auditory input is converted to a form that resembles the patients' stored representations of auditory input so seamlessly that the difference is not consciously recognizable. Observations of this kind are consistent with our present findings concerning visual input. J.W.'s left hemisphere maintains that he sees the objects presented to the right hemisphere; since the evidence suggests that there is no actual sensory transfer, J.W.'s interpretive system appears to be constructing this reality from speech cues that are provided by the right hemisphere. Again, the mind is fooled by the brain.

Consequences of commissurotomy on some aspects of cognition

While there can be little doubt that the left hemisphere of split-brain patients retains its abilities in terms of most higher-order cognitive activities such as verbal processing and problem solving, it is also true that there are some costs to having a divided brain. These costs do not appear to arise as a result of the separation of the two cortical mantles producing a state of impaired functioning through a lessening of general processing capacity. Rather, it appears that the effects are due to specialized systems being prevented from working together to produce particular cognitive outcomes.

Separating the hemispheres produces deficits that range from the subtle to the substantive. In one recent study, split-brain patients were assessed in terms of their ability to form a mental image of their left or right hand (Parsons *et al.* 1995). Each hemisphere had little problem generating an image of the contralateral hand, but was impaired at generating an image of the ipsilateral hand. This discrepancy is thought to be due to the fact that generating an image of a body part involves the part of the brain that actually manages the sensory-motor processes of the part in question. Thus, in a split brain, the left hemisphere is easily able to access the left pre- and post-central processes of the left hemisphere and thus the right hand. At the same time, it is no longer privy to the processes in the right pre- and post-central gyrus, which creates a problem for mental imaging of the left hand.

A more substantive deficit can be seen in the area of memory. We noted several years ago that following commissurotomy, patients had difficulty learning paired associate tasks (Gazzaniga *et al.* 1975). We also noted that this deficit was ameliorated in part by providing subjects with an imaging strategy, a finding that has now been confirmed (Milner *et al.* 1990). There have also been reports that split-brain patients suffer from an overall memory deficit, evidenced by subnormal scores on standardized tests (Zaidel and Sperry 1974). While these results were not in keeping with other observations (LeDoux *et al.* 1977), the issue of some sort of recall deficit was again observed in these patients if the test occurred at least two minutes after the test material was presented (Phelps *et al.* 1991).

Recently, the issue was carefully reexamined (Jha *et al.*, in press). Following commissurotomy, memory is definitely not normal. Although learning new skills and relationships is not a problem, memory of individual incidents is much impaired, not only in the laboratory, but also in everyday life. Testing to date suggests that this deficit may be more a function of impaired retrieval than impaired encoding. That is, with sufficient cueing, recall of complexes of information is possible. Recognition performance also seems to be a function of the information being presented to the subject in question in a more restrictive way, as if he has difficulty directing his own retrieval searches. These general findings fit well with the work by Phelps *et al.* (1991), as well as with a hemispheric encoding/retrieval asymmetry (HERA) model of prefrontal activation described recently by Tulving *et al.* (1994). In short, split-brain patients speaking from the left hemisphere do not have use of the right hemisphere's skill at retrieving episodic memories. Dividing the two hemispheres interferes with those cognitive processes that are normally distributed between the two cerebral hemispheres.

Summary and conclusions

Split-brain research has revealed an important dimension to the problem of under-standing conscious processes. The work is consistent with the view that the human brain manages specialized adaptations that have been established through natural selection for a variety of specific cognitive and perceptual tasks. These specific systems are monitored by yet another human adaptation, the left-brain interpreter, a system committed to building the narrative for the behaviour produced by the human brain's incessant activity.

Acknowledgements

Aided by NIH grants NINDS 5 RO1, NS22626-09, NINDS 5 PO1, and NS1778-012, and by the James S. McDonnell Foundation. Parts of this chapter have appeared in *The cognitive neurosciences* (ed. M.S. Gazzaniga (1995)), MIT Press, Cambridge, USA.

References

Baynes, K., Wessinger, C.M., Fendrich, R., and Gazzaniga, M.S. (1995). The emergence of the capacity of the disconnected right hemisphere to control naming: implications for functional plasticity. *Neuropsychologia*, **33**, 1225–42.

Gazzaniga, M.S. (1985). *The social brain*. Basic Books, New York.

Gazzaniga, M.S. (1992). Brain modules and belief formation. In *Self and consciousness* (ed. F.S. Kessel), pp. 88–102. Lawrence Erlbaum, Hillsdale, NJ.

Gazzaniga, M.S. and LeDoux, J.E. (1978). *The integrated mind*. Plenum Press, New York.

Gazzaniga, M.S. and Smylie, C.S. (1983). Facial recognition and brain asymmetries: clues to underlying mechanisms. *Annals of Neurology*, **13**, 536–40.

Gazzaniga, M.S. and Smylie, C.S. (1986). Right hemisphere superiorities: more apparent than real? *Society for Neuroscience Abstracts*, **2**, Part II, 1449.

Gazzaniga, M.S. and Smylie, C.S. (1990). Hemispheric mechanisms controlling voluntary and spontaneous facial expressions. *Journal of Cognitive Neuroscience*, **2**, 239–45.

Gazzaniga, M.S., Bogen, J.E., and Sperry, R.W. (1962). Some functional effects of sectioning the cerebral commissures in man. *Proceedings of the National Academy of Sciences of the United States of America*, **48**, 1765–9.

Gazzaniga, M.S., Risse, G.L., Springer, S.P., Clark, E., and Wilson D.H. (1975). Psychologic and neurologic consequences of partial and complete commissurotomy. *Neurology*, **25**, 10–15.

Gazzaniga, M.S., Eliassen, J.C., Nisenson, L., Wessinger, C.M., Fendrich, R., and Baynes, K. (1996). Collaboration between the hemispheres of a callosotomy patient: emerging right-hemisphere speech and the left hemisphere interpreter. *Brain*, **119**, 1255–62.

Jerne, N. (1967). Antibodies and learning: selection versus instruction. In *The neurosciences: a study program*, Vol. 1 (ed. G. Quarton, T. Melnechuck, and F.O. Schmidt), pp. 200–5. Rockefeller University Press, New York.

Jha, A.P., Kroll, N., Baynes, K., and Gazzaniga, M.S. Memory encoding following complete commissurotomy. *Journal of Cognitive Neuroscience*. (In press).

LeDoux, J.E., Wilson, D.H., and Gazzaniga, M.S. (1977). Manipulo-spatial aspects of cerebral lateralization: clues to the origin of lateralization. *Neuropsychologia*, **15**, 743–50.

Metcalfe, J., Funnell, M., and Gazzaniga, M.S. (1995). Right hemisphere memory superiority: studies of a split-brain patient. *Psychological Science*, **6**, 157–64.

Milner, B., Taylor, L., and Jones-Gotman, M. (1990). Lessons from cerebral commissurotomy: auditory memory, tic memory, and visual images in verbal associative learning. In *Brain circuits and functions of the mind: essays in honor of Roger W. Sperry* (ed. C.B. Trevarthen) pp. 293–303. Cambridge University Press, New York.

Nass, R.D. and Gazzaniga, M.S. (1987). Cerebral lateralization and specialization of the human nervous system. In *Handbook of physiology: the nervous system*, Vol. 5 (ed. V.B. Mountcastle, F. Plum, and S.R. Geiger), pp. 701–61. The American Physiological Society, Bethesda, MD.

Parsons, L.M., Gabrieli, J.D.E., and Gazzaniga, M.S. (1995). Cerebrally-lateralized mental representations of hand shape and movement. Presentation to the annual meeting of the Psychonomic Society, Los Angeles, California, November.

Phelps, E.A. and Gazzaniga, M.S. (1992). Hemispheric differences in mnemonic processing: the effects of left hemisphere interpretation. *Neuropsychologia*, **30**, 293–7.

Phelps, E.A., Hirst, W., and Gazzaniga, M.S. (1991). Deficits in recall following partial and complete commissurotomy. *Cerebral Cortex*, **1**, 492–8.

Rozin, P. and Schull, J. (1988). The adaptive–evolutionary point of view in experimental psychology. In *Steven's handbook of experimental psychology*. Vol. 1: Perception and motivation; Vol. 2: Learning and cognition, 2nd edn (ed. R.C. Atkinsin, R.J. Herristein, G. Lindzey, and R.D. Luce), pp. 503–46. Wiley, New York.

Schindler, R.A. and Kessler, D.K. (1987). The UCSF/Storz cochlear implant: patient performance. *American Journal of Otology*, **8**, 247–55.

Tulving, E., Kapur, S., Craik, F.I.M., Moscovitch, M., and Houle, S. (1994). Hemispheric encoding/retrieval asymmetry in episodic memory: positron emission tomography findings. *Proceedings of the National Academy of Sciences of the United States of America*, **91**, 2016–20.

Updike, J. (1989). *Self-consciousness*. Knopf, New York.

Weiskrantz, L., Warrington, E.R., Sanders, M.D., and Marshall, J. (1974). Visual capacity in the hemianopic field following a restricted occipital ablation. *Brain*, **97**, 709–28.

Zaidel, E. (1990). Language in the two hemispheres following complete cerebral callosotomy and hemispherectomy. In *Handbook of neuropsychology*, Vol. 4 (ed. F. Boller and J. Grafman). Elsevier, Amsterdam.

Zaidel, D. and Sperry, R.W. (1974). Memory impairment after cerebral commissurotomy in man. *Brain*, **97**, 263–72.

6

Brain mechanisms of vision, memory, and consciousness

EDMUND T. ROLLS

Introduction

We are starting to understand *how* the brain could perform some of the processing involved in perception and memory. These advances come in part from neuro-physiological experiments in which the processing involved in vision and memory is analysed by recording the activity of single neurons in primates during these types of processing, and incorporating this information into computational models at the network level which provide an account of the ways in which many neurons in a network could perform the required computations. Examples of this approach are described in this chapter. Understanding this processing provides some constraints on the neural basis of consciousness.

Having considered brain mechanisms involved in visual object recognition and memory, I then go on to consider whether, once this processing is fully understood, we will have produced an account of the brain mechanisms underlying conscious-ness. I argue that we will not, and that it is a different type of information processing that is involved in consciousness. I outline a theory of what the processing is that is involved in consciousness, of its adaptive value in an evolutionary perspective, and of how processing in our visual and other sensory systems can result in subjective or phenomenal states, the 'raw feels' of conscious awareness.

Brain mechanisms involved in visual object recognition

I focus on the nature of the representation of objects in the world that is found by the time information has reached the higher parts of the visual system, the temporal cortical visual areas, and on how that representation is built by passing through multiple connected cortical processing stages. Particular attention is paid to neural systems involved in processing information about faces, because with the large number of neurons devoted to this class of stimuli, this system has proved amenable to experimental analysis; and because of the importance of face recognition and expression identification in primate behaviour. Further elaboration of these ideas is provided by Rolls (1994*a*, 1995*a* and 1996*a*).

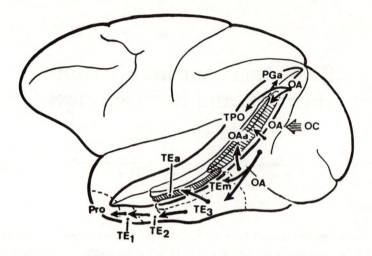

Fig. 6.1 Forward projections to and within the temporal lobe from earlier visual areas in the macaque. OC is the primary (striate) visual cortex. The TE areas form the inferior temporal gyrus, and the superior temporal sulcus (the margins of which are shown by a thick line) has been opened to reveal some of the areas within it. (From Seltzer and Pandya 1978.)

Visual cortical areas in the temporal lobes

Visual pathways project by a number of cortico-cortical stages from the primary visual cortex until they reach the temporal lobe visual cortical areas (Seltzer and Pandya 1978; Maunsell and Newsome 1987; Baizer *et al.* 1991). The inferior temporal visual cortex, area TE, is divided into a set of subareas, and in addition there is a set of different areas in the cortex in the superior temporal sulcus (Seltzer and Pandya 1978; Baylis *et al.* 1987) (see Fig. 6.1). Of these latter areas, TPO receives inputs from temporal, parietal, and occipital cortex, PGa and IPa from parietal and temporal cortex, and TS and TAa primarily from auditory areas (Seltzer and Pandya 1978). There is considerable specialization of function in these areas (Baylis *et al.* 1987). For example, areas TPO, PGa, and IPa are multimodal, with neurons which respond to visual, auditory, and/or somatosensory inputs; the inferior temporal gyrus and adjacent areas (TE3, TE2, TE1, TEa, and TEm) are primarily unimodal visual areas; areas in the cortex in the anterior and dorsal part of the superior temporal sulcus (e.g. TPO, IPa, and IPg) have neurons specialized for the analysis of moving visual stimuli; and neurons responsive primarily to faces are found more frequently in areas TPO, TEa, and TEm (Baylis *et al.* 1987), where they comprise approximately 20% of the visual neurons responsive to stationary stimuli, in contrast to the other temporal cortical areas in which they comprise 4–10%. The neurons which respond to non-face stimuli often require two or more simple features to be present in the correct spatial relationship in order to respond (Tanaka *et al.* 1990). The neurons with responses selective for faces are described in the remainder of this section, for the reasons given above, although we have recently described neurons in the anterior part of the temporal lobe which code for objects in what appears to be an analogous way (Rolls *et al.* 1996*a*).

Distributed encoding of facial identity

The neurons described in our studies as having responses selective for faces are selective in that they respond 2–20 times more (and statistically significantly more) to faces than to a wide range of gratings, simple geometrical stimuli, or complex 3D objects (see Rolls 1984, 1992*a*; Baylis *et al.* 1985, 1987). The selectivity of these neurons for faces has been quantified recently using information theory. This showed that these neurons reflected much more information about which (of 20) face stimuli had been seen (on average 0.4 bits) than about which (of 20) non-face stimuli had been seen (on average 0.07 bits) (Tovee and Rolls 1995).

These neurons thus reflect information not just that a face has been seen, but about which face has been seen. They respond differently to different faces. An important question for understanding brain computation is whether a particular object (or face) is represented in the brain by the firing of one or a few gnostic (or 'grandmother' or 'cardinal') cells (Barlow 1972), or whether instead the firing of a group or ensemble of cells each with somewhat different responsiveness provides the representation, as the data indicate for faces (Baylis *et al.* 1985). A recent way in which the fineness of tuning of these neurons to individual faces has been quantified is by measurement of the sparseness of the representation, *a*:

$$a = (\Sigma_{s=1,S} \; r_s/S)^2 \, / \, \Sigma_{s=1,S}(r_s^2/S)$$

where r_s is the mean firing rate to stimulus s in the set of S stimuli. The sparseness has a maximum value of 1.0, and a minimum value close to zero ($1/S$, if a neuron responded to only one of the S stimuli in a set of stimuli). (To interpret this measure, if the neurons had binary firing rate distributions, with a high rate to some stimuli and a rate of zero to the other stimuli, then if a neuron responded to 50% of the stimuli, the sparseness of its representations would be 0.5, and if it responded to 10% of the stimuli, the sparseness of its representation would be 0.1.) For a sample of these cells for which the responses were tested to a set of 23 faces and 45 natural scenes, it was found that the sparseness of the representation of the 68 stimuli had an average for the set of neurons of 0.65 (Rolls and Tovee 1995). If the spontaneous firing rate was subtracted, then the 'response sparseness' for these neurons was 0.33 (Rolls and Tovee 1995). It is suggested that the utility of this rather distributed encoding within the class faces is that it may enable the maximum information about a set of stimuli to be provided by a population of neurons (subject to a constraint on the average firing rate of the neurons; see Baddeley *et al.* 1996). Such a distributed representation would be ideal for *discrimination*, for the maximum information suitable for comparing fine differences between different stimuli would be made available across the population (if 50% were active to each stimulus). In contrast, it is suggested that more sparse representations are used in memory systems such as the hippocampus, because this helps to maximize the number of different memories that can be stored (see Rolls and Tovee 1995; Treves and Rolls 1994).

Although this rather distributed representation is present in the temporal cortical visual areas, it is certainly not fully distributed. If the information provided by a single neuron about each of the stimuli in a set of stimuli is calculated, then it is found that the amount of information about some stimuli can be as high as 1.5–2 bits for some stimuli, usually the most effective, and may approach zero for the stimuli in the set which produce responses which are close to the mean response of the neuron to the stimuli (Rolls *et al.* 1997*a*). The advantages of this type of sparse distributed representation for cognitive processing include generalization to similar stimuli (in the Hamming distance sense), graceful degradation (fault tolerance), and some locality to the representation, so that some single neurons which receive inputs from such a representation can obtain sufficient information without requiring an enormous fan in, that is number of synapses. (The number of synapses per neuron in the cerebral cortex is in the order of 5000, and only a proportion of these inputs will be active in any one 20 ms period.)

This information–theoretic approach has focused on how visual information about what is being looked at in the world is represented by the activity of individual neurons. How does the process scale when we take large numbers of such visual neurons? We have recently obtained evidence that the information available about which visual stimulus (which of 20 equiprobable faces) had been shown increases linearly with the number of neurons in the sample (Rolls *et al.* 1996*b*; Abbott *et al.* 1996). Because information is a logarithmic measure, this indicates that the number of stimuli encoded rises approximately exponentially, as the number of cells in the sample increases. The consequence of this is that large numbers of stimuli, and fine discriminations between them, can be represented without having to measure the activity of an enormous number of neurons. For example, the results of the experiments of Rolls *et al.* (1997*b*) indicate that the activity of 15 neurons would be able to encode 192 face stimuli (at 50% accuracy), of 20 neurons 768 stimuli, of 25 neurons 3072 stimuli, of 30 neurons 12 288 stimuli, and of 35 neurons 49 152 stimuli (Abbott *et al.* 1996; the values are for an optimal decoding case). This means that we can now effectively read the code from the end of this part at least of the visual system. By measuring the firing rates of relatively small numbers (tens) of neurons, we know which (of potentially hundreds or thousands of) visual stimuli are being looked at by the monkey.

A neuronal representation of faces showing invariance

One of the major problems which must be solved by a visual system used for object recognition is the building of a representation of visual information which allows recognition to occur relatively independently of size, contrast, spatial frequency, position on the retina, and angle of view, etc. We have shown that many of the neurons whose responses reflect face identity have responses that are relatively invariant with respect to size and contrast (Rolls and Baylis 1986); spatial frequency

(Rolls *et al.* 1985, 1987); and retinal translation, i.e. position in the visual field (Tovee *et al.* 1994). Some of these neurons even have relatively view-invariant responses, responding to different views of the same face but not of other faces (Hasselmo *et al.* 1989*a*). It is clearly important that invariance in the visual system is made explicit in the neuronal responses, for this simplifies greatly the output of the visual system to memory systems such as the hippocampus and amygdala, which can then remember or form associations about *objects*. The function of these memory systems would be almost impossible if there were no consistent output from the visual system about objects (including faces), for then the memory systems would need to learn about all possible sizes, positions, etc. of each object, and there would be no easy generalization from one size or position of an object to that object when seen with another retinal size or position.

Although the neurons just described have view-invariant responses, there is another population of face-selective neurons, found particularly in the cortex in the superior temporal sulcus, which tends to have view-dependent responses (Hasselmo *et al.* 1989*a*). Some of these neurons have responses which reflect the facial expression but not the facial identity of the stimulus (Hasselmo *et al.* 1989*b*). These neurons could be useful in providing information of potential use in social interactions (Rolls 1984, 1990*a*, 1992*b*; Perrett *et al.* 1985). Damage to this population and to brain areas to which these neurons project may contribute to the deficits in social and emotional behaviour produced by temporal or ventral frontal lobe damage (see Rolls 1984, 1990*a*, 1991, 1992*b*, 1995*b*, 1996*a*; Leonard *et al.* 1985; Hornak *et al.* 1996).

Learning of new representations in the temporal cortical visual areas

Given the fundamental importance of a computation which results in relatively finely tuned neurons which across ensembles, but not individually, specify objects including individual faces in the environment, we have investigated whether experience plays a role in determining the selectivity of single neurons which respond to faces. The hypothesis being tested was that visual experience might guide the formation of the responsiveness of neurons so that they provide an economical and ensemble-encoded representation of items actually present in the environment. To test this, we investigated whether the responses of temporal cortex face-selective neurons were at all altered by the presentation of new faces which the monkey had never seen before. It might be, for example, that the population would make small adjustments in the responsiveness of its individual neurons, so that neurons would acquire filter properties which would enable the population as a whole to discriminate between the faces actually seen. We thus investigated whether, when a set of totally novel faces was introduced, the responses of these neurons were fixed and stable from the first presentation, or instead whether there was some adjustment of responsiveness over repeated presentations of the new faces. First, it was shown for each neuron tested that its responses were stable over 5–15 repetitions of a set of familiar faces. Then a set of new faces was shown in random order (with 1 s for each

presentation), and the set was repeated with a new random order over many iterations. Some of the neurons studied in this way altered the relative degree to which
they responded to the different members of the set of novel faces over the first few
(1–2) presentations of the set (Rolls *et al.* 1989). If in a different experiment a single
novel face was introduced when the responses of a neuron to a set of familiar faces
was being recorded, it was found that the responses to the set of familiar faces were
not disrupted, while the responses to the novel face became stable within a few
presentations. Thus there is now some evidence from these experiments that the
response properties of neurons in the temporal lobe visual cortex are modified by
experience, and that the modification is such that when novel faces are shown, the
relative responses of individual neurons to the new faces alter (Rolls *et al.* 1989). It
is suggested that alteration of the tuning of individual neurons in this way results in
a good discrimination over the population as a whole of the faces known to the
monkey. This evidence is consistent with the categorization being performed by self-
organizing competitive neuronal networks, as described below and elsewhere (Rolls
1989*a,b,c*; Rolls and Treves, 1997).

Further evidence that these neurons can learn new representations very rapidly
comes from an experiment in which binarized black and white images of faces
which blended with the background were used. These did not activate face-selective
neurons. Full grey-scale images of the same photographs were then shown for ten
0.5 s presentations. It was found in a number of cases, if the neuron happened to be
responsive to the face, that when the binarized version of the same face was shown
next, the neurons responded to it (Rolls *et al.* 1993). This is a direct parallel to the
same phenomenon which is observed psychophysically, and provides dramatic evidence that these neurons are influenced by only a very few seconds (in this case 5) of
experience with a visual stimulus.

Such rapid learning of representations of new objects appears to be a major type
of learning in which the temporal cortical areas are involved. Ways in which this
learning could occur are considered below. It is also the case that there is a much
shorter-term form of memory in which some of these neurons are involved, for
whether a particular visual stimulus (such as a face) has been seen recently, in that
some of these neurons respond differently to recently seen stimuli in short-term
visual memory tasks (Baylis and Rolls 1987; Miller and Desimone 1994). A tendency of some temporal cortical neurons to associate together visual stimuli when
they have been shown over many repetitions separated by several seconds has also
been described by Miyashita (1988).

The speed of processing in the temporal cortical visual areas

Given that there is a whole sequence of visual cortical processing stages including
V1, V2, V4, and the posterior inferior temporal cortex to reach the anterior temporal
cortical areas, and that the response latencies of neurons in V1 are about 40–50 ms,
and in the anterior inferior temporal cortical areas approximately 80–100 ms, each
stage may need to perform processing for only 15–30 ms before it has performed

sufficient processing to start influencing the next stage. Consistent with this, response latencies between V1 and the inferior temporal cortex increase from stage to stage (Thorpe and Imbert 1989). This seems to imply very fast computation by each cortical area, and therefore to place constraints on the type of processing performed in each area that is necessary for final object identification. We note that rapid identification of visual stimuli is important in social and many other situations, and that there must be strong selective pressure for rapid identification. For these reasons, we have investigated the speed of processing quantitatively, as follows.

In a first approach, we measured the information available in short temporal epochs of the responses of temporal cortical face-selective neurons about which face had been seen. We found that if a period of the firing rate of 50 ms was taken, then this contained 84.4% of the information available in a much longer period of 400 ms about which of four faces had been seen. If the epoch was as little as 20 ms, the information was 65% of that available from the firing rate in the 400 ms period (Tovee *et al.* 1993). These high information yields were obtained with the short epochs taken near the start of the neuronal response, for example in the post-stimulus period 100–120 ms. Moreover, we were able to show that the firing rate in short periods taken near the start of the neuronal response was highly correlated with the firing rate taken over the whole response period, so that the information available was stable over the whole response period of the neurons (Tovee *et al.* 1993). We were able to extend this finding to the case when a much larger stimulus set, of 20 faces, was used. Again, we found that the information available in short (e.g. 50 ms) epochs was a considerable proportion (e.g. 65%) of that available in a 400 ms long firing rate analysis period (Tovee and Rolls 1995). These investigations thus showed that there was considerable information about which stimulus had been seen in short time epochs near the start of the response of temporal cortex neurons.

The next approach was to address the issue of for how long a cortical area must be active to mediate object recognition. This approach used a visual backward masking paradigm. In this paradigm there is a brief presentation of a test stimulus which is rapidly followed (within 1–100 ms) by the presentation of a second stimulus (the mask), which impairs or masks the perception of the test stimulus. This paradigm used psychophysically leaves unanswered for how long visual neurons actually fire under the masking condition at which the subject could just identify an object. Although there has been a great deal of psychophysical investigation with the visual masking paradigm (Turvey 1973; Breitmeyer 1980; Humphreys and Bruce 1989), there is very little direct evidence on the effect of visual masking on neuronal activity. For example, it is possible that if a neuron is well tuned to one class of stimulus, such as faces, that a pattern mask which does not activate the neuron will leave the cell firing for some time after the onset of the pattern mask. In order to obtain direct neurophysiological evidence on the effects of backward masking on neuronal activity, we analysed the effects of backward masking with a pattern mask on the responses of single neurons to faces (Rolls and Tovee 1994). This was performed to clarify both what happens with visual backward masking, and to show how long neurons may respond in a cortical area when perception and identification are just possible.

When there was no mask the cell responded to a 16 ms presentation of the test stimulus for 200–300 ms, far longer than the presentation time. It is suggested that this reflects the operation of a short-term memory system implemented in cortical circuitry, the importance of which is considered below. If the mask was a stimulus which did not stimulate the cell (either a non-face pattern mask consisting of black and white letters N and O, or a face which was a non-effective stimulus for that cell), then as the interval between the onset of the test stimulus and the onset of the mask stimulus (the Stimulus Onset Asynchrony, SOA) was reduced, the length of time for which the cell fired in response to the test stimulus was reduced. This reflected an abrupt interruption of neuronal activity produced by the effective face stimulus. When the SOA was 20 ms, face-selective neurons in the inferior temporal cortex of macaques responded for a period of 20–30 ms before their firing was interrupted by the mask (Rolls and Tovee 1994). We went on to show that under these conditions (a test-mask stimulus onset asynchrony of 20 ms), human observers looking at the same displays could just identify which of six faces was shown (Rolls *et al.* 1994*a*).

These results provide evidence that a cortical area can perform the computation necessary for the recognition of a visual stimulus in 20–30 ms, and provide a fundamental constraint which must be accounted for in any theory of cortical computation. The results emphasize just how rapidly cortical circuitry can operate. This rapidity of operation has obvious adaptive value, and allows the rapid behavioural responses to the faces and face expressions of different individuals which are a feature of primate social and emotional behaviour. Moreover, although this speed of operation does seem fast for a network with recurrent connections (mediated by, for example, recurrent collateral or inhibitory interneurons), recent analyses of networks with analog membranes which integrate inputs, and with spontaneously active neurons, show that such networks can settle very rapidly (Treves 1993; Simmen *et al.*, 1996; Treves *et al.*, 1997).

These experiments also have implications for visual processing in relation to top-down processing and consciousness. The evidence just described indicates that visual recognition can occur (the subjects say which face they saw) with largely feed-forward processing. There is not time in the experiments described for visual information to pass from V1 to V2 to V4 and thus to posterior and then anterior inferior temporal cortex, and back again all the way to V1, before V1 has started to process the second visual input, that is to have its processing of the first visual stimulus cut off by the mask.

Possible computational mechanisms in the visual cortex for learning invariant representations

The neurophysiological findings described above on the existence of ensemble-encoded invariant representations in the inferior temporal cortical areas (see also Rolls 1990*b*, 1991, 1994*a*), and wider considerations on the possible computational properties of the cerebral cortex (Rolls 1989*a,b*, 1992*a*, 1996*b*), lead to the following outline working hypotheses on object recognition by visual cortical mechanisms.

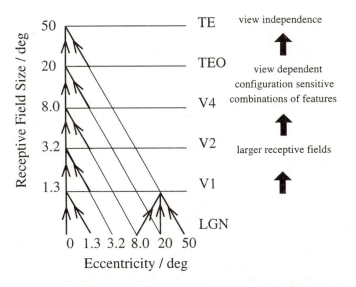

Fig. 6.2 Schematic diagram showing convergence achieved by the forward projections in the visual system, and the types of representation that may be built by competitive networks operating at each stage of the system from the primary visual cortex (V1) to the inferior temporal visual cortex (area TE) (see text). LGN is the lateral geniculate nucleus. Area TEO forms the posterior inferior temporal cortex. The receptive fields in the inferior temporal visual cortex (e.g. in the TE areas) cross the vertical midline (not shown).

The principles underlying the processing of faces and other objects may be similar, but more neurons may become allocated to represent different aspects of faces because of the need to recognize the faces of many different individuals, that is to identify many individuals within the category faces.

Cortical visual processing for object recognition is considered to be organized as a set of hierarchically connected cortical regions consisting at least of V1, V2, V4, posterior inferior temporal cortex (TEO), inferior temporal cortex (e.g. TE3, TEa, and TEm), and anterior temporal cortical areas (e.g. TE2 and TE1). (This stream of processing has many connections with a set of cortical areas in the anterior part of the superior temporal sulcus, including area TPO.) There is convergence from each small part of a region to the succeeding region (or layer in the hierarchy) in such a way that the receptive field sizes of neurons (e.g. 1 degree near the fovea in V1) become larger by a factor of approximately 2.5 with each succeeding stage (and the typical parafoveal receptive field sizes found would not be inconsistent with the calculated approximations of, for example, 8 degrees in V4, 20 degrees in TEO, and 50 degrees in inferior temporal cortex; Boussaoud *et al.* 1991) (see Fig. 6.2). Such zones of convergence would overlap continuously with each other (see Fig. 6.2). This connectivity would be part of the architecture by which translation invariant representations are computed. Each layer is considered to act partly as a set of local self-organizing competitive neuronal networks with overlapping inputs. (The region within which competition would be implemented would depend on the spatial properties of inhibitory interneurons, and might operate over distances of 1–2 mm in the cortex.) These competitive nets operate by a single set of forward inputs leading to (typically non-linear, e.g. sigmoid) activation of output neurons; of competition between the output neurons mediated by a set of feedback inhibitory interneurons which receive from many of the principal (in the cortex, pyramidal) cells in the net and project back to many of the principal cells which serves to decrease the firing rates of the less active neurons relative to the rates of the more active neurons (i.e. soft competition); and then of synaptic modification by a modified Hebb rule, such that synapses to strongly activated output neurons from active input axons strengthen, and from inactive input axons weaken (see Rolls 1989c; Rolls and Treves, 1997). (A biologically plausible form of this learning rule that operates well in such networks is

$$\delta w_{ij} = k \cdot m \, (r'_j - w_{ij})$$

where k is a constant, δw_{ij} is the change of synaptic weight, r'_j is the firing rate of the jth axon, and m is a non-linear function of the output activation of neuron i which mimics the operation of the NMDA receptors in learning; see Rolls 1989a,b,c; Rolls and Treves, in press.) Such competitive networks operate to detect correlations between the activity of the input neurons, and to allocate output neurons to respond to each cluster of such correlated inputs. These networks thus act as categorizers. In relation to visual information processing, they would remove redundancy from the input representation, and would develop low entropy representations of the information (see Barlow 1985; Barlow *et al.* 1989). Such competitive nets are biologically plausible, in that they utilize Hebb-modifiable forward excitatory connections, with competitive inhibition mediated by cortical inhibitory neurons. The competitive scheme I suggest would not result in the formation of 'winner-take-all' or 'grand-mother' cells, but would instead result in a small ensemble of active neurons representing each input (Rolls 1989a,b,c). The scheme has the advantages that the output neurons learn better to distribute themselves between the input patterns (see Bennett 1990), and that the sparse representations formed have utility in maximizing the number of memories that can be stored when, towards the end of the visual system, the visual representation of objects is interfaced to associative memory (Rolls 1989a,b; Rolls and Treves 1990). In that each neuron has graded responses centred about an optimal input, the proposal has some of the advantages with respect to hypersurface reconstruction described by Poggio and Girosi (1990a). However, the system I propose learns differently, in that instead of using perhaps non-biologically plausible algorithms to locate optimally the centres of the receptive fields of the neurons, the neurons use graded competition to spread themselves throughout the input space, depending on the statistics of the inputs received, and perhaps with some guidance from backprojections (see below and Rolls 1989a). The finite width of the response region of each neuron which tapers from a maximum at the centre is important for enabling the system to generalize smoothly from the examples with which it has learned (see Poggio and Girosi 1990*a,b*), to help the system to respond, for example, with the correct invariances as described below.

Translation invariance would be computed in such a system by utilizing competitive learning to detect regularities in inputs when real objects are translated in the physical world. The hypothesis is that because objects have continuous properties in space and time in the world, an object at one place on the retina might activate feature analysers at the next stage of cortical processing, and when the object was translated to a nearby position, because this would occur in a short period (e.g. 0.5 s), the membrane of the postsynaptic neuron would still be in its 'Hebb-modifiable' state (caused, for example, by calcium entry as a result of the voltage-dependent activation of NMDA receptors), and the presynaptic afferents activated with the object in its new position would thus become strengthened on the still-activated postsynaptic neuron. It is suggested (Rolls 1992*a*) that the short temporal window (e.g. 0.5 s) of Hebb-modifiability helps neurons to learn the statistics of objects moving in the physical world, and at the same time to form different representations of different feature combinations or objects, as these are physically discontinuous and present less regular correlations to the visual system. Foldiak (1991) has proposed computing an average activation of the postsynaptic neuron to assist with the same problem. One idea here is that the temporal properties of the biologically implemented learning mechanism are such that it is well suited to detecting the relevant continuities in the world of real objects. Another suggestion is that a memory trace for what has been seen in the last 300 ms appears to be implemented by a mechanism as simple as continued firing of inferior temporal neurons after the stimulus has disappeared, as we have shown in masking experiments (see also Rolls and Tovee 1994; Rolls *et al.* 1994*a*). I also suggest that other invariances, for example size, spatial frequency, and rotation invariance, could be learned by a comparable process. (Early processing in V1 which enables different neurons to represent inputs at different spatial scales would allow combinations of the outputs of such neurons to be formed at later stages. Scale invariance would then result from detecting at a later stage which neurons are almost conjunctively active as the size of an object alters.) It is suggested that this process takes place at each stage of the multiple-layer cortical processing hierarchy, so that invariances are learned first over small regions of space, and then over successively larger regions. This limits the size of the connection space within which correlations must be sought.

Increasing complexity of representations could also be built in such a multiple layer hierarchy by similar mechanisms. At each stage or layer the self-organizing competitive nets would result in combinations of inputs becoming the effective stimuli for neurons. In order to avoid the combinatorial explosion, it is proposed, following Feldman (1985, p. 279), that low-order combinations of inputs would be what is learned by each neuron. (Each stimulus would not be represented by activity in a single input axon, but instead by activity in a set of active input axons.) Evidence consistent with this suggestion that neurons are responding to combinations of a few variables represented at the preceding stage of cortical processing is that some neurons in V2 and V4 respond to end-stopped lines, to tongues flanked by inhibitory subregions, or to combinations of colours (see references cited by Rolls 1991), in posterior inferior temporal cortex to stimuli which may require two or more simple features to be present (Tanaka *et al.* 1990), and in the temporal cortical face processing areas to images that require the presence of several features in a face (such as eyes, hair, and mouth) in order to respond (see Perrett *et al.* 1982; Yamane *et al.* 1988). (Precursor cells to face-responsive neurons might, it is suggested, respond to combinations of the outputs of the neurons in V1 that are activated by faces, and might be found in areas such as V4.) It is an important part of this suggestion that some local spatial information would be inherent in the features which were being combined. For example, cells might not respond to the combination of an edge and a small circle unless they were in the correct spatial relation to each other. (This is in fact consistent with the data of Tanaka *et al.* (1990) and with our data on face neurons, in that some face neurons require the face features to be in the correct spatial configuration, and not jumbled—see Perrett *et al.* 1982; Rolls *et al.* 1994a.) The local spatial information in the features being combined would ensure that the representation at the next level would contain some information about the (local) arrangement of features. Further low-order combinations of such neurons at the next stage would include sufficient local spatial information so that an arbitrary spatial arrangement of the same features would not activate the same neuron, and this is the proposed, and limited, solution which this mechanism would provide for the feature binding problem (see Malsburg 1990). By this stage of processing a view-dependent representation of objects suitable for view-dependent processes such as behavioural responses to face expression and gesture would be available.

It is suggested that view-independent representations could be formed by the same type of computation, operating to combine a limited set of views of objects. The plausibility of providing view-independent recognition of objects by combining a set of different views of objects has been proposed by a number of investigators (Poggio and Edelman 1990). Consistent with the suggestion that the view-independent representations are formed by combining view-dependent representations in the primate visual system is the fact that in the temporal cortical visual areas, neurons with view-independent representations of faces are present in the same cortical areas as neurons with view-dependent representations (from which the view-independent neurons could receive inputs) (Hasselmo *et al.* 1989a,b; Perrett *et al.* 1987). This solution to 'object-based' representations is very different from that traditionally proposed for artificial vision system, in which the coordinates in 3D space of objects are stored in a database, and general-purpose algorithms operate on these to perform transforms such as translation, rotation, and scale change in 3D space. In the present, much more limited but more biologically plausible scheme, the representation would be suitable for recognition of an object, and for linking associative memories to objects, but would be less good for making actions in 3D space to particular parts of, or inside, objects, as the 3D coordinates of each part of the object would not be explicitly available. It is therefore proposed that visual fixation is used to locate in foveal vision part of an object to which movements must be made, and that local disparity and other measurements of depth then provide sufficient information for the motor system to make actions relative to the small part of space in which a local, *view-dependent* representation of depth would be provided (see Ballard 1990).

The computational processes proposed above operate by an unsupervised learning mechanism, which utilizes regularities in the physical environment to enable representations with low entropy to be built. In some cases it may be advantageous to utilize some form of mild teaching input to the visual system, to enable it to learn, for example, that rather similar visual inputs have very different consequences in the world, so that different representations of them should be built. In other cases, it might be helpful to bring representations together, if they have identical consequences, in order to use storage capacity efficiently. It is proposed elsewhere (Rolls 1989a,b) that the backprojections from each adjacent cortical region in the hierarchy (and from the amygdala and hippocampus to higher regions of the visual system) play such a role by providing guidance to the competitive network suggested above to be important in each cortical area. This guidance, and also the capability for recall, are it is suggested implemented by Hebb-modifiable connections from the backprojecting neurons to the principal (pyramidal) neurons of the competitive networks in the preceding stages (Rolls 1989a,b).

The computational processes outlined above use coarse coding with relatively finely tuned neurons with a graded response region centred about an optimal response achieved when the input stimulus matches the synaptic weight vector on a neuron. The coarse coding and fine tuning would help to limit the combinatorial explosion, to keep the number of neurons within the biological range. The graded response region would be crucial in enabling the system to generalize correctly to solve, for example, the invariances. However, such a system would need many neurons, each with considerable learning capacity, to solve visual perception in this way. This is fully consistent with the large number of neurons in the visual system, and with the large number of, probably modifiable, synapses on each neuron (in the order of 5000). Further, the fact that many neurons are tuned in different ways to faces is consistent with the fact that in such a computational system, many neurons would need to be sensitive (in different ways) to faces, in order to allow recognition of many individual faces when all share a number of common properties.

A computational model of invariant visual object recognition

To test and clarify the hypotheses just described about how the visual system may operate to learn invariant object recognition, we have performed a simulation which implements many of the ideas just described, and is consistent and based on much of the neurophysiology summarized above. The network simulated can perform object, including face, recognition in a biologically plausible way, and after training shows, for example, translation and view invariance (Wallis *et al.* 1993; Wallis and Rolls 1996).

In the four-layer network, the successive layers correspond approximately to V2, V4, the posterior temporal cortex, and the anterior temporal cortex. The forward connections to a cell in one layer are derived from a topologically corresponding region of the preceding layer, using a Gaussian distribution of connection probabilities

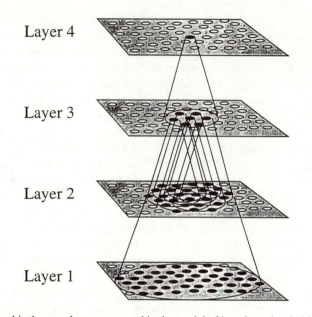

Layer 4

Layer 3

Layer 2

Layer 1

Fig. 6.3 Hierarchical network structure used in the model of invariant visual object recognition.

to determine the exact neurons in the preceding layer to which connections are made. This schema is constrained to preclude the repeated connection of any cells. Each cell receives 50 connections from the 32×32 cells of the preceding layer, with a 67% probability that a connection comes from within four cells of the distribution centre. Figure 6.3 shows the general convergent network architecture used, and may be compared with Fig. 6.2. Within each layer, lateral inhibition between neurons has a radius of effect just greater than the radius of feedforward convergence just defined. The lateral inhibition is simulated via a linear local contrast enhancing filter active on each neuron. (Note that this differs from the global 'winner-take-all' paradigm implemented by Foldiak (1991).) The cell activation is then passed through a non-linear cell output activation function, which also produces contrast enhancement of the firing rates.

In order that the results of the simulation might be made particularly relevant to understanding processing in higher cortical visual areas, the inputs to layer 1 come from a separate input layer which provides an approximation to the encoding found in visual area 1 (V1) of the primate visual system. These response characteristics of neurons in the input layer are provided by a series of spatially tuned filters with image contrast sensitivities chosen to accord with the general tuning profiles observed in the simple cells of V1. Currently, only even-symmetric (bar detecting) filter shapes are used. The precise filter shapes were computed by weighting the difference of two Gaussians by a third orthogonal Gaussian (see Wallis *et al.* 1993; Wallis and Rolls

1996). Four filter spatial frequencies (in the range 0.0625 to 0.5 pixels^{-1} over four octaves), each with one of four orientations (0° to 135°) were implemented. Cells of layer 1 receive a topologically consistent, localized, random selection of the filter responses in the input layer, under the constraint that each cell samples every filter spatial frequency and receives a constant number of inputs.

The synaptic learning rule can be summarized as follows:

$$\delta w_{ij} = k \cdot m \cdot r'_j$$

and

$$m_i^{(t)} = (1 - \eta)\, r_i^{(t)} + \eta m_i^{(t-1)}$$

where r'_j is the jth input to the neuron, r_i is the output of the ith neuron, w_{ij} is the jth weight on the ith neuron, η governs the relative influence of the trace and the new input (typically 0.4–0.6), and $m_i^{(t)}$ represents the value of the ith cell's memory trace at time t. In the simulation the neuronal learning was bounded by normalization of each cell's dendritic weight vector. An alternative, more biologically relevant implementation, using a local weight bounding operation, has in part been explored using a version of the Oja update rule (Oja 1982; Kohonen 1988). To train the network to produce a translation-invariant representation, one stimulus was placed successively in a sequence of seven positions across the input, then the next stimulus was placed successively in the same sequence of seven positions across the input, and so on through the set of stimuli. The idea was to enable the network to learn whatever was common at each stage of the network about a stimulus shown in different positions. To train on view invariance, different views of the same object were shown in succession, then different views of the next object were shown in succession, and so on.

One test of the network used a set of three non-orthogonal stimuli, based upon probable 3D edge cues (such as 'T, L, and +' shapes). During training these stimuli were chosen in random sequence to be swept across the 'retina' of the network, a total of 1000 times. In order to assess the characteristics of the cells within the net, a two-way analysis of variance was performed on the set of responses of each cell, with one factor being the stimulus type and the other the position of the stimulus on the 'retina'. A high F ratio for stimulus type (F_s), and low F ratio for stimulus position (F_p) would imply that a cell had learned a position-invariant representation of the stimuli. The discrimination factor of a particular cell was then simply the ratio F_s/F_p (a factor useful for ranking at least the most invariant cells). To assess the utility of the trace learning rule, nets trained with the trace rule were compared with nets trained without the trace rule and with untrained nets (with the initial random weights). The result of the simulations, illustrated in Fig. 6.4, show that networks trained with the trace learning rule do have neurons in layer 4 with much higher values of the discrimination factor. An example of the responses of one such cell in layer 4 is illustrated in Fig. 6.5. Similar position-invariant encoding has been demonstrated for a stimulus set consisting of eight faces. View-invariant coding has also been demonstrated for a set of five faces each shown in four views (see further, Wallis and Rolls 1996).

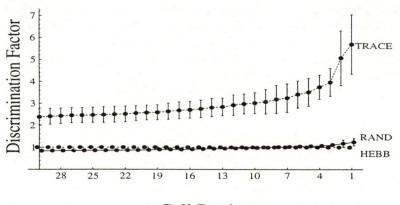

Fig. 6.4 Comparison of network discrimination when trained with the trace learning rule, with a Hebb rule (No trace), and when not trained (Random). The values of discrimination factor (see text) for the 50 most invariant cells in layer 4 are shown.

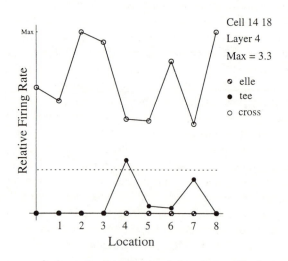

Fig. 6.5 The responses of a layer 4 cell in the simulation. The cell had a translation invariant response to stimulus 1.

These results show that the proposed learning mechanism and neural architecture can produce cells with responses selective for stimulus type with considerable position or view invariance. The ability of the network to be trained with natural scenes is currently helping to advance our understanding of how representations of objects are built and encoded in the primate visual system.

This combined neurophysiological and computational approach is thus leading to biologically plausible theories about how the brain operates when it performs face or object recognition. In addition, we now have quite considerable evidence about what happens in our higher cortical visual areas when we recognize faces, and about how information about at least some classes of object in the world is represented in the visual system. Yet does this understanding of visual object recognition help us directly with the problem of consciousness, of why it is that it feels the way it does when we recognize a face? Would a computer which operated in the way described above be conscious during object recognition? I suggest that it would not be, and that for the object recognition processes to be conscious, including to feel like something, the information from the type of visual processing system I describe would have to be projected to a different brain system, the nature of which will be described later. Before turning to that, I give an outline of some recent advances in understanding the brain processing that occurs when we store and then recall later everyday events, and ask whether these memory processes are closer to consciousness.

The hippocampus and memory

Evidence on how a part of the brain involved in memory, the hippocampus, operates is considered next. The hippocampus is involved in a particular type of memory, the memory for recent episodes. Advances in understanding how this brain region operates come again, in part, as a result of studies in which the information represented in the hippocampus has been analysed by recording the activity of single neurons in it while it is performing its memory functions, and from neuronal network theories which address *how* it could compute, given its structure, synaptic learning rules, and the information represented in it.

Effects of damage to the hippocampus on memory

First, it is necessary to consider what functions in memory are performed by the hippocampus, as shown by the effects of damage to it. Damage to the hippocampus and related structures in the temporal lobe in humans leads to anterograde amnesia, that is an inability to form many types of memory. Old memories are relatively spared. Recent memories, formed within the last few weeks or months, may be impaired (Squire 1992). The memory of particular past episodes, such as the place where one had lunch yesterday, what was for lunch, and who was present, provides an important example of the impairment. In analyses in monkeys of the contribution of the hippocampus itself to the memory impairments, it has been shown that a number of spatial memory tasks are involved (see Rolls 1990b, 1996c). They include object-place memory tasks, in which the locations of objects in space must be remembered (Gaffan and Saunders 1985; Gaffan 1994). This impairment is analogous to that shown by anterograde amnesic patients who cannot remember the locations of objects on a tray. In such tasks, rapid episodic memories of associations between visual information about objects originating from the inferior temporal visual cortex must be associated with information about their spatial position, originating from the parietal cortex. Another task that is impaired is 'whole scene memory', in which monkeys must remember the locations of objects in each scene (Gaffan and Harrison 1989; Gaffan 1994). Another task impaired by hippocampal system (e.g. fornix) lesions in monkeys is conditional spatial response learning, in which monkeys must learn to make one spatial response (e.g. touch on the left) when one object is shown, and a different spatial response (e.g. touch on the right) when a different visual image is shown (Rapniak and Gaffan 1987). In this task, new image–spatial response associations must be learned every day, so that this task also requires rapid (episodic-like) associations to be formed between visual object and spatial response (e.g. parietal) information, originating in different parts of the cerebral cortex. In contrast to these spatial tasks (in which associations to visual object information may be needed), it is now known that visual (and tactile) recency memory tasks (as tested in delayed match to sample tasks) are not affected by damage to the hippocampus *per se*, but that instead damage to the perirhinal cortex produces these (more unimodal) memory deficits. The hippocampus may thus especially be required when rapid spatial memories must be formed, frequently involving associations to information represented in remote association areas of the cerebral cortex, such as the temporal lobe association cortex. In the rat, hippocampal lesions also produce spatial memory deficits, for example in spatial reference memory in the water maze in which a rat must learn to use environmental spatial cues to find a hidden platform, and in working spatial memory tasks, for example in an eight-arm maze in which the rat must remember which of the arms it has already visited (Jarrard 1993).

On the basis of these findings in humans and other animals, the hypothesis is suggested that the importance of the hippocampus in spatial and other memories is that it can rapidly form 'episodic' representations of information originating from many areas of the cerebral cortex.

Systems-level connections of the hippocampus

Inputs converge into the hippocampus, via the parahippocampal gyrus and perirhinal cortex, which in turn feed into the entorhinal cortex and thus into the hippocampus, from virtually all association areas in the neocortex, including areas in the parietal cortex concerned with spatial function, temporal areas concerned with vision and hearing, and the frontal lobes (Fig. 6.6). An extensively divergent system of output projections enables the hippocampus to feed back into most of the cortical areas from which it receives inputs.

Information represented in the hippocampus

In order to understand the role of the hippocampus in memory, it is necessary to know what information is represented in the hippocampus. Whole series of findings have shown that hippocampal pyramidal cells (e.g. CA3 and CA1 neurons) in rats

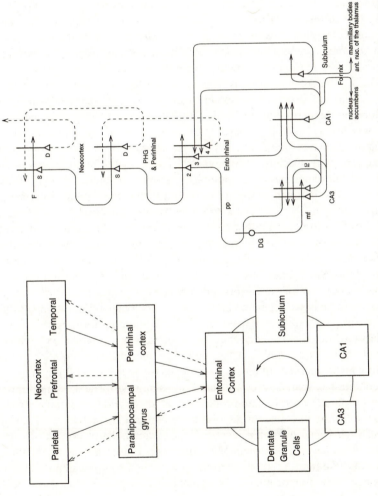

Fig. 6.6 Forward connections (solid lines) from areas of cerebral association neocortex via the parahippocampal gyrus and perirhinal cortex, and entorhinal cortex, to the hippocampus; and back-projections (dashed lines) via the hippocampal CA1 pyramidal cells, subiculum, and parahippocampal gyrus to the neocortex. There is great convergence in the forward connections down to the single network implemented in the CA3 pyramidal cells; and great divergence again in the back-projections. Left: block diagram. Right: more detailed representation of some of the principal excitatory neurons in the pathways. Abbreviations: D, deep pyramidal cells; DG, dentate granule cells; F, forward inputs to areas of the association cortex from preceding cortical areas in the hierarchy; mf, mossy fibres; PHG, parahippocampal gyrus and perirhinal cortex; pp, perforant path; rc, recurrent collateral of the CA3 hippocampal pyramidal cells; S, superficial pyramidal cells; 2, pyramidal cells in layer 2 of theentorhinal cortex;3, pyramidal cells in layer 3 of the entorhinal cortex. The thick lines above the cell bodies represent the dendrites.

respond when the rat is in a particular place in a spatial environment. In monkeys, it has been shown that there is a rich representation of space outside the monkey, in that (in the order of 10% of) hippocampal neurons in monkeys respond to particular positions in space (Rolls 1990a,b, 1991, 1996a,c; Rolls and O'Mara 1993). In many cases, this spatial encoding has been shown to be allocentric, that is coded in world coordinates, not in egocentric coordinates relative to the body axis (Feigenbaum and Rolls 1991). Moreover, 2.4% of hippocampal neurons combine information about the object shown and the place where it is shown, in that they respond in an object-place memory task differentially to the novel and familiar presentations of an object shown in a particular place (Rolls *et al.* 1989). Consistent with this, in a cue-controlled environment, some hippocampal neurons in primates respond to views of particular parts of the environment, irrespective of where the monkey is (Rolls and O'Mara 1993). Further, it has recently been possible to show that during active locomotion, 'spatial view' neurons respond to the location in space at which the monkey is looking (experiments of Rolls, Robertson and Georges-François, in preparation; see Rolls 1996b,e). These findings together show that there is a representation of space outside the organism in primates. This may be important, in that primates can explore space by moving the eyes to look at different places in the environment, and can remember the location of what they see there. In contrast, the hippocampal spatial cells found so far in rats respond when the rat is in a particular place, perhaps related to the fact that rats normally need to visit places in order to explore and store information about them, consistent with their use of olfactory cues, and their relatively poor vision compared to primates. Another type of spatial information that has been found in primates is information about whole-body motion (O'Mara *et al.* 1994). Such cells, for example, respond to clockwise but not counter-clockwise whole-body motion, or to forwards but not backwards linear translation. In some cases these neurons appear to be driven by vestibular information (in that they respond when the monkey is moved on a robot without performing the move-ment in the dark), while others are driven by the optic flow that is induced by whole-body motion (O'Mara *et al.* 1994). These cells may be important in short-range navigation, for which a memory of recent movements is needed. In addition, in mon-keys, when conditional spatial response tasks are being performed, some hippo-campal neurons respond to combinations of the visual image and the spatial response which must be linked by memory for the task to be performed correctly, and during the learning of such visual to spatial response associations, the responses of some hippocampal neurons become modified (Miyashita *et al.* 1989; Cahusac *et al.* 1993).

On the basis of these findings about neuronal activity in the hippocampus, and the effects of damage to the hippocampus, the hypothesis is suggested that the import-ance of the hippocampus in spatial and other memories is that it can rapidly form 'episodic' representations of information originating from many areas of the cerebral cortex. Synaptic modification within the hippocampus is probably involved in storing information during the learning (see Morris 1989). Whether this information is left in the hippocampus, or as a result of recall from the hippocampus is incor-porated into neocortical long-term memory, there is a need to retrieve information stored in the hippocampus (see Rolls 1995*c*, 1996*e*). Ways in which the recall could operate, and could reinstate in the cerebral neocortex the neuronal activity present during the original learning, are considered later.

In order to understand how the hippocampus could store the information it receives from the cerebral neocortex and form, for example, episodic memories which link spatial information with information about objects which originate from different regions of the cerebral cortex, we turn now to consider the internal circuitry of the hippocampus, and how it could operate (see Rolls 1989*a,b*, 1991, 1996*a,d,e*; Treves and Rolls 1994; compare with Marr 1971).

Hippocampal CA3 circuitry (see Fig. 6.6)

Projections from the entorhinal cortex reach the granule cells (of which there are 10^6 in the rat) in the dentate gyrus (DG) via the perforant path (pp). The granule cells project to CA3 cells via the mossy fibres (mf), which provide a *sparse* but possibly powerful connection to the 3×10^5 CA3 pyramidal cells in the rat. Each CA3 cell receives approximately 50 mossy fibre inputs, so that the sparseness of this connectivity is thus 0.005%. By contrast, there are many more—possibly weaker—direct perforant path inputs onto each CA3 cell, in the rat of the order of 4×10^3. The largest number of synapses (about 1.2×10^4 in the rat) on the dendrites of CA3 pyramidal cells is, however, provided by the (recurrent) axon collaterals of CA3 cells themselves. It is remarkable that the recurrent collaterals (rcs) are distributed to other CA3 cells throughout the hippocampus (Ishizuka *et al.* 1990; Amaral and Witter 1989; Amaral *et al.* 1990), so that effectively the CA3 system provides a single network, with a connectivity of approximately 4% between the different CA3 neurons.

CA3 as an autoassociation memory

Many of the synapses in the hippocampus show associative modification as shown by long-term potentiation, and this synaptic modification appears to be involved in learning (Morris 1989). On the basis of the evidence summarized above, Rolls (1987, 1989*a,b,c*, 1990*a,b*, 1991) has suggested that the CA3 stage acts as an autoassociation memory which enables episodic memories to be formed and stored for an intermediate term in the CA3 network, and that subsequently the extensive recurrent collateral connectivity allows for the retrieval of a whole representation to be initiated by the activation of some small part of the same representation (the cue). We have therefore performed quantitative analyses of the storage and retrieval processes in the CA3 network (Treves and Rolls 1991, 1992). We have extended previous formal models of autoassociative memory (see Amit 1989) by analysing a network with graded response units, so as to represent more realistically the continuously variable rates at which neurons fire, and with incomplete connectivity (Treves 1990; Treves and Rolls 1991). We have found that, in general, the maximum number p_{max} of firing patterns that can be (individually) retrieved is proportional to the number

C^{RC} of (associatively) modifiable RC synapses per cell, by a factor that increases roughly with the inverse of the sparseness a of the neuronal representation. (The sparseness of the representation provided by a neuron has been defined above.) Thus

$$P_{max} \approx \frac{C^{RC}}{a \ln(1/a)} k$$

where k is a factor that depends weakly on the detailed structure of the rate distribution, on the connectivity pattern, etc., but is roughly in the order of 0.2–0.3 (Treves and Rolls 1991).

The main factors that determine the maximum number of memories that can be stored in an autoassociative network are thus the number of connections on each neuron devoted to the recurrent collaterals, and the sparseness of the representation. For example, for $C^{RC} = 12\,000$ and $a = 0.02$ (realistic estimates for the rat), p_{max} is calculated to be approximately 36 000.

The requirement of the input systems to CA3 for the efficient storage of new information

By calculating the amount of information that would end up being carried by a CA3 firing pattern produced solely by the perforant path input and by the effect of the recurrent connections, we have been able to show (Treves and Rolls 1992) that an input of the perforant path type, alone, is unable to direct efficient information storage. Such an input is too weak, it turns out, to drive the firing of the cells, as the 'dynamics' of the network is dominated by the randomizing effect of the recurrent collaterals. This is the manifestation, in the CA3 network, of a general problem affecting storage (i.e. learning) in *all* autoassociative memories. The problem arises when the system is considered to be activated by a set of input axons making synaptic connections that have to compete with the recurrent connections, rather than having the firing rates of the neurons artificially clamped into a prescribed pattern.

In an argument developed elsewhere, we hypothesize that the mossy fibre inputs force efficient information storage by virtue of their strong and sparse influence on the CA3 cell firing rates (Treves and Rolls 1992; Rolls 1989*a,b*, 1996*e*).

A different input system is needed to trigger retrieval

An autoassociative memory network needs afferent inputs also in the other mode of operation, i.e. when it retrieves a previously stored pattern of activity. We have shown (Treves and Rolls 1992) that if the cue available to initiate retrieval is rather small, one needs a large number of associatively modifiable synapses. The number needed is of the same order as the number of concurrently stored patterns p. For such reasons we suggest that the direct perforant path system to CA3 (see Fig. 6.6) is the one involved in relaying the cues that initiate retrieval.

The dentate granule cells

The theory is developed elsewhere that the dentate granule cell stage of hippocampal processing which precedes the CA3 stage acts to produce during learning the sparse yet efficient (i.e. non-redundant) representation in CA3 neurons which is required for the autoassociation to perform well (Rolls 1989*a,b,c*, 1996*e*; see also Treves and Rolls 1992). One way in which it may do this is by acting as a competitive network to remove redundancy from the inputs producing a more orthogonal, sparse, and categorized set of outputs (Rolls 1987, 1989*a,b,c*, 1990*a,b*). A second way arises because of the very low contact probability in the mossy fibre–CA3 connections, which helps to produce a sparse representation in CA3 (Treves and Rolls 1992). A third way is that the powerful dentate granule cell–mossy fibre input to the CA3 cells may force a new pattern of firing onto the CA3 cells during learning.

The CA1 organization

The CA3 cells are connected to the CA1 cells. It is suggested that the CA1 cells, given the separate parts of each episodic memory which must be separately represented in CA3 ensembles, can allocate neurons, by competitive learning, to represent at least larger parts of each episodic memory (Rolls 1987, 1989*a,b,c*, 1990*a,b*). This implies a more efficient representation, in the sense that when eventually after many further stages neocortical neuronal activity is recalled (as discussed below), each neocortical cell need not be accessed by all the axons carrying each component of the episodic memory as represented in CA3, but instead by fewer axons carrying larger fragments (see further, Rolls 1996*e*).

Back-projections to the neocortex

It is suggested that the hippocampus is able to recall the whole of a previously stored episode for a period of days, weeks, or months after the episode, even when a fragment of the episode is available to start the recall. This recall from a fragment of the original episode would take place particularly as a result of completion produced by the autoassociation implemented in the CA3 network. It would then be the role of the hippocampus to reinstate in the cerebral neocortex the whole of the episodic memory. The cerebral cortex would then, with the whole of the information in the episode now producing firing in the correct sets of neocortical neurons, be in a position to incorporate the information in the episode into its long-term store in the neocortex, or use the recalled information for planning or action (see Rolls 1996*e*).

We suggest that during recall, the connections from CA3 via CA1 and the subiculum would allow activation of at least the pyramidal cells in the deep layers of the entorhinal cortex (see Fig. 6.6). These neurons would then, by virtue of their back-projections to the parts of cerebral cortex that originally provided the inputs to the hippocampus, terminate in the superficial layers of those neocortical areas, where synapses would be made onto the distal parts of the dendrites of the cortical pyramidal cells (see Rolls 1989*a,b,c*).

Our understanding of the architecture with which this would be achieved is shown in Fig. 6.6. The feed-forward connections from association areas of the cerebral neocortex (solid lines in Fig. 6.6) show major convergence as information is passed to CA3, with the CA3 autoassociation network having the smallest number of neurons at any stage of the processing. The back-projections allow for divergence back to neocortical areas. The way in which we suggest that the back-projection synapses are set up to have the appropriate strengths for recall is as follows (see also Rolls 1989*a,b*). During the setting up of a new episode memory, there would be strong feed-forward activity progressing towards the hippocampus. During the episode, the CA3 synapses would be modified, and via the CA1 neurons and the subiculum a pattern of activity would be produced on the back-projecting synapses to the entorhinal cortex. Here the back-projecting synapses from active back-projection axons onto pyramidal cells being activated by the forward inputs to entorhinal cortex would be associatively modified. A similar process would be implemented at preceding stages of neocortex, that is in the parahippocampal gyrus/perirhinal cortex stage, and in association cortical areas.

Quantitative constraints on the connectivity of back-projections

How many back-projecting fibres does one need to synapse on any given neocortical pyramidal cell, in order to implement the mechanism outlined above? Clearly, if the theory were to produce a definite constraint of that sort, quantitative anatomical data could be used for vertification or falsification.

Consider a polysynaptic sequence of back-projecting stages, from hippocampus to neocortex, as a string of simple (hetero-)associative memories in which, at each stage, the input lines are those coming from the previous stage (closer to the hippocampus). Implicit in this framework is the assumption that the synapses at each stage are modifiable and have been modified at the time of first experiencing each episode, according to some Hebbian associative plasticity rule. A plausible requirement for a successful hippocampo-directed recall operation is that the signal generated from the hippocampally retrieved pattern of activity, and carried backwards towards the neocortex, remains undegraded when compared to the noise due, at each stage, to the interference effects caused by the concurrent storage of other patterns of activity on the same back-projecting synaptic systems. That requirement is equivalent to that used in deriving the storage capacity of such a series of heteroassociative memories, and it was shown by Treves and Rolls (1991) that the maximum number of independently generated activity patterns that can be retrieved is given, essentially, by the same formula as above:

$$p \approx \frac{C}{a \ln(1/a)} k'$$

where, however, a is now the sparseness of the representation at any given stage, and C is the average number of (back-)projections each cell of that stage receives from cells of the previous one. (k' is a similar slowly varying factor to that introduced above.) If p is equal to the number of memories held in the hippocampal buffer, it is limited by the retrieval capacity of the CA3 network, p_{max}. Putting together the formula of the latter with that shown here, one concludes that, roughly, the requirement implies that the number of afferents of (indirect) hippocampal origin to a given neocortical stage (C^{HBP}), must be $C^{HBP} = C^{RC} a_{nc}/a_{CA3}$, where C^{RC} is the number of recurrent collaterals to any given cell in CA3, the average sparseness of a representation is a_{nc}, and a_{CA3} is the sparseness of memory representations there in CA3 (Treves and Rolls 1994).

One is led to a definite conclusion: a mechanism of the type envisaged here could not possibly rely on a set of monosynaptic CA3-to-neocortex back-projections. This would imply that, to make a sufficient number of synapses on each of the vast number of neocortical cells, each cell in CA3 has to generate a disproportionate number of synapses (i.e. C^{HBP} times the ratio between the number of neocortical cells and the number of CA3 cells). The required divergence can be kept within reasonable limits only by assuming that the back-projecting system is polysynaptic, provided that the number of cells involved grows gradually at each stage, from CA3 back to neocortical association areas (see Fig. 6.6).

The theory of the recall of recent memories in the neocortex from the hippocampus provides a clear view about why back-projections should be as numerous as forward projections in the cerebral cortex. The reason suggested for this is that as many representations may need to be accessed by back-projections for recall and related functions (see Rolls 1989a,b,c) in the population of cortical pyramidal cells as can be accessed by the forward projections, and this limit is given by the number of inputs onto a pyramidal cell (and the sparseness of the representation), irrespective of whether the input is from a forward- or a back-projection system.

Consciousness

It would be possible to build a computer which would perform all the above functions of visual object recognition, memory, and even emotion (Rolls 1990a, 1995b), using the same computational principles described above, and yet we might not want to ascribe subjective or phenomenal states, which I shall call qualia, to this computer. We might not want to say that it feels like something to the computer when the computer is performing these functions. This raises the general issue of consciousness and its functions. Because the topic of subjective or phenomenal feels or feelings (that it feels like something to be in that state) is of considerable interest, and is for the present purpose the defining aspect of consciousness, one view on consciousness, influenced by contemporary cognitive neuroscience, is outlined next. However, this view is only preliminary, and theories of consciousness are likely to develop considerably.

A starting point is that many actions can be performed relatively automatically, without apparent conscious intervention. An example sometimes given is driving a car. Such actions could involve control of behaviour by brain systems which are old in evolutionary terms such as the basal ganglia. It is of interest that the basal ganglia (and cerebellum) do not have back-projection systems to most of the parts of the cerebral cortex from which they receive inputs (see for example Rolls and Johnstone 1992; Rolls 1994*b*). In contrast, parts of the brain such as the hippocampus and amygdala, involved in functions such as episodic memory and emotion respectively, about which we can make (verbal) declarations, do have major back-projection systems to the high parts of the cerebral cortex from which they receive forward projections (Rolls 1992*a*; Treves and Rolls 1994). It may be that evolutionarily newer parts of the brain, such as the language areas and parts of the prefrontal cortex, are involved in an alternative type of control of behaviour, in which actions can be planned with the use of a (language) system which allows relatively arbitrary (syntactic) manipulation of semantic entities (symbols).

The general view that there are many routes to behavioural output is supported by the evidence that there are many input systems to the basal ganglia (from almost all areas of the cerebral cortex), and that neuronal activity in each part of the striatum reflects the activity in the overlying cortical area (Rolls and Johnstone 1992; Rolls 1994*b*). The evidence is consistent with the possibility that different cortical areas, each specialized for a different type of computation, have their outputs directed to the basal ganglia, which then select the strongest input, and map this into action (via outputs directed, for example, to the premotor cortex) (Rolls and Johnstone 1992). Within this scheme, the language areas would offer one of many routes to action, but a route particularly suited to planning actions, because of the syntactic manipulation of semantic entities which may make long-term planning possible. A schematic diagram of this suggestion is provided in Fig. 6.7. Consistent with the hypothesis of multiple routes to action, only some of which utilize language, is the evidence that split-brain patients may not be aware of actions being performed by the 'non-dominant' hemisphere (Gazzaniga and LeDoux 1978; Gazzaniga 1988, 1995). Also consistent with multiple, including non-verbal, routes to action, patients with focal brain damage, for example to the prefrontal cortex, may emit actions, yet comment verbally that they should not be performing those actions (Rolls *et al.* 1994). In both these types of patient, confabulation may occur, in that a verbal account of why the action was performed may be given, and this may not be related at all to the environmental event which actually triggered the action (Gazzaniga and LeDoux 1978; Gazzaniga 1988, 1995). It is possible that sometimes in normal humans when actions are initiated as a result of processing in a specialized brain region such as those involved in some types of rewarded behaviour, the language system may subsequently elaborate a coherent account of why that action was performed (i.e. confabulate). This would be consistent with a general view of brain evolution in which as areas of the cortex evolve, they are laid on top of existing circuitry connecting inputs and outputs, and that each level in this hierarchy of separate input-output pathways may control behaviour according to the specialized function it can perform

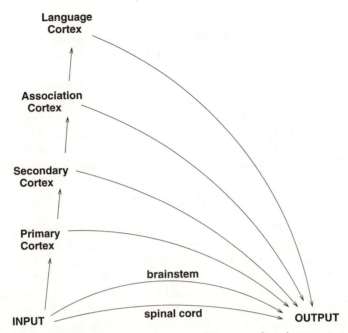

Fig. 6.7 Schematic illustration indicating many possible routes from input systems to action (output) systems. Cortical information processing systems are organized hierarchically, and there are routes to output systems from most levels of the hierarchy.

(see schematic in Fig. 6.7). (It is of interest that mathematicians may get a hunch that something is correct, yet not be able to verbalize why. They may then resort to formal, more serial and language-like, theorems to prove the case, and these seem to require more conscious processing. This is a further indication of a close association between linguistic processing, and consciousness. The linguistic processing need not, as in reading, involve an inner articulatory loop.)

We may next examine some of the advantages and behavioural functions that language, present as the most recently added layer to the above system, would confer. One major advantage would be the ability to plan actions through many potential stages and to evaluate the consequences of those actions without having to perform the actions. For this, the ability to form propositional statements, and to perform syntactic operations on the semantic representations of states in the world, would be important. Also important in this system would be the ability to have second-order thoughts (e.g. I think that he thinks that ...), as this would allow much better modelling and prediction of others' behaviour, and therefore of planning, particularly planning when it involves others. This capability for higher order thoughts would also enable reflection on past events, which would also be useful in planning. In contrast, non-linguistic behaviour would be driven by learned reinforcement associations, learned rules, etc., but not by flexible planning for many steps ahead involving a model of the world including others' behaviour. (For an earlier view which is close to this part of the argument see Humphrey 1980.) (The examples of behaviour from non-humans that may reflect planning may reflect much more limited and inflexible planning. For example, the dance of the honey-bee to signal to other bees the location of food may be said to reflect planning, but the symbol manipulation is not arbitrary. There are likely to be interesting examples of non-human primate behaviour, perhaps in the great apes, that reflect the evolution of an arbitrary symbol-manipulation system that could be useful for flexible planning, see Cheney and Seyfarth 1990.) It is important to state that the language ability referred to here is not necessarily human verbal language (though this would be an example). What it is suggested is important to planning is the syntactic manipulation of symbols, and it is this syntactic manipulation of symbols which is the sense in which language is defined and used here.

It is next suggested that this arbitrary symbol-manipulation using important aspects of language processing and used for planning but not in initiating all types of behaviour is close to what consciousness is about. In particular, consciousness may *be* the state which arises in a system that can think about (or reflect on) its own (or other peoples') thoughts, that is in a system capable of second- or higher-order thoughts (Rosenthal 1986, 1990, 1993; see also Dennett 1991). On this account, a mental state is non-introspectively (i.e. non-reflectively) conscious if one has a roughly simultaneous thought that one is in that mental state. Following from this, introspective consciousness is the attentive, deliberately focused consciousness of one's mental states. It is noted that not all of the higher-order thoughts need themselves be conscious (many mental states are not). However, according to the analysis, having a higher-order thought about a lower-order thought is necessary for the lower-order thought to be conscious. This analysis is consistent with the points made above that the brain systems that are required for consciousness and language are similar. In particular, a system which can have second- or higher-order thoughts about its own operation, including its planning and linguistic operation, must itself be a language processor, in that it must be able to bind correctly to the symbols and syntax in the first-order system. According to this explanation, the feeling of anything is the state which is present when linguistic processing that involves second- or higher-order thoughts is being performed.

It is suggested that part of the evolutionary adaptive significance of this type of higher-order thought is that is enables correction of errors made in first-order linguistic or in non-linguistic processing. Indeed, the ability to reflect on previous events is extremely important for learning from them, including setting up new long-term semantic structures. It was shown above that the hippocampus may be a system for such recall of recent memories. Its close relation to 'conscious' processing in humans (Squire (1992) has classified it as a declarative memory system) may be simply that it enables the recall of recent memories, which can then be reflected upon in conscious, higher-order processing. Another part of the adaptive value of a higher-order thought system may be that by thinking about its own thoughts in a given situation, it may be able to understand better the thoughts of another individual in a similar situation, and therefore predict that individual's behaviour better (Humphrey 1980).

As a point of clarification, I note that according to this theory, a language processing system is not *sufficient* for consciousness. What defines a conscious system according to this analysis is the ability to have higher-order thoughts, and a first-order language processor (that might be perfectly competent at language) would not be conscious, in that it could not think about its own or others' thoughts. In line with the argument on the adaptive value of higher-order thoughts and thus consciousness given above, that they are useful for correcting lower-order thoughts, I now suggest that correction using higher-order thoughts of lower-order thoughts would have adaptive value primarily if the lower-order thoughts are sufficiently complex to benefit from correction in this way. Such lower-order thoughts might involve a linked chain of 'if' ... 'then' statements that would be involved in planning. It is partly because complex lower-order thoughts such as these which involve syntax and language would benefit from correction by higher-order thoughts, that I suggest that there is a close link between this reflective consciousness and language.

This analysis does not yet give an account for sensory qualia ('raw sensory feels', for example why 'red' feels red), for emotional qualia (e.g. why a rewarding touch produces an emotional feeling of pleasure), or for motivational qualia (e.g. why food deprivation makes us *feel* hungry). The view I suggest on such qualia is as follows. Information processing in and from our sensory systems (e.g. the sight of the colour red) may be relevant to planning actions using language and the conscious processing thereby implied. Given that these inputs must be represented in the system that plans, we may ask whether it is more likely that we would be conscious of them or that we would not. I suggest that it would be a very special-purpose system that would allow such sensory inputs, and emotional and motivational states, to be part of (linguistically-based) planning, and yet remain unconscious. It seems to be much more parsimonious to hold that we would be conscious of such sensory, emotional, and motivational qualia because they would be being used (or are available to be used) in this type of (linguistically-based) higher-order thought processing, and this is what I propose.

The explanation of emotional and motivational subjective feelings or qualia that this discussion has led towards is thus that they should be felt as conscious because they enter into a specialized linguistic symbol-manipulation system that is part of a higher-order thought system that is capable of reflecting on and correcting its lower-order thoughts involved, for example, in the flexible planning of actions. It would require a very special machine to enable this higher-order linguistically-based thought processing, which is conscious by its nature, to occur without the sensory, emotional, and motivational states (which must be taken into account by the higher-order thought system) becoming felt qualia. The qualia are thus accounted for by the evolution of the linguistic system that can reflect on and correct its own lower-order processes, and thus has adaptive value.

This account implies that it may be especially animals with a higher-order belief and thought system and with linguistic symbol manipulation that have qualia. It may be that much non-human animal behaviour, provided that it does not require flexible linguistic planning and correction by reflection, could take place according to reinforcement-guidance (using, for example, stimulus reinforcement association learning in the amygdala and orbitofrontal cortex, see Rolls 1990*a*, 1996*a*), and rule-following (implemented, for example, using habit or stimulus-response learning in the basal ganglia, see Rolls 1994*b*; Rolls and Johnstone 1992). Such behaviour might appear very similar to human behaviour performed in similar circumstances, but would not imply qualia. It would be primarily by virtue of a system for reflecting on flexible, linguistic, planning behaviour that humans (and animals close to humans, with demonstrable syntactic manipulation of symbols, and the ability to think about these linguistic processes) would be different from other animals, and would have evolved qualia.

In order for processing in a part of our brain to be able to reach consciousness, appropriate pathways must be present. Certain constraints arise here. For example, in the sensory pathways, the nature of the representation may change as it passes through a hierarchy of processing levels, and in order to be conscious of the information in the form in which it is represented in early processing stages, the early processing stages must have access to the part of the brain necessary for consciousness. An example is provided by processing in the taste system. In the primate primary taste cortex, neurons respond to taste independently of hunger, yet in the secondary taste cortex, food-related taste neurons (e.g. responding to sweet taste) only respond to food if hunger is present, and gradually stop responding to the taste during feeding to satiety (see Rolls 1989*d*, 1993, 1995*c*). Now the quality of the tastant (sweet, salt, etc.) and its intensity are not affected by hunger, but the pleasantness of its taste is decreased to zero (neutral) (or even becomes unpleasant) after we have eaten it to satiety. The implication of this is that for quality and intensity information about taste, we must be conscious of what is represented in the primary taste cortex (or perhaps in another area connected to it which bypasses the secondary taste cortex), and not of what is represented in the secondary taste cortex. In contrast, for the pleasantness of a taste, consciousness of this could not reflect what is represented in the primary taste cortex, but instead what is represented in the secondary taste cortex (or in an area beyond it). The same argument arises for reward in general, and therefore for emotion, which in primates is not represented early on in processing in the sensory pathways (nor in or before the inferior temporal cortex for vision), but in the areas to which these object analysis systems project, such as the orbitofrontal cortex, where the reward value of visual stimuli is reflected in the responses of neurons to visual stimuli (see Rolls 1990*a*, 1995*b*,*c*). It is also of interest that reward signals (e.g. the taste of food when we are hungry) are associated with subjective feelings of pleasure (see Rolls 1990*a*, 1993, 1995*b*,*c*). I suggest that this correspondence arises because pleasure is the subjective state that represents in the conscious system a signal that is positively reinforcing (rewarding), and that inconsistent behaviour would result if the representations did not correspond to a signal for positive reinforcement in both the conscious and the non-conscious processing systems.

Do these arguments mean that the conscious sensation of, for example, taste quality is represented or occurs in the primary taste cortex, and of the pleasantness of taste in the secondary taste cortex, and that activity in these areas is sufficient for conscious sensations (qualia) to occur? I do not suggest that at all. Instead, the arguments I have put forward above suggest that we are only conscious of representations when we have high-order thoughts about them. The implication then is that pathways must connect from each of the brain areas in which information is represented about which we can be conscious, to the system which has the higher-order thoughts, which as I have argued above, requires language. Thus, in the example given, there must be connections to the language areas from the primary taste cortex, which need not be direct, but which must bypass the secondary taste cortex, in which the information is represented differently (see Rolls 1989*d*, 1995*c*). There must also be pathways from the secondary taste cortex, not necessarily direct, to the language areas so that we can have higher-order thoughts about the pleasantness of the representation in the secondary taste cortex. A schematic diagram incorporating this anatomical prediction about human cortical neural connectivity in relation to consciousness is shown in Fig. 6.8.

One question that has been discussed is whether there is a causal role for consciousness (see for example Armstrong and Malcolm 1984). The position to which the above arguments lead is that indeed consciousness does have a causal role in the elicitation of behaviour, but only under the limited set of circumstances when higher-order thoughts play a role in correcting or influencing lower-order thoughts. As we have seen, some behavioural responses can be elicited when there is not this type of reflective control of lower-order processing. There are many brain processing routes to output regions, and only one of these involves conscious, verbally represented processing which can later be recalled (see Fig. 6.7).

It is of interest to comment on how the evolution of a system for flexible planning might affect emotions. Consider grief which may occur when a reward is terminated and no immediate action is possible (see Rolls 1990*a*, 1995*b*). It may be adaptive by leading to a cessation of the formerly rewarded behaviour and thus facilitating the possible identification of other positive reinforcers in the environment. In humans, grief may be particularly potent because it becomes represented in a system which can plan ahead, and understand the enduring implications of the loss.

This account of consciousness also leads to a suggestion about the processing that underlies the feeling of free will. Free will would in this scheme involve the use of language to check many moves ahead on a number of possible series of actions and their outcomes, and then with this information to make a choice from the likely outcomes of different possible series of actions. (If, in contrast, choices were made only on the basis of the reinforcement value of immediately available stimuli, without the arbitrary syntactic symbol manipulation made possible by language, then the choice strategy would be much more limited, and we might not want to use the term free will, as all the consequences of those actions would not have been computed.) It is suggested that when this type of reflective, conscious, information processing is occurring and leading to action, that the system performing this processing

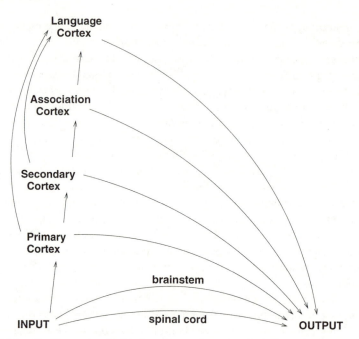

Fig. 6.8 Schematic illustration indicating that early stages in information processing may need access to language areas which bypass subsequent levels in the hierarchy, so that consciousness of what is represented in early cortical stages, and which may not be represented in later cortical stages, can occur. Higher-order linguistic thoughts (HOLTs) could be implemented in the language cortex itself, and would not need a separate cortical area. Back-projections, a notable feature of cortical connectivity, with many probable functions including recall (Rolls 1989*a,b*, 1996*a*), probably reciprocate all the connections shown.

and producing the action would have to believe that it could cause the action, for otherwise inconsistencies would arise, and the system might no longer try to initiate action. This belief held by the system may partly underlie the feeling of free will. At other times, when other brain modules are initiating actions, the conscious processor may confabulate and believe that it caused the action, or at least give an account (possibly wrong) of why the action was initiated. The fact that the conscious processor may have the belief even in these circumstances that it initiated the action may arise as a property of it being inconsistent for a system which can take overall control using conscious verbal processing to believe that it was overridden by another system.

In the operation of such a free will system, the uncertainties introduced by the limited information possible about the likely outcomes of series of actions, and the inability to use optimal algorithms when combining conditional probabilities, would be much more important factors than whether the brain operates deterministically or not. (The operation of brain machinery must be relatively deterministic, for it has evolved to provide reliable outputs for given inputs.)

These are my initial thoughts on why we have consciousness, and are conscious of sensory, emotional, and motivational qualia, as well as qualia associated with first-order linguistic thoughts. It is likely that theories of consciousness will continue to undergo rapid development, and current theories should not be taken to have practical implications.

Discussion points on consciousness

Some ways in which the current theory may be different from other related theories follow. The current theory holds that it is higher-order *linguistic* thoughts (HOLTs) that are closely associated with consciousness, and this may differ from Rosenthal's higher-order thoughts (HOTs) theory (Rosenthal 1986, 1990, 1993), in the emphasis in the current theory on language. Language here is defined by syntactic manipulation of symbols, and does not necessarily imply verbal language. The reason that strong emphasis is placed on language is that it is as a result of having a multistep flexible 'on the fly' reasoning procedure that errors which cannot be easily corrected by reward or punishment received at the end of the reasoning need 'thoughts about thoughts', that is some type of supervisory process to detect where errors in the reasoning have occurred. This suggestion on the adaptive value in evolution of such a higher-order linguistic thought process for multistep planning ahead, and correcting such plans, may also be different from earlier work. Put another way, this point is that credit assignment when reward or punishment is received is straightforward in a one-layer network (in which the reinforcement can be used directly to correct nodes in error, or responses), but is very difficult in a multistep linguistic process executed once 'on the fly'. Very complex mappings in a multilayer network can be learned if thousands of learning trials are provided. But once these complex mappings are learned, their success or failure in a new situation on a given trial cannot be evaluated and corrected by the network. Indeed, the complex mappings achieved by such networks (e.g. backpropagation nets) mean that after training they operate according to fixed rules, and are often quite impenetrable. In contrast, to correct a mulitstep linguistic process, recall of the steps just made in the reasoning or planning, and perhaps related episodic material, needs to occur, so that the link in the chain which is most likely to be in error can be identified. This may be part of the reason why there is a close relation between declarative memory systems, which can explicitly recall memories, and consciousness.

Some computer programs may have supervisory processes. Should these count as higher-order linguistic thought processes? My current response to this is that they should not, to the extent that they operate with fixed rules to correct the operation of a system which does not itself involve linguistic thoughts about symbols rooted semantically in the external world. If, on the other hand, it were possible to implement on a computer such a high-order linguistic thought supervisory correction process to correct first-order linguistic thoughts, then this process would *prima facie* be conscious. If it were possible in a thought experiment to reproduce the neural connectivity and operation of a human brain on a computer, then *prima facie* it would also have the attributes of consciousness. It might continue to have those attributes for as long as power was applied to the system.

Another possible difference from earlier theories is that raw sensory feels are suggested to arise as a consequence of having a system that can think about its own thoughts. Raw sensory feels, and subjective states associated with emotional and motivational states, may not necessarily arise first in evolution.

A property often attributed to consciousness is that it is unitary. The current theory would account for this by the limited syntactic capability of neuronal networks in the brain, which render it difficult to implement more than a few syntactic bindings of symbols simultaneously. This limitation makes it difficult to run several 'streams of consciousness' simultaneously. In addition, given that a linguistic system can control behavioural output, several parallel streams might produce maladaptive behaviour (apparent as for example in indecision), and might be selected against.

The current theory holds that consciousness arises by virtue of a system that can think linguistically about its own linguistic thoughts. The advantages for a system of being able to do this have been described, and this has been suggested as the reason why consciousness evolved. The evidence that consciousness arises by virtue of having a system that can perform higher-order linguistic processing is, however, and I think may remain, circumstantial. (Why must it feel like something when we are performing a certain type of information processing? The evidence described here suggests that it does feel like something when we are performing a certain type of information processing, but does not produce a strong reason why it has to feel like something. It just does, when we are using this linguistic processing system capable of higher-order thoughts.) The evidence, summarized above, includes the points that we think of ourselves as conscious when, for example, we recall earlier events, compare them with current events, and plan many steps ahead. Evidence also comes from neurological cases, from, for example, split-brain patients (who may confabulate conscious stories about what is happening in their other, non-language, hemisphere), and from cases such as frontal lobe patients who can tell one consciously what they should be doing, but nevertheless may be doing the opposite. (The force of this type of case is that much of our behaviour may normally be produced by routes about which we cannot verbalize, and are not conscious about.) This raises the issue of the causal role of consciousness. Does consciousness cause our behaviour?[1] The view that I currently hold is that the information processing which is related to consciousness (activity in a linguistic system capable of higher-order thoughts, and used for planning and correcting the operation of lower-order linguistic systems) can play a causal role in producing our behaviour (see Fig. 6.7). It is, I postulate, a property of processing in this system (capable of higher-order thoughts) that it feels like something to be performing that type of processing. This means that we do not need to invoke a causal role for the feeling *per se*. This makes the feeling rather like a property of this type of information processing. Nevertheless, the view I currently espouse is that it just happens to feel like something when this processing system is active.

This is of course quite testable: humans performing this type of higher-order linguistic processing, for example recalling episodic memories and comparing them with current circumstances, who denied being conscious, would *prima facie* constitute evidence against the theory.

Acknowledgements

The author has worked on some of the experiments described here with G.C. Baylis, M.J. Burton, M.E. Hasselmo, C.M. Leonard, F. Mora, D.I. Perrett, M.K. Sanghera, T.R. Scott, S.J. Thorpe, and F.A.W. Wilson, and their collaboration, and helpful discussions with or communications from M. Davies and C.C.W. Taylor (Corpus Christi College, Oxford), and M. Stamp Dawkins, are sincerely acknowledged. Some of the research described was supported by the Medical Research Council (PG8513579), and by The Human Frontier Science Program.

Endnote

[1] This raises the issue of the causal relation between mental events and neurophysiological events, part of the mind–body problem. My view is that the relation between mental events and neurophysiological events is similar (apart from the problem of consciousness) to the relation between the program running in a computer and the hardware in the computer. In a sense, the program causes the logic gates to move to the next state. This move causes the program to move to its next state. Effectively, we are looking at different levels of what is overall the operation of a *system*, and causality can usefully be understood as operating both within levels (causing one step of the program to move to the next), as well as between levels (e.g. software to hardware and vice versa).

References

Abbott, L.A., Rolls, E.T., and Tovee, M.J. (1996). Representational capacity of face coding in monkeys. *Cerebral Cortex*, **6**, 498–505.

Amaral, D.G. and Witter, M.P. (1989). The three-dimensional organization of the hippocampal formation: a review of anatomical data. *Neuroscience*, **31**, 571–91.

Amaral, D.G., Ishizuka, N., and Claiborne, B. (1990). Neurons, numbers and the hippocampal network. *Progress in Brain Research*, **83**, 1–11.

Amit, D.J. (1989). *Modelling brain function*. Cambridge University Press, New York.

Armstrong, D.M. and Malcolm, N. (1984). *Consciousness and causality*. Blackwell, Oxford.

Baddeley, R.J., Wakeman, E., Booth, M., Rolls E.T., and Abbott, L.F. (1997). The distribution of firing rates of primate temporal lobe visual neurons to 'natural' scenes. (In preparation.)

Baizer, J.S., Ungerleider, L.G., and Desimone, R. (1991). Organization of visual inputs to the inferior temporal and posterior parietal cortex in macaques. *Journal of Neuroscience*, **11**, 168–90.

Ballard, D.H. (1990). Animate vision uses object-centred reference frames. In *Advanced neural computers* (ed. R. Eckmiller), pp. 229–36. North Holland, Amsterdam.

Barlow, H.B. (1972). Single units and sensation: a neuron doctrine for perceptual psychology? *Perception*, **1**, 371–94.

Barlow, H.B. (1985). Cerebral cortex as model builder. In *Models of the visual cortex* (ed. D. Rose and V.G. Dobson), pp. 37–46. Wiley, Chichester.

Barlow, H.B., Kaushal, T.P., and Mitchison, G.J. (1989). Finding minimum entropy codes, *Neural Computations*, **1**, 412–23.

Baylis, G.C. and Rolls, E.T. (1987). Responses of neurons in the inferior temporal cortex in short term and serial recognition memory tasks. *Experimental Brain Research*, **65**, 614–22.

Baylis, G.C., Rolls, E.T., and Leonard, C.M. (1985). Selectivity between faces in the responses of a population of neurons in the cortex in the superior temporal sulcus of the monkey. *Brain Research*, **342**, 91–102.

Baylis, G.C., Rolls, E.T., and Leonard, C.M. (1987). Functional subdivisions of temporal lobe neocortex. *Journal of Neuroscience*, **7**, 330–42.

Bennett, A. (1990). Large competitive networks. *Network*, **1**, 449–62.

Boussaoud, D., Desimone, R., and Ungerleider, L.G. (1991). Visual topography of area TEO in the macaque. *Journal of Computational Neurology*, **306**, 554–75.

Breitmeyer, B.G. (1980). Unmasking visual masking: a look at the 'why' behind the veil of the 'how'. *Psychological Review*, **87**, 52–69.

Cahusac, P.M.B., Rolls, E.T., Miyashita, Y., and Niki, H. (1993). Modification of the responses of hippocampal neurons in the monkey during the learning of a conditional spatial response task. *Hippocampus*, **3**, 29–42.

Cheney, D.L. and Seyfarth, R.M. (1990). *How monkeys see the world*. University of Chicago Press, Chicago.

Dennett, D.C. (1991). *Consciousness explained*. Penguin, London.

Feldman, J.A. (1985). Four frames suffice: a provisional model of vision and space. *Behavioural Brain Sciences*, **8**, 265–89.

Foldiak, P. (1991). Learning invariance from transformation sequences. *Neural Computations*, **3**, 193–9.

Feigenbaum, J.D. and Rolls, E.T. (1991). Allocentric and egocentric spatial information processing in the hippocampal formation of the behaving primate. *Psychobiology*, **19**, 21–40.

Gaffan, D. (1994). Scene-specific memory for objects: a model of episodic memory impairment in monkeys with fornix transection. *Journal of Cognitive Neuroscience*, **6**, 305–20.

Gaffan, D. and Harrison, S. (1989). Place memory and scene memory: effects of fornix transection in the monkey. *Experimental Brain Research*, **74**, 202–12.

Gaffan, D. and Saunders, R.C. (1985). Running recognition of configural stimuli by fornix transected monkeys. *Quarterly Journal of Experimental Psychology*, **37B**, 61–71.

Gazzaniga, M.S. (1988). Brain modularity: towards a philosophy of conscious experience. In *Consciousness in contemporary science* (ed. A.J. Marcel and E. Bisiach), Chapter 10, pp. 218–38. Oxford University Press.

Gazzaniga, M.S. (1995). Consciousness and the cerebral hemisphere. In *The cognitive neurosciences* (ed. M.S. Gazzaniga). Chapter 92, pp. 1392–400. MIT Press, Cambridge, MA.

Gazzaniga, M.S. and LeDoux, J. (1978). *The integrated mind*. Plenum, New York.

Hasselmo, M.E., Rolls, E.T., Baylis, G.C., and Nalwa, V. (1989*a*). Object-centered encoding by face-selective neurons in the cortex in the superior temporal sulcus of the monkey. *Experimental Brain Research*, **75**, 417–29.

Hasselmo, M.E., Rolls, E.T., and Baylis, G.C. (1989*b*). The role of expression and identity in the face-selective responses of neurons in the temporal visual cortex of the monkey. *Behaviour Brain Research*, **32**, 203–18.

Hornak, J., Rolls, E.T., and Wade, D. (1996). Face and voice expression identification and their association with emotional and behavioural changes in patients with frontal lobe damage. *Neuropsychologia*, **34**, 247–61.

Humphrey, N.K. (1980). Nature's psychologists. In *Consciousness and the physical world* (ed. B.D. Josephson and V.S. Ramachandran), pp. 57–80. Pergamon, Oxford.

Humphreys, G.W. and Bruce, V. (1989). *Visual cognition*. Erlbaum, Hove.

Ishizuka, N., Weber, J., and Amaral, D.G. (1990). Organization of intrahippocampal projections originating from CA3 pyramidal cells in the rat. *Journal of Computational Neurology*, **295**, 580–623.

Jarrard, E.L. (1993). On the role of the hippocampus in learning and memory in the rat. *Behavioural and Neural Biology*, **60**, 9–26.

Kohonen, T. (1988). *Self-organization and associative memory*, (2nd edn). Springer-Verlag, New York.

Leonard, C.M., Rolls, E.T., Wilson, F.A.W., and Baylis, G.C. (1985). Neurons in the amygdala of the monkey with responses relective for faces. *Behavioural Brain Research*, **15**, 159–76.

Malsburg, C. von der (1990). A neural architecture for the representation of scenes. In *Brain organization and memory: cells, systems and circuits* (ed. J.L. McGaugh, N.M. Weinberger, and G. Lynch), Chapter 18, pp. 356–72. Oxford University Press, New York.

Marr, D. (1971). Simple memory: a theory for archicortex. *Philosophical Transactions of the Royal Society of London, Series B*, **262**, 24–81.

Maunsell, J.H.R. and Newsom, W.T. (1987). Visual processing in monkey extrastriate cortex. *Annual Review of Neuroscience*, **10**, 363–401.

Miller, E.K. and Desimone, R. (1994). Parallel neuronal mechanisms for short-term memory. *Science*, **263**, 520–22.

Miyashita, Y. (1988). Neuronal correlates of visual associative long-term memory in the primate temporal cortex. *Nature*, **335**, 817–20.

Miyashita, Y., Rolls, E.T., Cahusac, P.M.B., Niki, H., and Feigenbaum, J.D. (1989). Activity of hippocampal neurons in the monkey related to a conditional spatial response task. *Journal of Neurophysiology*, **61**, 669–78.

Morris, R.G.M. (1989). Does synaptic plasticity play a role in information storage in the vertebrate brain? In *Parallel distributed processing: implications for psychology and neurobiology* (ed. R.G.M. Morris), Chapter 11, pp. 248–85. Oxford University Press.

Oja, E. (1982). A simplified neuron model as a principal component analyser. *Journal of Mathematical Biology*, **15**, 267–73.

O'Mara, S.M., Rolls, E.T., Berthoz, A., and Kesner, R.P. (1994). Neurons responding to whole-body motion in the primate hippocampus. *Journal of Neuroscience*, **14**, 6511–23.

Perrett, D.I., Rolls, E.T., and Caan, W. (1982). Visual neurons responsive to faces in the monkey temporal cortex. *Experimental Brain Research*, **47**, 329–42.

Perrett, D.I., Smith, P.A.J., Mistlin, A.J., Chitty, A.J., Head, A.S., Potter, D.D., *et al.* (1985). Visual analysis of body movements by neurons in the temporal cortex of the macaque monkey: a preliminary report. *Behavioural Brain Research*, **16**, 153–70.

Perrett, D.I., Mistlin, A.J., and Chitty, A.J. (1987). Visual neurons responsive to faces. *Trends in Neuroscience*, **10**, 358–64.

Poggio, T. and Edelman, S. (1990). A network that learns to recognize three-dimensional objects. *Nature*, **343**, 263–6.

Poggio, T. and Girosi, F. (1990*a*). Networks for approximation and learning. *Proceedings of the IEEE*, **78**, 1481–97.

Poggio, T. and Girosi, F. (1990*b*). Regularization algorithms for learning that are equivalent to multilayer networks, *Science*, **247**, 978–82.

Rolls, E.T. (1984). Neurons in the cortex of the temporal lobe and in the amygdala of the monkey with responses selective for faces. *Human Neurobiology*, **3**, 209–22.

Rolls, E.T. (1987). Information representation, processing and storage in the brain: analysis at the single neuron level. In *The neural and molecular bases of learning* (ed. J.-P. Changeux and M. Konishi), pp. 503–40. Wiley, Chichester.

Rolls, E.T. (1989*a*). Functions of neuronal networks in the hippocampus and neocortex in memory. In *Neural models of plasticity: experimental and theoretical approaches* (ed. J.H. Byrne and W.O. Berry), Chapter 13, pp. 240–65. Academic Press, San Diego.

Rolls, E.T. (1989*b*). The representation and storage of information in neuronal networks in the primate cerebral cortex and hippocampus. In *The computing neuron* (ed. R. Durbin, C. Miall, and G. Mitchison), Chapter 8, pp. 125–59. Addison-Wesley, Wokingham, England.

Rolls, E.T. (1989*c*). Functions of neuronal networks in the hippocampus and cerebral cortex in memory. In *Models of brain function* (ed. R.M.J. Cotterill), pp. 15–33. Cambridge University Press.

Rolls, E.T. (1989*d*). Information processing in the taste system of primates. *Journal of Experimental Biology*, **146**, 141–64.

Rolls, E.T. (1990*a*). A theory of emotion, and its application to understanding the neural basis of emotion. *Cognition and Emotion*, **4**, 161–90.

Rolls, E.T. (1990*b*). Functions of the primate hippocampus in spatial processing and memory. In *Neurobiology of comparative cognition* (ed. D.S. Olton and R.P. Kesner), Chapter 12, pp. 339–62. Lawrence Erlbaum, Hillsdale, NJ.

Rolls, E.T. (1990*c*). Theoretical and neurophysiological analysis of the functions of the primate hippocampus in memory. *Cold Spring Harbor Symposia in Quantitative Biology*, No. 55, 995–1006.

Rolls, E.T. (1991). Neural organisation of higher visual functions. *Current Opinion in Neurobiology*, **1**, 274–8.

Rolls, E.T. (1992*a*). Neurophysiological mechanisms underlying face processing within and beyond the temporal cortical visual areas. *Philosophical Transactions of the Royal Society of London*, **335**, 11–21.

Rolls, E.T. (1992*b*). Neurophysiology and functions of the primate amygdala. In *The amygdala* (ed. J.P. Aggleton), pp. 143–65. Wiley-Liss, New York.

Rolls, E.T. (1993). The neural control of feeding in primates. In *Neurophysiology of ingestion* (ed. D.A. Booth), Chapter 9, pp. 137–69. Pergamon, Oxford.

Rolls, E.T. (1994*a*). Brain mechanisms for invariant visual recognition and learning *Behavioural Processes*, **33**, 113–38.

Rolls, E.T. (1994*b*). Neurophysiology and cognitive functions of the striatum. *Revue Neurologique*, **150**, 648–60.

Rolls, E.T. (1995*a*). Learning mechanisms in the temporal lobe visual cortex. *Behavioural Brain Research*, **66**, 177–85.

Rolls, E.T. (1995*b*). A theory of emotion and consciousness, and its application to understanding the neural basis of emotion. In *The cognitive neurosciences* (ed. M.S. Gazzaniga), Chapter 72, pp. 1091–106. MIT Press, Cambridge, MA.

Rolls, E.T. (1995*c*). Central taste anatomy and neurophysiology. In *Handbook of olfaction and gustation* (ed. R.L. Doty), Chapter 24, pp. 549–73. Dekker, New York.

Rolls, E.T. (1996*a*). The orbitofrontal cortex. *Philosophical Transactions of the Royal Society of London, Series B*, **351**, 1433–44.

Rolls, E.T. (1996*b*). A neurophysiological and computational approach to the functions of the temporal lobe cortical visual areas in invariant object recognition. In *Computational and biological mechanisms of visual coding* (ed. L. Harris and M. Jenkin). Cambridge University Press. (In press.)

Rolls, E.T., (1996*c*). The representation of space in the primate hippocampus, and its relation to memory. In *Brain processing and memory* (ed. K. Ishikawa, J.C. McGough, and H. Sakata) pp. 203–27. Elsevier, Amsterdam. (In press.)

Rolls, E.T., (1996*d*). The representation of space in the primate hippocampus, and episodic memory. In *Perception, memory and emotion: frontier in neuroscience* (ed. T. Ono, B.L. McNaughton, S. Molotchnikoff, E.T. Rolls, and H. Nishijo), pp. 375–400. Elsevier, Amsterdam.

Rolls, E.T. (1996*e*). A theory of hippocampal function in memory. *Hippocampus*, **6**, in press.

Rolls, E.T. and Baylis, G.C. (1986). Size and contrast have only small effects on the responses to faces of neurons in the cortex of the superior temporal sulcus of the monkey. *Experimental Brain Research*, **65**, 38–48.

Rolls, E.T. and Johnstone, S. (1992). Neurophysiological analysis of striatal function. In *Neuropsychological disorders associated with subcortical lesions* (ed. G. Vallar, S.F. Cappa, and C.W. Wallesch), Chapter 3, pp. 61–97. Oxford University Press.

Rolls, E.T. and O'Mara, S. (1993). Neurophysiological and theoretical analysis of how the hippocampus functions in memory. In *Brain mechanisms of perception and memory: from neuron to behaviour* (ed. T. Ono, L.R. Squire, M.E. Raichle, D.I. Perrett, and M. Fukuda), Chapter 17, pp. 276–300. Oxford University Press, New York.

Rolls, E.T. and Tovee, M.J. (1994). Processing speed in the cerebral cortex, and the neurophysiology of visual masking. *Proceedings of the Royal Society of London, Series B*, **257**, 9–15.

Rolls, E.T. and Tovee, M.J. (1995). Sparseness of the neuronal representation of stimuli in the primate temporal visual cortex. *Journal of Neurophysiology*, **73**, 713–26.

Rolls, E.T. and Treves, A. (1990). The relative advantages of sparse versus distributed encoding for associative neuronal networks in the brain. *Network*, **1**, 407–21.

Rolls, E.T. and Treves, A. *Neural networks and brain function.* Oxford University Press, Oxford.

Rolls, E.T., Baylis, G.C., and Leonard, C.M. (1985). Role of low and high spatial frequencies in the face-selective responses of neurons in the cortex in the superior temporal sulcus. *Vision Research*, **25**, 1021–35.

Rolls, E.T., Baylis, G.C., and Hasselmo, M.E. (1987). The responses of neurons in the cortex in the superior temporal sulcus of the monkey to band-pass spatial frequency filtered faces. *Vision Research*, **27**, 311–26.

Rolls, E.T., Baylis, G.C., Hasselmo, M.E., and Nalwa, V. (1989). The effect of learning on the face-selective responses of neurons in the cortex in the superior temporal sulcus of the monkey. *Experimental Brain Research*, **76**, 153–64.

Rolls, E.T., Tovee, M.J., and Ramachandran, V.S. (1993). Visual learning reflected in the responses of neurons in the temporal visual cortex of the macaque. *Society for Neuroscience Abstracts*, **19**, 27.

Rolls, E.T., Tovee, M.J., Purcell, D.G., Steward, A.L., and Azzopardi, P. (1994*a*). The responses for neurons in the temporal cortex of primates, and face identification and detection. *Experimental Brain Research*, **101**, 474–84.

Rolls, E.T., Hornak, J., Wade, D., and McGrath, J. (1994*b*) Emotion-related learning in patients with social and emotional changes associated with frontal lobe damage. *Journal of Neurology, Neurosurgery and Psychiatry*, **57**, 1518–24.

Rolls, E.T., Booth, M.C.A., and Treves, A. (1996). View-invariant representations of objects in the inferior temporal visual cortex. *Society of Neuroscience Abstracts*, **22**, 445–5.

Rolls, E.T., Tovee, M., and Treves, A. (1997*a*). Information in the neuronal representation of individual stimuli in the primate temporal visual cortex. *Journal of Computational Neuroscience*, in press.

Rolls, E.T., Treves, A., and Tovee, M.J. (1997*b*). The representational capacity of the distributed encoding of information provided by populations of neurons in the primate temporal visual cortex. *Experimental Brain Research*, in press.

Rosenthal, D.M. (1986). Two concepts of consciousness. *Philosophical Studies*, **49**, 329–59.

Rosenthal, D. (1990). *A theory of consciousness*, ZIF Report No. 40. Zentrum fur Inter-disziplinaire Forschung, Bielefeld, Germany.

Rosenthal, D.M. (1993). Thinking that one thinks. In *Consciousness* (ed. M. Davies and G.W. Humphreys), Chapter 10, pp. 197–223. Blackwell, Oxford.

Rupniak, N.M.J. and Gaffan, D. (1987). Monkey hippocampus and learning about spatially directed movements. *Journal of Neuroscience*, **7**, 2331–7.

Seltzer, B. and Pandya, D.N. (1978). Afferent cortical connections and architectonics of the superior temporal sulcus and surrounding cortex in the rhesus monkey. *Brain Research*, **149**, 1–24.

Simmen, M.W., Rolls, E.T., and Treves, A. (1996). On the dynamics of a network of spiking neurons. In *Computations and neuronal systems: proceedings of CNS95* (ed. F.H. Eekman and J.M. Bower). Kluwer, Boston.

Squire, L.R. (1992). Memory and the hippocampus: a synthesis from findings with rats, monkeys and humans. *Psychological Review*, **99**, 195–231.

Tanaka, K., Saito, C., Fukada, Y., and Moriya, M. (1990). Integration of form, texture, and color information in the inferotemporal cortex of the macaque. In *Vision, memory and the temporal lobe* (ed. E. Iwai and M. Mishkin), Chapter 10, pp. 101–9. Elsevier, New York.

Thorpe, S.J. and Imbert, M. (1989). Biological constraints on connectionist models. In *Connectionism in perspective* (ed. R. Pfeifer, Z. Schreter, and F. Fogelman-Soulie), pp. 63–92. Elsevier, Amsterdam.

Tovee, M.J. and Rolls, E.T. (1995). Information encoding in short firing rate epochs by single neurons in the primate temporal visual cortex. *Visual Cognition*, **2**, 35–58.

Tovee, M.J., Rolls, E.T., Treves, A., and Bellis, R.P. (1993). Information encoding and the responses of single neurons in the primate temporal visual cortex. *Journal of Neurophysiology*, **70**, 640–54.

Tovee, M.J., Rolls, E.T., and Azzopardi, P. (1994). Translation invariance and the responses of neurons in the temporal visual cortical areas of primates. *Journal of Neurophysiology*, **72**, 1049–60.

Treves, A. (1990). Graded-response neurons and information encodings in autoassociative memories. *Physical Review A*, **42**, 2418–30.

Treves, A. (1993). Mean-field analysis of neuronal spike dynamics. *Network*, **4**, 259–84.

Treves, A. and Rolls, E.T. (1991). What determines the capacity of autoassociative memories in the brain? *Network*, **2**, 371–97.

Treves, A. and Rolls, E.T. (1992). Computational constraints suggest the need for two distinct input systems to the hippocampal CA3 network. *Hippocampus*, **2**, 189–99.

Treves, A. and Rolls, E.T. (1994). A computational analysis of the role of the hippocampus in memory. *Hippocampus*, **4**, 374–91.

Treves, A., Rolls, E.T., and Simmon, M.W. (1997). Time for retrieval in recurrent associative nets. *Physica D*, in press.

Turvey, M.T. (1973). On the peripheral and central processes in vision: inferences from an information processing analysis of masking with patterned stimuli. *Psychological Review*, **80**, 1–52.

Wallis, G. and Rolls, E.T. (1996). Invariant face and object recognition in the visual system. *Progress in Neurobiology*, in press.

Wallis, G., Rolls, E.T., and Foldiak, P. (1993). Learning invariant responses to the natural transformations of objects. *International Joint Conference on Neural Networks 2*, **2**, 1087–90.

Yamane, S., Kaji, S., and Kawano, K. (1988). What facial features activate face neurons in the inferotemporal cortex of the monkey? *Experimental Brain Research*, **73**, 209–14.

7

Single neurons, communal goals, and consciousness

HORACE BARLOW

Introduction

Together with many other scientists I have a strong bias towards a reductionist approach to consciousness, but at the same time I cannot believe that a reductionist account of the working of my brain will ever give a satisfactory explanation for my own subjective experiences; these have vividness, excitement, colour, and personal qualities that seem to lie quite outside the scientific realm. How can one stick to reductionism and avoid the disappointment that seems inevitable when it is applied to consciousness? I think the frustration results from asking the wrong questions about the wrong system, so let me first point out where consciousness plays a role that can hardly be denied.

Humans differ from other species in pursuing communal goals that persist for many generations in large fractions of the population, yet are determined to an important extent culturally, not mainly genetically. What makes the pursuit of communal goals possible is our ability to communicate fluently with each other, and to hold concepts in our brains about other individuals, about our institutions, and about those communal goals themselves. Furthermore, the ability to communicate fluently about these concepts is surely the direct and obvious result of our being conscious. If this is accepted one cannot possibly regard it as a mere epiphenomenon, for it is a crucial and causal step that determines the nature of human communities, and has been an important factor leading to our domination of the world. Even though consciousness appears to be an attribute of each individual, to understand its workings one must look at an interacting social group, not at a single brain, and certainly not at an isolated part of a single brain. Only in the context of the social group can one see how consciousness—our ability to know and communicate about states of our own brain—has brought about our cultural evolution.

The system important for a reductionist approach to consciousness is therefore the social group, but the question asked is equally important. Curiosity about our subjective experience naturally prompts the question 'What *is* consciousness?' just as the experience of heat and light prompted the same questions about them. But the results obtained by reductionist experimentation do not tell one what the experiences of heat and light *are*: they tell one what heat and light *do*. In the same way we are unlikely to find out what consciousness *is*, but we can hope to find out what consciousness *does* for the individual and the species. Notice, however, that although our knowledge of physics does not answer the '*is*' question, either about our experience of physical stimuli or about light and heat, this knowledge does change our attitude to our sensory experiences: the '*is*' question somehow becomes less mysterious and imperative when we understand the physical basis by which our senses keep us informed about the world around us. In the same way, even though the reductionist approach cannot tell us what our private subjective experience *is*, private experience acquires a different flavour once one appreciates its biological role in promoting social communication, for it then has an obvious functional role and equally obvious survival value.

In order to present the above arguments more completely this paper is divided into three parts. The first explains how far one can get in explaining subjective experience in terms of neuronal activity, and why this approach must ultimately be abandoned. The second is about what consciousness *does*; since conscious introspection can hardly be expected to provide an unbiased answer, we try to imagine how a totally alien creature would view human history and human behaviour. This longer section is itself formed around two imaginary reports, the first pointing out that the success of the human species depends very largely on the unique pattern of our cooperative behaviour, and the second suggesting that this depends upon what we call consciousness, with a section in between about the role of communal goals and institutions in human life. Finally, the third section compares the characteristics of consciousness that would be expected if it had evolved to expand social communication with its 'particulars' as described by William James and others.

How well do cardinal cells explain consciousness?

Let me start with the suggestion (Barlow 1972) that there is a simple and direct relationship between the activity of single neurons in sensory centres and conscious perception, and why there is still much to be said for this view. First go back to Müller's Law of specific energies; this originally stated that the different sense organs each give a distinct quality of sensation, regardless of the means by which the organ is stimulated. It was then extended (but not by Müller himself) to nerve fibres, and the surprising thing is that by and large this extension holds: there are arguments about itching and pain, and the chemical senses do not fit as well as the somatosensory, auditory, and visual systems, but the fact of the matter is that the *verbal* categorization of sensations has been found to correspond quite well with the *physiological* and *anatomical* categorization of types of nerve. This is a fact that needs to be taken into account, for why should a verbally categorized sensation correspond with the activity of a specific physiological and anatomical category? Why should it not correspond to *any* logical function of the activity of the sensory nerve fibres? At the very least, the truth of Müller's Law leads one to hope that there might be a simple and direct relationship between the activity of sensory neurons and conscious perception.

When neurons in the visual system were found to respond selectively to specific patterns of sensory input it was natural to suppose that this expectation was being fulfilled, and that these patterns correspond to simple perceptions built out of more elementary sensations. Analysis of the properties of these neurons showed that they were sensitive enough, and selective enough, to account for many aspects of perceptual psychophysics, which would be hard to explain if perception depended on a complex pattern in a very large number of neurons, as the opponents of a simple relationship are wont to suggest.

The notion of this simple relation was developed into that of 'cardinal cells' Barlow (1972, 1995). The idea is that sensory scenes are represented in the cortex by the activity of a relatively small number of neurons picked from a very large ensemble, each element of which has selective properties that make it suitable, in relatively sparse combinations, for representing the enormous number of scenes we actually experience and discriminate from each other. This notion is not contradicted by any of the experimental facts I know, it is further testable experimentally, it would be efficient for learning, it is subjectively plausible, and it accords well with modern analyses of sensory coding (e.g. Field 1994). However there is much more to consciousness than could ever be explained simply by the activity of such cardinal cells, as the following argument shows.

In order to illustrate the idea that neurons might represent concepts and ideas, in 1969 Jerry Lettvin (see Appendix to Barlow 1995) whimsically postulated that there was a group of 'mother cells' in the fictional *von Seelendonck's area* that responded to the image of 'mother', whenever and however such an image was presented. Suppose we had confirmed this finding, and with our improved techniques were able to preserve and activate such cells in a brain slice, and perhaps even grow them in tissue culture. Under such conditions, would their activity still correspond to the conscious perception of 'mother'? I find that utterly implausible, but perhaps you might say that there *is* an element of consciousness in the responses of those cells in the slice; they might be the basic elements of the 'feel' of mother, but be unable to communicate this 'feel' for want of appropriate connections. This won't do, however, for it is the 'feel' itself, not its communication to other parts, that we are trying to understand. I think we must mean something more by 'the conscious experience of mother' than could possibly be explained by knowledge of the biophysics of those isolated cells, however complete that knowledge was.

I have framed this argument to knock down the idea of a simple correlation between the activity of specific groups of cells and the occurrence of specific perceptions, because that, with the modifications implied for cardinal cells, seems to me the most plausible current idea about the relationship between neural activity and conscious experience. But of course the argument destroys *any* hypothesis defining a relationship between activity in a group of nerve cells and conscious experience, whether these be oscillations or some other kind of magic tingle; the difficulty stems from considering an isolated group of cells, not from the nature of the relationship postulated.

Obviously, not all neural activity is associated with conscious experience, and we need to know what kind of activity in which cells is so associated, but in spite of the upbeat review of the reductionist approach given by Crick (1994), new information along these lines will be hard to interpret without understanding the functional role of consciousness, and I do not believe this can be done if one confines one's attention to a single brain or an isolated part of a single brain.[1] We must therefore look in another direction.

The biological approach

There are several directions one might turn in trying to escape the brick wall that the ultra-reductionist approach leads to; one could for instance consider introspective ideas about consciousness, or spend a long time in a philosophical library. But for a biological scientist the overriding question must surely be 'What is its survival value: what types of behaviour does consciousness make possible that would not be possible without it, or that would be performed less advantageously for the individual and the species without it?' Some consider this a foolish question: unconscious people cannot do anything properly, and we could not do anything properly ourselves without consciousness. But this is wrong, for no one knows the limits to what an automaton can do. Long ago, Nietzsche (1887) recognized this and said, 'Consciousness is really only a net of communication between human beings; it is only as such that it had to develop; a solitary human being who lived as a beast of prey would not have needed it.' The question was discussed at length by William James (1879, 1890), but he was not satisfied by any answers then forthcoming. I think he abandoned the search prematurely and shall suggest how to continue it, but first there is a related problem that can be approached by the same method.

It is an age-old question how we know that others are conscious, except by analogy with ourselves. The usual argument goes as follows: I know that I am conscious; the other human beings I see around me are similar to me in very many ways, and I must therefore assume that they too are conscious. Put like that it is not a very strong argument, for however like me they are in some ways, they differ in many others; I do not assume that others have the same name as I do, so why should I assume that, if they are conscious at all, they are conscious in the same way as me? But in practice the assumption of consciousness in others involves much more than the assumption that they have similar private experiences to my own. If I fail to assume consciousness in others and fail to modify my behaviour in the light of this assumption, I shall make a mess of my social affairs on a day-to-day basis. Baron-Cohen *et al.* (1985) have shown rather convincingly that this failure leads to the devastating consequences exhibited by autistic children. Such children apparently do not understand that other people receive a different view of the world which, like their own, is sometimes incomplete or incorrect. This shows dramatically that the important aspect of the assumption of consciousness in others is not the belief that they have private experiences like me, but accepting that they are eligible to join my

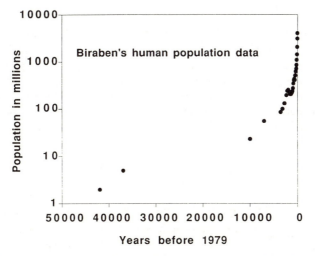

Fig. 7.1 Biraben's estimate of the human population at various dates before 1979 (from Thatcher 1983). The early estimates are obviously not very reliable.

group of consciously communicating individuals. Private experience like mine may be necessary for them to be eligible, but it is a mistake to consider such private experience as sufficient for full consciousness, since they also require a 'theory of mind' in order to participate in a consciously communicating group.

The approach that I suggest for gaining insight into these two problems—the selective advantage of consciousness, and why we assume that other humans are conscious—is a thought-experiment in which a very wise Alien visits planet Earth in order to advise us about its crisis and that of the Earthlings. We would show him the population data shown in Fig. 7.1, so that he would know that we have conquered the world, and understands that we are putting it in peril through overpopulation, attempting limitless economic expansion, and pollution. He does not know, any more than we do, precisely why this has come about, but we want him to take a look and give us his views about it.

The reason for introducing the Alien is that he is totally unlike an Earthling and therefore has not the faintest idea of what it is like to *be* a human being. He cannot understand our feelings or intuit our motives, so he is forced to start out by being a behaviourist: all he can observe is what we *do* and the consequences of our actions. In this way the Alien provides a thought-tool for exploring how much of our behaviour could be explained if we had no conscious experience, and perhaps by using him we can appreciate the types of behaviour for which conscious experience is necessary. Of course you may think you already know this, but there are good reasons for doubting the validity of such introspective conclusions (see for instance Barlow 1987).

The Alien would want to know how we differ from other species, and there is little doubt that the differences of greatest interest concern our brains. So we would tell him, in résumé, that humans are swollen-headed animals, that we think each swollen head contains a mechanism for extracting reliable knowledge of the world from the unreliable sensory messages that the world provides, and for storing this knowledge for future use. The postulated skill in understanding the physical and natural events around us is derived from Kenneth Craik's concept that 'the brain models reality' and E.C. Tolman's notion of 'cognitive maps' (Craik 1943; Tolman 1948). There is little doubt that Jerison (1991) is right in saying that we are the most knowing of animals, and perhaps with this basic idea about how we differ from other animals the Alien would be encouraged to conduct his first tour of inspection.

The first Alien report

I can imagine him reporting, after such a tour, as follows:

Humans do indeed seem to be the most knowing of earthly animals, and I can well believe that the most difficult and important task for their brains is to acquire, store, and organize knowledge acquired through their senses. However, the monkeys in the trees also seem to know a lot, judging from the tricks they get up to, yet their limited population shows that they are not nearly as successful as you, nor have they changed the environment to anything like the same extent. Furthermore, you were only a moderately successful species ten or twenty thousand years ago, but your individual brains cannot have been very different then from what they are now. The ability to acquire knowledge would not by itself have allowed your population to increase to the point where you endanger the planet, and I think there must be something more about earthlings that you have not yet revealed.

It may be presumptuous to make a suggestion, but I notice that large groups of humans cooperate over long periods of time as if all the individuals in a group possessed a common mind. Monkeys do not do that, but fritter away their efforts in a succession of enterprises that are only briefly coherent. It is this long-term cooperative behaviour that has made humans uniquely successful—and uniquely dangerous. I therefore wonder if human heads are swollen, not just to accommodate the superior equipment for acquiring knowledge that you have told me about, but also in order to accommodate equipment that facilitates cooperation with other humans.

To be blunt, I do not think that you are such remarkable animals taken individually, but anything can happen when a large group of you becomes animated by the same spirit for a prolonged period. It is as if part of each swollen head does not wholly belong to the individual that carries it, but is shared with other human beings around it.

Before considering these frank comments, notice that the résumé we gave to the Alien—man is the most knowing of animals—is unsatisfactory to Earthlings for a reason that is apparently quite different from those advanced above by the Alien. It omits any mention of conscious awareness—that magic distillation of experience, intentions, hopes, and fears that is the thing we know best of all and cannot help regarding as our most important possession. One reason for the omission is that we really would not know what to tell him, for there is certainly no consensus to report. A more rational defence is that, according to most ways of thinking, a good account of what the brain *does* need not contain any hint of what it is like to *be* a brain. But this excuse jars with our conviction that we have control over what we do, and hence that consciousness is not just a matter of *being* a brain; if consciousness has any influence on our lives at all, then some account of the *being* should be included in an account of what the brain *does*.

In the remainder of this chapter I hope to make you understand that the Alien's complaint about unexplained *cooperative behaviour* is very closely related to the Earthling's complaint about the omission of *consciousness*; they are opposite sides of the same coin, and realizing this brings the *being* and *doing* a little closer together.

Knowing each other

Craik's brain models were of the physical objects and laws that cause our sensations, and Tolman's cognitive maps referred mainly to the geographical layout of the mazes his rats were running. But physical objects and geography are not the most important things for a newborn infant to know about, and it is doubtful if they are most important at any subsequent period of human life. 'No man is an island, entire of it self'; we are profoundly social animals and depend on other humans not only immediately after birth, but throughout life. It follows that the physical objects around us are not what we need to model most urgently; instead it is the people— their distinguishing characteristics, the actions each of them takes, and the way they each respond to our demands and actions. Humphrey (1976) has argued that the key task for intelligence is to facilitate social cooperation, and that the ability to do this is the main benefit derived from our large brains. Mastering physical phenomena and geography are easy compared with mastering (or arranging to be beneficially mastered by) each other, and it is this accomplishment, reviewed in the book edited by Byrne and Whiten (1988), that has the greater survival value for individual humans.

It is not of course a new idea that human relationships are important and mould our lives even when we are not aware of it. It would be hard to state an origin for it in the arts and humanities; perhaps, like the idea that consciousness is only important socially, its modern form can be traced back to Friedrich Nietzsche, but scientifically it is often attributed to Freud, and is perhaps his most lasting legacy. The infant interacts with its entourage, and the residues of these interactions in the infant's brain persist throughout life. The same is true for the human relationships formed in childhood, adolescence, and adulthood, many of which leave influential residues. We are hopelessly bad at consciously tracing the origins of our ideas, thoughts, and opinions, but few would nowadays deny the strong influence of other people through the interactions sketched above, even though this may offend our sense of the privacy, originality, and individuality of our own conscious thoughts. Above all, a high proportion of all the work done by our brains must consist of modelling the behaviour of other humans. Each brain contains a representation of many other brains inside itself and the Alien was absolutely right: a large part of each of our swollen heads is devoted to forming, storing, and using models of what goes on in other people's heads;[2] in that sense we share our brains with each other.

How far does this go towards explaining the devastating power of humans compared with other species? One naturally surveys in one's mind the historical steps that led to this power: the development of spoken language, agriculture, and animal husbandry; the exploitation of the mineral wealth of the world; the creation of surpluses that engendered trade, cities, money, wealth, and empire; the invention of writing to meet the requirements for permanent records; the formation and dissemination of the belief-systems characteristic of the great religions; and finally the development of the science and technology associated with materials, crops and livestock, energy and information, together with the accumulation of the reliable knowledge that science produces. The ability to acquire knowledge of geography and the material world fits Tolman's and Craik's paradigms, but cities, money, wealth, empire, the spread of religious beliefs, and the development of scientific knowledge require just that cooperation of large groups of people and the accumulation of knowledge over long periods of time that the Alien identified as the unique and power-giving characteristics of humans. For these, our ability to model each other is a very important component, but these widespread and long-lasting tides of human endeavour require something more.

Communal goals and social institutions

If they depended simply on each of us modelling other individuals, the range of cooperation would be limited to a few times the range of personal acquaintanceship, and the duration of cooperation would similarly be limited to a few working lifetimes; instead, the same spirit appears to animate populations of millions, and can persist for hundreds or even thousands of years. The feature of human society that brings this about, and at the same time differentiates our own social organization from anything else seen in the natural world, is our propensity to create communal goals together with social institutions to foster them and guard any acquired knowledge; these have usually been created by our remote ancestors and persist for generations, though they are not dictated by our genes.

The family or tribe must be the prototypical social institution, but the term can be extended to cover any organization that influences several individuals and persists for several working lifetimes. Church, army, state, football club, bingo group, educational institutions, and libraries all qualify, but it is clearly those that foster a serious communal goal with which we are most concerned. The associates of each institution intermingle and overlap, so the full extent to which they influence our lives might not be too obvious to the visiting Alien, but a moment's reflection suggests that the human mind makes models of the behaviour of institutions as avidly as it models the minds of individuals. And it is personally advantageous to do so, for institutions have power over us and look after us in ways that are analogous to the prototypical family or tribe, in addition to acting as the depository and guardians of acquired knowledge.

Furthermore, institutions are like individuals in many ways. They must defend their own selfish interests if they are to survive, while they have to live at peace with other institutions and therefore sometimes act altruistically for the common good. It is no accident that they are granted property and legal rights. We do not ordinarily attribute a 'mind' or consciousness to them, though we come close to it when we say that the club (or church, or bingo group) would not *like* that, or *believes* this. And it is clear that we are easily influenced by the likes, dislikes, and beliefs of institutions, just as we are by the likes, dislikes, and beliefs of individual people in our lives. Possibly as much of the average person's brain is devoted to modelling institutions as is devoted to modelling individual people.

This is not the place to discuss actual goals, purposes, and institutions, but three points are worth making. The first is that an institution can amplify and perpetuate the influence of an individual mind; religions claim to amplify and continue the teaching of great spiritual leaders, and the political institutions founded by megalomaniacal kings and conquerors amplify and continue their temporal powers. It may seem wrong to describe such institutions as fostering *communal* goals, but although they may stem from a single mind, that mind is itself the product of a community and its teachings are seldom left unmodified. On a smaller scale, writers, artists, and scientific discoverers produce ideas that 'catch on' and become widely known; Dawkins (1976) suggests the term *meme* for the smallest unit of such culturally transmissible ideas.

The second point is that our own individual beliefs and allegiances tend to become aligned for or against these powerful belief systems and centres of power, with the result that the number of different belief systems and allegiances of the human species is reduced by a vast factor. There are 5000 million individuals, but because of our tendency to model institutions, the number of distinguishable ideas we hold about the universe, as well as the number of distinguishable ideals we strive to achieve, is enormously less. Thus social institutions crystallize beliefs and focus power, and they control the direction in which the human race is headed. While institutions are conservative by their very nature, it is only by changing them that one can realistically hope to change the direction we are going.

Thirdly, it is worth emphasizing that these human tides of purpose and belief do not ebb and flow without leaving any trace. Popper (1972) defined three worlds: 'first, the world of physical objects ... secondly, the world of states of consciousness ... and thirdly, the world of *objective contents of thought*, especially of scientific and poetic thoughts and of works of art'. Communal goals sometimes result in objective knowledge, and subsequent generations benefit greatly by not having to start from scratch.

Our visiting Alien pointed out the importance of cooperative behaviour for the dominance of mankind, and this was attributed to the human propensity to model each other. We now see that the range and duration of these waves of cooperation are enormously extended by the formation of social institutions and by our propensity to model them, as well as individuals, in our minds. Furthermore, they have resulted in the accumulation of the large store of public knowledge contained in our libraries. If we shared the above discussion with the visiting Alien, what might he say after a second tour of inspection?

The second Alien view

How well would the revised account of the human mind explain, and perhaps predict, what he observed? I think he would still be puzzled, because he would ask 'What exactly is it that spreads this wave of cooperation? How can a belief system, an ideal, or a spirit of allegiance gain possession of large groups of human brains for prolonged periods?' Tolman (who invented cognitive maps) started as a pure behaviourist, yet was eventually led to make remarks, such as '*rat behaviour reeks of purpose*', quite out of keeping with the tenets of that school. This was because he observed repeatedly that the common feature in the behaviour of his rats was the attainment of an identifiable goal, not the particular route each took in order to attain it. An Alien as smart as Tolman might say of us '*human history reeks of communal purpose*', for the important feature of our behaviour that repeats itself again and again is the generation of communal goals and their spread through a population. The propensity to model and understand each other is not by itself sufficient to account for our acceptance of communal goals, and he might be prompted to ask if we can ourselves explain how it happens.

I do not think the average participant in the spread of Agriculture, or Muhammedanism, or the Industrial Revolution, would be able to give a very cogent account of the motive for his actions. He would probably say something like 'I chose to take part after I had talked to a number of people and considered the alternative opportunities open to me'. This does not tell one much, but it does contain the all-important phrase 'I chose', for choosing is what William James and most of the rest of us consider to be the most characteristic product of *consciousness*. Perhaps many drifted into participating in the industrial revolution without making a conscious choice, but surely it is the making of conscious choices that one regards as the most important things one does; if consciousness is not important here, it is not important anywhere. So we see that those tides of human effort that so impressed (and frightened) the Alien are composed of vast numbers of individual conscious choices based on communications with other humans.

This vital role justifies our intuitive judgment that consciousness is supremely important, but how would it appear to our visiting Alien, who has no understanding of human feelings, motives, and experience? What would persuade him that we were not behaviouristic robots each controlled entirely by individual past experience? The fact that human behaviour *reeks of communal goals and purposes* requires an explanation, and the Alien might put it like this:

It is clear to me that there must be a special type of activity in your brains that takes place when each of you reports to others what is going on in your individual brain, and interacts with the reports from others. This activity will presumably be mediated by neural mechanisms similar to those that control the rest of your behaviour, but it is in some way kept distinct from much of the activity in your brains that it would be unnecessary, or even undesirable, to report to others. I suspect this special activity that often precedes communication is what you call *conscious awareness*, though you have for some reason hardly mentioned this to me. If I am right, you are conscious of what others say to you, and of what you say and are preparing to

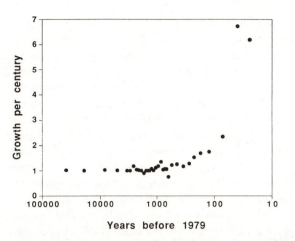

Fig. 7.2 The factor by which the human population has increased per century (from Biraben's data, see Thatcher 1983). The really rapid increase is extremely recent and coincides better with the communication revolution than with the agricultural or industrial revolutions. Note the reversed logarithmic scale of time before 1979. Note also that the earlier figures represent averages over long epochs, and these may conceal extensive fluctuations.

say to others, including an account of what you are seeing, feeling, and smelling; when alone, you are still conscious because you are preparing future interactions or recalling past ones. This is all done against a background of extensive knowledge of each other and of those institutions that have such a powerful influence over you, but this background of knowledge is shared amongst you and is not unique to each individual; therefore, you do not often communicate about it, and, as my hypothesis predicts, you are indeed largely unconscious of it.

In your species there is the beginning of a communal forum for decision-making, and what you call *consciousness* accompanies the activity of the part of your brain that connects each of you with this forum.

Is the Alien's statement that consciousness creates a communal forum obvious and trivial? First look at Fig. 7.2 where the population data of Fig. 7.1 have been replotted. The ordinate is now the factor by which human population increased per century, while the abscissa is a logarithmic scale of time before 1979, when Biraben published the data (see Thatcher 1983). Plotted thus, it can be seen that the high rate of population increase is a very recent phenomenon. It started about three hundred years ago, but the really rapid increase seems timed by the occurrence of the revolution in world communication rather than by the agricultural or industrial revolutions. The communication revolution has vastly enlarged the communal forum, and the almost catastrophic increase in growth rate may be the result.

This brings up the obvious point that many other factors as well as conscious choice decide human history; slaves built the pyramids but are unlikely to have contributed much to the decisions that caused them to be built. But even if the decision was made by a single individual, it must have emerged from the conscious interactions of that individual with others, for we all have an ear tuned to the communal forum, whether we admit it or not.

Is the biological role of consciousness in forming and accepting communal goals widely recognized? The earliest statement of the social importance of consciousness that has been pointed out to me consists of a few hundred words by Nietzsche (1887) containing the quote given earlier in this chapter. But although he says very clearly that '... consciousness has developed only under the pressure of the need for communication', he barely hints that this makes possible the communication of knowledge and formulation of long-term communal goals, which I maintain is what gives consciousness its survival value; instead he emphasizes the negative aspects: '... all becoming conscious involves a great and thorough corruption, falsification, reduction to superficialities, and generalization'. An evolutionary attitude to the mind and society was revived by Wilson's *Sociobiology* (1975), and has been followed up by Lumsden and Wilson (1981) and Barkow *et al.* (1992), but many recent works that claim to shed light on the mind (Churchland 1986; Humphrey 1992; Zeki 1993; Crick 1994) almost completely ignore its social aspects. Earlier papers by Humphrey (1979, 1983) and myself (Barlow 1979, 1987, 1990) have argued for the social importance of consciousness, and Dennett (1991) gives an elegant account of how the conscious mind might have evolved as a culturally acquired meme-system, but he says less about the reciprocal effect of the conscious mind on evolution.

The next section makes some predictions from the hypothesis that consciousness has evolved to act as the agent of cultural evolution and is adapted to this specific role, and compares these predictions with the 'particulars of the distribution of consciousness' as described by William James (1879, 1890) and discussed by Glynn (1993).

William James' 'particulars'

In his illuminating discussion James starts by saying that consciousness is primarily a selecting agency and appears to be an organ of choice. We seem to be most conscious at precisely those points where the choice between alternative actions is being taken, whereas we act more like a true automaton when the course of action is certain or habitual. If consciousness forms the social forum as my hypothetical Alien suggested, we see that our conscious decisions are inevitably communal decisions, made in the light of the attitudes and opinions of our fellow creatures and our social institutions. Individually, we contribute to the social forum and thus influence the conscious decisions of others, and as I write these words I am trying to make such a contribution; as you read them you will perhaps be influenced by them, one way or another. It is this habitual behaviour that gives to humans their unique social characteristic, and it provides the survival value that William James felt that consciousness must have.

As well as mere intellectual opinions, the brain mechanisms of consciousness also mediate those waves of long-lasting cooperation among vast numbers of humans, and they thus underly the feature that has been responsible for the astounding success of the human race. The fact that consciousness sits at the interface between each individual and the society he is part of means that it sits at the nodal point, or rather the millions of nodal points, that determine these enterprises. Our intuition that it is important is fully justified, for how could anything be more important than something occupying this position and acting as the agent of our history and evolution?

Several other characteristics also take their natural place. For instance, the fact that we are not conscious of habitual actions should be traced back to the fact that other humans do not need to be told about them. And the prominence of language is expected, for that is the main medium of communication within a social group. But there are some aspects that may still appear puzzling, namely the incompleteness and deceptiveness of our conscious awareness that Freud emphasized, and the fact that to each of us it seems such a private and personal thing, uninfluenced by others.

The deceptiveness would arise from the fact that each person's consciousness is directed outward towards society, and it is not necessary for that person to understand all the reasons for his or her actions. Nature's policy, if it can be put like that, is to inform each of us strictly on a 'need to know' basis. Thus when I am injured I retreat and avoid the injury in future, and when my appetites are gratified I seek the same pleasurable circumstances again, but I only need to be guided to these actions; introspection does not reveal to me the benefits my body is deriving and the reason why these help me, and ultimately assist the dissemination of my genes. The same occurs when boy meets girl: we are naturally guided towards the appropriate actions during courtship, and subsequent to courtship, but the natural consequences of these actions are not prominent in our awareness. Consciousness provides the means to explain your actions to society, but it does not provide a backward look at the true biological roles of those actions. Many people suffer from the delusion that they can consciously explain *all* their actions, but this is not the case; one can explain one's actions to the extent that such explanations are likely to form worthy contributions to the social forum.

When it comes to the sense of uniqueness and privacy each of us has about our own consciousness, we can again see that this is an expected feature on the current hypothesis. Each individual is a separate actor in the social interactions we are talking about, and what he or she has to contribute depends, not upon what is shared with others, but upon the way the individual's innate abilities and experience differ from others. That is what the rest of society requires in the reports people make of what they are doing, why they are doing it, and what they think should be done; the individuality of self-awareness simply reflects this need. The tendency to deny the influence of other people and institutions fits in because these influences are part of the shared background that everyone has experienced, and denial is just the means of preventing their redundant communication. Our awareness feels unique for the simple reason that what we have worth communicating to others is the unique part of our thoughts and experience.

Jackendoff (1987) has recently made a well-reasoned attempt to fit a computational model of the working of our brains to our awareness of these workings. His model distinguishes between representational structures, which contain the incoming information, and computational processes that transform these structures. His initially surprising conclusion is that in the three examples he considers, language, vision, and music, it is not the highest level of representation or structures that we are consciously aware of, nor of course a very low level close to the sensory input; instead it is an intermediate level corresponding to the phonology in language, Marr's $2\frac{1}{2}$ D sketch in vision, and the surface structure in music. On the current hypothesis, conscious experience gives one the facility of communicating one's own experience to others; that is its point, purpose, and survival value. On this hypothesis, if you were asked 'What did he say?', 'What did you see?', or 'Play it again', the appropriate response would be to attempt to produce the same experience in your interlocutor as you experienced yourself. This implies that you should repeat the phonology, describe the $2\frac{1}{2}$ D sketch, or recreate the musical surface structure. These are the highest levels that include the whole experience but exclude as far as possible elements of interpretation due to your individual viewpoint; they are therefore the appropriate levels for communicating with others about that experience. Jackendoff expressed concern about this for he could not see the point of consciousness being restricted to this intermediate level, but I think his result provides a nice example of the way the current hypothesis gives additional understanding and insight.

The hypothesis that consciousness enables us to participate in a communal forum and is evolutionarily adapted to that role seems to explain some of its characteristics. The mystery of private experience, what it is like to *be* conscious, remains relatively untouched and unexplained, but I personally find that the nature of this experience[3] is itself changed considerably by appreciating that it connects us with each other and has played an important part in our history. The nature of subjective awareness becomes more intelligible and less puzzling when one appreciates its crucial social and biological role.

Conclusions

The first conclusion must be a negative one: the reductionist analysis of consciousness at the neuronal level is inappropriate. It does not matter if the elements of our perception correspond to cardinal cells, or to patterns of activity in Sherrington's 'millionfold democracy' of cells, for the biologically important aspect of consciousness concerns communication between individuals, not communication among the nerve cells of a single individual. We might one day be thrilled to hear that the neurons important for consciousness stain differently, or have characteristic rhythms of activity, but such discoveries would not show us how consciousness performs its characteristic biological role, and this role is its most important feature because it confers survival value.

What I have tried to bring out in this article is that consciousness is not just the *product* of recent human evolution, but also its *agent*: it is only because we each have access to our individual sensations, perceptions, intuitions, and emotions that we can participate in the long-term goals of the communities we live in, both understanding these goals and potentially making some contribution to them. Such participation is the hallmark of human communities and an important component of the biological success of our species. Our population increase gives an objective measure of this success, but quite obviously it cannot continue at the present rate, and even the most superficial knowledge of current affairs and recent history makes us realize that our communal goals urgently require modification. Consciousness makes it possible for us to attempt this.

Acknowledgements

The views expressed here have been developed through discussions with many people over many years, but I would particularly like to mention Graeme Mitchison, Ian Glynn, Francis Crick, and Semir Zeki, whose disagreements have made me refine the argument at many points. I am particularly indebted to Martha Nussbaum, who drew my attention to the few hundred words by Nietzsche (1887) that, more than a century ago, concisely expressed an important part of the view developed here.

Endnotes

[1] In the discussion of my paper I was asked how much more than a brain slice would be needed before I would admit that a preparation could be conscious. The answer, as I hope will become clear later, is that you need more than a single brain, you need a community of interacting brains, before consciousness can perform its biologically useful work. The biophysical mechanisms for performing this work can certainly be studied in isolated preparations, but you will not be able to see what job these mechanisms are doing.

[2] It is sometimes said that theorizing about the goal of consciousness has no practical implications, but this is quite untrue. If the above statements are correct, neuropathologists and neuropsychologists interested in the effects of local brain damage should spend much more time on tests devised to detect impaired social function, and also (see below) impaired behaviour in relation to social institutions.

[3] Christoph von der Malsburg said at one point in the discussion, 'I have this light in my head, and I want to know what it is'. But he will remain unsatisfied: science tells us what an electron *does* in glorious quantitative detail, but it cannot say what it *is*. In the same way we shall not be able to tell Christoph what the light in his head *is*, but we can already say what it *does*: it enables him to describe his thoughts and experiences to the rest of us. He has billions of cells and billions of metres of connecting fibre in his brain that enable it to make its own decisions, but to enable Christoph's brain to influence our decisions it needs the 'light' that gives him knowledge, partial but expressible, of what underlies these decisions.

References

Barkow, J.H., Cosmides, L., and Tooby, J. (ed.) (1992). *The adapted mind: evolutionary psychology and the generation of culture*. Oxford University Press, New York.

Barlow, H.B. (1972). Single units and sensation: a neuron doctrine for perceptual psychology? *Perception*, **1**, 371–94.

Barlow, H.B. (1979). Nature's joke: a conjecture on the biological role of consciousness. In *Consciousness and the physical world* (ed. B.D. Josephson and V.S. Ramachandran), pp. 81–90. Pergamon Press, Oxford.

Barlow, H.B. (1987). The biological role of consciousness. In *Mindwaves* (ed. C. Blakemore and S. Greenfield). Basil Blackwell, Oxford.

Barlow, H.B. (1990). The mechanical mind. *Annual Review of Neuroscience*, **13**, 15–24.

Barlow, H.B. (1995). The neuron doctrine in perception. In *The Cognitive Neurosciences* (ed. M. Gazzaniga). MIT Press, Cambridge, MA.

Baron-Cohen, S., Leslie, A.M., and Frith, U. (1985). Does the autistic child have a 'theory of mind'? *Cognition*, **21**, 37–46.

Byrne, R. and Whiten, A. (ed.) (1988). *Machiavellian intelligence: social expertise and the evolution of intellect*. Clarendon Press, Oxford.

Churchland, P.S. (1986). *Neurophilosophy: towards a unified science of the mind-brain*. MIT Press, Cambridge, MA.

Craik, K.J.W. (1943). *The Nature of explanation*. Cambridge University Press.

Crick, F. (1994). *The astonishing hypothesis: the scientific search for the soul*. Charles Scribner's Sons, New York.

Dawkins, R. (1976). *The selfish gene*. Oxford University Press.

Dennett, D.C. (1991). *Consciousness explained*. Allan Lane, London.

Field, D.J. (1994). What is the goal of sensory coding? *Neural Computation*, **6**, 559–601.

Glynn, I.M. (1993). The evolution of consciousness: William James's unresolved problem. *Biological Reviews*, **69**, 599–616.

Humphrey, N.K. (1976). The social function of intellect. In *Growing points in ethology* (ed. P.P. Bateson and R.A. Hinde), pp. 303–17. Cambridge University Press.

Humphrey, N.K. (1979). Nature's psychologists. In *Consciousness and the physical world* (ed. B.D. Josephson and V.S. Ramachandran), pp. 57–80. Pergamon, Oxford.

Humphrey, N. (1983). *Consciousness regained*. Oxford University Press.

Humphrey, N. (1992). *A history of the mind*. Chatto and Windus, London.

Jackendoff, R. (1987). *Consciousness and the computational mind*. MIT Press, Cambridge, MA.

James, W. (1879). Are we automata? *Mind*, **4**, 1–22.

James, W. (1890). *The principles of psychology* (two volumes). Henry Holt and Co., Boston (also MacMillan 1891 and Dover Publications 1950).

Jerison, H.J. (1991). *Brain size and the evolution of mind (The fifty-ninth James Arthur lecture on the evolution of the human mind 1989)*. American Museum of Natural History, New York.

Lumsden, C.J. and Wilson, E.O. (1981). *Genes, mind and culture: the co-evolutionary process*. Harvard University Press, Cambridge, MA.

Nietzsche, F. (1887). *Die Fröhliche Wissenschaft* #354 (translated as *The gay science* by W. Kaufmann, Vintage Books, Random House, New York, 1974 edn). Verlag von E.W. Fritzsch, Leipzig.

Popper, K. (1972). *Objective knowledge*. Clarendon Press, Oxford.

Thatcher, A.R. (1983). How many people have ever lived on earth? In *44th Session of the International Statistical Institute*, Vol. 2, pp. 841–3. Madrid. International Statistical Institute, London.

Tolman, E.C. (1948). Cognitive maps in rats and men. *Psychological Review*, **55**, 189–208.

Wilson, E.O. (1975). *Sociobiology: the new synthesis*. Harvard University Press, Cambridge, MA.

Zeki, S. (1993). *A vision of the brain*. Blackwell Scientific Publications, Oxford.

8

Automaticity: from reflective to reflexive information processing in the human brain

MARCUS E. RAICHLE

As I write my mind is not preoccupied with how my fingers form the letters; my attention is fixed simply on the thoughts the words express. But there was a time when the formation of the letters, as each one was written, would have occupied my whole attention.

Sir Charles Sherrington (1906)

How do we communicate through the medium of spoken and written language in such an effortless manner? How does this remarkable process evolve from a conscious, effortful endeavour to one that exhibits remarkable elements of automaticity? As Sherrington's comments indicate, the importance of our capacity to automate aspects of behaviour has been appreciated for some time. From comments such as Sherrington's and must subsequent research, the idea has emerged that the manner in which the brain handles a particular type of information processing differs depending upon whether the task is novel or familiar (Reason and Mycielska 1982; Shallice 1988; Shiffrin 1988). Shallice and Norman (see Shallice 1988) have been quite specific in postulating the existence of unique brain circuitry for the production of willed, reflective, or conscious behaviour as compared to automatic, reflexive, or non-conscious behaviour.

In parallel with such observations and conjectures on conscious and non-conscious information processing have been a number of clinical observations in patients with deficits in speech production tasks that are often explained by the existence of two information processing routes. In its earliest instantiation (see for example Jackson 1874; Lichtheim 1885; McCarthy and Warrington 1984) the two-route model for speech production postulated separate routes for the routine production of spontaneous speech (like repeating aloud common words) and more complex language tasks such as dealing with a new idiom. It seems reasonable to suggest that such a two-route hypothesis for speech production is likely to be a specific instance of a more general feature of brain organization designed to ensure efficiency of operation through automation while at the same time maintaining flexibility in the face of ever-changing contingencies. Recent work in functional neuroimaging in normal humans provides us with a unique opportunity to examine such a question in detail.

Emerging from this recent work are not only suggestions about how single word processing is instantiated in the human brain under both novel and familiar circumstances, but also how we might begin to consider the distinction between the neural circuitry for conscious and non-conscious behaviour. These points will be illustrated from functional brain imaging work done in normal human subjects processing single words while being studied with position emission tomography (PET).

The introduction of modern brain imaging techniques such as X-ray computed tomography (CT), PET, and, more recently, magnetic resonance imaging (MRI) has dramatically changed the way in which we can examine safely the normal human brain. It is now possible to examine not only the physical anatomy of the living human brain with X-ray CT and MRI but also its functional anatomy (i.e. the actual areas involved in specific tasks) with PET (Raichle 1987; Posner and Raichle 1994; Raichle *et al.* 1994) and, more recently, with MRI (Kwong *et al.* 1992; Ogawa *et al.* 1992). We can now visualize the brain circuitry involved in a variety of cognitive tasks including various speech production tasks (see for example Peterson *et al.* 1988, 1989; Friston *et al.* 1991; Frith *et al.* 1991; Wise *et al.* 1991; Raichle *et al.* 1994) and determine the validity of the hypothesis that more than one route underlies speech production and that familiarity plays an important role in the selection of a particular route. From this rapidly evolving brain imaging literature emerges not only strong support for multiple routes and the circumstances surrounding their use, but also a clear indication of the actual anatomical circuits involved (Raichle *et al.* 1994).

In earlier work performed in our laboratory on normal adult subjects using PET, speaking an appropriate verb for a seen noun resulted in increased blood flow in the left prefrontal, left temporal, and anterior cingulate cortices, and the right cerebellar hemisphere (Fig. 8.1, row 4; see also Petersen *et al.* 1988, 1989). These responses were in addition to the changes in local blood flow occurring during visual word perception (Fig. 8.1, row 2; bilateral extrastriate visual cortices), and the reading aloud of a noun (Fig. 8.1, row 3; bilateral primary motor and Sylvian-insular cortices, supplementary motor area, and the paramedian cerebellum).

Following the publication of our earlier work (Petersen *et al.* 1988, 1989) three additional pieces of information came to light which led to the experiments that are summarized here. First, further analysis of the original data (for summary see Fiez *et al.* 1996) revealed an apparent reciprocal relationship between the left prefrontal cortex (active during speaking an appropriate verb for a seen or heard noun but reduced during speaking a seen or heard noun itself but reduced during speaking a seen or heard noun) and the Sylvian-insular cotex bilaterally (active when speaking the seen or heard noun itself but reduced during speaking an appropriate verb for a seen or heard noun). Second, in a pilot study (J.V. Pardo and M.E. Raichle, unpublished data) involving six subjects, we observed that after as little as 15 minutes of practice in generating verbs from the same list of seen nouns, the areas of the brain activated were no different than those activated when speaking the seen noun. Third, performance studies prompted by these observations demonstrated that there was a significant reduction in response times and the occurrence of stereotyped responses across practice blocks (Raichle *et al.* 1994).

The above work led us to the hypothesis that two distinct routes can be used for speech production (Fig. 8.2), one involving the anterior cingulate, left temporal and

Composite

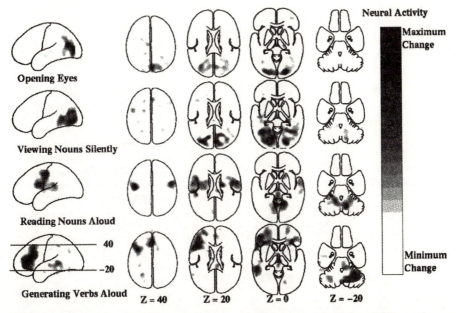

Opening Eyes

Viewing Nouns Silently

Reading Nouns Aloud

40

-20

Generating Verbs Aloud Z = 40   Z = 20   Z = 0   Z = -20

Neural Activity

Maximum Change

Minimum Change

Fig. 8.1 Four different task states are represented in these mean blood flow difference images obtained with positron emission tomography (PET) from a group of normal subjects performing a hierarchically designed set of language tasks. Each row represents the mean difference images between the designated task state and a control state. The images of the left represent projections of the changes as seen through the lateral surface of the brain with the front of the brain at the reader's left. The horizontal lines through these images denote the orientation of the horizontal slice through the same data as seen to the right of these first images. These horizontal images are oriented with the front of the brain on top and the left side to the reader's left. The markings 'Z = 40' indicate millimetres above and below a horizontal plane throughthe brain marked 'Z = 0'.

The row labelled 'Opening Eyes' indicates the difference between a control state of lying quietly awake with eyes closed and lying quietly with eyes open fixating on a small cross-hair in the middle of a television monitor. Note the changes in the visual cortices associated with visual fixation on a small dot of light on a television monitor.

The row labelled 'Viewing Nouns Silently' indicates the differences between the control state of lying quietly awake with eyes open fixating on a small cross-hair (row 1) and passively viewing the same television monitor with common English nouns appearing once a second just below the cross-hair. Note the increased blood flow, over and above that observed with opening the eyes (row 1), in the back of the brain in areas known to be concerned with visualperception.

The row labelled 'Reading Nouns Aloud' indicates the differences between the control state of passively viewing the nouns (row 2) and reading the same nouns aloud as they appeared on the television monitor. Note the changes in primary motor cortices (Z = 40), Sylvian-insular cortices (Z = 20), and cerebellum (Z = -20) associated with speaking aloud words seen on atelevision monitor.

The row labelled 'Generating Verbs Aloud' indicates the difference between the control state of reading nouns aloud (row 3) and saying aloud an appropriate verb for each noun as it appears on the screen. Note the extensive changes in the left frontal and temporal cortices and the right cerebellar hemisphere. Not shown are increases in the anterior cingulate gyrus and decreases in activity in Sylvian-insular cortices in the areas seen active in reading nounsaloud (row 3, Z = 20).

Taken together, these difference images, arranged in this hierarchical fashion, are designed to demonstrate the spatially distributed nature of the processing by task elements going on in the normal human brain during a language task.

Reading Words Aloud

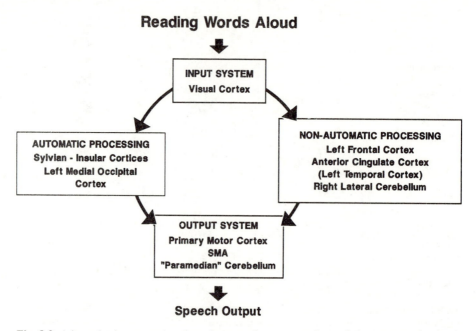

Fig. 8.2 A hypothesis concerning the existence of two routes for verbal response selection in the normal human brain developed from experiments presented in Figs 8.1 and 8.3 and described in detail elsewhere (Raichle *et al.* 1994). See text for a more complete description.

left prefrontal cortices, and the right cerebellar hemisphere, and the other involving areas of Sylvian-insular cortices bilaterally. Furthermore, the use of these two routes reflects the degree to which a given response is willed, reflective, and conscious or, alternatively, automatic, reflexive, and non-conscious. As a test of this hypothesis, we conducted a study (Raichle *et al.* 1994) to determine the functional anatomical effects of practice on this simple speech production task (say an appropriate verb for a seen noun) in normal adult humans using PET measurements of local blood flow. A detailed report of this work is available elsewhere (Raichle *et al.* 1994). A summary of this work is presented below.

The study (Raichle *et al.* 1994) consisted of three tasks: passive viewing of common English nouns as they appeared on a television monitor at the rate of one every 1.5 seconds; reading aloud these same nouns; and generating an appropriate action word or verb for each noun. Two word lists were used. The first word list was used during the initial experience with each of the three tasks just described. Following completion of these three tasks and their associated PET scans, eight additional practice blocks of verb generation were performed on the first word list while the subjects remained in the PET camera (no scans were performed during these practice blocks). For these practice blocks the subjects were instructed to come up with whatever response was fastest and easiest for them. Following completion of these practice blocks, five additional PET scans were performed: one of practised verb generation on the first word list and one of reading aloud the first list one final time. Then a new list of words was introduced and the three tasks repeated.

Approximately 15 minutes of practice in saying a verb for a seen noun produced dramatic changes in the cortical organization supporting the task (Fig. 8.3). There was a statistically significant effect of condition on blood flow in all seven areas chosen for analysis. In the anterior cingulate, left prefrontal cortex, left temporal cortex, and right cerebellar hemisphere blood flow decreased with practice, whereas in the Sylvian-insular cortices bilaterally (Fig. 8.3) and the left medial extrastriate cortex it rose (not shown; see Raichle *et al.* 1994). In effect, the practice condition could not be distinguished from the simple read aloud condition with the exception of the left medial extrastriate cortex which became more active as the result of practice.

Behaviourally, practice induced a significant decrease in response onset times and the development of stereotyped responses (i.e. the subjects tended, with increasing frequency, to choose the same verb for a particular noun as practice proceeded). Introduction of a novel list of words after practice caused reactivation of the left frontal, left temporal, and anterior cingulate cortices, and the right cerebellar hemisphere. Deactivation (relative to reading nouns aloud) occurred in the left Sylvian-insular and the left medial extrastriate cortices while the right Sylvian-insular cortex did not change. Behaviourally, introduction of a novel list of nouns reversed the practice-induced changes in reaction times. These results are consistent with the existence of two routes for speech production.

We hypothesize that reading aloud *familiar* words utilizes a pathway from word perception areas to speech production via areas in Sylvian-insular cortices bilaterally. We have observed repeatedly that Sylvian-insular cortices are active during repetition and reading aloud of familiar English nouns (Petersen *et al.* 1988, 1989; Raichle *et al.* 1994). We also observe this same pathway active when the more complex task of saying aloud appropriate action words, or verbs, for visually presented nouns has been well practised (Raichle *et al.* 1994). Prior to practice a completely different pathway connects word perception areas to speech production areas. This pathway includes areas of left prefrontal and anterior cingulate cortices and the right cerebellar hemisphere. The fact that one group of areas (i.e. Sylvian-insular cortices bilaterally) are substituted for another group of areas (i.e. left prefrontal and anterior cingulate cortices and the right cerebellar hemisphere) as a task is learned makes it unlikely that practised performance is simply the more efficient use of areas initially recruited for task performance.

How are we to think about these two pathways and the circumstances under which they are utilized. What is their relationship, if any, to the several instantiations of dual route ideas in speech production as well as automatic and non-automatic behaviour enumerated in the introduction? What, if anything, does this have to say about conscious versus non-conscious behaviour?

To begin, the two routes revealed by our studies of the verb generation task (Petersen *et al.* 1988, 1989; Raichle *et al.* 1994) would qualify for the two routes envisioned

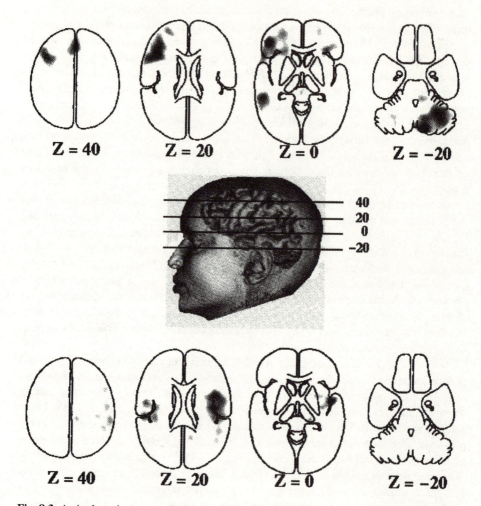

Fig. 8.3 A single task state studied under two different conditions (naive [top] and practised [bottom]) is represented in the images in this figure. In this task subjects were asked to generate (i.e. speak aloud) an appropriate verb for a series of visually presented nouns appearing on a television monitor at the rate of one every second and a half. The control state for these subtraction images was simply reading aloud the nouns as they appeared on the monitor. In the naive state, the areas in the left frontal, left temporal, and cingulate (not shown) cortices, and the right cerebellar hemisphere were active in the performance of the task. In the practised state a completely different set of areas were active. These resided within Sylvian-insular cortices bilaterally. It should be noted that these latter areas were active during simple reading of nouns aloud (see Fig. 8.1, row 3) but were inactivated during the naive performance of the verb generation task (Raichle *et al.* 1994). When the task was learned the neural architecture supporting the task could not be distinguished from that supporting noun reading itself (see Fig. 8.1, row 3 for reference). The details of this study can be found in Raichle *et al.* (1994).

in Lichtheim's original theoretical formulation (Lichtheim 1885; McCarthy and Warrington 1984). Although probably first suggested by John Hughlings Jackson (1874), the idea of two pathways was first advanced most clearly by Lichtheim (1885), a Swiss neurologist. In an attempt to provide a conceptual framework for the various forms of aphasia reported by Broca, Wernicke and others, he devised a scheme centred around three brain systems: an auditory word-form area concerned with the perceptual aspects of language; a centre for the motor representations of words, or a motor centre of speech; and a very distributed system 'for the elaboration of concepts'. As he envisioned it, information coming from the auditory word-from system could advance to the motor centre for speech either directly or via the concept system. The latter route via the concept system he characterized as more 'conscious' and less fluent than the former (Lichtheim 1885, p. 474). One pathway utilized a direct route from perception to production, whereas the other utilized a more indirect route involving a distributed system of widely separated areas of the cerebral cortex.

In a very telling discussion Lichtheim (1885, p. 474) said,

[I]t would appear as if, in naming objects, the auditory representations once found had to react in consciousness. This variety of language is a much more 'conscious' one than fluent speaking, in which *we are aware of the sense of what we are saying, rather than of every word we say* [italics added]. Under certain circumstances conversational language is carried on in a similar way to naming, as, for instance, when we use an idiom not quite familiar to us. Here we must seek the words by the complicated process just mentioned; the direct communication between concept and motor center without cooperation of sound-representation does not exist; the subconscious act of speaking is not yet possible. A greater psychical exertion is obviously required, and consequently more fatigue is entailed.

Lichtheim (1885) also envisioned that acquisition of language occurred by imitation, 'as observed in the child, and upon the reflex arc which this process presupposes.' He went on to say that 'When intelligence of the imitated sounds is superimposed, a connection is established between the auditory center [for word-representations] and the part [of the brain] where concepts are elaborated.'

Shallice and Norman (see Shallice 1988) formulate such issues more generally in terms of what they call *contention scheduling* and a *supervisory attentional system*. Contention scheduling is the process by which selection is made of routine actions or thought processes. It is considered to be a decentralized process involving a very large but finite set of discrete programmes, hierarchically organized. Routine activities of our daily lives such as driving a car back and forth to work are managed in a non-conscious manner through contention scheduling (Lichtheim, I am sure, would have used spontaneous speech as an example). A particular set of programmes or schemata has a level of activation dependent upon the triggering inputs it receives. While summarized nicely in the model of Norman and Shallice (Shallice 1988), this general idea has much support in the psychological literature (see summary discussion by Shallice 1988, p. 333). We would suggest that in the case of the verb-generation paradigm (Raichle 1994), areas within Sylvian-insular cortices are involved in the process of contention scheduling as formulated by Norman and Shallice (Shallice 1988).

The above formulation of the functional organization of our mental lives is obviously incomplete. A moments reflection suggests that, useful as they may be under a majority of circumstances, routine actions and thought processes are sometimes inappropriate, occasionally embarrassing and even potentially dangerous. Therefore, there has to exist a means by which routine, reflexive behaviours and thoughts can be inhibited and replaced, situationally or long term, by more appropriate behaviour and thoughts (Reason and Mycielska 1982). Norman and Shallice (Shallice 1988) postulate the existence of a second system to accomplish this which they call the supervisory attentional system.

The supervisory attentional system of Norman and Shallice (Shallice 1988) provides a mechanism whereby elements or schemata within the lower level contention-scheduling system for routine, reflexive behaviour and thoughts can be temporarily modified by activating or inhibiting particular elements within it. This facilitates coping with novel situations in which the routine selections are unsatisfactory. As Shallice (1988, p. 345) states: 'The primary function of the Supervisory System is that of producing a response to novelty that is planned rather than one that is routine or impulsive.' In a general sense this fits nicely with Lichtheim's concept of a centre for the elaboration of concepts.

While Lichtheim (1885) and Norman and Shallice (Shallice 1988) envisioned a *superimposition* of higher centres for the conscious guidance of behaviour over more routine, reflexive responses, our data would suggest a *substitution* of areas (Figs 8.2 and 8.3). In our example, areas guiding non-automatic or conscious speech acts are preferentially selected, by a process yet to be defined, over those areas concerned with automatic or non-conscious speech acts when well-learned, reflexive responses (e.g. substituting verb generation for reading words aloud) are not appropriate. As a corollary, one must also envision circumstances in which the reverse is true: automatic responses are preferred and, hence, selected. As Sutherland (1996) has pointed out, '[w]hen confronted by a predator, it is surely better to climb a non-optimal tree than to be eaten while weighing the respective merits of different trees.' The manner in which the brain is biased *either* way (i.e. towards or away from automatic behaviour) remains a most important and challenging question.

Lichtheim (1885) did not specify the neural correlates of his higher centres but he was quite clear that he did not believe them to be housed in a single area. 'Though in the diagram point B [Lichtheim 1885, p. 436, diagram 1] is represented as a sort of center for the elaboration of concepts, this has been done for simplicities sake; with most writers, I do not consider the function to be localized in one spot of the brain, but rather to result from the combined action of the whole sensorial sphere. Hence, the point B should be distributed over many spots' (Lichtheim 1885, p. 477).

Shallice and Norman (Shallice 1988) were much more specific in drawing attention to the role of a specific area of the brain, the frontal lobe, in their supervisory attentional system. They review extensive evidence, primarily from neuropsychology, showing that patients with frontal lobe injury often act in an impulsive and reflexive manner as if they lacked a supervisory attentional system.

Reviewing the evidence that has now been gained from functional imaging studies in normal subjects, one would have to conclude that Lichtheim and Norman and Shallice were correct in anticipating the neural architecture of a centre or system for conscious, reflective behaviour. On the one hand it is clear from Figs 8.1 and 8.3 that multiple, widely-distributed areas of the normal human brain are involved in the performance of a novel speech production act as Lichtheim (1885) would have predicted. Likewise, it is also clear that the frontal lobe plays a prominent, although not exclusive, role in the process as Norman and Shallice (Shallice 1988) would have predicted.

The current functional anatomical evidence would suggest at least two things: caution in utilizing performance abnormalities in patients with frontal lobe lesions to characterize fully the brain systems utilized for human performance under novel circumstances; and the need for performance information on patients with lesions elsewhere in such circuits as defined by functional imaging studies in normal subjects. Particularly illustrative in this regard was the work of Fiez *et al.* (1992) in a patient with a right cerebellar infarction. This study was directly prompted by the finding (see Fig. 8.1, bottom row, Z = –20) of striking right cerebellar hemisphere activation in the naive performance of the verb generation task. Because the motoric aspects of the task had been subtracted out in the control task (Reading Aloud Words, Fig. 8.1, line 3, Z = –20), it was reasonable to suspect that the right cerebellum was contributing to the cognitive aspects of the task and, indeed, it was (Fiez *et al.* 1992).

While the experiments used for illustrative purposes in this work (i.e. verb generation, Raichle 1994) and in the work of Lichtheim (1885) have focused specifically on language, the work of Norman and Shallice (Shallice 1988) as well as others (see for example Shiffrin 1988) suggest that in discussing automatic and non-automatic behaviour and their neural instantiation we are talking about issues that transcend a single domain of human performance such as language. What other evidence do we have for this from a neurobiological perspective? Are the general principles of neural organization emerging from imaging studies of language in normal subjects applicable to other domains of human performance as Norman and Shallice would suggest? It is useful to look at several examples.

The data most directly comparable to our verb generation study (Raichle *et al.* 1994) is a PET functional imaging study of maze learning in strongly right-handed subjects by van Mier and her colleagues (van Mier *et al.* 1994, 1995). In the maze learning study, subjects used a stylus to trace a complex maze etched on the surface of a bit pad. Two groups of subject were studied, those who used their right hand and those who used their left hand to perform the maze task. Performance was recorded in the naive state, after a period of practice, and then with a novel maze. The tasks were designed to parallel directly the design of the learning study of the verb generation task (Raichle *et al.* 1994). The objective was to determine whether the same principles of neural organization supported learning in a performance domain outside of language. The answer to this question was a clear yes.

The naive performance of the maze task utilized a set of areas (right premotor cortex; right parietal cortex: Brodmann Areas 7 and 40; and the left cerebellar hemisphere) regardless of the hand used. These areas of activation were in addition to primary motor and sensory areas associated with task performance. A brief period of practice with either hand resulted in marked improvement in performance. None of the areas listed above were active after practice. In the practice state the afore-mentioned areas were replaced by activity in the supplementary motor area (SMA). The introduction of a novel maze completely reversed these changes in neural organization. Three things are striking about these results. First, they parallel exactly the type of changes observed in the transition from the naive to the practised performance of the verb generation task (Raichle *et al.* 1994). Second, the areas involved in both the naive and practised performance of the maze task were unique to the task. Third, the changes associated with learning were independent of the hand used. These results suggest that a general principle of brain organization and allocation of resources is observed in both instances, but that the details of that organization are task specific. Thus, when one thinks in terms of concepts like a supervisory attentional system (Shallice 1988), it must be viewed as a distributed system that is task specific.

Do we have other instances of this type of neural organization that distinguishes naive from practised performance? Two illustrative examples come to mind, acquisition of conditional motor associations in the monkey (Mitz *et al.* 1991; Chen and Wise 1995*a,b*) and learning song in songbirds (for review see Nottebohm 1991).

In a series of innovative experiments Wise and his colleagues (Mitz *et al.* 1991; Chen and Wise 1995*a,b*) studied the learning of conditional motor responses in the monkey correlating unit activity in the cerebral cortex with performance. In the most detailed of these studies for the purposes of this discussion (Chen and Wise 1995*a,b*), monkeys learned to saccade to specific targets in their visual field based on an association between the appearance of a visual cue and a particular target location. In the naive state the monkeys had to guess which locus in their visual field was indicated by a particular stimulus. Correct guesses were rewarded with juice. Performance was measured as the number of correct responses. As expected, performance improved with practice as the monkeys learned the correct association between target location and a particular stimulus. Unit recording of neuronal activity was performed in two cortical locations, the supplementary eye field (SEF) and the frontal eye field (FEF).

The results of these studies in monkeys show a remarkable parallel to the verb generation (Raichle *et al.* 1994) and maze learning (van Mier *et al.* 1994, 1995) studies in normal humans. In the SEF of the monkey, Chen and Wise (1995*a*) identified two populations of neurons which they termed respectively *learning-selective* and *learning-dependent*. The learning-selective neurons were only active in the presence of a novel cue. As the monkey learned the relationship between a novel cue and its associated saccade location, activity in the learning-selective neurons ceased. The converse was true for the learning-dependent cells. The learning-dependent cells only became active as the monkey learned the correct association between target and cue. While similar classes of neurons were also found in the FEF, their proportions were much less. This difference suggested that the role of the SEF and FEF in the learning of conditional motor responses differed significantly.

The second illustrative example of alternate neural organizations underlying the naive and practised performance, respectively, of a task is the acquisition of song in birds such as canaries and zebra finches. Work by a variety of groups (for review see Nottebohm 1991) has provided a detailed description of the areas within the song-bird brain responsible for the acquisition and production of song. Central to this organization is an area known as the high vocal centre or HVC. This area plays an important role in the acquisition and production of song. Two pathways emerge from the HVC. One pathway projects directly from the HVC to the robust nucleus of the archistriatum or RA. Not surprisingly it is known as the *direct pathway*. From the RA fibres pass through a series of areas leading to brainstem nuclei which control the vocal apparatus responsible for the actual production of song. The second pathway also leaves the HVC on its way to the RA but only arrives at the latter location after passing through a number of intermediate areas in the songbird brain. This is, not surprisingly, know as the *recursive loop*. Thus, there are two pathways from the HVC to the RA: a short, direct one and the long, recursive one. The recursive loop is of particular interest because it is critical for song learning but not for the production of a learned song. Alternatively, the direct loop is quite capable of supporting a song after the skill has been mastered but is not capable of supporting the learning process.

The parallel in the principles of neural organization supporting learning in these very different tasks (i.e. verb generation and maze learning in humans, conditional oculomotor association learning in monkeys and song learning in birds) is striking. Selective brain areas, populations of neurons, and pathways active in the naive performance of a task are replaced by other areas, population of neurons, and pathways when the task has been learned. While the details differ within and across species, the general principles remain the same. It seems possible to make a clear distinction between the neural circuitry underlying the unpractised, presumably conscious, reflective performance of a task, on the one hand, and the practised, presumably non-conscious, reflexive performance of the same task, on the other. The general organizational principles underlying such a distinction appear to transcend species and tasks. The detailed organization surrounding individual tasks, however, appears to be unique to each task.

What contribution might these findings make to our understanding of consciousness? First, it should be appreciated that much of our behaviour, although conscious in appearance, is governed by non-conscious processes which have obviously evolved to allow us to perform in a sophisticated and efficient manner. Henry Maudsley (1878) succinctly captured this idea when he stated that 'if an act became no easier after being done several times, if the careful direction of consciousness were necessary to its accomplishment on each occasion, it is evident that the whole activity of a lifetime might be confined to one or two deeds'. Second, paradigms have emerged for study in humans and laboratory animals in which the neural instantiation of given behaviour can be studied as a conscious, reflective act as well as a non-conscious, reflexive act. The neural architecture underlying these two different modes of the same task are clearly different. As such they give us a glimpse of the manner in which a conscious act is neurally distinguished from a non-conscious one. Third, while a common theme emerges from the work reviewed in this chapter in terms of the principles governing the neural instantiation of conscious and non-conscious behaviour in the brain, striking differences exist among tasks in terms of the specific brain areas involved. Put another way, no single, unique architecture yet emerges as a unifying feature of conscious, reflective performance. The cerebral cortex appears like the sections of a great symphony orchestra. Relationships determine performance and performance can be infinitely variable. 'Subtracting' two different states of a performing orchestra might well distinguish who was playing on one state and not the other. However, a conductor who is always performing would always be subtracted out.

References

Chen, L.L. and Wise, S.E. (1995*a*). Neuronal activity in the supplementary eye field during acquisition of conditional oculomotor associations. *Journal of Neurophysiology*, **73**, 1101–21.

Chen, L.L. and Wise, S.E. (1995*b*). Supplementary eye field contrasted with the frontal eye field during acquisition of conditional oculomotor associations. *Journal of Neurophysiology*, **73**, 1121–34.

Fiez, J.A., Petersen, S.E., Cheney, M.K., and Raichle, M.E. (1992). Impaired nonmotor learning and error detection associated with cerebellar damage: a single case study. *Brain*, **115**, 155–78.

Fiez, J.A., Petersen, S.E., and Raichle, M.E. (1996). Identification of two pathways used for verbal response selection. In *Development dyslexia* (ed. C.D. Chase, G.D. Rosen, and G.F. Sherman), pp. 227–58. York Press, Baltimore, MD.

Friston, K.J., Frith, C.D., Liddle, P.F., and Frackowiak, R.S.J. (1991). Investigating a network model of word generation with positron emission tomography. *Proceedings of the Royal Society of London, Series B*, **244**, 101–6.

Frith, C.D., Friston, K., Liddle, P.F., and Frackowiak, R.S.J. (1991). Willed action and the prefrontal cortex in man: a study with PET. *Proceedings of the Royal Society of London, Series B*, **244**, 241–6.

Jackson, J.H. (1874). On the nature of the duality of the brain. *Medical Press and Circular*, **1**, 19, 41, 63.

Kwong, K.K., Bellieveau, J.W., Chesler, D.A., Goldberg, I.E., Weisskoff, R.M., Poncelet, B.P. *et al.* (1992). Dynamic magnetic resonance imaging of human brain activity during primary sensory stimulation. *Proceedings of the National Academy of Sciences of the United States of America*, **89**, 5675–9.

Lichtheim, L. (1885). On asphasia. *Brain*, **7**, 433–84.

Maudsley, H. (1878). *The physiology of mind*, pp. 149–56. Appleton, New York.

McCarthy, R. and Warrington, E.K. (1984). A two route model of speech production. *Brain*, **107**, 463–85.

Mitz, A.R., Godshalk, M., and Wise, S.E. (1991). Learning-dependent neuronal activity in the premotor cortex: activity during the acquisition of conditional motor associations. *Journal of Neuroscience*, **11**, 1855–72.

Nottebohm, F. (1991). Reassessing the mechanisms and origins of vocal learning in birds. *Trends in Neuroscience*, **14**, 206–11.

Ogawa, S., Tank, D.W., Menon, R. *et al.* (1992). Intrinsic signal changes accompanying sensory stimulation: function brain mapping with magnetic resonance imaging. *Proceedings of the National Academy of Sciences of the United States of America*, **89**, 5951–5.

Petersen, S.E., Fox, P.T., Posner, M.I., Mintun, M.A., and Raichle, M.E. (1988). Positron emission tomographic studies of the cortical anatomy of single word processing. *Nature*, **331**, 585–9.

Petersen, S.E., Fox, P.T., Posner, M.I., Mintun, M.A., and Raichle, M.E. (1989). Positron emission tomographic studies of the processing of single words. *Journal of Cognitive Neuroscience*, **1**, 153–70.

Posner, M.I. and Raichle, M.E. (1994). *Images of mind*. W.H. Freeman, New York.

Raichle, M.E. (1987). Circulatory and metabolic correlates of brain function in normal humans. In *The handbook of physiology*. Part 2: The nervous system, Vol. V. Higher function of the brain. Part 1 (ed. F. Plum and V. Mountcastle), pp. 643–74. American Physiology Society, Bethesda, MD.

Raichle, M.E., Fiez, J., Videen, T.O., Fox, P.T., Pardo, J.V., and Petersen, S.E. (1994). Practice-related changes in human brain functional anatomy during non-motor learning. *Cerebral Cortex*, **4**, 8–26.

Reason, J. and Mycielska, K. (1982). *Absent minded? The psychology of mental lapses and everyday errors*. Prentice-Hall, Englewood Cliffs, NJ.

Shallice, T. (1988). *From neuropsychology to mental structure*, pp. 328–52. Cambridge University Press, New York.

Sherrington, C. (1906). *The integrative action of the nervous system*. Yale University Press, New Haven.

Shiffrin, R.M. (1988). Attention. In *Steven's handbook of experiment psychology* (2nd edn) (ed. R.C. Atkinson, R.J. Herrnstein, G. Lindsay, and R.D. Luce), pp. 739–811. Wiley, New York.

Sutherland, N.S. (1996). The biological causes of irrationality. In *Neurobiology of decision making* (ed. A.R. Damasio, H. Damasio, and Y. Christen), pp. 145–56. Springer-Verlag, Berlin.

van Mier, H., Petersen, S.E., Tempel, L.W., Perlmutter, J.S., Snyder, A.Z., and Raichle, M.E. (1994). Practice related changes in a continuous motor task measured by PET. *Society of Neuroscience Abstracts*, **20**, 361.

van Mier, H., Tempel, L., Perlmutter, J.S., Raichle, M.E., and Petersen, S.E. (1995). Generalization of practice-related effects in motor learning using the dominant and non-dominant hand measured by PET. *Society of Neuroscience Abstracts*, **21**, 1441.

Wise, R., Chollet, F., Hadar, U., Friston, K., Hoffner, E., and Frackowiak, R. (1991). Distribution of cortical neural networks involved in word comprehension and word retrieval. *Brain*, **114**, 1803–17.

9

Neuronal origin of visual imagery

YASUSHI MIYASHITA

Introduction

'Create an image of the Pantheon in your mind. Can you count the columns that support its pediment?' (Alain 1926) (Fig. 9.1). Our ability to 'see with the mind's eye', *mental imagery*, has been of interest to philosophers and scientists for a long time. When the nature of reflective consciousness was investigated by reflection, it was often asked whether '(strong) image' and '(weak) perception' are distinguishable in both psychological and epistemological dimensions (Sartre 1938). The Pantheon's columns are among the most known litmus tests for such a distinction. I agree that

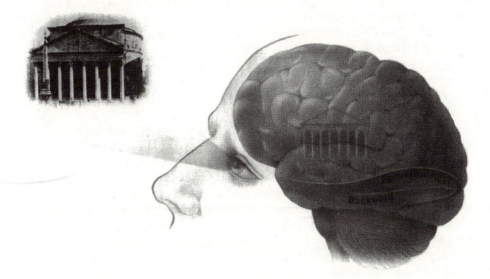

Fig. 9.1 Visual perception mainly relies on the forward, bottom-up flow of information. Imagery experience, in contrast, highlights the backward projections as an anatomical substrate of top-down mental operations. We may predict that, if an imagery task requires reconstruction of the detailed local geometry of the image (such as counting the columns of the Pantheon), backward signals from higher-order representations would reach topographically organized visual areas. This cartoon does not indicate that mental images are actual pictures in the brain; obviously, we cannot assume any homunculus in the brain who looks at the images. (Adapted from Miyashita 1995; artwork by K. Sutliff.)

many open questions remain when the origin of imagery is described from a phenomenological viewpoint, as discussed in other chapters of this book (see for example Chapter 3 by Murata). Figure 9.1 does not indicate that mental images are actual pictures in the brain; obviously, we cannot assume any homunculus in the brain who looks at the images (see Chapter 6 by Rolls in this book). Nevertheless, I find imagery an important topic, since it is one of the first higher cognitive abilities that will be firmly rooted in the brain and since understanding this ability would provide some constraints on the neural basis of consciousness.

Historically, imagery played a major role in theories of conscious phenomena, especially during the eighteenth century with the British Associationists or during the birth of philosophical psychology with William James and Wilhelm Wundt (Farah 1990; Tye 1991; Kosslyn 1994). While radical behaviourism dominated experimental psychology and physiology, imagery was not regarded as an appropriate subject for scientific study. With the advent of cognitive psychology after the 1960s, it once again became acceptable. The discovery of 'mental rotation' (Cooper and Shepard 1973) convinced us that complex properties of imagery could be studied with the methodological purity of empirical science. Today there are many approaches (including neuroimaging, electrophysiological, psychophysical, and neuropsychological ones) asking where and how in the brain the images of objects, scenes, and living beings are generated, stored, and maintained (Roland 1993; Kosslyn 1994; Miyashita 1995). Even the question of to what degree the processes involved in visual perception and imagery share a common neural substrate was partially answered (see below). In this chapter I will sketch the current status of our understanding of imagery problems.

The visual system and the backward-projection hypothesis of imagery

The visual system in the primate consists of a mosaic of more than 30 visual areas, starting from the primary visual cortex (V1 or striate cortex), which are functionally heterogeneous and hierarchically organized (Van Essen *et al.* 1992). A visual stimulus on the retina is analysed in terms of its elementary features, such as orientation, colour, texture, and depth, by low-level visual processing in the striate cortex and the prestriate areas, most of which are organized retinotopically. The analysed features are integrated, using high-level visual processing in the temporal and parietal cortex, into a unique configuration that functions as the internal representation of an object and its spatial properties. A notable point here is that the connections among the visual areas are reciprocal via both forward and backward projections (Van Essen *et al.* 1992; Miyashita 1993). I propose a hypothesis ('backward-projection hypothesis') (Miyashita 1993, 1995) that visual perception mainly relies in the forward, bottom-up flow of information and that imagery experience, in contrast, highlights the backward projections as a possible anatomical substrate of top-down mental operations (Fig. 9.1). The hypothesis predicts that, if an imagery task requires reconstruction of the detailed local geometry of the image (such as counting the columns of the Pantheon), backward signals from higher-order representations would reach topographically organized visual areas (Farah 1990; Kosslyn 1994; Miyashita 1995).

The backward-projection hypothesis of imagery contains several components to be substantiated and tested. The first is on the nature of the internal representation. There has been debate as to whether depictive (quasi-pictorial) or propositional representation lies in the deepest structure for image generation (Pylyshyn 1981: Tye 1991; Kosslyn 1994). The depictive theory assumes that the processes which produce and utilize visual images most probably rely on high-level visual mechanisms. At present there are several lines of evidence for involvement of high-level visual mechanisms. Studies performed using positron emission tomography (PET) consistently revealed activation of the dorsal (area 19) and ventral (fusiform gyrus) visual association areas, superior and inferior parietal cortex, as well as other non-visual cortices such as the dorsolateral prefrontal cortex and angular gyrus, for example, when subjects imagined that they started at their front door and then walked alternately to the left or the right each time they reached a corner (Roland and Friberg 1985; Roland 1993), or when subjects imagined a letter in a grid and decided whether the letter would have covered a mark presented in the grid (Kosslyn 1994). Perhaps one of the strongest supports for depictive representation in image generation was given by single-unit recording from the visual association cortex. In monkey inferior temporal cortex, which is a candidate for the monkey homologue of the human visual area in the fusiform gyrus, single neurons revealed picture-specific discharges when the monkey generated from its long-term memory store the image (paired associate) that was instructed by a previous cue stimulus (Sakai and Miyashita 1991; Naya *et al.*, 1996). Before considering the neuronal correlate of image generation, we briefly look at the neuronal representation of visual long-term memory in the temporal cortex.

Neuronal representation of long-term visual memory in the temporal cortex

Along the occipito-temporal visual pathway from the primary visual cortex (Fig. 9.1), the physical properties of a visual object are analysed in the multiple subdivisions of the prestriate-posterior temporal cortices, and the inferotemporal cortex synthesizes the analysed attributes into a unique configuration (Mishkin 1982; Van Essen *et al.* 1992; Miyashita 1993). The inferotemporal cortex has been proposed to be the memory storehouse for object vision on the basis of behavioural experiments (Mishkin 1982; Squire 1987). But how are the memories of objects represented by neuronal networks in the inferotemporal cortex?

Most of our long-term memories of episodes are organized so that we can retrieve them by association. I propose that visual memory is organized by the same principle and encodes forms of objects as structured bundles of associations between elementary views of objects (Miyashita *et al.* 1993). Evidence for the associative mechanism was obtained by training monkeys to memorize artificial associative relations among visual patterns, and then by examining whether picture-selective activities of inferotemporal neurons encode the stimulus–stimulus association imposed in the learning

(Miyashita 1988, 1993). One example of such studies used the pair-association learning task (Sakai and Miyashita 1991; Higuchi and Miyashita 1996) developed by Murray *et al.* (1993); computer-generated coloured pictures were sorted randomly into pairs (Fig. 9.2(A)). The combination of the paired associates cannot be predicted without memorizing them beforehand, and macaque monkeys (*Macaca fuscata*) were trained to memorize these pairs. In each trial of the experiment, a cue stimulus was presented on a video monitor for 0.5 s. After a delay period, two choice stimuli, the paired associate of the cue (correct choice) and a distracter (incorrect choice), were shown. The monkey obtained a fruit juice reward when a correct choice was made. It is noted that this task is essentially a memory *recall* task, which demands memory retrieval and thus generation of images from long-term memory.

In the inferotemporal cortex, we recorded single-neuron activity using a micro-electrode and tested whether a cell preferentially responded to both of the paired associates. Figure 9.2(B) shows the stimulus selectivity of a cell which responded reproducibly to only a few pictures. The strongest and the second-strongest responses were ascribed to a particular pair which had no apparent geometrical similarity. We called this type of neuron a 'pair-coding neuron' that manifested selective responses to both of the paired associates. Some other cells showed broader tuning and responded to more than three pictures. Nevertheless, paired pictures were found to be among the most effective stimuli for these cells (Fig. 2(C)).

We analysed sampled cells by calculating the response correlation with a pair index or correlation coefficient (Sakai and Miyashita 1991; Higuchi and Miyashita 1996). The frequency distribution of either index demonstrated that the paired associates elicited significantly correlated responses. This result provides strong evidence that inferotemporal neurons acquire stimulus selectivity through associative learning and that the selectivity reflects a stimulus–stimulus association among geometrically different complex forms. It also suggests that the neuronal mechanisms for flexibly creating those associations are crucial in memorizing complex visual forms that consist of many simpler local figures (Miyashita *et al.* 1993).

Fig. 9.2 Associative representation of pictures in neurons of the temporal cortex. Stimulus-selectivity of neurons encodes stimulus–stimulus associations among geometrically different complex forms, which were learned in the visual pair association task. (A) Twelve pairs of Fourier descriptors (1 and 1' to 12 and 12') used as stimuli in the pair association task. When one member of each pair is shown, trained monkeys can retrieve and choose the other member of the paired associates. (B) Stimulus-selectivity of a pair-coding neuron. The ordinate shows mean discharge rates for each cue presentation relative to the spontaneous discharge rate (denoted by an arrowhead). Cue stimuli are labelled as 'Pair No.' on the abscissa (light histogram bar at No.1 is #1, dark histogram bar at No.1 is #1', etc.). This neuron selectively responded to both pictures of the paired associates #6 and #6'. (C) Similar to B but for another neuron.

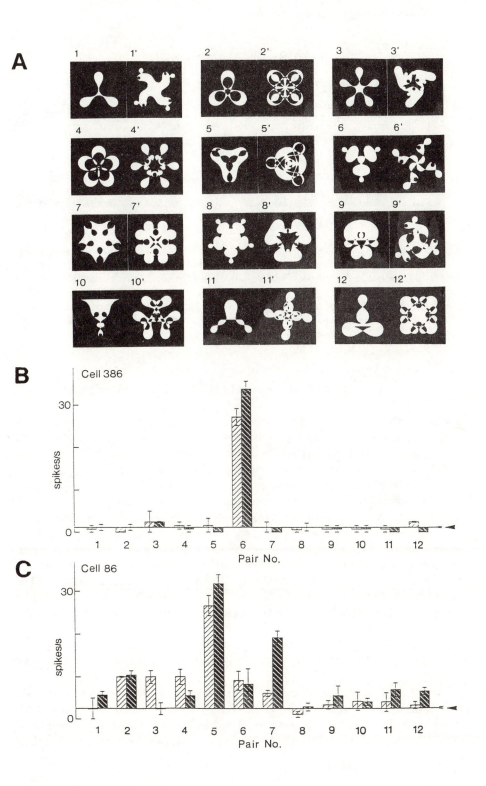

PAIR-RECALL NEURON

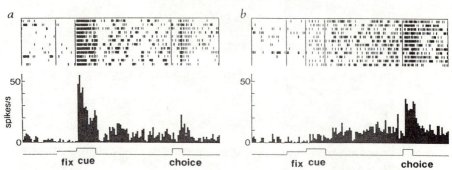

Fig. 9.3 A neuronal correlate of image-retrieval in the temporal cortex. Responses of a pair-recall neuron, which exhibits picture-selective activity while the subject retrieves the image of the paired associate in the pair associate task. (a) Trials for cue 12 that elicited the strongest cue response. (b) Trials for cue 12′ that elicited the delay response, reflecting retrieval of the paired associate 12. Note the tonic increasing activity during the delay period, which is much stronger than the cue response. Fix, fixation period; cue, cue stimulus presentation period; choice, choice stimuli presentation period.

Neuronal correlate of image-generation in the visual association cortex

The associative code in the inferotemporal cortex would be used in the image generation process. Indeed, single-unit recording provided evidence for this (Miyashita 1993; Naya *et al.*, 1996). Recall that in the pair-association task the monkey was required to recognize the paired associate of a cue stimulus after a delay period. In an earlier experiment with the pair-association task (Sakai and Miyashita 1991), we found an interesting category of neurons (*pair-recall neuron*) that exhibited picture-selective activity during the delay period. Figure 9.3 shows an example. One picture elicited the strongest response during the cue period from a single neuron (Fig. 9.3(a)). In the trial when the paired associate of this cue-optimal picture was used as a cue, the same cell had the highest tonic activity during the delay period, in contrast to a weak response during the cue period (Fig. 9.3(b)). Other pictures evoked small or no responses. The increasing delay activity of the pair-recall neurons is not related to motor response because the monkey could not predict the spatial position of the correct paired associate in the task. This activity is not only picture-selective, but also closely coupled with the paired associate that is not actually seen but retrieved. The discovery of the pair-recall neuron was the first demonstration of a neuronal correlate of visual imagery.

These neural mechanisms were further investigated by developing a novel task, the pair-association with colour switch (PACS) task, in which the necessity for image generation and its time were controlled by a colour switch in the middle of the delay period (Naya *et al.*, 1996). A control task, in which there is no colour switch, corresponds to the conventional delayed matching-to-sample (DMS) task where the monkey chooses the same picture as a cue. In both trials, 12 pairs of Fourier descriptors were used as visual stimuli (G1 and C1–G12 and C12), each pair containing a green picture and a cyan picture (Fig. 9.4(A), plate section). When the monkey started pressing a lever in front of the video monitor, a grey square was presented at the centre of the screen for 1 s (warning). Following the cue presentation of one of the 24 pictures for 0.5 s, a square was presented during the delay period. The square's colour was the same as the cue's colour during the first part of the delay period (Delay Period 1) for 2 s in the PACS trial or for 5 s in the DMS trial. In the PACS trial, the square's colour changed into the colour of the paired associate after Delay Period 1, signalling the initiation of retrieval, and the second part of the delay period (Delay Period 2) for 3 s started. Delay Period 2 was not included in the DMS trial. To balance the visual stimulus conditions in the two trials, a grey square was presented for 1 s during the third part of the delay period (Delay Period 3). After Delay Period 3, a choice of two stimuli was shown randomly in two of four possible positions (arranged in two rows of two columns). The choice stimuli were the paired associate of the cue (correct) and a distracter (error) in the PACS trial, while the choice stimuli were the same picture as the cue (correct) and a distracter (error) in the DMS trial. The animal obtained a reward for touching the correct picture within 1.2 s. The PACS trials and the DMS trials were randomized. Extracellular discharges of single neurons were recorded in three hemispheres with a glass-insulated tungsten microelectrode.

Figure 9.5 (see plate section) shows typical responses of a single inferotemporal neuron in the PACS task. One picture (G7; green) elicited the strongest response during the Cue Period (Fig. 9.5 top; here we call this cue-optimal picture the best picture, irrespective of its delay response). The excitatory response was maintained in Delay Period 1 (Fig. 9.5 middle). The paired associate (C7; cyan) of the best picture (G7) elicited little response during the Cue Period and Delay Period 1; however, this neuron started to respond just after the onset of Delay Period 2 when the square's colour changed from the cue's colour (C7; cyan) to that of the paired associate (G7; green). The picture-selective activation after the colour switch in the PACS task is called the 'pair-recall' effect. The pair-recall effect continued from Delay Period 2 into Delay Period 3 in which the square's colour was the same grey in both tasks (Fig. 9.5 bottom). Thus the pair-recall effect was not due to the square's colour; this was also confirmed by the fact that the pair-recall effect was observed in trials with cue C7 but not in trials where other cyan pictures were used as cues. In the DMS task, the response selectivity was the same as that in the PACS task during the Cue Period and Delay Period 1. However, the colour switch of the square had no effect in the DMS task. These results suggest that this delay discharge, which is specific to the PACS task, was triggered by image generation.

To characterize the pair-recall effect in 15 task-related cells, we collected trials whose cue was the best picture's associate. The effect of the task on the delay response was significant ($F (1, 14) = 19.8$, $P < 0.001$), and there was an interaction between task and period ($F (1, 28) = 12.2$, $P < 0.005$). We further analysed responses among periods in each task, and responses between the tasks in each period. In both the PACS and DMS tasks, responses in Delay Period 1 remained equal to the warning responses. These Delay Period 1 responses were thus task independent. In Delay Period 3 of the PACS task, the responses were significantly stronger than those in Delay Period 1 ($t = 3.5$, $P < 0.005$), while the Delay Period 3 responses in the DMS task remained equal to the Delay Period 1 responses. The Delay Period 3 responses in the PACS task were significantly stronger than those in the DMS task ($t = 5.2$, $P < 0.001$). These results indicate that the pair-recall effect is triggered by the colour switch.

All of the above results support the hypothesis that these neural discharges represent active images of a specific object. However, how does this neural firing come about? Alternatively, what kind of machinery can drive the pair-recall neuron in Delay Period 2 in spite of null activity in Delay Period 1? Obviously we cannot assume any homunculus or 'quantum microtubule'. You may assume an excitatory input from a non-visual association cortex such as the dorsolateral prefrontal cortex. However, the activity in Delay Period 2 is highly stimulus-selective, and we must remember that the inferotemporal cortex is the highest visual centre of the primate brain that has specific visual information of an object. The neural mechanism for image generation remains to be further identified, but it should involve the pair-recall neurons in the temporal cortex.

Imagery generation requires the backward projection to the primary visual cortex

So far I have described the neuronal origin of visual imagery in the inferotemporal cortex in the case of a visual object, or more generally, the higher-order association areas in the temporal and parietal lobes in the case of images of scenes or living beings. At present, there is general agreement on this issue with neurophysiological and neuroimaging approaches. Contrary to this agreement on high-level visual mechanisms, evidence from neuroimaging appears both to support and contradict the hypothesis that visual imagery is based upon contributions of the early visual areas (Roland 1993; Kosslyn 1994). There are some possible sources of the conflicting observations. The first is the difference in task paradigms, which would result in different requirements for scrutinizing local features of objects or for attention. The second is the contribution of weak signals near the threshold of detection sensitivity; intersubject averaging, used to enhance signal-to-noise ratios in PET, might mask physiological and morphological variances among subjects. This difficulty might be overcome partially by the use of fMRI (Le Bihan *et al.* 1993).

Psychophysical studies have also addressed this problem on the basis of neuronal response characteristics in the primary visual cortex (V1), which are specific to the stimulated eye as well as to orientation and retinal location of the stimulus (Fig. 9.6). For example, subjects decided whether two line segments were perfectly aligned (a 'vernier acuity' task), and accuracy decreased from 80 to 65% when the subjects

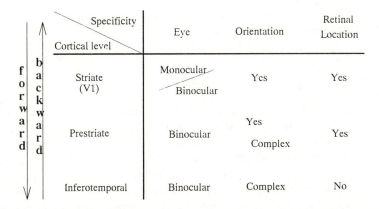

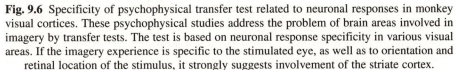

Specificity Cortical level	Eye	Orientation	Retinal Location
Striate (V1)	Monocular Binocular	Yes	Yes
Prestriate	Binocular	Yes Complex	Yes
Inferotemporal	Binocular	Complex	No

Fig. 9.6 Specificity of psychophysical transfer test related to neuronal responses in monkey visual cortices. These psychophysical studies address the problem of brain areas involved in imagery by transfer tests. The test is based on neuronal response specificity in various visual areas. If the imagery experience is specific to the stimulated eye, as well as to orientation and retinal location of the stimulus, it strongly suggests involvement of the striate cortex.

formed images compared to when they did not (Craver-Lemley and Reeves 1987). Moving the image away from the target almost eliminated the effect (location specificity); however, effects observed when the subjects formed images of vertical lines were comparable to those observed when the subject formed images of horizontal lines (no orientation specificity). It was demonstrated (Kaufman *et al.* 1981) that the McCullough effect (orientation-specific colour after-effect) could be induced via imagery. However, the imagery effect was transferred from one eye to the other, while the actual McCullough effect is not. Thus from the results of these psychophysical experiments, the involvement of early visual areas (especially V1) in visual imagery has been unable to be ascertained.

Recently, a new approach was devised (Ishai and Sagi 1995), which investigated imagery effects on visual perception in a psychophysical detection paradigm. They compared human subjects' abilities to detect a computer-generated 'Gabor target' under two conditions; one was the perceptual condition in which the target was flanked by two peripheral Gabor masks, and the other was the imagery condition in which the subjects imagined the absent masks. Experiments under the perceptual condition showed enhancement of detection of a visual target when the subjects perceived actual visual mask stimuli, revealing the existence of facilitatory interactions between spatial channels. The enhancement under the perceptual condition was specific to the stimulated eye, and the orientation, spatial frequency, and retinal location of the stimulus (Polat and Sagi 1994). Surprisingly, the same facilitatory characteristics were found under the imagery condition, such as monocularity, and orientation- and retinal location-specificity. This observation strongly suggests that the mental images can be interfaced with perceptual representations at early stages of visual information processing (Fig. 9.6).

Discussion

I have examined several lines of empirical evidence that support the backward-projection hypothesis of visual imagery. The PACS task, in which the necessity for image generation and its initiation time were controlled by a colour switch, provided particularly compelling evidence for the role of temporal cortical neurons. The hypothesis also predicted that backward signals from higher-order representations would reach topographically organized visual areas when an imagery task requires reconstruction of the detailed local geometry of the image (such as counting the columns of the Pantheon). This prediction was confirmed by an elegant psychophysical experiment with a Gabor-target detection task.

However, in those experiments the image was generated only in a simple way, in which a subject recalled a previously seen object or event. We use imagery in more flexible ways. First, we can combine or arrange objects in novel configurations in images. Second, we can also mentally draw patterns that we have never actually seen, or we can visualize novel patterns that are not based on rearranging familiar components (see Farah 1990). To make these image computations possible, the imagery system should contain another subsystem that uses associative memory and that constructs local representations on the basis of a global image by a top-down attentional shift (Kosslyn 1994). Anatomical localization of the subsystem might be hypothesized to be in the dorsolateral prefrontal cortex, but evidence is still scanty (Fuster 1989; Roland 1993). It is noted that, although I believe depictive representation lies in the deepest structure for image generation (as described above), propositional representation also may generate imagery by the use of this subsystem, especially in humans (Pylyshyn 1981). Characterization and neurophysiological analysis of this subsystem would provide further constraints on the neural basis of imagery and its conscious activation.

References

Alain, E.A.C. (1926). *Systeme des beaux-art*, Nouvelle édition, Gallimard, Paris.

Cooper, L.A. and Shepard, R.N. (1973). Chronometric studies of the rotation of mental images. In *Visual information processing* (ed. W.G. Chase), pp. 76–176. Academic Press, New York.

Craver-Lemley, C. and Reeves, A. (1987). Visual imagery selectively reduces vernier acuity. *Perception*, **16**, 533–614.

Farah, M.J. (1990). *Visual agnosia*. MIT Press, Cambridge.

Fuster, J.M. (1989). *The prefrontal cortex*. Raven Press, New York.

Higuchi, S. and Miyashita, Y. (1996). Formation of mnemonic neuronal responses to visual paired associates in inferotemporal cortex is impaired by perirhinal and entorhinal lesions.

Proceedings of the National Academy of Sciences of the United States of America, **93**, 739–43.

Ishai, A. and Sagi, D. (1995). Common mechanisms of visual imagery and perception. *Science*, **268**, 1772–4.

Kaufman, J.H., May, J.G., and Kunen, S. (1981). Interocular transfer of orientation-contingent color aftereffects with external and internal adaptation. *Perception and Psychophysics*, **30**, 547–51.

Kosslyn, S.M. (1994). *Image and brain*. MIT Press, Cambridge.

Kosslyn, S.M., Alpert, N.M., Tompson, W.L. *et al.* (1993). Visual mental imagery activates topographically organized visual cortex: PET investigations. Journal of *Cognitive Neuroscience*, **5**, 263–87.

Le Bihan, D., Turner, R., Zeffiro, T.A., Cuenod, C.A., Jezzard, P., and Bonnerot, V. (1993). Activation of human primary visual cortex during visual recall: a magnetic resonance imaging study. *Proceedings of the National Academy of Sciences of the United States of America*, **90**, 11802–5.

Mishkin, M. (1982). A memory system in the monkey. *Philosophical Transactions of the Royal Society of London, Series B*, **298**, 85–95.

Miyashita, Y. (1988). Neuronal correlate of visual associative long-term memory in the primate temporal cortex. *Nature*, **335**, 817–20.

Miyashita, Y. (1993). Inferior temporal cortex: where visual perception meets memory. *Annual Review of Neuroscience*, **16**, 245–63.

Miyashita, Y. (1995). How the brain creates imagery. *Science*, **268**, 1719–20.

Miyashita, Y. and Chang, H.S. (1988). Neuronal correlate of pictorial short-term memory in the primate temporal cortex. *Nature*, **331**, 68–70.

Miyashita, Y., Date, A., and Okuno, H. (1993). Configurational encoding of complex visual forms by single neurons of monkey temporal cortex. *Neuropsychologia*, **31**, 1119–32.

Murray, E.A., Gaffan, D., and Mishkin, M. (1993). Neural substrates of visual stimulus–stimulus association in rhesus monkey. *Journal of Neuroscience*, **13**, 4549–61.

Naya, Y., Sakai, K., and Miyashita, Y. (1996) Activity of primate inferotemporal neurons related to a sought target in a pair-association task. *Proceedings of the National Academy of Sciences of the United States of America*, **93**, 2664–9.

Pylyshyn, Z.W. (1981). The imagery debate: analogue media versus tacit knowledge. *Psychological Review*, **87**, 16–45.

Polat, U. and Sagi, D. (1994). Spatial interactions in human vision: from near to far via experience-dependent cascades of connections. *Proceedings of the National Academy of Sciences of the United States of America*, **91**, 1206–9.

Roland, P.E. (1993). *Brain activation*. Wiley, New York.

Roland, P.E. and Friberg, L. (1985). Localization of cortical areas activated by thinking. *Journal of Neurophysiology*, **53**, 1219–43.

Sakai, K. and Miyashita, Y. (1991). Neural organization for the long-term memory of paired associates. *Nature*, **354**, 152–5.

Squire, L.R. (1987). *Memory and brain*. Oxford University Press, London.

Sartre, J.P. (1938). *L'imaginare*. Gallimard, Paris.

Tye, M. (1991). *The imagery debate*. MIT Press, Cambridge.

Van Essen, D.C., Anderson, C.H., and Felleman, D.J. (1992). Information processing in the primate visual system: an integrated systems perspective. *Science*, **255**, 419–23.

10

Awareness of memory deficit

HIROTAKA TANABE

Introduction

The famous amnesic patient, HM, with bilateral medial temporal lesions involving the hippocampal region is always referred to as a representative case of complete anterograde amnesia that causes someone to forget the episodes of daily life as rapidly as they occur. Even this profoundly amnesic patient is said to be to some extent aware of his memory deficit (Schacter 1991), probably based on descriptions such as 'his frequent apologies for what he fears may be considered lapses from good manners, such as forgetting the names of persons to whom he has just been introduced' and 'he often volunteers stereotyped descriptions of his own state, by saying that it is "like waking from a dream"' (Milner *et al.* 1968). There are, however, no direct descriptions in this article (Milner *et al.* 1968) demonstrating that HM is aware of his inability to form new memories. Are patients with a total inability to lay down new memory traces really aware of their memory deficits?

In the present study, I examined whether or not patients with complete global amnesia could be aware of their inability to record ongoing information, observing their speech and behaviour during the amnesic episode in three cases of transient global amnesia (TGA) with transient dysfunction confined to the bilateral medial temporal lobe including the hippocampal area.

Clinical features of Transient Global Amnesia (TGA)

TGA is a well-recognized clinical entity characterized as follows (Tanabe *et al.* 1991; Frederiks 1993). Patients suffer sudden anterograde and retrograde memory loss without other neurological signs or symptoms. They retain personal identity and are able to carry on normal activities. However, they are unable to acquire any new information, namely they show complete anterograde amnesia. In addition, their inner world goes back to a certain point of the past (i.e. there is some retrograde amnesia), while the outer world including their appearance is in real time. As a result, various things incomprehensible to them develop in their immediate environment and situation. For example, one patient was astonished at a scar from a burn on her hand she had received 5 months before and asked her husband about it. Patients ask questions such as 'What day is today?' and 'Why am I here?' to try and grasp things incomprehensible to them or orient themselves with respect to their situation.

However, they cannot retain answers due to the complete anterograde amnesia, so that they repeat the same questions despite repeated explanations. The retrograde memory loss, extending back for days, months, or even years before the attack, gradually or quickly shrinks as the patients recover. No or only a brief period of permanent retrograde amnesia persists, but memory for events during the acute phase is permanently impaired. The amnesic episodes generally last several hours.

Thus, a TGA episode gives a rare chance to examine 'awareness' of memory deficit throughout different degrees of amnesia in a single subject, and it is considered to be the best material with which to consider the current issue.

Subjects

ST is a 63-year-old, right-handed housewife. One morning she became suddenly perplexed and repeatedly asked her son the same questions over and over despite repeated explanations. For instance, she asked him where her husband was, evidently not remembering that he had been hospitalized with a fracture of his foot one month before. Her son, who is a medical doctor, took her immediately to our hospital by car. On the way, she repeatedly asked where they were going, despite the fact that she was given the same replies each time. She showed complete inability to form any new memories; she could readily remember three object names immediately after they were hidden. However, she could recall none of the objects after distraction such as five seriated subtractions of the digit '7' from 100 or after a delay of a couple of minutes. Moreover, she could not remember at all that she had seen them. Her immediate or short-term memory was preserved; digit spans were 7 forward and 5 backward. Her behaviour also reflected her dramatic memory loss. At one point, the examiner left the room and returned 5 minutes later. She behaved as if she had never seen the doctor before. Her retrograde amnesia was considered to cover at least 10 months with fragments of memory during the acute phase.

This case gave me the first experience with this striking amnesic episode of TGA and called my attention to the question whether or not TGA patients are really aware of their memory deficits themselves. In the article on this case (Tanabe *et al*. 1991), we wrote as follows: 'During the TGA, our patient appeared perplexed and asked a series of questions repeatedly as if to try to orient herself, but she did not definitely realize her inability to acquire new information.'

AS is a 57-year-old, right-handed neuropsychiatrist with experience in lecturing on TGA. He had occasionally complained of a migraine for the preceding three years. One morning he complained of a headache at his office. Before noon, his secretary wondered why he did not leave his office because he was due to meet his colleagues at noon. When she asked him about the appointment, he had forgotten it and repeatedly asked her the date despite being given the same answer. On the way to our hospital by car, he repeatedly demanded to know where he was going and why he must go to hospital, despite always being given the same reply, like the first case. When he arrived at our hospital, he was still in the acute phase. His digit spans were

8 forward and 7 backward. He shortly became able to retain fragments of some events, so that he had left the acute phase and entered the recovery stage. His retrograde amnesia was considered to cover six weeks at that point, and one week 30 minutes later.

During the acute stage when he not only could recall none of three object names after distraction or after a few minutes, but also could not even remember the fact that he had seen them, he never admitted that he suffered from TGA, although he said to us that he knew TGA well and lectured on it to medical students. In the recovery stage when he became able to remember or choose from multiple choice one of three objects after distraction or a delay of a few minutes, he admitted at last that he had some problems with his memory.

The examination of the second case demonstrated the following. While he had a complete anterograde amnesia with some retrograde amnesia, he indeed admitted to feeling strange or disorientated in time, but he did not identify the problems as a memory disorder.

MY is a 63-year-old, right-handed white-collar worker of a pharmaceutical company. For a few days before the attack of TGA, he had been fatigued due to overwork. One day just after taking a dessert at lunch, his actions suddenly became strange. After he was brought to our hospital, he still repeated the same questions: 'Did I do anything wrong?' and 'Why am I here?', even after receiving adequate replies. At that point, retrograde amnesia covered a few years and he could not remember even his first son's marriage which had been held in Hawaii one year earlier. Like the former cases, his short-term memory was preserved; digit spans were 8 forward and 4 backward.

In this third case, I asked the patient more direct questions of whether or not he was aware that he was suffering from a failure to remember events while at the same time exhibiting a complete inability to store new memories.

MY's awareness of the nature of his memory deficit is clearly revealed in the following conversation with the author (A = author; P = patient).

A: You have a problem with your memory.

P: Really?

A: You're aware that you forget things?

P: No, but I can't quite remember why I'm here now.

A: How about now? Do you have trouble remembering things?

P: Oh, I haven't had much trouble with my memory before.

A: You don't have any problems now?

P: No.

Thus, it is demonstrated that in the acute phase of TGA, patients were aware of particular situations incomprehensible to them resulting from their memory deficits, but unaware of their memory deficits themselves; and that in the recovery phase they at last became aware of their memory problems.

In all three cases, single photon emission computed tomography (SPECT) scans taken during the TGA episode revealed hypoperfusion restricted to the bilateral medial aspect of the temporal lobe involving the hippocampal region, while those taken after TGA showed no abnormalities (see Fig. 10.1, plate section) (Tanabe *et al.* 1991, 1994*a,b*; Kazui *et al.* 1995).

Conclusion

Concerning TGA patients' insight or judgement with respect to their amnesic condition, some authors (Fisher 1989; Schacter, 1991) argue that they are aware of their memory loss or profound anterograde amnesia, while other authors (Caplan 1985; Kushner and Hauser 1985) contradict this argument. For instance, Kushner and Hauser (1985) and Caplan (1985) gave the following descriptions, respectively: 'nine patients exhibited insight by observing that something was amiss, but no patient identified the problem as a memory disorder' and 'some patients admit to feeling strange, disorientated, frightened or somehow ill, though it was rare for them to identify the problem as one involving poor memory'.

This discrepancy in opinion seems to be partly due to the phase of TGA during which these doctors examined the patients, that is, whether in the acute or recovery phase, and partly to the difference in their judgements on 'awareness of deficit'. For the latter point, the following should be mentioned. Complaints of TGA patients described in the literature, such as: 'I'm having a stroke' and 'I'm losing my mind' (Fisher and Adams 1964), 'Am I going mad? I can't remember anything' (Evans 1966), and 'There's something wrong with me' (Fisher 1982), do not directly imply that patients are aware of their memory problems themselves, even though they do indicate that patients are aware of an unusual situation.

Our investigations into the three cases of TGA revealed that during the acute phase of TGA, patients were aware of a particular situation incomprehensible to them resulting from their memory deficits, but were unaware of their memory deficits themselves; and that in the recovery phase, that is, only after they become able to encode some memories, did they at last become aware of this deficit. This demonstrates that subjects with complete anterograde amnesia are not aware of their total inability to acquire new memories.

In other words, awareness of memory deficit is impaired in patients with complete global amnesia in the context that their consciousness is preserved, if consciousness is defined as the awareness of the environment and the self (Frederiks 1969), or a mechanism that combines attention with short-term memory (Crick and Koch 1992). Their behaviour during the TGA episode in which they try to clarify the development and components of that particular situation to try to orient themselves into that particular situation reflects that they are aware of the 'environment and the self'. In addition, they retain personal identity and have normal short-term memory.

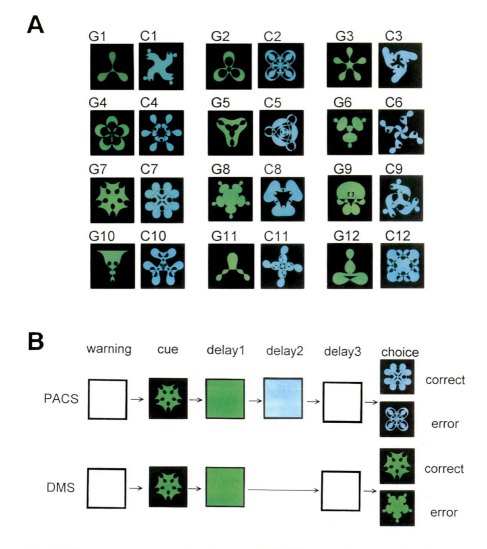

Fig. 9.4 The pair-association with colour switch (PACS) task and an example of neuronal responses in the temporal cortex. (A) Twelve pairs of coloured Fourier descriptors used as stimuli in both the PACS task and the DMS task. Similar to Fig. 9.2(A), but now stimuli are colour-coded for controlling the necessity for image generation and its initiation time. The first pair is picture G1 (green) and picture C1 (cyan), the second pair is G2 and C2, and so on. (B) The sequence of events in a trial of the PACS task or the DMS task. Cue stimuli and squares were presented at the centre of a video monitor. Choice stimuli were presented randomly in two of four positions on the video monitor. Warning, grey square (1 s in both tasks); cue, one of 24 pictures in (A) as a cue stimulus (0.5 s); Delay Period 1, square with has the same colour as the cue picture (2 s in the PACS task, 5 s in the DMS task); Delay Period 2, square which has the same colour as the paired associate of the cue picture (3 s in the PACS task); Delay Period 3, grey square (1 s in both tasks); choice, a choice of two stimuli (1.2 s in both task), the paired associate of the cue (correct) and one from a different pair (error) in the PACS task, or the same picture as the cue (correct) and one from a different pair (error) in the DMS task.

STIMULUS SELECTIVITY
OF AIT NEURON IN PACS

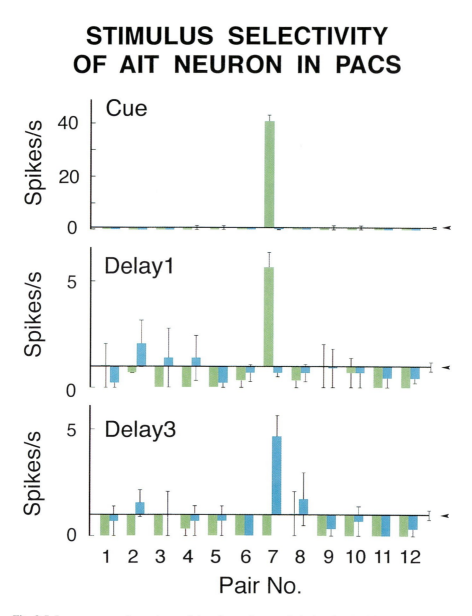

Fig. 9.5 Image generation triggered by the colour switch in the PACS task. Stimulus-selectivity of a neuron in the temporal cortex is shown in different task periods (top, Cue Period; middle, Delay Period 1; bottom, Delay Period 3). The ordinate shows the mean discharge rate in each task period after the presentation of a cue stimulus; cue stimuli are labelled as 'Pair No.' on the abscissa (green histogram bar at No.1 is G1, cyan histogram bar at No.1 is C1, etc.). This neuron selectively responded to the cue stimulus G7 during the Cue Period. Note that the cue stimulus C7 does not elicit any response during the Cue Period and Delay Period 1, but this neuron became active during Delay Periods 2 and 3.

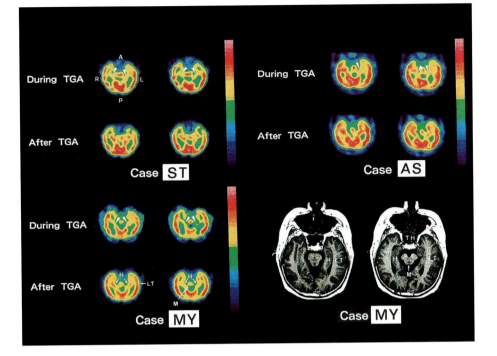

Fig. 10.1 Hippocampal SPECT images during and after the episode of TGA, using *N*-isopropyl-(I-123)-*p*-iodoamphetamine (IMP) in case ST and Tc-99m hexamethylpropyleneamine oxime (HM-PAO) in cases AS and MY. These special images are taken parallel to the longitudinal axis of the hippocampus, so that they enable the evaluation of total blood flow of the hippocampal area in one or two slices (Tanabe *et al.* 1994*a,b*; Kazui *et al.* 1995). During TGA, SPECT scans were performed 6 or 7 h after the onset. After TGA, SPECT scans were administered, one week later in case ST, one week later in case AS, and the next day in case MY. In each case, the upper row of images was taken during the episode and those on the lower row after the episode. In each case, the left and right images are images involving the lower and upper hippocampal regions, respectively. Hippocampal MR (magnetic resonance) images of case MY, approximately corresponding to the level of the hippocampal slices of SPECT, are shown at the bottom right for anatomical identification of hippocampal SPECT images. In the SPECT and MR images, the left side of the slices corresponds to the right side of the brain. Pink indicates to the highest level of cerebral blood flow and blue the lower level. White arrow heads indicate areas with reduced blood flow. Compared with after-TGA images, those taken during TGA demonstrate a definite hypoperfusion in the medial portion of the temporal lobe bilaterally in all the cases. Blood flow in other areas including the frontal cortex and thalamus was preserved. A, anterior; P, posterior; R, right; L, left; H, hippocampus; TH, temporal horn; LT, lateral aspect of the temporal lobe; M, midbrain.

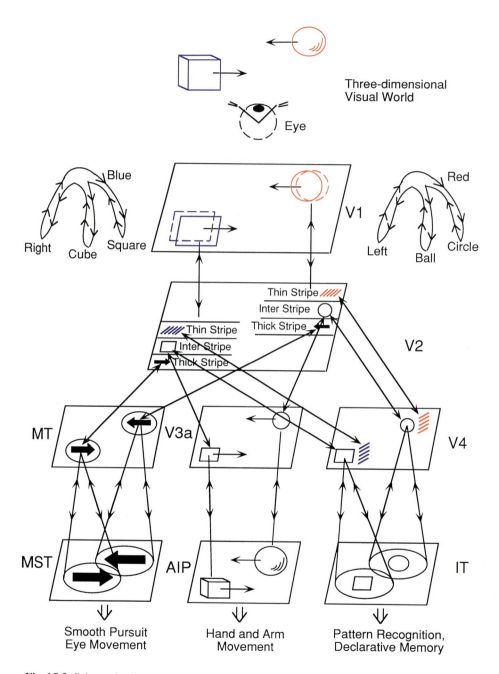

Fig. 15.3 Schematic diagram showing how the bidirectional theory provides the computational mechanism to solve the binding problem in the parallel and hierarchical pathways within the visual cortical areas.

References

Caplan, L.R. (1985). Transient global amnesia. In *Handbook of clinical neurology*, Vol. 45 (ed. P.J. Vinken, G.W. Bruyn, H.L. Klawans, and J.A.M. Frederiks), pp. 205–18. Elsevier, Amsterdam.

Crick, F. and Koch, C. (1992). The problem of consciousness. *Scientific American*, **267**, (3), 152–9.

Evans, J.H. (1966). Transient loss of memory, an organic mental syndrome. *Brain*, **89**, 539–48.

Fisher, C.M. (1982). Transient global amnesia: precipitating activities and other observations. *Archives of Neurology*, **39**, 605–8.

Fisher, C.M. (1989). Neurologic fragments. II. Remarks on anosognosia, confabulation, memory, and other topics; and appendix on self-observation. *Neurology*, **39**, 127–32,

Fisher, C.M. and Adams, R.D. (1964). Transient global amnesia. *Acta Neurologica Scandinavica*, **40**, Suppl. 9, 1–83.

Frederiks, J.A.M. (1969). In *Handbook of clinical neurology*, Vol 3 (ed. P.J. Vinken and G.W. Bruyn), pp. 48–61. Elsevier, Amsterdam.

Frederiks, J.A.M. (1993). Transient global amnesia. *Clinical Neurology and Neurosurgery*, **95**, 265–83.

Kazui, H., Tanabe, H., Ikeda, M., Nakagawa, Y. Shiraishi, J., and Hashikawa, K. (1995). Memory and cerebral blood flow in cases of transient global amnesia during and after the attack. *Behavioural Neurology*, **8**, 93–101.

Kushner, M.J. and Hauser, W.A. (1985). Transient global amnesia; a case-control study. *Annals of Neurology*, **18**, 684–91.

Milner, B., Corkin, S., and Teuber, H.L. (1968). Further analysis of the hippocampal amnesic syndrome; 14-year follow up study of H.M. *Neuropsychologia*, **6**, 215–34.

Schacter, D.L. (1991). Unawareness of deficit and unawareness of knowledge in patients with memory disorders. In *Awareness of deficit after brain injury; clinical and theoretical issues* (ed. G.P. Prigatano and D.L. Schacter), pp. 127–51. Oxford University Press.

Tanabe, H., Hashikawa, K., Nakagawa, Y. *et al.* (1991). *Acta Neurologica Scandinavica*, **84**, 22–27, 463.

Tanabe, H., Ikeda, M., and Hashikawa, K. (1994a). Neuroimaging of the human hippocampus in the context of disturbance of the higher brain functions. *Shinkei Kenkyu no Shinpo*, **38**, 161–72.

Tanabe, H., Kazui, H., Ikeda, M., Hashimoto, M., Yamada, N., and Eguchi, Y (1994b). Slowly progressive amnesia without dementia. *Neuropathology*, **14**, 105–14.

11

Body awareness and its disorders

ATSUSHI YAMADORI

Introduction

What is consciousness? What kind of mechanism produces this enigmatic phenomenon?

Hughlings Jackson (Jackson 1884) maintained that physiology and psychology belong to a different dimension and that it is impossible to think of causality between the two levels. He wrote that states of consciousness are utterly different from nervous states of the highest centres. The two things occur together; for every mental state there is a correlative nervous state. Although the two things occur in parallel, there is no interference of one with the other. This doctrine of concomitance is logical and persuasive. The physico-chemical world has its own laws and is complete within itself. A neuronal network, however complex, is a physical network. How are psychological phenomena related to physical networks?

On the other hand, it is also a fact that we can consciously control our actions, that is, our brain states. If someone decides to commit suicide, he can destroy his own organ of mind by himself. Is this concomitance? Jackson would have argued that if someone decided to commit suicide, it was not a psychological state of mind but a neurological physico-chemical activity occurring simultaneously with the state that would cause subsequent neurological brain events leading to its termination of activity.

I cannot help but believe that I, a conscious person, can control my brain to a certain degree at least. I can shift my attention. I can move my fingers. I can write. I can stop writing. I agree with Eccles (1992) that the self can control the brain. If so, there must be some kind of causal relation bridging the difference of dimension.

There have been many arguments on these almost impossible questions. I am aware that I am clearly incapable of dealing with these philosophical and epistemological questions. But for a clinician who believes that a conscious idea can be the driving force of the brain state, a venture to leap over this cognitive impasse may be permitted.

Michael Polanyi (1958), a proponent of emergence theory, argued that a life in its individuality cannot be defined in terms of physics and chemistry. In his terminology it is characterized by an ordering principle. Through generations of operations of an ordering innovative principle, human consciousness has emerged. It is a new level of evolution. Psychic states and nervous states are not separated by an abyss. They are continuous. There exist operational systems in between. We have to observe human conscious behaviour carefully and find out what kinds of transformations are taking place.

I can approach the problem only through my clinical experience. Two peculiar syndromes in which a part of a patient's own body or a part of his actions is felt alien to himself are described. One is the classical syndrome of anosognosia for hemiplegia (Babinski 1914). In extreme cases the syndrome is not only characterized by non-recognition of the fact of hemiplegia but also by flat denial of the existence of the hemiplegia and above all by irrational perception and interpretation of his own paralysed arm.

The other is the alien hand syndrome (Feinberg 1992). In one type of this syndrome for which we proposed the name 'compulsive manipulation of tools' (Mori and Yamadori 1982), a patient might be unable to inhibit his own right hand from reaching for an object and feel that the action is controlled by someone else.

Denial of left hemiparalysis, and misinterpretation of his own paralysed limb

A left hemiplegic patient with an acute stroke in the right perisylvian area will sometimes deny the fact that his left limbs do not move. This denial of the plain fact is so bizarre that one never forgets the experience.

Intriguing and thought-provoking phenomena often observed in cases of this type of denial of the hemiplegia are positive symptoms which accompany the negative state of inability of motion (paralysis). Not only would the patient deny the fact of paralysis (denial of a defect), but he might also insist that he could move the paralysed limb (motor hallucination). If the paralysed limb was shown to him and if its immobility was logically demonstrated to him, he would claim that the limb was not his and belonged to someone else, e.g. his sister's arm (objectification), or even that it was not a limb but someone, e.g. his baby (personification phenomenon), or something else, e.g. a mass of flesh (objectification). If in such a case an examiner further pursued the whereabouts of the limb, the patient would answer that he had his own limb apart from the paralysed one (supernumerary phantom). The following case is typical (Yamadori 1989).

A 45-year-old right-handed man suddenly developed a left hemiparalysis, left homonymous hemianopia, and left hemisensory deficit of all modalities, due to a massive haemorrhage in the right putamen. During his hospital stay it became clear that he had a denial of the left hemiparalysis, a supernumerary phantom limb, a motor hallucination of the left limb, and a left unilateral spatial neglect.

The following is part of a dialogue between the patient and me.

After he claimed that he had no trouble with his left hand, he added that he had a new left arm in addition to the old one:

A.Y.:   Where is the new arm?

Patient: It was there last night.

A.Y.:   Is it gone now?

Patient: How can the hand disappear? I had it all night.

A.Y.:   How many arms do you have?

Patient: I have three now.

A.Y.:   Raise your hands.

Patient: OK.

A.Y.:   Raise the left hand also.

Patient: I raised it.

I had him grasp his paralysed left forearm by his right hand:

A.Y.:   What is this?

Patient: This is a new one.

A.Y.:   Which one?

Patient: This is an old one. I had it just now.

A.Y.:   Is this an old one?

Patient: Yes.

These bizarre statements by patients have been thrown into a category of confusion, hallucination, or delusion, and further exploration of the pathophysiology has rarely been tried.

Denial of hemiplegia and concept of body schema

All the denial patients with these positive symptoms whom I have seen had, without exception, dense left-sided weakness and hemisensory deficits of all modalities, demonstrating the predominance of this syndrome in right hemispheric patients. Among the sensory deficits, impairment of proprioception (or kinaesthesia) is usually most prominent. How can we explain this complex of bizarre syndromes in a coherent way?

Head and Holmes (1911) were the first to hypothesize the body schema as a basis for normal bodily movements and bodily sensations. According to them the body schema is a physiological system serving as a frame of reference for ever-changing body positions. Without this type of organization it would be impossible to obtain meaningful information that can relate temporal and spatial information coming from one part of the body to that from another. Benton and Sivan (1993) recently defined it as 'a long-standing spatially organized model of one's body that provides a framework within which perceptual, motor, and judgmental reactions directed towards one's body occur.'

Head and Holmes (1911), among others, tried to explain anosognosia in terms of the body schema. Thus the non-perception of the left hemiparalysis was explained as being caused by a breakdown of the body schema which is assumed to exist in the right hemisphere. The theory, however, is not persuasive. It is difficult to explain the one-sidedness of the phenomenon. Can the body schema be split in half? And only the left half disappear? Because of many obvious shortcomings, the hypothesis of the body schema as a cause of anosognosia has long ceased to be discussed. In place of the body schema, inattention theory is now on stage (Bisiach and Geminiani 1991). I believe that it is difficult to explain positive symptoms in terms of neglect.

However, if we shift a responsible hemisphere housing the body schema from the right to the left as was once proposed by Gerstmann (1942), the body-schema theory becomes a powerful means of interpretation. An appropriately placed extensive lesion in the right hemisphere would destroy pyramidal tract fibres issuing from the motor cortex causing paralysis of the left limbs as well as sensory fibres reaching the parietal cortex causing left-sided hemisensory deficits of all modalities, especially of proprioception. My hypothesis starts from here.

The body-schema system continually receives information about the changing states of the joints and skin from all over the body. It is a system of abstraction. According to Head and Holmes (1911) it is maintained at the physiological level, that is, away from awareness. But if attention is directed to a particular part of the body, it floats up to the level of consciousness. The self not only becomes aware of the presence of that part but also identifies it as a particular part of his own body. I assume that this awareness of the part of the body as his own becomes possible because it is represented in the body schema as an integral part. The body schema inherently belongs to the self, or to be more exact constitutes the basis of selfness.

Suppose the right hemisphere is damaged and bodily information from the left side of the body stops arriving at the hemisphere. The body schema in the left hemisphere would also stop receiving information about the left half of the body. The activity of the body schema would become semi-autonomous. It keeps functioning without information from the left side. How would a patient feel? What would he experience? It is highly likely that he would feel nothing unusual with his body since the body schema itself remains intact. He would keep having a complete body image without any defects. But it is also highly likely that he would lose touch with an exact image of the left limbs because new information is not arriving. The left limbs are there but to him they are foggy.

If questioned about his body status he would answer that everything is all right (denial of the paralysis). He would even claim that he can move his paralysed left arm when asked to move it (motor hallucination). When the paralysed left arm was brought by the clinician to the front of his face to provide indisputable evidence of paralysis, and when he was persuaded by many means to recognize that he could not move it, he might finally understand the reality that the limb was paralysed. But confrontation with the reality would not necessarily lead to true comprehension of the situation. His inner experience based on the body-schema activity may be too strong to be denied.

One solution to this contradiction would be to exclude the shown limb, i.e. the paralysed limb, from his body image. The limb would be interpreted as alien to him. It would become an object. It would variously be called an examiner's hand, a sister's hand, a baby, 'you', or even a mass of warm flesh. The other solution would be to conclude that the limb belongs to him all right, but that there must be an extra one since the body schema keeps sending the conscious self signals that the body is normal. The third limb or supernumerary phantom would thus be created. However, since this imaginary limb is not supported by an actual inflow of proprioceptive information, some metamorphosis could not be avoided. The result would be a fluctuating and non-confident description of the phantom limb as budding directly from the trunk or lacking a part of the arm, etc. This experience would be further complicated by the fact that the linguistic system is closely associated with the body schema, both being in the same hemisphere. Disconnection of the speech area from the information concerning the left limb would cause confabulatory responses about the status of the left limb (Geschwind 1965). In an extraordinary case, the patient would not only insist that he has an extra left arm, but would produce many confabulatory reasons for it.

Syndrome of the alien left hand

In a patient with callosal damage you may find a symptom called 'alien hand sign'. According to a description by Bogen (1993) it was first described by Brion and Jedynak in 1972. The left hand in the right-handed patient behaves in a way that the patient finds foreign, alien, or at least uncooperative. Bogen added his own experience in which a patient complained about 'my little sister' in referring to whomever or whatever it was that made her left hand behave peculiarly. In most of the reported cases the sign was limited to the left hand and the lesion was in the corpus callosum. Because of this fact the sign was also called 'callosal' alien hand (Feinberg 1992).

I have observed this type of movement disorder on several occasions. Although the alien hand is an appropriate name, in my experience no patients regarded their left hand itself as alien. They knew for certain that the hand was theirs. On examination, no one showed impairment of sensation in all modalities. The essence of their complaints was they could not control a strange movement of their own left hand. As Bogen rightly put it, 'something' made the hand move whatever that something might be. Or the left hand moved by itself. The hand belongs to the self but the movement does not. Only the 'motion' of the hand is pushed outside the realm of his awareness.

Even more complex actions can be performed by the left hand in these patients without self-awareness.

Compulsive manipulation of tools by the right hand

In 1982 we reported a bizarre right-hand mode of behaviour and proposed to call it 'compulsive manipulation of tools' (Mori and Yamadori 1982). A 60-year-old right-handed patient suffered from an embolic stroke and developed a lesion in the medial aspect of the left frontal lobe involving the supplementary motor area and the genu of the corpus callosum.

When a tool was placed on a desk in front of him, his right hand reached for the tool, grasped it, and started using it against his will. For instance, when a comb was placed on the desk and he was ordered not to use it, his right hand nonetheless picked it up and started combing. His comprehension capacity of language was normal and he clearly understood that he had to refrain from such an action. But he could not help reaching and manipulating it. In order to comply with the order he had to use his left hand. It grasped the right hand and stopped its motion. Manipulative actions thus released were all consistent with what was expected with a particular tool. Given a spoon, he brought it to his mouth. With a pencil, he scrawled something on the desk. With a pair of scissors, he tried to cut his clothes. When an unfamiliar object like a spanner was provided, he reached and grasped it, but did not use it.

To summarize, this pathological behaviour was characterized by: the involuntary and compulsive use of a presented tool with the right hand; the inability to inhibit the action by the patient's will; and the necessity to mobilize the left hand to stop the right hand's action. Since our publication of the case more than 10 case studies reporting almost identical behavioural disorders have appeared in the literature. The distribution of lesions was also identical, with a combination of lesions in the left medial frontal lobe and the anterior part of the corpus callosum including the genu.

In all the reported cases sensory functions including proprioception of the right limbs were normal. All the cases showed no abnormalities of the bodily image. They knew the right hand belonged to them. An experience of strangeness was confined to actions themselves, and the patients complained that the hand started moving by itself against their will. Here again, as in the case of callosal alien hand, only the movement was dissociated from the awareness of the self.

In patients with a total callosal section, it has been repeatedly reported that the right hemisphere can perform relatively higher cognitive tasks without being aware of the performance (Sperry *et al.* 1969; see also Gazzaniga, Chapter 5). In these callosotomized cases subjects did not know what the stimulus was when it was presented to the right hemisphere and what the response should be. The whole process is shielded from consciousness, i.e. from the left hemisphere. But in cases of compulsive manipulation of tools, the patient knew clearly the nature of the given stimulus and what the response should be. What is shielded from his awareness is only the action.

The correct manipulation of a tool is a complex type of behaviour requiring the concerted action of the visual system, semantic system, motor memory, and motor executive system at least. The fact that such complex behaviour can be realized without awareness that the behaviour is being controlled by the performing self seems to provide more questions than answers.

Body schema and body image

From these experiences I would like to speculate that awareness of the body, i.e. body image, is built on activity of the body schema. Under normal conditions this schema functions at the physiological level. It does not emerge into the consciousness.

Thus we can recognize at least three organizing levels concerning body experience. At the lowest level there is an assembly of neuronal information coming from all parts of the body, which is distributed in the cerebral cortex of either side of the hemispheres. Let me call it the somaesthetic information assembly. At the middle level the body schema as defined by Head and Holmes (1911) is situated. Here the information assembly concerning body somaesthesis is organized into a system with a frame of reference, and the body is represented as a functional entity. This body schema secures the emergence of the conscious body image at the third level.

When abnormal information comes in to the somaesthetic information assembly, the signal is transformed into information relevant to the body-schema system: a location and a posture in relation to the rest of the body become specified. Then this information is again transformed into another type of information relevant to conscious experience: a name (or rather a description), and a feeling of a particular part of the body. Usually the activities of the body schema do not rise to the level of the body image. Only in necessary conditions is it transformed into a conscious image. When a contradiction occurs between an internally felt intact body image and the external reality of a left hemiplegia, the body image seems to take the upper hand. Denial of the reality, motor hallucination, objectification, or a supernumerary phantom, can all be understood as a logical result that the patient retains an intact whole body image despite the reality that part of the body is damaged. Descriptions of these experiences by patients might be ambiguous and fluctuating because they are based on internal information and not on external reality.

A mismatch can also happen between the body-schema system and a motor executive system. In this instance an action performed by a part of the body would be felt alien. Unlike a mismatch between the body schema and a pattern of incoming neural information concerning the status of the body, this type of disconnection would not lead to an impairment of a body image. The body belongs to the self but the action is controlled by the non-self.

Conclusion

Consciousness depends on an ordering system whose principle we have yet to understand. But the system must be continuous with systems organizing neural activity. The syndromes of anosognosia and alien hand seem to give us a glimpse of the relation of part of this hierarchical neurological system to consciousness (see further, Ramachandran and Rogers-Ramachandran 1996).

References

Babinski, M.J. (1914). Contribution a l'etude des troubles mentaux dans l'hemiplegie organique cerebrale (anosognosie). *Revue Neurologique*, **27**, 845–8.

Benton, A. and Sivan, A.B. (1993). Disturbances of the body schema. In *Clinical neuropsychology*, (3rd edn) (ed. K.M. Heilman and E. Valenstein), pp. 123–40. Oxford University Press, New York.

Bisiach, E. and Geminiani, G. (1991). Anosognosia related to hemiplegia and hemianopia. In *Awareness of deficit after brain injury* (ed. G.P. Prigatano and D.L. Schacter), pp. 17–39. Oxford University Press, New York.

Bogen, J.E. (1993). The callosal syndrome. In *Clinical neuropsychology* (3rd edn) (ed. K.M. Heilman and E. Valenstein), pp. 337–407. Oxford University Press, New York.

Eccles, J.C. (1992). *How the self controls its brain*. Springer-Verlag, Berlin.

Feinberg, T.E., Schindler, R.J., Flanagan, N.G., and Haber, L.D. (1992). Two alien hand syndrome. *Neurology*, **42**, 19–24.

Gerstmann, J. (1942). Problem of imperception of disease and of impaired body territories with organic lesions. *Archives of Neurology and Psychiatry*, **48**, 890–913.

Geschwind, N. (1965). Disconnexion syndromes in animal and man, II. *Brain*, **34**, 585–644.

Head, H. and Holmes, G. (1911). Sensory disturbances from cerebral lesions. *Brain*, **34**, 102–254.

Jackson, H. (1884). Remarks on evolution and dissolution of the nervous system. In *Selected writings of Hughlings Jackson* (ed. J. Taylor), pp. 76–91. Hodder and Stoughton, London (1988).

Mori, E. and Yamadori, A. (1982). Compulsive manipulation of tools and pathological grasp phenomenon. *Clinical Neurology (Tokyo)*, **22**, 329–35. (In Japanese.)

Polanyi, M. (1958). *Personal knowledge*, pp. 381–405. Routledge & Kegan Paul, London.

Ramachandran, V.S. and Rogers-Ramachandran, D. (1996). Synaesthesia in phantom limbs induced with mirrors. *Proceedings of the Royal Society of London, Series B*, **263**, 377–86.

Sperry, R.W., Gazzaniga, M.S., and Bogen, J.E. (1969). Interhemispheric relationships: the neocortical commissures; syndromes of hemisphere disconnection. In *Handbook of Clinical Neurology*, Vol. 4 (ed. P.J. Vinken and G.W. Bruyn), pp. 273–90. North-Holland, Amsterdam.

Yamadori, A. (1989). Anosognosia. *Neurological Medicine*, **30**, 364–9. (In Japanese.)

12

Language, spatial cognition, and the brain

URSULA BELLUGI AND EDWARD S. KLIMA

Introduction

For a book on consciousness, cognition, and computation, the study of language and its representation in the brain is clearly crucial. There is general agreement that language expression, processing, and even aspects of internal representation may be co-extensive with consciousness and that language, at the minimum, considerably enriches consciousness. The scientific study of language, until recently, has involved primarily the study of spoken languages; in fact, nearly all that was known about language and its representation in the brain had come from the study of spoken languages. New research into signed languages has revealed that there are primary linguistic systems, passed down from one generation of deaf people to the next, which have been forged into autonomous languages and are not derived from spoken languages. Thus, we can now examine properties of linguistic systems that have developed in alternate modes of transmission. Studies of signed languages have shown that fully expressive languages can arise outside of the mainstream of human spoken languages, and exhibit the same kinds of linguistic organization found in the thousands of spoken languages the world over (Bellugi and Hickok 1995; Bellugi and Studdert-Kennedy 1980; Klima and Bellugi 1988).

Although spoken and signed languages are structurally similar at their core, the surface properties of the two modes are radically different—each deeply rooted in the modalities involved in its production and perception. Both spoken and signed languages involve the same kinds of organization (phonology, morphology, syntax, semantics, hierarchically governed complex rule systems, argument structure, lexical categories, and syntactic constraints). Signed languages serve not only everyday conversation, but intellectual argument, scientific discussion, wit, and poetry. Yet, on the surface, the formal devices subserving signed and spoken languages are markedly different. Whereas spoken languages rely primarily on rapid temporal sequencing for each of their linguistic layers, signed languages are deeply rooted in their modes of perception and production. Multilayering of linguistic elements and the structured use of space in the service of syntax are major modality-determined aspects of signed languages. Thus, the most striking surface difference between signed and spoken language is the reliance on *spatial* contrasts at all linguistic levels. We describe a programme of studies, illuminated by new techniques in brain imaging, leading toward a deeper understanding of the neural systems that subserve language and other higher cognitive functions. Using a multidisciplinary approach we seek to gain insight into the often inaccessible workings of the brain by studying unusual languages and populations with differing cognitive and language abilities (Bellugi 1980; Bellugi *et al.* 1990; Poizner *et al.* 1990).

Perspectives from language in a different modality

Experimental findings concerning the neural basis of language necessarily bear on neurolinguistic systems only as they relate to auditory and phonetic processing. In fact, it has been assumed that the organizational properties of language are inseparably connected with the sounds of speech, and that the fact that language is normally spoken and heard determines the basic principles of grammar, as well as the organization of the brain for language. Studies of brain organization indicate that the left cerebral hemisphere is specialized for processing linguistic information in the auditory–vocal mode; thus the link between biology and behaviour has been identified with the particular sensory modality in which language has developed.

Although evolution in humans has been for spoken language (there is no group of hearing people that has a sign language as its primary linguistic system), recent research into sign languages has revealed the existence of primary linguistic systems that have developed naturally in visual/manual modalities. These signed languages have all of the complexities of spoken languages, and are passed down from one generation of deaf people to the next. Importantly, these sign languages are not derived from the spoken language of the surrounding community: rather, they are autonomous languages with their own grammatical form. Indeed, the sign language developed by deaf people in Great Britain is *mutually incomprehensible* with the sign language that has developed among deaf people in the United States. There are now numerous studies of primary signed languages arising independently in different countries around the world, including Bali, Brazil, China, Japan, and many more. The existence of these primary visual/manual linguistic systems can provide a new perspective on the determinants of brain organization for language: how is language organized when it is based instead on moving the hands in space, and on visually processing? We can now investigate the neurobiology of language when language itself is spatially realized (Bellugi *et al.* 1993).

American Sign Language (ASL) exhibits formal structuring at the same levels as spoken languages, and similar kinds of organizational principles as spoken languages. At the core, spoken and signed languages are essentially identical in terms of rule systems. Nevertheless, on the surface, signed and spoken languages differ markedly. The formal grammatical structuring assumed by a visual/manual language is deeply influenced by the modality in which the language is cast, at all structural levels. ASL displays complex *linguistic* structure, but unlike spoken languages, conveys much of its structure by manipulating *spatial* relations, making use of spatial contrasts at all linguistic levels.

In our research, we have been specifying the ways in which the formal properties of language are shaped by their modalities of expression; sifting properties peculiar to a particular language mode from more general properties common to all languages. As noted, the most striking surface difference between signed and spoken languages is the reliance on *spatial* contrasts, most evident in the grammar of the language. Figure 12.1 shows some aspects of grammatical structure in ASL and its reliance on spatial contrasts. Instead of relying on linear order for inflectional marking, as in English (*act, acting, acted, acts*), ASL grammatical processes nest sign stems in spatial patterns of considerable complexity; thereby marking grammatical functions such as number, aspect, and person. Grammatically complex forms can be spatially nested, one inside the other, with different orderings producing different meanings (A). Similarly, the syntactic structure specifying relations of signs to one another in sentences of ASL is also essentially spatially organized. Nominal signs may be associated with abstract positions in a plane of signing space, and direction of movement of verb signs between such end-points marks grammatical relations. Pronominal signs directed towards these previously established loci clearly function to refer back to nominals, even with many signs intervening (B). This spatial organization underlying syntax is a unique property of visual–gestural systems.

Neural systems subserving a visuospatial language

Not only is sign language independent from spoken language, it is transmitted in a different modality and encodes linguistic structure in essentially *spatial* distinctions rather than temporal distinctions. These differences between signed and spoken languages provide an especially powerful tool for understanding the neural systems subserving language. Consider the following: in hearing/speaking individuals, language processing is mediated by the left cerebral hemisphere, whereas visuospatial processing is mediated by the right cerebral hemisphere. But what about a language that is communicated using spatial contrasts rather than temporal contrasts? On the one hand, the fact that sign language has the same kind of complex linguistic structure as spoken languages and the same expressivity might lead one to expect left hemisphere mediation. On the other hand, the spatial medium so central to the linguistic structure of sign language clearly suggests right hemisphere mediation. In fact, the answer to this question is dependent on the answer to another, deeper question concerning the *basis* of the left hemisphere specialization for language. Specifically, is the left hemisphere specialized for language processing *per se* (i.e. is there a brain basis for language as an independent entity)? Or is the left hemisphere's dominance generalized to processing any type of information that is presented in terms of temporal contrasts? If the left hemisphere is indeed specialized for processing language itself, sign language processing should be mediated by the left hemisphere just as spoken language is. If however, the left hemisphere is specialized for processing fast temporal contrasts in general, we would expect sign language processing to be mediated by the right hemisphere. The study of sign languages in deaf signers permits us to pit the nature of the signal (auditory/temporal vs. visual/spatial) against the type of information (linguistic vs. non-linguistic) that is

A. Three-dimensional morphology in ASL

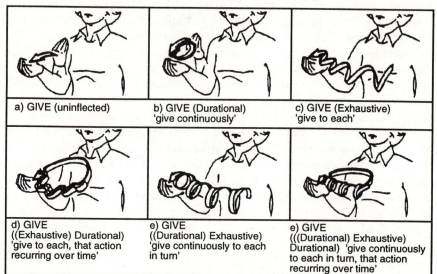

a) GIVE (uninflected)	b) GIVE (Durational) 'give continuously'	c) GIVE (Exhaustive) 'give to each'
d) GIVE ((Exhaustive) Durational) 'give to each, that action recurring over time'	e) GIVE ((Durational) Exhaustive) 'give continuously to each in turn'	e) GIVE (((Durational) Exhaustive) Durational) 'give continuously to each in turn, that action recurring over time'

B. Spatially organized syntax

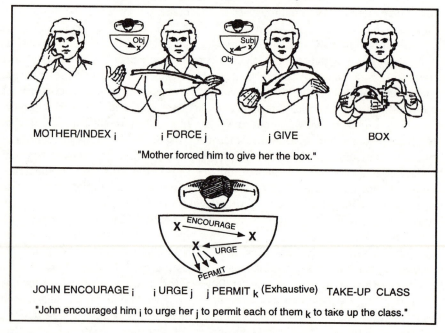

MOTHER/INDEX ᵢ   ᵢ FORCE ⱼ   ⱼ GIVE   BOX

"Mother forced him to give her the box."

JOHN ENCOURAGE ᵢ   ᵢ URGE ⱼ   ⱼ PERMIT ₖ (Exhaustive)   TAKE-UP CLASS

"John encouraged him ᵢ to urge her ⱼ to permit each of them ₖ to take up the class."

Fig. 12.1 Morphology and syntax in ASL.

encoded in that signal as a means of examining the neurobiological basis of language.

We address these questions through a large programme of studies of deaf signers with focal lesions to the left or the right cerebral hemisphere. We investigate several major areas, each focusing on a special property of the visual–gestural modality as it bears on the investigation of brain organization for language. We have now studied intensively more than twenty deaf signers with left or right hemisphere focal lesions; all are highly skilled ASL signers and all used sign as a primary form of communication throughout their lives. Our subjects are examined with an extensive battery of experimental probes, including formal testing of ASL at all structural levels, spatial cognitive probes sensitive to right hemisphere damage in hearing people, and new methods of brain imaging. Figure 12.2 shows the superimposition of lateral reconstructions of lesions from a large number of deaf signers, separated into those with left hemisphere lesions versus those with right hemisphere lesions. This programme allows us to begin to map out the differential effect of lesions in various regions of the brain on language and cognitive systems. The large pool of well-studied and thoroughly characterized subjects thus allows a new perspective on the determinants of brain organization for language (Bellugi and Hickok 1995; Hickok *et al.* 1995, 1996; Damasio *et al.* 1986).

Left hemisphere lesions and sign language grammar

Our first major finding is that only deaf signers with damage to the left hemisphere show sign language aphasias. Marked impairment in sign language after left hemisphere lesions was found in the majority of the left hemisphere damaged (LHD) signers but not in any of the right hemisphere damaged (RHD) signers, whose language profiles were much like matched controls. Figure 12.3(a) presents a comparison of LHD, RHD, and normal control profiles of sign characteristics from our Sign Diagnostic Aphasia Examination—a measure of sign aphasia. The RHD signers showed no impairment at all in any aspect of ASL grammar; their signing was rich, complex, and without deficit, even in the spatial organization underlying sentences of ASL. By contrast, LHD signers showed markedly contrasting profiles: one was agrammatic after her stroke, another made frequent paraphasias at the sign internal level, and a third showed grammatical paraphasias, particularly in morphology. A fourth deaf signer showed deficits in the capacity to perform the spatially encoded grammatical operations which link signs in sentences, a remarkable failure in the spatially organized syntax of the language. Figure 12.3(b) presents illustrations of aphasic errors at the lexical level, a movement substitution and a location substitution, made by two different left lesioned signers. In contrast, none of the RHD signers showed any within-sentence deficits; they were completely unimpaired in sign sentences and not one showed any hint of aphasia for sign language (in contrast to their marked non-language spatial deficits, described below).

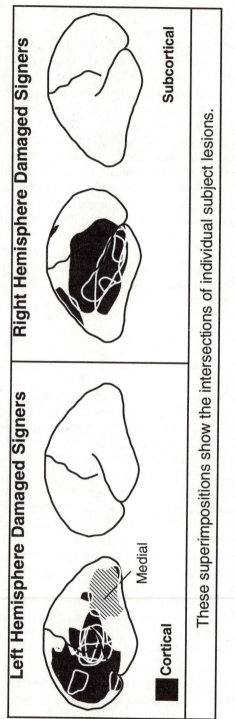

Fig. 12.2 Superimpositions of lesions from left- and right-lesioned deaf signers, lateral reconstructions.

A. Sign Profiles of Left and Right Lesioned Signers

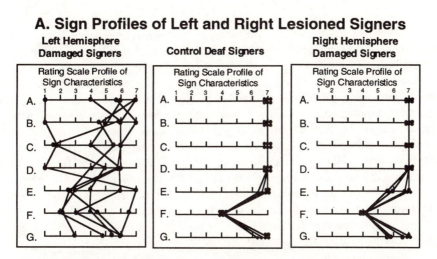

Left Hemisphere Damaged Signers — Rating Scale Profile of Sign Characteristics

Control Deaf Signers — Rating Scale Profile of Sign Characteristics

Right Hemisphere Damaged Signers — Rating Scale Profile of Sign Characteristics

LHD deaf signers show marked and different sign language aphasias; RHD deaf signers are much like controls.

A. Melodic Line: 1=absent; 4=limited to short phrases andstereotyped expressions; 7=runs through entire sentence
B. Phrase Length: 1=1 sign; 4=4 signs; 7=7 signs
C. Articulatory Agility: 1=always impaired or impossible; 4=normal only in familiar signs and phrases; 7=never impaired
D. Grammatical Form: 1=none available; 4=limited to simple descriptives and stereotypes; 7=normal range
E. Paraphasia in Running Sign: 1=present in every utterance; 4=once per minute of conversation; 7=absent
F. Sign Finding: 1=fluent without information; 4=information proportional to fluency; 7=exclusively content signs
G. Sign Comprehension: 1=absent (z= -2); 2 (z= -1.5); 3 (z= -1); 4 (z= -.5); 5 (z=0); 6 (z= +.5); 7=normal (z= +1)

B. Lexical Errors by Deaf Left-Lesioned Signers

A. Movement error (subject LHD 130)

THEN   **THEN w/error**

B. Place of Articulation error (subject LHD 108)

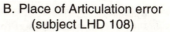

FROG   **FROG w/error**

Fig. 12.3 (a) Sign profiles of left- and right-lesioned signers. LHD deaf signers show marked and different sign language aphasias; RHD deaf signers are much like controls. (b) Lexical errors by left-lesioned deaf signers.

Moreover, we find dramatic differences in performance between left and right hemisphere damaged signers on formal experimental probes of sign competence. For example, we developed a test of the equivalent of rhyming in ASL, a probe of phonological processing. Two signs 'rhyme' if they are similar in all but one phonological parametric value such as handshape, location, or movement. To tap this aspect of phonological processing, subjects are presented with an array of pictured objects and asked to pick out the two objects whose signs 'rhyme', that is, differ only in one parameter (e.g. handshape) but are identical on other parameters (e.g. location and movement). LHD signers are significantly impaired relative to RHD signers and controls on this test, another sign of the marked difference in effects of right and left hemisphere lesions on signing. On other tests of ASL processing at different structural levels, we found similar distinctions between left- and right-lesioned signers: with the right-lesioned signers much like the controls, but the signers with left hemisphere lesions significantly impaired (Bellugi *et al.* 1990; 1993).

Right hemisphere lesions and non-language spatial processing

These results from language testing contrast sharply with results on tests of non-language spatial cognition. RHD signers are significantly more impaired on a wide range of spatial cognitive tasks than LHD signers, who show little impairment. Drawings of many of the RHD signers (but not those with LHD) show severe spatial distortions, neglect of the left side of space, and lack of perspective. On tasks of spatial construction, such as a block design task, there is strong evidence of a spatial deficit following right hemisphere damage, similar to that found in hearing people. We note RHD signers' tendencies to break the overall configuration of the design in the block design task and their spatial disorganization, compared to deaf signers with LHD. Yet, astonishingly, these sometimes severe spatial deficits among RHD signers do not affect their competence in a spatially nested language, ASL.

The finding that sign aphasia follows left hemisphere lesions but not right hemisphere lesions provides a strong case for a modality-independent *linguistic* basis for the left hemisphere specialization for language. These data suggest that the left hemisphere is biologically predisposed for language itself, independent of language modality. Thus, hearing and speech are not necessary for the development of hemisphere specialization—sound is not crucial. Furthermore, the finding of a dissociation between competence in a spatial language and competence in non-linguistic spatial cognition demonstrates that it is the type of information that is encoded in a signal (i.e. linguistic vs. spatial information) rather than the nature of the signal itself (i.e. spatial vs. temporal) that determines the organization of the brain for higher cognitive functions (Poizner *et al.* 1987; Bellugi *et al.* 1990).

Sign language has been found to be preserved in right-lesioned signers. Signers with right hemisphere damage present special issues, since they often show non-language spatial deficits. Several right-lesioned signers have severe left hemispatial neglect—that is, selective inattention to the left side of space, which is apparent in

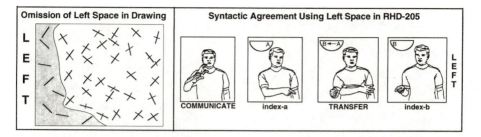

Fig. 12.4 Neglect for spatial cognition but not sign language in a right-lesioned signer.

drawings, where the left side is frequently omitted. In a task where they are asked to cross out all the lines on a page, they characteristically omit several lines on the left side of space (Fig. 12.4, left portion). This left field neglect shows up on almost all visual tasks. Such a distortion in spatial cognitive abilities might certainly be expected to impact the processing and production of a visual spatial language. Remarkably, this does not impact signing or ability to understand signing, which is unimpaired. Inattention to the left portion of the visual field *does not hold* for linguistic stimuli.

In one experiment, we contrasted presentation of signs with presentation of objects to both visual fields. The sign trials used bimanual signs which have one meaning if information from both hands was processed, but have a different meaning if information from only one hand was taken into account. The object trials involved simultaneous presentation of different objects in the two visual fields presented in the same spatial relations as the signs. The subject was nearly perfect on the sign identification task, but only half of the object trials were correctly identified, with all the errors involving omission of the object in left hemispace. This pattern of left hemispace omission was not observed in the sign trials. Moreover, although his drawings show left neglect, he used the left side as well as the right in producing signs, and even used the left side of his signing space for establishing nominals and verb agreement appropriately in his sign language syntax (Fig. 12.4, right portion). This shows what little effect right hemisphere damage can have on core linguistic functions, even when the language is essentially visuospatial (Corina *et al.* 1996).

The contrast between spatial syntax and spatial mapping in ASL

Until now, we have considered the spatial organization underlying grammatical contrasts, most notably syntax in ASL. That is, ASL uses spatial relations to encode syntactic information, such as grammatical subjects and objects of verbs, through manipulation of arbitrary loci and relations among loci in a plane of signing space. As opposed to its syntactic use, space in ASL also functions in a topographic way. The same plane of signing space may also be used in spatial mapping: that is, the

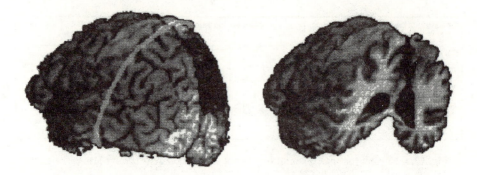

Fig. 12.5 RHD lesion reconstructed by BrainVox (Damasio and Frank 1992). The images are from MRI reconstructions of RHD-207. The reconstructions may be viewed from any perspective desired, and may be sliced and re-sliced to examine both cortical and sub-cortical structures.

space within which signs are articulated can also be used to describe the layout of objects in space. In such mapping, spatial relations among signs correspond topographically to actual spatial relations among the objects described, as opposed to representing arbitrary grammatical information. We investigate the breakdown of two uses of space within sign language, one for spatially organized syntax and the other for directly representing spatial relations in ASL. Right- and left-lesioned deaf signers provide striking dissociations between processing spatial syntax versus spatial mapping. They were given tests designed to probe their competence in ASL spatial syntax, and spatial topographic processing. The combined results on the spatial syntax tests reveal significant differences between the two groups: left-lesioned signers were significantly impaired on syntax tests, but right-lesioned signers' performance was not distinguishable from normal controls. Contrastingly, on the tests of spatial topographic processing, right-lesioned signers revealed significant deficits whereas left-lesioned signers performed well (Hickok *et al.*, in press; Bellugi *et al.* 1993).

A powerful example of the dissociability of spatial syntax from spatial mapping comes from an RHD signer (RHD 207). Her lesion involves the right superior parietal cortex with medial extension to the corpus callosum. This is illustrated in a three-dimensional reconstruction from *in vivo* MRI images using BrainVox, a system developed by Damasio and Frank (1992) (see Fig. 12.5). Like other right-lesioned signers, she is not at all aphasic. Her processing on ASL grammar tests was nearly perfect, and her use of spatially organized syntax is error free. However, when she was asked to repeat short stories in ASL that involved spatial descriptions—describing the layout of a particular dentist's office, for example—she was severely impaired. This right-lesioned signer does quite well in remembering and reproducing the actual items within a description (unlike some of our normal controls), but she completely fails in her ability to place these objects in their correct spatial locations in her signed story. Control subjects correctly locate nearly all the items

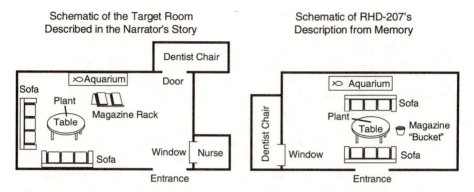

Fig. 12.6 Disorganization in spatial mapping in right-lesioned signer.

that they remember from the story, whereas she correctly locates only about a third of the items she remembers. Figure 12.6 illustrates the reconstructed layout of her signed description of a dentist's office in comparison to the ASL description in the experiment. Her signed description shows a marked spatial disorganization of elements within the room; she incorrectly specified the orientation and locations of items of furniture. She tended to 'lump' all of the furniture within the centre of the room, thus showing marked impairment in spatial mapping in ASL. Thus, even with signing, the use of space to represent *syntactic* relations and the use of space to represent *spatial* relations may be differentially affected by brain damage, with the syntactic relations disrupted by the left hemisphere damage and the spatial relations disrupted by right hemisphere damage (Emmorey *et al.* 1995; Bellugi *et al.* 1993).

Language, modality, and the brain

We are investigating similarities as well as differences between the neural systems subserving signed versus spoken language. Our growing database of deaf and hearing signers, combined with powerful new techniques in brain imaging including functional magnetic resonance imaging (fMRI), allows us to explore *within*-hemisphere neural systems subserving signed and spoken language. We are now beginning to amass evidence that suggests both some central commonalities and some peripheral differences between the neural systems underlying signed and spoken languages. Patterns of language breakdown and preservation in left- as opposed to right-lesioned signers lead us to the following conclusions. Because the left-lesioned signers show frank sign language aphasias and the right-lesioned signers show preserved language function, it appears that it is, indeed, the left cerebral hemisphere which is specialized for sign language. Thus, there appear to be neural systems within the left hemisphere that emerge as special-purpose linguistic processors in persons who have profound and lifelong auditory deprivation and who communicate with linguistic systems that use radically different channels of reception and transmission from those of speech. In this crucial respect, brain organization for language in deaf signers parallels that in hearing, speaking individuals.

Furthermore, our data indicate that differential damage within the left hemisphere produces different forms of sign language aphasia, and suggest the possibility that those anatomical structures within the left hemisphere that subserve visual–gestural language differ in part from those that subserve auditory–vocal language. We are now mapping out the differences between spoken and signed language neural systems within the left hemisphere which may arise from the nature of the different visual input pathways and manual output pathways. Several left-lesioned signers exhibit sign language aphasias from lesions to systems that would not be expected to lead to language disruption in spoken language. Nonetheless, it is the similarities between signed and spoken language in interhemispheric organization that are most revealing. These studies of language in a different modality show that the left hemisphere in man is biologically predisposed for language itself, independent of language modality. These findings lead towards a neurobiology of language, and are critical for a new understanding of consciousness and cognition.

Acknowledgements

This research was supported in part by National Institutes of Health grants RO1 DC00146, RO1 DC00201, R37 HD13249, as well as grants from the March of Dimes. Illustrations copyright Ursula Bellugi, The Salk Institute for Biological Studies, La Jolla, CA.

References

Bellugi, U. (1980). The structuring of language: clues from the similarities between signed and spoken language. In *Signed and spoken language: biological constraints on linguistic form*, Dehlem Konferenzen (ed. U. Bellugi and M. Studdert-Kennedy), pp. 115–40. Verlag Chemie, Weinheim/Deerfield Beach, FL.

Bellugi, U. and Hickok, G. (1995). Clues to the neurobiology of language. In *Neuroscience, memory, and language*, Decade of the Brain Series, Vol. 1 (ed. R. Broadwell), pp. 89–107. Library of Congress, Washington, DC.

Bellugi, U. and Studdert-Kennedy, M. (ed.) (1980). *Signed and spoken language: biological constraints on linguistic form*, Dahlem Konferenzen. Verlag Chemie, Weinheim/Deerfield Beach, FL.

Bellugi, U., Poizner, H., and Klima, E.S. (1990). Mapping brain functions for language: evidence from sign language. In *Signal and sense: local and global order in perceptual maps* (ed. G. M. Edelman, W.E. Gall, and W.M. Cowan), pp. 521–43. Wiley-Liss, New York.

Bellugi, U., Poizner, H., and Klima, E.S. (1993). Language, modality and the brain. In *Brain development and cognition* (ed. M. Johnson), pp. 403–23. Blackwell Publishers, Cambridge, MA.

Corina, D., Kritchevsky, M., and Bellugi, U. (1996). Visual language processing and unilateral neglect: evidence from American Sign Language. *Cognitive Neuropsychology*, **13**, 321–56.

Damasio, H. and Frank, R. (1992). Three-dimensional *in vivo* mapping of brain lesions in humans. *Archives of Neurology*, **49**, 137–43.

Damasio, A., Bellugi, U., Damasio, H., Poizner, H., and Van Gilder, J. (1986). Sign language aphasia during left hemisphere amytal injection. *Nature*, **322**, 363–65.

Emmorey, K., Corina, D., and Bellugi, U. (1995). Differential processing of topographic and referential functions of space. In *Language, gesture, and space* (ed. K. Emmorey and J. Reilly), pp. 43–62. Erlbaum, Hillsdale, NJ.

Hickok, G., Klima, E.S., Kritchevsky, M., and Bellugi, U. (1995). A case of 'sign blindness' following damage in the left occipital cortex in a deaf signer. *Neuropsychologia*, **33**, 1597–1606.

Hickok, G., Bellugi, U., and Klima, E.S. (1996). The neurobiology of signed language and its implications for the neural organization of language. *Nature*, **381**, 699–702.

Hickok, G., Say, K., Bellugi, U., and Klima, E.S. The basis of hemispheric asymmetries for language and spatial cognition: clues from focal brain damage in two deaf native signers. *Aphasiology*, Special Issue, **10(6)**, 577–91.

Klima, E.S. and Bellugi, U. (1988). *The signs of language*. Harvard University Press, Cambridge, MA.

Poizner, H., Klima, E.S., and Bellugi, U. (1987). *What the hands reveal about the brain*. MIT Press/Bradford Books, Cambridge, MA.

Part III
Computational approaches

13

The coherence definition of consciousness

CHRISTOPH VON DER MALSBURG

Introduction

I am not sure it is not a mistake to write about consciousness—too little is my chance of adding anything to what the Great have already said, too thickly the issue becomes overgrown with philosophical argument, and too diverse are the viewpoints emphasized by different people. Most discouraging of all, little progress is in sight regarding the *qualia* issue, the question of how a material thing, our brain, can create the vivid sensations we experience. I feel that essential scientific and technical breakthroughs are required before the consciousness issue can be made to progress substantially. The next major impulse may have to await the advent of artificial organisms that we can talk to and that give us the impression they are conscious. It is my belief that this venture of building artificial conscious organisms will not encounter insurmountable barriers (although progress will be difficult), and that once they are here we will have to revise our notions on a basic level, just as biologists had to do so vis-à-vis the *vis vitalis* issue after the organic chemistry revolution.

I will focus in this essay on a riddle that in my view is central to the consciousness issue: how does the mind or brain create the unity we perceive out of the diversity that we know is there? I contend this is a technical issue, not a philosophical one, although its resolution will have profound philosophical repercussions, and although we have at present little more than the philosophical method to attack it.

A profound revolution has swept across the intellectual world in the last one or two decades, as a result of which we are now ready to see the creation of order in complex systems, not as the result of extraneous pre-existing plans, but of spontaneous interactions of simple agents. In my view this was an essential philosophical adaptation, putting us in a much better position now to attack the consciousness issue.

The unity of mind

Our introspective experience is one of unity, of monolithic coherence. This unity characterizes consciousness and awareness, attention, perception and action, our decisions and our will, our personality and self and, to a large extent, our value judgments. This unity prevails in spite of the diversity of aspects, influences, perceptions, impulses, memories, processes, and agents that we find as components of our mind, or, from a different perspective, in spite of the tremendous mass of building elements in our brain—areas, nuclei, nerves, neurons, fibres, synapses, membranes, and molecules. Creating the mind's unity out of the brain's diversity, the problem of nervous integration, is now, after the aforementioned revolution, an issue of a scientific, technical nature: how does the brain manage to let its myriad elements cooperate to create a coherent functional whole?

A now essentially defunct view sees all of the underlying diversity of the brain essentially as passive material arranged and ordered by a separate perceiving and planning entity, sometimes insisting on an immaterial nature of the mind. Very often this view sees itself tempted to squeeze the unity-creating entity into a tight place— the pineal gland (as did Descartes 1662) or some other small anatomical part of the brain—maybe just trying to deprive the poor thing of space for internal disagreement, or falling prey to the deeply ingrained prejudice that order is to be created with the help of central control—a centre being, of course, a separate entity of small extent. It is perhaps just another attempt to understand the mind's unity when identifying consciousness with just one modality, for instance short-term memory (Erdelyi 1974), the ability to enact plans (Shallice 1978), the ability to detect and put away obstacles encountered in unconscious processes (Mandler 1975), language (Sperry 1966), or the self (Minsky 1988). Unfortunately, even single modalities are not natural, monolithic units, and on closer inspection they become themselves extensive and diverse systems, creating the same riddle as before.

One attempt at the unity-out-of-diversity problem relies on unity of action, on the impossibility for our limbs and muscles to move in more than one direction at a time. This alone would not explain coherent motion flowing from a chaotic brain. It would instead have to be seen as a persistent influence on the brain to weed out self-contradiction and incoherence. Although this certainly is an important factor, the argument still shuns the original question of how the brain creates those coherent states.

Perhaps the most grotesque—although at the same time so strangely compelling —device to deal with the unity problem is the homunculus, the idea of a separate planning and perceiving agent, hidden somewhere in the brain and structured after the model of a coherently acting, deciding, and perceiving human. The origin of this compulsion is evidently the basic experience of ours that confronted with diverse stuff before our eyes our mind creates a coherent whole out of it. So rapid and effortless is this process that we have long since come to incorporate it in our basic conception of the world as a primary constituent, as elementary as gravity and air. And in the same way that it is difficult to discover even the problem of how gravity works, the phenomenon already being deeply ingrained in our mind when we start thinking, it is difficult to recognize as such the problem of how the mind creates order. Consequently, man has used this phenomenon of 'spontaneous' creation of order by the mind as one of the fundamental metaphors to understand the world: wherever there is order, there must have been a mind to create it. The concept of the homunculus results very naturally from the application of this metaphor to the enigma of creation of order and unity in the mind itself! The infinite regress arising from the question how the homunculus creates his own internal order has been gloated over enough to need more comment.

Consciousness as a degree of coherence of the mind

Introspectively, we can easily distinguish different degrees of consciousness. Driving your car you are entertaining a conversation with this attractive person. All of a sudden, your passenger asks why you go so fast. You immediately slow down and reply you had not been conscious of your driving, paying attention to the conversation. Now you are conscious of it, perhaps feeling like an idiot to take orders from that person, or to have given the impression of being overexcited.

In this example, a large sector of your mind (the one occupied with driving) was first shut off from communication with other modalities and was then suddenly opened to interact with them, so that you can now comment on it, place it in a social context, remember details and draw conclusions. Along similar lines, you find states of mind that are more or less fractionated into disconnected activities and distracted by various influences, one part of your mind not being able to react to the events in other parts; and other states where all your capacities are highly focused on one point, ready to react should anything important be noticed by any one agent of your mind.

Typical states of high consciousness are those involving intense perceived danger, when we are readying all of our senses and faculties to save us from a threat. Another potent stimulus to raise our level of consciousness is the detection of an obstacle in the performance of a routine task. When thus alerted, we start bringing to bear creative infrastructure to help us solve the problem—diagnostic tools, reference to underlying goals and strategies, memories of similar situations and analogous problems. We perceive such states of mind as on a higher level of consciousness (Mandler 1975), albeit in a temporally more drawn-out way than the more acute states of alert.

Observations of this kind lead us to the conclusion that, even in the waking state, we experience mind states of different degrees of consciousness, and that the difference is made by the degree of coherence, or order, or readiness to communicate, between parts of the brain. Let us, then, describe a state of highest consciousness as one characterized by global order among all the different active processes going on simultaneously in your mind, by maximal coherence and consistency between the different aspects of, and perspectives on, the current subject matter, one in which the full mental power you can muster is thrown onto the same issue, one in which only such material is activated as is relevant to the present interest.

The mind in a state of consciousness can be described as an organism composed of subsystems that are causally connected with each other. Each of the subsystems is actively observing what the others are doing and is ready to react to any significant change in them. (The mind as a 'society of agents' has been discussed by Minsky (1988), although without reference to the consciousness issue.) These reactions are necessary to maintain coherence across all larger and smaller changes in subject matter as they occur. Sometimes very drastic and global changes of state happen, all subsystems switching to a new topic almost instantly, and it may not be easy or possible to track the change back to a local cause in one of the communicating modalities. In other instances the cause for a change may be obvious, such as when an external event hits our senses, draws the attention of many agents to it and causes them to react.

A perhaps enlightening physical metaphor for the conscious state of the brain is a system of communicating cavity resonators supporting acoustic or electromagnetic oscillations. A globally coupled state could be one in which all the different cavities are phase-locked to each other. A local event would shift the phase or frequency of one of the cavities, and the rest of the system could adjust to it by altering phases and frequencies accordingly. A 'subconscious' state would be one in which the system decomposed into subsystems without fixed phase relationships between them, and in a fractionated state like that the oscillations in many cavities would not adjust in response to a local change elsewhere in any consistent way. Another meta- phor from physics refers to systems capable of phase transitions. A good example, discussed as such by Toulouse *et al.* (1986), is a spin glass. Any configuration change in a subsystem of sufficient size can precipitate a more or less global phase transition, many other subsystems reacting such as to lead to minimum free energy again.

What is coherence?

My definition of consciousness as a brain state of a high level of coherence between subsystems requires a definition of the term 'coherence'. One could be tempted to base a definition of mental coherence on insight into the semantic content of the modalities involved and on judgment about mutual relevance of their present state. However, such a definition would be impractical or impossible. In fact, there is reason to believe that it is not necessary to refer explicitly to the semantic content of different modalities and that a simple and quite general definition of coherence can be found.

The essence of coherence is successful collaboration of modalities in solving problems. In order to function properly, the brain needs general mechanisms to diag- nose and establish such collaboration. The brain's creation by evolution antedates the generation of many of the specific agents present in modern man's mind. The structure of the mechanisms of organization must therefore be independent of specific subject matters, and consequently, fairly simple.

Let me speculate a little on what those mechanisms could be. When inspecting an object, it gets reflected differently in different modalities. One important mechanism for defining coherence might be the associative mechanism, by which the patterns simultaneously appearing in the different modalities are synaptically linked to each other. This mechanism can be very potent if attention is quickly shifted between sub- components of a perceived situation and associations are established between all sets of patterns simultaneously lighting up in different places in the brain. Such coincidences as appear only accidentally will not have lasting effects, whereas reliable cross-predictions of events in different modalities will establish permanent relationships.

This establishment of functional relations between modalities makes sense only for fairly elementary sub-patterns of actual situations. Only these have a chance of recurring, entire situations being unique events. (How appropriate sub-patterns of situations are picked out for storage during learning still is to a large extent unknown.) Confronted with a new situation, all modalities are active with new complex patterns that cannot be related directly to each other. If the situation is, however, decomposed into known elementary patterns, the relationships between the complex patterns in the different modalities can be disambiguated and useful maps between them can be pieced together. The price for this disambiguation and structuring of relationships is narrowly focused attention and the necessity to scan sequentially previously learned sub-patterns.

According to this analysis, coherence and consequently consciousness are only possible at the expense of restricting scenes to definite interpretations in terms of known sub-patterns. This point has been emphasized by Kahneman (1973), and according to Posner (1987, p. 153) 'the key to understanding the nature of conscious attention is its limited capacity'. The significance and depth of this connection between coherence and restriction or limitation of substance is far from being fully grasped.

The mind as a historical process

According to the coherence definition I am advocating here, only those brain states are conscious in which as many modalities as possible are functionally coupled to each other. One important aspect of this coupling is that modalities have to be disposed to react to changes and events taking place in any of the others. This leads to an operational test and a basis for an experimental procedure: create some appropriate and unexpected changes in individual modalities and see whether the others react in appropriate ways: if they do, that mind is conscious. There are several difficulties with this experiment, not the least of which is the danger of altering the subject's state of consciousness. Nevertheless, we use it all the time to test the state of consciousness or awareness of others, creating test stimuli too weak to attract attention, but able to arouse a perceptible reaction in an attentive mind (whispering, for instance, the question: are you awake?).

Any definition of coherence based on causal connectedness within the mind and with the environment must rely on the introduction of events that could not have been expected. Otherwise any 'effect' could be the result of anticipation or of stored patterns rather than a causal effect of the observed event. It is therefore important to make the distinction between logical and historical processes. In a logical process all events can be foreseen in principle. Simple examples are periodic processes and processes produced by play-back from a record. Others are those in which events can be anticipated on the basis of fixed sets of rules. A historic process is one that is dominated by unforeseeable events. Only historic processes attract our attention for any period of time. Our brain is very good at catching regularities and has memory mechanisms to store and retrieve them, in this way quickly trivializing logical processes by detecting their regularity.

Imagine a brain state in which the different modalities all ran down their own process, going through the same sequence of topics, each speaking its own language, but synchronized as a logical process like clockwork, not by interaction. (An approximation to this Gedanken-experiment may be the stereotyped performance of an over-learned piece of music.) We probably would not admit this as a highly conscious process. We would rather be inclined to require an additional test, in which one of the modalities was made to trip, and unless the others adapted to re-establish coherence, we would not call the state conscious. By the same token, were we to discover that on the third planet of Sirius there was a civilization that had gone through the exact same stages of development like ours in perfect synchrony, we would not conclude that one of them had been aware of the other all along, but would rather insist on signs of causal connection before according that attribute. These would have to be based on random, unforeseen events in one civilization and reactions to them in the other.

From the causal criterion for the state of consciousness, it is clear that a snapshot of a brain or of a mind, taken with a super-cerebroscope, cannot tell us at all whether that organism was in a conscious state: we could not perform causal tests. Indeed, the argument makes clear that it is misleading to speak of a conscious *state* at all: we should always speak of a process to be observed over some stretch of time. The empirical test for causality requires the creation of sets of events and could not possibly be due to accidental coincidence, or to relations pre-established at an earlier time (like Leibniz' 'pre-stabilized harmony' between mind and body). Our method for doing so is to create events that could not possibly have been predicted (in their timing, for instance) and to test whether they have consistent consequences.

Thus, consciousness cannot be conceived as a static configuration, but only as a historic process in time. This, then, leads to another Gedanken-experiment: use the super-cerebroscope to record the brain process over a whole interval of time and store the result on a magnetic tape. Would that tape (or a 'slave brain' controlled in detail by it) be conscious? To make the question more pointed, assume the recorded period contained clear examples of events that evidently were unexpected by the brain, and the record showed that each and every time all the different agents had reacted appropriately. I think we are all inclined to say that the recorded brain process was a conscious one, but that nevertheless the tape itself was not conscious, because it certainly could not react to stimuli thrown at it: the replay of the tape would be a logical, not a historical, process.

Subconscious states (and their role in creativity)

Subconscious states can be interpreted as those in which many of the agents in the brain are not functional or are not coherent with each other. Dreams, for instance, can be understood in many of their aspects as a result of temporary dysfunction in important modalities. In a dream I may imagine events as real—I fly, or I meet a person actually deceased, or I walk through a door in my house into a non-existent room—that my waking brain would perhaps allow me to imagine, but not without telling me at the same time that they were unreal and should not be taken as a basis for action. So in my dream, the machinery for handling the reality status of an event —real and present, or real and past, or future but quite possible, or pure fancy, etc.— is not functional. For a discussion of subconscious, hypnotic states as states of reduced communication between sub-systems, see Hilgard (1977).

Subconscious activity may go on in our mind while we are consciously engaged in another matter. We usually find out about such activity in indirect ways, by discovering effects that cannot be attributed to mind processes that we remember, or if we remember them, cannot be traced back to a reason or purpose or to an act of will. Our basis for classifying mind processes as subconscious is the judgment that one or several important modalities have not contributed properly to the process.

Apparently, the lack of functionality of modalities, or their lack of coordination, does not correspond to sheer lack of neural activity. In fact, electroencephalograms and other signals recorded from the healthy brain suggest that the whole brain is always active. The lack of mutual engagement of modalities, or the total absence of some of them as active agents, in our mind is probably due instead to the lack of correspondence, or coordination, or resonance, and therefore proper interaction, between sub-processes. A completely unconscious state of mind, in this image, is one in which there is a very low level of coherence between subsystems, to the extent that one cannot talk of a functional state at all, the brain not capable of reacting to any event altogether.

A thought can establish itself in the mind only if none of the participating modalities throws in its veto. In a fully conscious state this is a very restrictive condition. Since among the modalities there are some that tell us how similar situations have been handled in the past, the conscious state has a tendency to restrict us to trodden paths. Disengaging modalities from a process liberates it from constraints and gives it more freedom to be creative (but also to err, of course). Poincaré's (1954) description of creative processes is very instructive: work at the problem intensely and consciously (and just bear the frustration of not being able to solve it right away). Then do something else: engage your conscious mind in other activities and let your subconscious silently do its work. When you come back to the problem, you may find that all of a sudden the pieces fall into place and you see the solution in a flash. This account easily jibes with the coherence definition of consciousness: while many of the usual modalities are out, being engaged in everyday activities, some idle agents are on their own, engaged in play among themselves in ways that would never be permitted by some others, and before those come back patterns have been found and locked in that are novel and crucial to the solution sought.

Minimal requirements for consciousness

It would be a ridiculous proposition to expect a system of coupled cavities, which I used as a physical metaphor, to be conscious as soon as it is pervaded by intimate causal connections. The difference to the brain must lie in the nature of the modalities and the relationships among them and with the environment. The essential property of the brain and its modalities is appropriate perceptual and motor coupling to the environment: the agents of the brain are there to organize behaviour. In order to be able to do so, any significant change in the environment must be appropriately reflected in the brain. This condition is a direct continuation of the coherence theory of consciousness and establishes the connection between consciousness and biological significance.

When speaking of the set of modalities required for a conscious mind, one might consider a concept of simple additiveness, each sensory modality contributing just one more facet to the model of the world created internally. The collection of modalities that we require would then just be an accident of our own evolutionary history. We happen to have a certain complement of modalities and customarily require all of them to be involved in a mental state to be called conscious. If we were dolphins, we would also ask for echo-acoustic processes to be part of a conscious thought. Turning this argument around, the debate about the existence of consciousness in a monkey or dog would be more of a quantitative issue than a qualitative one.

Brains may differ along several dimensions. One is the resolution of the raster with which modalities describe the world, the number of fibres in the optic or auditory nerves or the number of muscle fibres that can be controlled independently, for instance. An important difference between a mouse and a monkey is certainly one of resolution. Another dimension is extra perceptual modalities, such as colour vision or echo-location. Still another is complements of functional schemata with which to structure the environment. Examples relevant to man are the usage of tools, long-range planning, language, or cultural activities such as music or mathematics.

All of these dimensions add to the volume of consciousness and make it richer, or functionally more effective. But let us pose the question whether there is a clear-cut threshold below which we cannot possibly speak of consciousness, or whether it will always remain a matter of taste where we stop talking about consciousness, or a matter of just gradual reduction, when going down the ladder of complexity in the animal kingdom.

The decisive issue is whether the organism can couple to the environment in a meaningful way, whether it can successfully react to external events, whether it can survive in a historical world (and not just a logical world, for which an automaton may be fit). A minimal arrangement must certainly include two modalities, a sensory and a motor one, plus an adaptive translation mechanism between the two. To be sure, the two are required already for the more trivial reason that the organism has to be able to sense trouble and to move to avoid it. But beyond that the coupling of sensation and motility seem to be required for the establishment of functional coherence with the environment, a purely perceptual organism never being able to create a sensible reflection of the environment. It has been argued (Dru *et al.* 1975; Held and Hein 1963) that in order for learning to occur there has to be a motor system to create sensory events actively, that passive learning is not possible.

The situation relevant for the appearance of consciousness, then, is an environment characterized by a historical process and an organism with sensory and motor modalities between which translation is a non-trivial matter. We *want* this translation to be a non-trivial problem because otherwise we would call the organism an automaton, a purely logical entity (like a protozoan swimming up a chemical gradient). And the translation *has to be* non-trivial for the organism to establish coherence with the environment: the only source of reliable knowledge is the establishment of highly non-trivial and therefore highly significant relationships between modalities.

It may be that coherence between modalities and with the environment can only be established with the help of objective representations. When my finger touches an object in front of me, my eye is able with great precision to predict the moment when my sense of touch will record the actual contact. This agreement can only be reached reliably if the participating modalities, vision, kinaesthesia, and touch, separately have a correct representation of the actual situation. Similarly, translation of Chinese into English (taken as two modalities) is not possible as a logical process without reference to a representation of the subject matter spoken about. Representation and meaning (Mephisto's 'Schein des Himmelslichts' in Goethe's Faust), so much taken as the very essence of consciousness, would therefore be a functional must and not a superfluous luxury.

The representation a brain possesses of its environment is not a static entity, perhaps something like a description to some degree of precision, akin to a photograph, to which the brain converged after some time of exploration and learning (a view criticized by Freeman and Skarda (1990)). We know an environment only relative to the activities we have organized in it. A tool with which we are intimately familiar will, for instance, take on a totally new life if we want to depict it in a drawing. The combinations of scenes and functional aspects are inexhaustible. When I speak of representation, then, I have to speak as much of the brain's potential to establish new objective properties of the environment relative to new activities as of the knowledge accumulated in past activities.

Turning to the simple end of the scale of animals, does a fly have its own low level of consciousness? After all, even a fly has modalities that can be in coherent functional states. To me the issue boils down to asking whether the fly is a logical device, an automaton, or whether it can flexibly react to new situations and create its own primitive representation of environmental facts. I would not be surprised if it could.

What about machines? An automaton has a fixed (though possibly large) set of reaction patterns all of which are premeditated by the designer: an automaton is a logical and not a historical animal. It cannot create representations of the world (although the designer may put some of his in the machine). Any talk about machines that translate natural languages (Searle 1980) belongs to the realm of science fiction. No existing automaton displays any faculty to put us in doubt whether it had consciousness. The situation will be fundamentally changed once we understand the principle of autonomously learning organisms (as discussed by von der Malsburg (1985)). That this principle can certainly be formulated algorithmically itself is as irrelevant as the fact that a thermodynamic system can be simulated on a computer—nobody takes it as an automaton for that reason.

Conclusion

Unfortunately, my definition of consciousness as a state of high coherence among modalities has to rely intensely on implicit features of the environment and of the working brain itself. Compare this to the delightful explicitness of formal systems and universal Turing machines! My definition is not constructive: there is a proof of existence in the working brain, but before we can perform the test of building experimental organisms endowed with consciousness we will have to understand the brain much better.

Some authors discuss consciousness as if it were pure luxury, a largely super-fluous feature over and above the biological function of the brain. If my definition does indeed address the essence of the phenomenon, then consciousness and proper function of the brain are just two sides of the same coin.

Much of the confusion that sometimes dominates discussions of consciousness arises because different people take very different aspects of our mind as the essence of the matter. One reaction to this could be that the definition of consciousness is an ill-defined issue, or a personal one, or both. I am, to the contrary, convinced that consciousness is fundamentally a rather well-defined phenomenon.

I take it as a reassuring sign that the aspect of inter-agent communication posited in my definition of consciousness is well reflected in traditional terminology. The Latin roots of the word 'conscious' mean 'being privy to', 'sharing knowledge'. The words 'attention' or 'to attend to' seem to derive their meaning from the image of a person orienting himself towards a thing or matter, getting ready to react to it. In the English language there are, in addition, the words 'awareness' and 'being aware of', which are translated in many languages synonymously with 'consciousness' and 'conscious of', although they are slightly more specialized to processes of per-ception. We use all of these expressions also when speaking of inter-human rela-tions, as when I ask you, for instance, whether you are aware that we have a lunch appointment later today, meaning: do you know of it and are you ready to take the necessary action? This usage is simply to be applied to the mind itself as if it was composed of different persons interacting with each other—in the example just given: 'Is the memory and action-planning part of your brain coherent with the past lunch-appointment event in the linguistic modality of it?' Here, as in so many cases, expressions of common parlance contain very deep insight, a fact of which philosophy has profited so extensively.

With my basic stance—that consciousness does not reside in any specialized faculty of mind or localized structure of the brain, but is a cooperative phenomenon of the whole brain or mind—I am far from being alone. It is highly recommendable to read in this context a discussion of the problem by the famous neuropsychologist Luria (1978), which may be summed up in the citation (on p. 31): 'The cerebral basis of man's complex, semantic, system-based conscious activity must be sought in the combined activity of discrete brain systems, each of which makes its own special contribution to the work of the functional system as a whole.' The electrophysiologist E. Roy John (1976) expresses similar opinions: 'I believe that "mind", under which rubric are subsumed such phenomena as consciousness, subjective experience, the concept of self, and self-awareness, is an *emergent property* of sufficiently complex and appropriately organized matter.' (p. 1). 'The content of consciousness is the sum of all information processes in all the various functional systems of the brain. The information in each area comprises a coherent temporal pattern.' (p. 39). Many others could be cited.

Although I cannot easily see a way to prove it, I find it conceivable that the *qualia* issue may be solved by stating that the quality of the taste of strawberries, or of the colour red, or of the pain when my toe hits an obstacle is identical with all the processes and reactions that the sensation provokes or could provoke in my mind. (Maybe the most puzzling examples are those where the rational mind, represented by language, is most incapable of expressing those reactions.) So the colour red may be gone for me when the colour area of my brain is destroyed (accepting for the moment that claim in the literature), but that does not prove that the essence of colour resides in that area. You still need the whole brain to get to that essence, although all those reflection patterns aroused from the colour area may vanish forever with its destruction. The point is illuminated to some extent by a metaphor. When trying to grasp the meaning of money it does not help to stare at a dollar bill. The bill by itself has little value. It derives its significance entirely from the patterns of beliefs and habits of people out there: hand it to a merchant and he is ready to give you something for it, his reaction depending in turn entirely on his expectation what others would sell for the bill or how much money they would be ready to pay for the object. Similarly, it does not help staring at the neuron whose signal is linked with some elementary sensation—the essence of that sensation is in the reaction patterns of the whole brain (and body!).

If my discussion of consciousness is of any validity, the issue can be seen to run very much against the grain of science as we know it. Science has always had its great triumphs when and where it succeeded in subdividing complex phenomena into very simple paradigms. Doing the same to the brain we are in danger of being left with bits and pieces in our hand. Using the simile of just now, in order to understand the value of money, we should not stare at dollar bills, but rather try to understand the system of beliefs and habits that give money its power. By the same token, none of the isolated components of the brain can be expected to hold the essence of consciousness. That is rather in the modes of interaction of all parts of the brain, and maybe even in the way the brain is integrated into the social world and the world at large. In this sense science may never understand consciousness in its substance. Nevertheless, it may still be a subject for good science, finding, for instance, ways to measure the level of consciousness of brain states. One such approach could just concentrate on statistical properties of signals exchanged between different modalities, or signal correlations between them, as a measure of the extent to which they are functionally coupled. Nature may, after all, have been friendly enough to provide us with an easily picked-up signature of the state. Who knows, perhaps this signature is indeed nothing but a simple oscillatory signal, as advocated by Crick and Koch (1990)?

References

Crick, F. and Koch, C. (1990). Towards a neurobiological theory of consciousness. *Seminars in the Neurosciences*, **2**, 263–75.

Descartes, R. (1662). *Traité de l'Homme*. Paris. (1662/1972) Treatise on man. Translated by T.S. Hall. Harvard University Press.

Dru, D., Walker, J.P., and Walker, J.B. (1975). Self-produced locomotion restores visual capacity after striate lesions. *Science*, **187**, 265–6.

Erdelyi, M.H. (1974). A new look at the new look: perceptual defense and vigilance. *Psychological Review*, **81**, 1–25.

Freeman, W.J. and Skarda, C.A. (1990). Representations: who needs them? In *Brain, organization and memory: cells, systems, and circuits* (ed. J.L. McGaugh, N.M. Weinberger, and G. Lynch), pp. 375–80. Oxford University Press, New York.

Held, R. and Hein, A. (1963). Movement-produced stimulation in the development of visually guided behaviour. *Journal of Comparative and Physiological Psychology*, **56**, 872–6.

Hilgard, E.R. (1977). *Divided consciousness: multiple controls in human thought and action*. Wiley, New York.

John, E.R. (1976). A model of consciousness. In *Consciousness and self-regulation* (ed. G.E. Schwartz and D. Shapiro), pp. 1–50. Wiley, Chichester.

Kahneman, D. (1973). *Attention and effort*. Prentice Hall, Englewood Cliffs, NJ.

Luria, A.R. (1978). The human brain and conscious activity. In *Consciousness and self-regulation*, Vol. 2 (ed. G.E. Schwartz and D. Shapiro), pp. 1–36. Wiley, Chichester.

Mandler, G. (1975). *Mind and emotion*. Wiley, New York.

Minsky, M. (1988). *The society of mind*. Simon and Schuster, New York.

Poincaré, H. (1954). Cited in *The creative process* (ed. M.T. Ghiselin and J. Brewster), pp. 22–31. University of California Press, Berkeley.

Posner, M.I. (1987). *Chronometric explorations of mind*. Erlbaum, Hillsdale, NJ.

Searle, J.R. (1980). Minds, brains and programs. *Behavioural and Brain Sciences*, **3**, 417–58.

Shallice, T. (1978). The dominant action system: an information processing approach to consciousness. In *The stream of consciousness: scientific investigations into the flow of human experience* (ed. K.S. Pope and J.L. Singer), pp. 117–57. Plenum, New York.

Sperry, R.W. (1966). Brain bisection and consciousness. In *Brain and conscious experience* (ed. J. Eccles), p. 298. Springer, Berlin.

Toulouse, G., Dehaene, S., and Changeux, J.P. (1986). A spin glass model of learning by selection. *Proceedings of the National Academy of Sciences (USA)*, **83**, 1695.

von der Malsburg, C. (1985). Algorithms, brain, and organization. In *Dynamical systems and cellular automata* (ed. J. Demongeot, E. Golès, and M. Tchuente), pp. 235–46. Academic Press, London.

14

Neurodynamics and brain mechanisms

JACK D. COWAN

Consciousness is the creature of Rhythm ... If consciousness is the product of rhythm all things are conscious, for all have motion, and all motion is rhythmic ...

Ambrose Bierce 1924

Introduction

Whatever the nature of consciousness, everyone will agree that it needs a brain, and that brain states at some level (from single neurons to entire cortices and beyond) are involved in it. Following the neurologist Sherwood (1957), define *awareness* as a state in which an organism reacts to stimuli in a way determined by its nervous system and its history, and *consciousness* as a state in which an organism is able to make an observation[1] of reality[2] and is aware of this, its own act. As Sherwood notes,

... such a state can be recognised only through logical communication from the organism, which must bear witness to its own state. The substrate for consciousness—the central nervous system—must be such that its ability to accept, sort, and transmit information is superior to [that of] a system capable only of awareness.

In this paper, I assume that large-scale brain states involving the activities of at least 10^2 neurons form the substrate for consciousness, and give an account of some of the dynamics of such neural groups. My intention throughout this paper is to illustrate the point that many aspects of awareness and consciousness that are generally ascribed to higher cognitive functions can be explained simply in terms of the low-level activities of neural groups or networks.

Neurons as synchrony detectors

In building a useful mathematical model of the dynamics of neurons and neural groups or networks, one must compromise between the complexities involved in the triggering of action potentials, and the simplifications required to obtain analytical tractability. The Hodgkin–Huxley equations (Hodgkin and Huxley 1952) provide a comprehensive account of the action potential, but are far too complicated to be used in network modelling. The 'integrate-and-fire' model introduced by Uttley (1956) and Beurle (1956) provides a simpler basis to begin the analysis of neural networks.

In such a model, neurons can be in one of three states: *quiescent, activated,* or *refractory.* In the quiescent state, neurons act like leaky integrators—incoming action potentials act across synapses to generate post-synaptic potentials of about 1 mV which slowly decay with a time constant of from 3 to 5 ms. These potentials are summed (generally in a non-linear fashion) and if the sum exceeds a *threshold,* the neuron is activated; if not the sum decays back to the resting potential. Following activation, which lasts for about 1 ms (the duration of the action potential), the neuron enters the (relative) refractory state in which its effective threshold is initially much larger than the (resting) threshold. The neuron can be reactivated during the refractory state, but only by a strong stimulus; if not its threshold returns to rest with a time constant of from 5 to 50 ms. Thus each neural state has a time constant associated with it. Given that in the resting state neural transmembrane potentials are about −70 mV, and neural resting thresholds correspond to a transmembrane potential of about −55 mV, at least 15 more-or-less simultaneous action potentials are needed to trigger a neural response. Cortical neurons are not of course point objects, but can be as large as 2 to 3 mm in vertical extent, and the neural membrane, that is the dendrite, is the site of thousands of synapses. Thus only a very small fraction of such synapses need be simultaneously activated to trigger a neural response. This is sometimes referred to as *spatial summation.* It is also possible to trigger a response via a single synapse through a *burst* of action potentials—a phenomenon referred to as *temporal summation.* Such properties lead to the notion that neurons are specialized, not only to transmit information, but to detect *synchronous activity* in the set of neurons (or receptors) from which they receive signals. One might expect networks of neurons to generate and propagate such activity. In such a case, one might also expect the refractory properties of neurons to shape the patterns of activation. In what follows I describe a variety of such effects and try to use them as part of the substrate referred to above.

Neurodynamics

The relevant equations were developed some twenty years ago by Wilson and Cowan (1972, 1973). If refractory states are neglected, these equations take the form:

$$\tau \frac{dE(\underline{x},\ t)}{dt} = -E(\underline{x},t) + [1 - \Delta_a E]\Phi_e[\tau \int_{-\infty}^{\infty} w_{ee}(\underline{x} - \underline{x}')\ E(\underline{x}',\ t)d\underline{x}'$$

$$-\tau \int_{-\infty}^{\infty} w_{ei}(\underline{x} - \underline{x}')\ I(\underline{x}',\ t)d\underline{x}' - \theta_{eq}]$$

$$\tau \frac{dI(\underline{x},\ t)}{dt} = -I(\underline{x},\ t) + [1 - \Delta_a I]\Phi_i[\tau \int_{-\infty}^{\infty} w_{ie}(\underline{x} - \underline{x}')\ E(\underline{x}',t)d\underline{x}'$$

$$-\tau \int_{-\infty}^{\infty} w_{ii}(\underline{x} - \underline{x}')\ I(\underline{x}',t)d\underline{x}' - \theta_{iq}] \tag{14.1}$$

where $E(\underline{x},t)$ and $I(\underline{x},t)$ are, respectively, the proportions of excitatory and inhibitory cells becoming activated per unit time at the location $\underline{x}$ in a sheet or slab of neural tissue (averaged over a duration of τ ms), Δ_a is the duration of the active state, and $w_{ij}(\underline{x} - \underline{x}')$ gives the synaptic strength or weight of connections at $\underline{x}$ to cells of class i (excitatory or inhibitory) from all cells of class j (excitatory or inhibitory), a distance $|\underline{x} - \underline{x}'|$ away.

Attractor dynamics

It is instructive to examine the solutions of these equations for the total proportions of activated excitatory and inhibitory neurons, $E(t) = \int_{-\infty}^{\infty} E(\underline{x}, t)\, dx$ and $I(t) = \int_{-\infty}^{\infty} I(\underline{x}, t)dx$, respectively, in which case the equations reduce to

$$\tau \frac{dE}{dt} = -E(t) + [1 - \Delta_a E]\Phi_e[k_{ee}E - k_{ei}I + P]$$

$$\tau \frac{dI}{dt} = -I(t) + [1 - \Delta_a I]\Phi_i[k_{ie}E - k_{ii}I + Q] \tag{14.2}$$

where P and Q are external stimuli. These equations can be analysed by *phase plane* methods in which the two loci $E = $ constant and $I = $ constant are plotted in the (E,I) plane, as shown in Fig. 14.1(a). Such a phase plane portrait is obtained when k_{ee} is large and $P = Q = 0$. It can be shown that the stationary state $E = I = 0$ is stable and that there is a second stable state at $E \approx 0.4$, $I \approx 0.13$. Such a state can be realized with initial conditions or by stimulation of suitable intensity. Fig. 14.1(b) shows the steady-state value of E as a function of P with $Q = 0$. It will be seen that switching occurs between $E = 0$ to $E \approx 0.4$ as P varies from -0.3 to $+0.3$ and back. The associated *hysteresis* loop is characteristic of systems which are known as *excitable* (Winfree 1987). Such effects were predicted by Cragg and Temperley (1954), and first found in simulations by Harth *et al.* (1970). Such stable states are now called stationary *attractors*. Thus according to this analysis a slab of neural tissue can exhibit either 'resting' behaviour in which, on average, there is no activity, or 'excited' behaviour in which, on average, approximately 40% of the cells are activated. If $Q \neq 0$ a third stationary attractor exists corresponding to $E = I = 0.23$. Thus, on average about 23% of the cells are activated. In addition to stationary attractors, networks with strong inhibition can instead exhibit stable periodic or oscillatory attractors, known technically as *limit cycles*. Fig. 14.2(a) shows the phase plane and corresponding cycle for such a state, and Fig. 14.2(b) the corresponding values of $E(t)$ averaged over one period and the limit cycle frequency, as functions, of P. It will be seen that there is a threshold value of $P = P_0$, below which the limit cycle is non-existent. At P_0 the average value of $E(t)$ is about 11%, and the limit cycle frequency about 9–10 Hz. The properties described above are stimulus dependent. Any network exhibiting limit cycles for one set of stimuli will show switching and hysteresis for some other set. Recently, Borisyuk and Kirillov (1992) found that

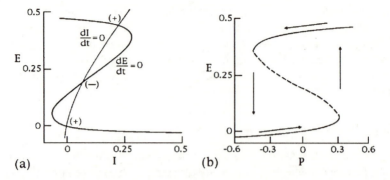

Fig. 14.1 (a) Phase plane diagram of constant excitatory vs. constant inhibitory activity in a spatially homogeneous network of neural elements. Their intersections are either stable (+) or unstable (−). (b) Steady-state values of E as a function of the stimulus $P(Q = 0)$. Solid lines indicate stable states, dashed lines unstable ones. A hysteresis loop is indicated by arrows. This is generated when P is slowly varied through the range ±0.3. Redrawn from Wilson and Cowan (1972).

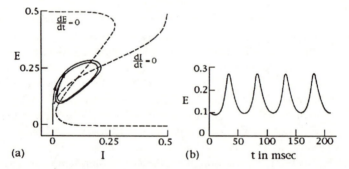

Fig. 14.2 (a) Phase plane diagram of excitatory vs. inhibitory activity in a spatially homogeneous network of neural elements. (b) $E(t)$ for limit cycle shown in (a). $\tau = 8$ ms. Redrawn from Wilson and Cowan (1972).

initial conditions could also affect this outcome. In addition, they found that for some parameter values, long-period oscillations are possible.

Localized vs. propagating activity

These properties can be shown to exist for the more general networks characterized by eqn 14.1. Thus hysteretic switching and cycling of activity can exist in lines, sheets, and slabs of neural tissue. However, with space-dependent interactions new phenomena can emerge. Consider the function $w(\underline{x} - \underline{x}')$, the weight of connections

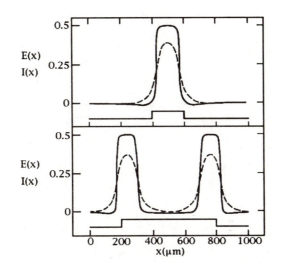

Fig. 14.3 Spatially localized stationary attractors generated in a line of neural tissue by two line stimuli of different widths. $E(x)$ (solid lines), $I(x)$ (dashed lines). Redrawn from Wilson and Cowan (1973).

at the point $\underline{x}$ from all neurons a distance $|\underline{x} - \underline{x}'|$ away. Let this be of the form assumed by Beurle (1956), that is

$$w(\underline{x} - \underline{x}') = b \exp(-|\underline{x} - \underline{x}'|/\sigma)$$

where b is the density of synaptic connections, and σ the space constant giving the decay of $w(\underline{x} - \underline{x}')$ with distance. It follows that in the one-dimensional case, the total synaptic weight is $\int_{-\infty}^{\infty} w(\underline{x} - \underline{x}')d\underline{x}' = 2b\sigma = W$. With reference to eqn 14.1 let us now suppose that $\sigma_{ie} > \sigma_{ee}$, i.e. excitatory to inhibitory connections are longer ranged than excitatory to excitatory ones. This condition on the space-constants leads to what is known as *lateral inhibition*, since local excitation leads to inhibition rather than excitation at distances $|\underline{x} - \underline{x}'| \geqslant \sigma_{ie}$. Under such a condition, stationary states or periodic cycles can remain spatially localized if lateral inhibition is sufficiently strong. Figure 14.3 shows, for example, spatially localized stationary attractors generated in a line of neural tissue by two line stimuli of different widths. The longer one produces edge-enhancement effects that are characteristic of lateral inhibition. Similarly, Fig. 14.4 shows a spatially localized limit cycle generated in response to a constant line stimulus.

In addition, there is also a third possibility: a *metastable* state called 'active transient' (Wilson and Cowan 1973). In this state, the response to a brief localized stimulus continues to increase even after the stimulus ceases, reaches a maximum, and then decays back to the resting state. Figure 14.5 shows two examples of the active transient. In each case the stimulus $P(x,t)$ is a spatial square-wave of width L and amplitude P applied for a duration Δt. By assumption, $P(x,t)$ excites only excitatory

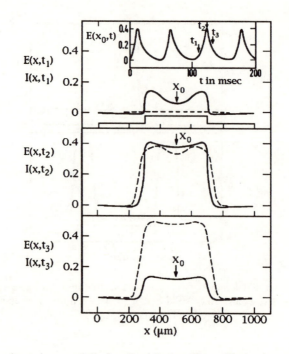

Fig. 14.4 Three phases in a spatially localized limit cycle oscillation in response to a maintained stimulus with the rectangular profile shown at the bottom of the first diagram. $E(x)$ (solid lines), $I(x)$ (dashed lines). Inset shows temporal details of the cycle at the point x_0. Redrawn from Wilson and Cowan (1973).

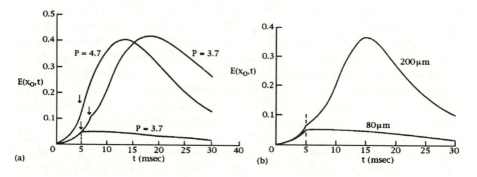

Fig. 14.5 (a) Temporal summation and latency effects in the active transient mode. (b) Spatial summation. Redrawn from Wilson and Cowan (1973).

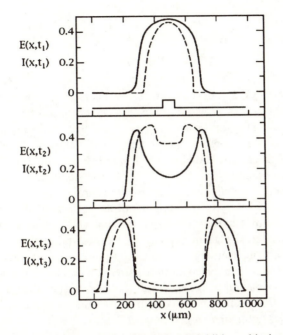

Fig. 14.6 Generation of travelling wave pair under disinhibitory biasing in the limit cycle mode. $E(x)$ (solid lines), $I(x)$ (dashed lines). The region initially stimulated is indicated in the top graph. $t_1 = 20$ ms, $t_2 = 30$ ms, $t_3 = 50$ ms. Redrawn from Wilson and Cowan (1973).

neurons within the tissue. If L is sufficiently small, the response $E(x,t)$ develops a single spatial maximum located at the centre of the stimulated region, and remains localized within it. Figure 14.5 indicates that there is a threshold for the generation of active transients, and that both *temporal* and *spatial summation* are involved: a stimulus $P(x,t)$ generates an active transient only if the product $P \times \Delta t \times L$ is sufficiently large. This indicates that the active transient threshold is a 'charge' threshold, just as is the case for action potentials in axons stimulated by brief shocks.

Finally, if the action of inhibitory neurons is blocked, for example with a constant bias $Q(x,t)$ of amplitude $-Q$, so that the network is 'disinhibited', another new state emerges from the limit cycle state—the propagating wave. Instead of remaining localized, the peak excitatory phase of each limit cycle gives rise to a pair of waves travelling in opposite directions from the region of stimulation. Figure 14.6 shows such an effect. Wave pairs are generated once per cycle as long as the stimulus $P(x,t)$ persists, and each wave travels away from the locus of stimulation without attenuation. It follows that a very brief stimulus will generate a single wave pair, whereas a stimulus of longer duration will generate a succession of such pairs. The propagation velocity is a function of Q and the connectivity parameters b_{ij} and

σ_{ij}, whereas the wavelength depends upon P. For $Q = -30$ and $\sigma_{ie} = 50\,\mu m$ the propagation velocity is 4 cm s^{-1}.

Applications

Wilson and Cowan (1972, 1973) used these results to try to account for numerous experimental observations of neural networks in the neocortex and thalamus of various vertebrates. They suggested, for example, that stationary attractors were the basis for *short term memory* (STM). Cragg and Temperley (1954) had earlier suggested hysteresis effects, and Hebb (1949), in his influential book *Organization of behaviour*, reverberations as a basis for STM. The stationary attractors described above are reverbatory: activity circulates among neurons in excited regions in such a manner that the total activity at each point of the region remains constant and, as described above, shows hysteresis effects. Wilson and Cowan cited the work of Fuster and Alexander (1971) in support of the possibility that cortical neurons exhibit such effects. Concerning the limit cycle or oscillatory mode, Wilson and Cowan suggested that maintained stimulus strengths might be encoded in the frequency of *bursts* of neural activity which would be triggered in this mode. They further suggested that oscillatory activity in various nuclei of the thalamus is in the form of limit cycles, citing the observations of Purpura (1970), who found that under certain conditions, neurons in the ventro-laminar nucleus could only respond to every second pulse in a long train of stimuli, i.e. they showed *frequency demultiplication*. Wilson and Cowan also suggested that the metastable active transient mode was relevant to the interpretation of cortical responses to brief stimuli, such as visual patterns. They noted that active transient responses show both latency effects (it takes longer to develop edge enhancement in response to a weak stimulus than to a stronger one), and size–intensity effects (a strong stimulus appears wider than a weaker one), and that such effects need lateral *excitation* as well as inhibition. Thus some enhancement of the initial effects produced by brief bursts of activity from the retina and lateral geniculate nucleus is needed in the cortex. The implication is that the active transient mode characterizes the responses of primary sensory cortex. Finally, Wilson and Cowan suggested that the propagating wave mode characterizes disinhibited or 'undercut' cortical slabs (Burns 1958, 1968).

Refractory effects

The properties described above are obtained in sheets or slabs of excitatory and inhibitory neurons without refractory states. If one incorporates such states, the dynamics become even more complex. In fact, even a sheet of excitatory neurons can generate and sustain suprisingly complex patterns. Figure 14.7 shows, for example, what occurs in such a sheet following point stimulation. Initially, circular waves know as 'target patterns' propagate from the source of stimulation. After some time such patterns break up and are replaced by *spiral waves*, which continue indefinitely, even in the absence of stimulation. Thus such waves are also stable attractors of the sheet's dynamics.

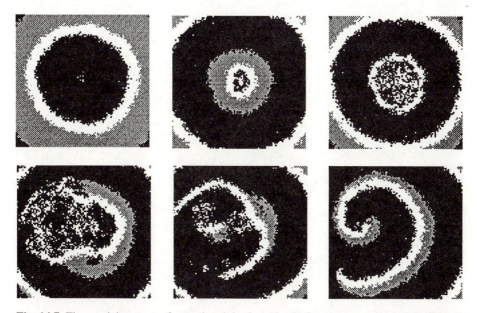

Fig. 14.7 The spatial pattern of neural activity in a sheet of excitatory cells with refractory states, as a function of generation time t: (a) 175, (b) 345, (c) 465, (d) 503, (e) 536, and (f) 749 ms. At $t = 0$ all neurons except the central source are quiescent. At $t = 500$ ms the source is shut off. Colour code: grey = quiescent; white = activated; black = relatively refractory. Redrawn from Milton *et al.* (1993).

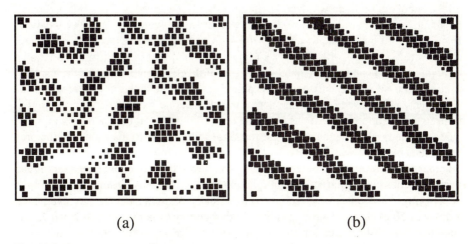

(a)   (b)

Fig. 14.8 (a) Blob pattern formed in the early stages of self-organized pattern formation. (b) Stripe pattern formed in late stages.

Sheets comprising both excitatory and inhibitory neurons with refractory states exhibit even more complex patterns. Figure 14.8 shows, for example, the patterns generated in a spatially homogeneous sheet with isotropic lateral inhibition—i.e. weight patterns are the same everywhere in the sheet—inhibition is longer ranged than excitation, and all patterns are radially symmetric (Ermentrout and Cowan 1979, von der Malsburg and Cowan 1982, Fohlmeister *et al.*, in press). It will be seen that at first such sheets tend to make patches or *blobs* of activated neurons, in a doubly periodic array. Eventually, such a pattern loses its stability, and *stripes* of activated neurons appear in the sheet[3]. Although refractory states are not necessary for the generation of blob and stripe patterns, if they are obtained, the patterns tend to move.

Some 'low-level' explanations of apparently complex phenomena

In this section I discuss a number of applications of the attractor dynamics described previously. The underlying assumptions are that such dynamics provide a substrate for neural information processing, and that many puzzling phenomena usually attributed to higher interpretive or *cognitive* processing can actually be explained in terms of attractor dynamics at a fairly low level of network operation.

Metacontrast or 'backward masking'

As a first example, consider the perceptual masking of a brief visual target stimulus, say a disc, by a second subsequent stimulus, for example an annulus, presented at a location in the visual field that does not overlap that of the disc (Kahneman 1968). A one-dimensional analogue of this experiment was simulated using the active transient mode described earlier. Thus a line of model neural tissue is stimulated with a target bar of given width and (suprathreshold) intensity for 5 ms. Subsequently, masking bars of the same width but greater intensity were presented at locations flanking that of the target. To measure the degree of masking, responses to the target alone were compared with responses to the target and mask. The results are shown in Figure 14.9. It can be seen that the mask has little effect on the maximum response to the target—it mainly affects the decaying phase of the active transient response. However, as discussed earlier, the active transient mode exhibits temporal summation, so that an appropriate measure of the response to the target is not the maximum value reached, but the integral of the response over its entire duration, i.e. the area under the curve shown in Figure 14.9, $\int_0^t E(x,t')dt'$. With this measure it will be seen that masking is a monotonic decreasing function of the delay between the target and mask presentations. Such a masking function is called 'type A' (Kohlers 1962). Type A masking functions measured psychophysically show strong effects even with a delay of 50 ms if the mask is of much higher contrast than the target. However, as shown in Fig. 14.5, stronger stimuli generate active transients with shorter peak latencies, so the neural response to a high-contrast mask may be expected to propagate through the visual pathway at a much higher velocity than the target response,

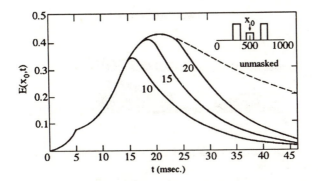

Fig. 14.9 Type A metacontrast effects in the active transient mode. $E(x_0, t)$ is the excitatory response at the point of target presentation, as shown in the upper right. Figures on the curves are times when the masking bars are presented. The dashed line indicates the unmasked response. Redrawn from Wilson and Cowan (1973).

and in fact to reach the cortex concurrently with the target response even if initiated some 50 ms later. This implies that cortical interactions underlie type A masking, a conclusion supported by dichoptic experiments in which masking is obtained with the target in one eye and the mask in the other (Kohlers 1962; Kahneman 1968).

There is another type of masking (Kohlers and Rosner 1960) called 'type B' by Kohlers (1962), in which the mask is presented about 50 ms after the target, in the same location and at the same contrast. Under such conditions masking is obtained. If the delay is shorter or longer, the effect diminishes. This cannot be simulated with a simple sheet of excitatory and inhibitory neurons. One possibility raised by Wilson and Cowan (1973) is that a two-sheet model of the lateral geniculate nucleus (LGN) and cortex, with *corticofugal fibres* back-projecting from the visual cortex to the LGN, could account for type B masking. The appropriate delay from the LGN to the cortex back to the LGN would have to be about 50 ms. On one model this implies a delay from the LGN to the cortex of about 25 ms, corresponding to a temporal frequency of 40 Hz. Can this be the source of the ubiquitous 40 Hz oscillations in visual cortex responses observed by Gray and Singer (1989)? Another interesting and related possibility is suggested by Kawato's bidirectional theory of visual processing (Kawato *et al.* 1993) in which the 50 ms masking delay (and the 40 Hz oscillations) could be a consequence of the loop required to compute forward and inverse optic models.

Short-term active memory

As a second example, we consider the phenomenon known as 'short-term active memory'. As noted previously, early observations by Fuster and Alexander (1971) of persistent firing of cortical neurons following training for delayed response discriminations led Wilson and Cowan (1973) to propose that localized stationary attractors form the substrate for such effects. Recently, Zipser (1991) and Zipser

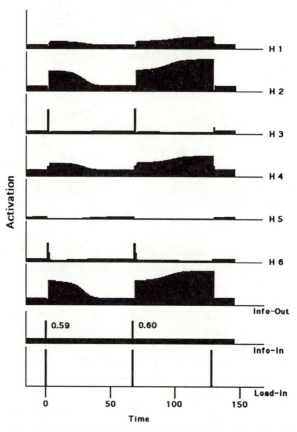

Fig. 14.10 Attractor dynamics of the Zipser *et al.* model. Redrawn from Zipser *et al.* (1993).

et al. (1993) have developed a much more elaborate model for such discriminations, based on essentially the same idea. What Zipser *et al.* did was to use the technology of supervised learning in artificial neural networks, that is recurrent back-propagation (Williams and Zipser 1989) to train such a network on the same task. The results were striking—neurons developed in the network that showed more or less the same kind of persistent firing during the interval between cue presentation and task execution as observed in cortical neurons. At first the training was performed in a noise-free situation. Under noisy conditions, the resulting model firing patterns followed even more closely the observed cortical patterns. Figures 14.10 and 14.11 show some of the details. In Fig. 14.10, the noise-free case, firing patterns are shown which indicate clearly the tendency for model neurons to fire at persistent rates consistent with the existence of a stationary attractor. In Fig. 14.11, the noisy case, the similarity between model neuron firing patterns and cortical

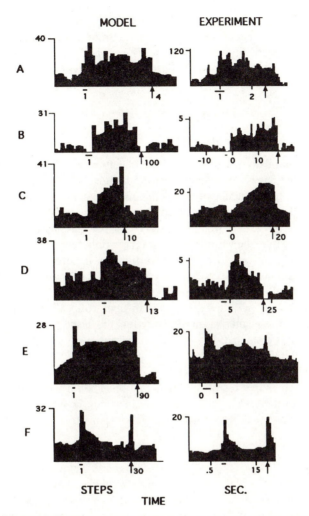

Fig. 14.11 Comparison of the temporal activity patterns of cortical neurons with hidden unis from model networks during real and simulated delayed response discriminations. Redrawn from Zipser *et al.* (1993).

neurons is clear. Note also the last comparison, labelled F in Fig. 14.11, in which two instances are shown of the second class of neurons found in both the model networks after training, and in the cortex, namely those which fire only at cue presentation and task execution. Such neurons may be said to 'gate' the attractor neurons, switching them on and off whenever it is appropriate.

It is evident that the attractor dynamics model described above, *mutatus mutandis* can also be used to provide an account of the observations described by Miyashita (this volume, Chapter 9). Interestingly, another model for such data has been published recently (Amit *et al.* 1994) based on the training of an associative memory network. The results are similar to those of Zipser *et al.* in that the resulting model neuron firing patterns can be made to correspond closely to observed patterns, and they also support the idea that cortical networks store information in the form of stationary attractors.

Geometric visual hallucinations

As a third and final example of low-level explanatory models for complex pheno-mena, consider the nature of geometric visual hallucinations. These are commonly experienced under the influence of psychedelic substances or certain anaesthetics, or on waking or falling asleep, or during conditions of sensory deprivation or medita-tion. Similar patterns can be found preserved in petroglyphs and cave paintings. Klüver (1971) classified the various reported images into four groups, which he called *form constants*: (a) gratings, lattices, fretworks, filigrees, honeycombs, and chessboards, (b) cobwebs, (c) tunnels and funnels, alleys, cones, vessels, and (d) spirals. Typical funnel and spiral hallucinations are shown in Figs 14.12 and 14.13. Various reports indicate that such images, although they are difficult to localize in space, are stable with respect to eye movements; that is, they remain in the visual field despite eye movement. This suggests that they are generated not in the eyes, but in the brain.

Assuming that hallucinations arise spontaneously in the visual cortex, and given the fact that all observers report seeing Klüver's form constants or variations on them, the common properties of the hallucinations should yield information about the architecture of the visual cortex. We can, in effect, investigate that architecture on the hypothesis that such patterns determine the geometry of visual hallucinations.

Eye–brain maps

The first step in the investigation is to calculate what visual hallucinations look like, not in the standard coordinates of the visual field—polar coordinates—but in the coordinates of the primary visual cortex. It is well established that there is a topo-graphic map of the visual field in the primary visual cortex. However, the metric of the map is highly distorted. The central portion of the visual field from $r = 0°$ to $r = 1°$ or so, has a much bigger representation in the visual cortex than it does in the visual field. The reason for this is that there is a non-uniform distribution of retinal ganglion cells, each of which sends an *axon* to the brain. This allows one to calculate the details of the eye–brain map (Ermentrout and Cowan 1979). Let ρ_R be the pack-ing density of nerve cells in the retina, and let ρ_C be the corresponding density in visual cortex. Then $\rho_R r_R dr_R d\theta_R$ is the number of retinal axons in a retinal element of area $r_R dr_R d\theta_R$. By hypothesis, these axons connect topographically to the cells in an element of area $dx_C dy_C$ in the primary visual cortex, i.e. to $\rho_C dx_C dy_C$ cortical cells. (Thus the assumption is that the visual cortex is effectively flat and locally Cartesian.) Evidence indicates that ρ_C is approximately constant, whereas ρ_R falls off

Fig. 14.12 A typical funnel hallucination. Redrawn from Oster (1970).

Fig. 14.13 A typical spiral hallucination. Redrawn from Oster (1970).

from the origin of the visual field, i.e. from the *fovea*, with an inverse square law. From this one can calculate the Jacobian of the retino-cortical transformation, and hence cortical coordinates $\{x_c, y_c\}$ as functions of the retinal coordinates $\{r_R, \theta_R\}$. The resulting coordinate transformation takes the form:

$$x_C = \frac{1}{\varepsilon^{\frac{1}{2}}} \ln\left[\frac{\varepsilon^{\frac{1}{2}}}{w_0} r_R + \left(1 + \frac{\varepsilon}{w_0^2} r_R^2\right)^{\frac{1}{2}}\right], \quad y_C = \frac{r_R}{w_0} \frac{\theta_R}{\left(1 + \frac{\varepsilon}{w_0^2} r_R^2\right)^{\frac{1}{2}}}.$$

Data from human visual psychophysics allow one to fix the constants at $w_0 = 0.295$ and $\varepsilon = 0.051$.

The transformation has two important limiting cases: (a) close to the fovea, $r_R < 1°$, it reduces to:

$$x_C = \frac{r_R}{w_0}, \quad y_C = \frac{r_R \theta_R}{w_0}.$$

and (b), sufficiently far away from the fovea, $r_R \geq 1°$, it becomes:

$$x_C = \frac{1}{\varepsilon^{\frac{1}{2}}} \ln \frac{\varepsilon^{\frac{1}{2}} r_R}{w_0}, \quad y_C = \frac{\theta_R}{\varepsilon^{\frac{1}{2}}}.$$

Figure 14.14 shows the corresponding retino-cortical map in case (b), with y_C scaled by a factor $2/\pi$. (a) is just a scaled version of the identity transformation, and (b) is a scaled version of the *complex logarithm*.[4] To see this let $z_R = x_R + iy_R = r_R \exp[i\theta_R]$ be the complex representation of a retinal point $(x_R, y_R) = (r_R, \theta_R)$, then $z_C = x_C + iy_C = \ln(r_R \exp[i\theta_R]) = \ln r_R + i\theta_R$.

Hallucinations as cortical stripes

Given that the retino-cortical map is generated by the complex logarithm (except very near the fovea), it is easy to calculate the action of the transformation on *circles*, *rays*, and *logarithmic spirals* in the visual field. Circles of constant r_R in the visual field simply become vertical lines in the cortex, whereas rays of constant θ_R become horizontal lines in the cortex. Interestingly, logarithmic spirals become *oblique* lines in the visual field: the equation of such a spiral is just $\theta_R = a \ln r_R$, whence $y_C = ax_C$ under the action of $z_R \rightarrow z_C$. It follows from this that many of the geometric visual hallucinations seen as circles, rays, and spirals, in fact logarithmic spirals, in the visual field correspond roughly to *stripe* patterns of nerve cell excitation at various angles in the visual cortex. Figures 14.15 and 14.16 show the action of the transform on the funnel and spiral hallucinations shown in Figs 14.12 and 14.13. It follows from this that if one can construct a network of model nerve cells which will spontaneously become active in a variety of stripe patterns, whenever it is destabilized,

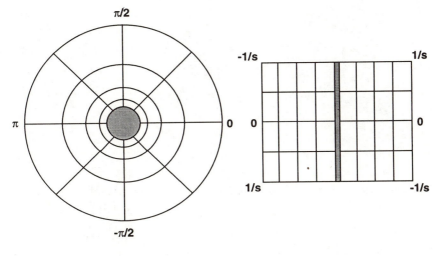

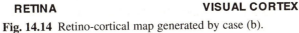

RETINA   **VISUAL CORTEX**

Fig. 14.14 Retino-cortical map generated by case (b).

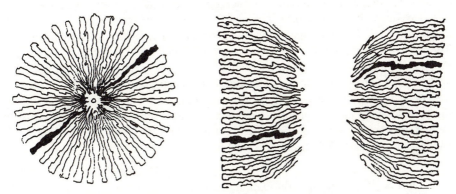

Fig. 14.15 Action of the retino-cortical transform on the funnel hallucination.

then one will have provided a very plausible theory for the generation of geometric visual hallucination patterns. The way to do this is described in the earlier section on refractory effects. It was in fact the content of the paper by Ermentrout and Cowan (1979).

Edge detectors in the cortex

The discussion above describes the theory of geometric visual hallucination patterns as it was formulated a decade ago. It is in fact rather naive in the sense that the visual

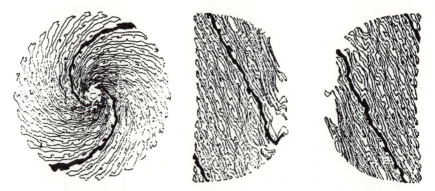

Fig. 14.16 Action of the retino-cortical transform on the spiral hallucination.

cortex is represented as if it were just a *cortical retina*. In fact cortical cells do much more than just signalling the position in a transformed version of the visual field. In particular, most cortical cells signal the local *orientation* of a contour in the visual field.

How are such cells interconnected? Recent developments with voltage-sensitive dyes have made it possible to see how the cells are actually distributed in the cortex, and a variety of vital stains have made it possible to see how they are interconnected. The results indicate that the distribution of edge detectors is roughly π-periodic, in that approximately every millimetre there is an *iso-orientation patch* to be found of a given orientation, and that the cells within any such patch are highly selective in the connections they make: roughly speaking they make contacts only every milli-metre of so along their axons, and they tend to make such connections with cells in similar or nearly similar iso-orientation patches. These findings clearly have impli-cations for any theory of geometric visual hallucinations.

A new theory for geometric visual hallucinations

The observations described above make it clear that a reasonable hypothesis on the generation of geometric visual hallucinations is that they are in large part the result of intercortical connectivity, specifically the connectivity described above, generally referred to as 'intrinsic horizontal', found in layers II, III, and V of the six-layered visual cortex. The model described here (Wiener and Cowan, in preparation) is based on such findings, and is essentially an extension of the Ermentrout–Cowan model to incorporate edge detectors.

The visual cortex as a lattice

Given the various complexities described above it is necessary to introduce a greatly reduced description of the visual cortex as a whole, at least in so far as edge detectors

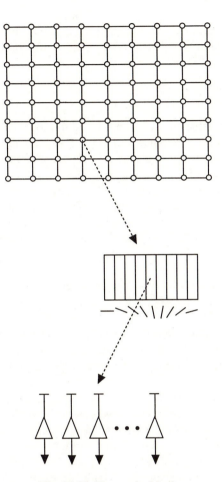

Fig. 14.17 The cortical lattice.

are concerned. The visual cortex is therefore represented as a two-dimensional *lattice*, each point of which corresponds not to a single element, or even to a single iso-orientation patch, but to all the iso-orientation patches which occupy a cortical *hypercolumn* 1.5–2.0 mm in diameter. Roughly speaking it includes all iso-orientation patches in the range $-\pi/2 \leqslant \phi_c \leqslant +\pi/2$. Such a set is found twice in a hypercolumn, one set for each eye. In the model described here, binocular aspects are neglected, so each lattice point can be thought of as occupying a cortical region about 1 mm in diameter, and since the cortex as a whole is about 36×36 mm^2, neglecting binocularity, this gives $36 \times 36 = 1296$ lattice points. Each lattice point comprises some number of iso-orientation patches, each of which itself comprises a number of edge detectors. Figure 14.17 shows a representation of such a scheme. For the purposes of our model, we lump together the action of these detectors in a single edge-detecting *element* at each lattice point. That is, we consider only the first two levels shown in Fig. 14.17.

A new weighting function

It follows that new variables must be introduced to model edge-detecting elements and their interactions in such a lattice. Let $w(\underline{x},\underline{x}',\phi_c,\phi'_c)$ be the weight of connections between the element at $\underline{x}$ tuned to the orientation ϕ_c and that at $\underline{x}'$ tuned to ϕ'_c. What is the form to be assumed for $w(\underline{x},\underline{x}',\phi_c,\phi'_c)$? The weighting function is therefore chosen to be strongest between elements of the same orientation preference along the orientation axis, weaker at right angles to the axis, and weakest at other angles. Interactions between elements with differing orientation preferences are allowed only at a single lattice point, and not between two or more lattice points. Thus $w(\underline{x},\underline{x}',\phi_c,\phi'_c)$ can be written as

$$
\begin{aligned}
w(\underline{x},\underline{x}',\phi_c,\phi'_c) = {} & w(\underline{x} - \underline{x}',\phi_c,\phi'_c)\delta(\phi_c - \phi'_c) \\
& + \delta(\underline{x} - \underline{x}')w(\underline{x},\underline{x}',\phi_c - \phi'_c)
\end{aligned}
\tag{14.3}
$$

In most cases studied, interactions between elements of the same orientation preference at differing lattice points are assumed to be excitatory (positive weights), while those between elements of differing orientation preferences at the same lattice point are assumed to be inhibitory (negative weights). From data obtained using vital dyes (Rockland and Lund 1982) similar to that described earlier, Mitchison and Crick (1982) hypothesized that the connectivity was as shown in Fig. 14.18. Thus, cortical edge detectors on the Mitchison–Crick hypothesis should be connected to detectors of the same orientation, either in a direction parallel to their orientation preference, or at right angles to it, every millimetre or so along the cortex. The model introduced in this paper incorporates Mitchison and Crick's two possibilities. Given such weight patterns supplemented by local *inhibitory* interactions between elements signalling differing ϕ_c, we find patterns in which a unique ϕ_c, is activated at every lattice point. If we reduce the mutual inhibition at each point, we obtain patterns in which several different ϕ_cs (but not all) are activated at each lattice point, giving rise to multiple patterns in the visual field. Under the action of the retino-cortical map, or rather its inverse, some of these activation patterns correspond to geometric visual hallucinations.

It is worth noting that this theory makes a prediction regarding the maximum number of rays or arms possible in a geometric hallucination. Since each ray or arm must be set off from the background by two edges, we expect the same number of distinct components as detected directions (not half as many, because we repeat the detected directions on both sides of the cortex). As mentioned in the previous section, the cortex is approximately 36 mm in each direction, each lattice point in our model represents a square with side 1 mm, and we expect a distinct detected direction for each distinct y coordinate in the lattice. Therefore, we would expect no more than 36 rays or arms of a spiral in geometric hallucinations. Reported hallucinations

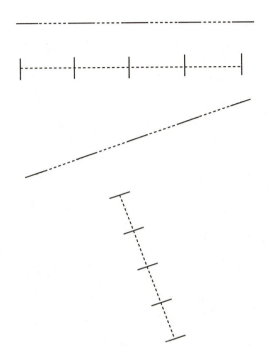

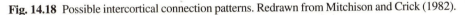

Fig. 14.18 Possible intercortical connection patterns. Redrawn from Mitchison and Crick (1982).

conform to this limitation, and some (including those reproduced in this article) do show the maximum predicted number of arms.

Numerical results

A variety of simulations were carried out to test the analysis. It was shown that circles, rays, and logarithmic spirals, both individually and in a variety of combinations could arise in the network, from a variety of random initial conditions. Figure 14.19 shows a typical result in which a cobweb, one of Klüver's form constants, forms after some competition with a logarithmic spiral pattern, from random initial excitation of the cortex. Further simulations show that other solutions are possible.

The results presented in this paper were obtained using elements with inhibitory local and excitatory long-range weights. Other patterns can be obtained using inhibitory weights for both local and long-range interactions. Random initial conditions give a somewhat disorganized set of edges that look something like the lattice spiral patterns sometimes reported (see Figs 14.20 and 14.21). This is the case even though they do not actually contain spirals. The fact that different patterns are obtained using differing weights does not interfere with our conclusions. If the effect of hallucinogens is to disinhibit the cortex, then both lattice spiral patterns (early in an episode, when limited disinhibition may have taken place) and the ray, circle, and spiral

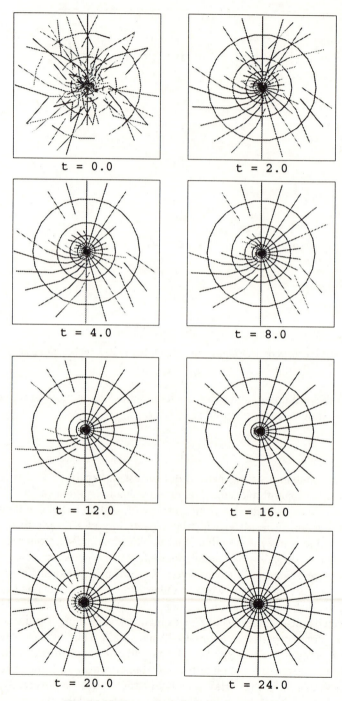

Fig. 14.19 Formation of a cobweb pattern.

Fig. 14.20 Result of simulation using inhibitory weights.

Fig. 14.21 A reported image of a lattice spiral pattern. Redrawn from Siegel (1977).

patterns (later, when more disinhibition has taken place, making some weights excitatory) could be obtained. Both excitatory and inhibitory connections are known to exist in the primary cortex.

Discussion

In this article I have argued that many aspects of awareness and consciousness can be explained in terms of the low-level activities of neural networks. The main network property I have utilized to advance the argument is the (universal) tendency for network activity to self-organize into stable patterns, either stationary (neurons firing at high maintained levels) or oscillatory (neurons firing in bursts).[5] Although I have chosen to describe only phenomena occurring on the relatively fast timescales associated with perception and delayed discriminations, similar arguments could be applied to the neurodynamics of long-term memory. Some of the alternative models for semantic memory discussed by Lauro Grotto *et al.* in Chapter 16 of this book, or the model for delayed discrimination advanced by Amit *et al.* (1994), fall within this category.

The three phenomena I did discuss, metacontrast effects, delayed response discriminations, and geometric visual hallucinations, can all be explained directly in terms of the properties of stable patterns or attractors, rather than in terms of the language and concepts of cognitive psychology and philosophy. Consider, for example, the approach to metacontrast effects described by Dennett in his interesting book *Consciousness Explained* (Dennett 1991). Dennett (1991, p. 135) rightly takes issue with Cartesian ideas about perception and consciousness, and argues instead for a *Multiple Drafts* model:

As soon as any ... discrimination has been accomplished, it becomes available for eliciting some behaviour ... or for modulating some internal informational state ... this multi-track process occurs over hundreds of milliseconds, during which time various additions, incorporations, emendations, and overwritings of content can occur, in various orders ... Contents arise, get revised, contribute to the interpretation of other contents or to the modulation of behaviour ... and in the process leave their traces in memory, which then eventually decay or get incorporated into or overwritten by later contents, wholly or in part.

Reference to Fig. 14.9 shows clearly that in terms of the attractor hypothesis, the target response is indeed *overwritten* by the mask response. However, one needs to be careful not to overinterpret the content of Fig. 14.9. As Rolls and Tovee (1994) have shown, neurons in the visual cortex are actually turned off during the course of backward masking. Figure 14.9 actually describes simulation within the framework of a continuum model. It is clear from Rolls and Tovee's work that the *network* model is needed to account correctly for the data. In such a model, the active transient model can be shown to have all the properties required to account correctly for type A metacontrast effects, at both neural and psychic levels. I consider it very likely that a similar model can account for observations such as Libet's (1985) on backwards referral in time.

Similar arguments hold for the perception of geometric visual hallucinations. On one hypothesis (Dennett 1993), hallucinations occur when the brain tries to make sense out of noise. In this article I have argued that geometric visual hallucinations are stable patterns (attractors), generated from visual noise by self-organization, and simply reflect the architecture of the visual cortex. I also consider it to be very likely that the non-geometric hallucinations seen in the later stages of hallucinosis (Klüver 1928) can also be accounted for in terms of simple neural circuit properties. In this context, let me note the similarity between drug-induced visual hallucinations, and the content of REM-sleep dreams as described by Flanagan in Chapter 4 of this book. Both are 'vivid, bizzare, and full of multimodal imagery', to use Flanagan's terms. In fact Flanagan describes the genesis of such dreams in terms similar to Dennett's explanation of hallucinations:

[phenomenal]-dreams are ... noise the system creates while it is doing what it was designed to do, but because the cerebral cortex is designed to make sense out of stimuli it tries half successfully to put dreams into narrative structures already in place, structures which involve modes of self-representation, present concerns, and so on.

On the hypothesis of this paper such dreams are generated by the same processes of self-organization of attractors that we assert lead to geometric visual hallucinations. It is interesting in this light to note that the pharmacological action of psychedelic drugs such as LSD and THC (Pieri *et al.* 1978) produces a chemical state which is thought to be very similar to that described by Flanagan for REM-sleep dreams: the action of *noradrenaline* and *serotonin* is greatly altered (Posner and Peterson 1990). I consider it very likely that REM-sleep dreams are produced by essentially the same neurodynamic mechanisms as visual hallucinations.

Endnotes

[1] Relating the stimulus to previous stimuli or to memory.
[2] External stimuli which evoke similar responses in similar organisms.
[3] It is not a coincidence that such patterns dominate the architectonics of the visual cortex.
[4] This was first recognized by Schwartz (1977).
[5] There is also the possibility of stable chaotic patterns—neurons firing apparently in bursts of random activity. However, this does not lead to any new phenomena.

References

Amit, D., Brunel, N., and Tsodyks, M.V. (1994). Correlations of cortical Hebbian reverberations: theory versus experiment. *Journal of Neuroscience*, **14**, 6435–45.

Beurle, R.L. (1956). Properties of a mass of cells capable of regenerating pulses. *Philosophical Transaction of the Royal Society of London, Series B*, **669**, 55–94.

Bierce, A. (1924). *Can such things be*. Boni, New York.

R.M. Borisyuk and A.B. Kirillov. (1992). Bifurcation analysis of a neural network model. *Biological Cybernetics*, **66**, 319–25.

Burns, B.D. (1958). *The mammalian cerebral cortex*. Arnold, London.

Burns, B.D. (1968). *The uncertain nervous system*. Arnold, London.

Cragg, B.G. and Temperley, H.N.V. (1954). The organisation of neurones: a cooperative analogy. *EEG Clinical Neurophysiology*, **6**, 85–92.

Dennett, D. (1991). *Consciousness explained.* Little, Brown and Co., Boston.

Dennett, D. (1993). In *Secrets of the inner mind*, Vol. 84, pp. 110–11. Time-Life Books, Alexandria, VA.

Ermentrout, G.B. and Cowan, J.D. (1979). A mathematical theory of visual hallucination patterns. *Biol. Cybernetics*, **34**, 137–50.

Fohlmeister, C., Gerstner, W., Ritz, R., and van Hemmen, J.L. Spontaneous excitations in the primary visual cortex. *Neural Computation*, 7, 5, 905–14.

Fuster, J.M. and Alexander, G.E. (1971). Neuron activity related to short term memory. *Science*, **173**, 652–4.

Gray, C.M. and Singer, W. (1989). Stimulus-specific oscillations in orientation columns of cat visual cortex. *Proceedings of the National Academy of Sciences of the United States of America*, **86**, 1698–702.

Harth, E.M., Csermely, T.J., Beek, B., and Lindsay, R.D. (1970). Brain functions and neural dynamics. *Journal of Theoretical Biology*, **26**, 93–120.

Hebb, D.O. (1949). *Organization of behaviour: a neuropsychological theory.* Wiley, New York.

Hodgkin, H. and Huxley, A.F. (1952). A quantitative description of membrane current and its application to conduction and excitation in nerve. *Journal of Physiology* (London), **117**, 500–44.

Kahneman, D. (1968). Methods, findings, and theory in studies of visual masking. *Psychological Bulletin*, **70**, 404–25.

Kawato, M., Hayakawa, H., and Inui, T. (1993). A forward-inverse optics model of reciprocal connections between visual areas. *Network: Computation in Neural Systems*, **4**, 415–22.

Klüver, H. (1971). *Mescal and mechanisms of hallucinations.* University of Chicago Press, IL.

Kohlers, P.A. (1962). Intensity and contrast effects in visual masking. *Vision Research*, **2**, 277–94.

Kohlers, P.A. and Rosner, B.S. (1960). On visual masking (metacontrast): dichoptic observation. *American Journal of Psychology*, **73**, 2–21.

Libet, B. (1985). Subjective antedating of a sensory experience and mind–brain theories. *Journal of Theoretical Biology*, **114**, 563–70.

Milton, J.G., Chu, P.H., and Cowan, J.D. (1993). Spiral waves in integrate-and-fire neural networks. In *Advances in neural information processing systems*, Vol. 5 (ed. S.J. Hanson, J.D. Cowan, and C.L. Giles), pp. 1001–7. Morgan Kaufmann, San Mateo, CA.

Mitchison, G. and Crick, F. (1982). Long axons within the striate cortex: their distribution, orientation, and patterns of connection. *Proceedings of the National Academy of Sciences of the United States of America*, **79**, 3661–5.

Oster, G. (1970). Phosphenes. *Scientific American*, **222**, (2), 83–7.

Pieri, L., Keller, H.H., Burkard, W., and DaPrada, M. (1978). Effects of lisurside and LSD on cerebral monoamine systems and hallucinosis. *Nature*, **272**, 278–80.

Posner, M.I. and Peterson, S.E. (1990). The attention system of the human brain. *Annual Review of Neuroscience*, **13**, 25–42.

Purpura, D.R. (1970). Operations and processes in thalamic and synaptically related neural subsystems. In *The neurosciences: second study program* (ed. F.O. Schmitt). Rockefeller University Press, New York.

Rockland, K.S. and Lund, J.S. (1982). Widespread periodic intrinsic connections in the tree shrew visual cortex. *Science*, **215**, 1532–4.

Rolls, E.T. and Tovee, M.J. (1994). Processing speed in the cerebral cortex and the neurophysiology of visual masking. *Proceedings of the Royal Society of London, Series B*, **257**, 9–15.

Schwartz, E. (1977). Spatial mapping in the primate sensory projection: Analytic structure and relevance to perception. *Biol. Cybernetics*, **25**, 181–94.

Sherwood, S.L. (1957). Consciousness, adaptive behaviour and schizophrenia. In *Schizophrenia: somatic aspects* (ed. D. Richter). Pergamon Press, New York.

Siegel, R.K. (1977). Hallucinations. *Scientific American,* **237**, (4), 132–40.

Uttley, A.M. (1956). A theory of the mechanism of learning based on the computation of conditional probabilities. Proceedings of the 1st International Conference on Cybernetics, Namur. Gauthier-Villars, Paris.

Von der Malsburg, C. and Cowan, J.D. (1982). Outline of a theory for the ontogenesis of iso-orientation columns in visual cortex. *Biol. Cybernetics*, **45**, 49–56.

Williams, R.J. and Zipser, D. (1989). A learning algorithm for continually running fully recurrent neural networks. *Neural Computation*, **1**, 270–80.

Wilson, H.R. and Cowan, J.D. (1972). Excitatory and inhibitory interactions in localized populations of model neurons. *Biophysical Journal*, **12**, 1–24.

Wilson, H.R. and Cowan, J.D. (1973). A theory of the functional dynamics of cortical and thalamic nervous tissue. *Kybernetik*, **13**, 55–79.

Winfree, A.T. (1987). *When time breaks down*. Princeton University Press, New Jersey.

Zipser, D. (1991). Recurrent network model of the neural mechanism of short-term active memory. *Neural Computation*, **3**, 179–93.

Zipser, D., Kehoe, B., Littlewort, G., and Fuster, J. (1993). A spiking network model of short-term active memory. *Journal of Neuroscience*, **13**, 3406–20.

15

Bidirectional theory approach to consciousness

MITSUO KAWATO

Introduction

This chapter proposes computational hypotheses about consciousness based on our recent studies on motor control and vision. Consciousness could be classified into three different levels: vigilance, coherent perception and behaviour, and self-consciousness. I will not deal with the first level because our bidirectional theories developed in computational studies of motor control and vision primarily have significant implications for the latter two.

In the following three sections, I will explain the background of the development of the bidirectional theory for visually guided arm-reaching movements, the bidirectional theory itself, and its extension to different voluntary movements such as handwriting and speech motor control The next section will introduce a bidirectional theory for vision. Then, the first hypothesis about coherent perception and behaviour will be stated in the framework of sensory-motor integration. Finally, the second hypothesis about self-consciousness will be stated.

The first hypothesis involves coherent perception and behaviour. We assume that coherent perception and behaviour (I was very much influenced by von der Malsburg (see Chapter 13) for this definition) can be achieved only if parallel and multiple sensory-motor transformation modules talk to each other and settle down into a coherent state. Our proposal is that this coherent state is achieved by fast relaxation computation through bidirectional information flow between different levels of the hierarchy.

The second hypothesis concerns self-consciousness. By extending our internal model hypothesis, we propose that some network within the brain (possibly including the prefrontal cerebral cortex, the lateral part of the cerebellum, and the caudate nucleus part of the basal ganglia) models the interactions between the above sensory-motor modules. These internal models of the brain itself are acquired by continuous monitoring of activities of the other part of the brain through learning and synaptic plasticity. This hypothesis is similar to the philosophical theory of Rosenthal (1986, 1993) because the specific network within the brain is above the other part of the brain and monitors and controls its activities.

Computational studies of goal-directed arm movements

Fast and coordinated arm movements should be executed under feedforward control since biological feedback loops, in particular those via the periphery, are slow and have small gains. Recent estimates show dynamic stiffness is low during movement (Bennett *et al.* 1992; Gomi *et al.* 1992; Bennett 1993; Gomi and Kawato 1996). This necessitates internal, neural models such as an inverse dynamics model (Katayama and Kawato 1993; Kawato *et al.* 1993*a*). Analysis of the activity of single Purkinje cells suggests the existence of an inverse dynamics model in the cerebellum (Shidara *et al.* 1993).

Trajectories of point-to-point arm movements using multi-joints are characterized by roughly straight hand paths and bell-shaped speed profiles (Morasso 1981). Kinematic and dynamic optimization principles have previously been proposed to account for these invariant features (Flash and Hogan 1985; Uno *et al.* 1989; Kawato 1992). Experimental data support the dynamic optimization theory, which requires both forward and inverse models of the motor apparatus and the external world.

The problem of controlling goal-directed limb movements can be conceptually categorized into a set of information-processing sub-processes: trajectory planning, coordinate transformation from extracorporal space to intrinsic body coordinates, and motor command generation. These sub-processes are required to translate the spatial characteristics of the target or goal of the movement into an appropriate pattern of muscle activation. Over the past decade, computational studies of motor control have become much more advanced by concentrating on these three computational problems.

Unidirectional versus bidirectional theory

Many of the models can be broadly classified into one of two alternative classes of theories: unidirectional and bidirectional (Fig. 15.1).

Both types assume a hierarchical arrangement of the three computational problems to be solved for visually guided reaching and a corresponding hierarchy in the neural representations of these problems. Accordingly, the trajectory planning problem, the coordinate transformation problem, and the motor command generation problem are on one side, and the desired trajectory in extrinsic space, the desired trajectory in intrinsic space, and the motor commands are on the other.

In the unidirectional theory framework, the three computational problems must be solved sequentially without taking into account the lower levels because the information flow is only downward, that is, unidirectional.

On the other hand, the bidirectional theory framework allows both downward and upward information flow, and thus high-level trajectory planning can be done while taking into account smoothness in the motor command space. In this way, the three computational problems can be solved simultaneously. The downward information flow is mediated by the inverse kinematics model (IKM) and the inverse dynamics

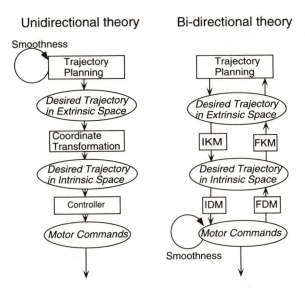

Fig. 15.1 Comparison of the unidirectional and bidirectional theories for goal-directed arm movements in their computational structures. Hierarchical arrangement of computational problems and internal representations of visually guided arm movements are equally assumed. The left side shows a block diagram of the unidirectional theory, and the right side a block diagram of the bidirectional theory. IKM, inverse kinematics model; IDM, inverse dynamics model; FKM, forward kinematics model; FDM, forward dynamics model.

model (IDM) of the controlled object and the environment. The upward information flow is mediated by the forward kinematics model (FKM) and the forward dynamics model (FDM).

In unidirectional theories, information flows only downward from the higher level to the lower level. As a result, the higher-level computational problem is solved without reference to the lower-level computational problems. For example, trajectory planning is solved without knowledge of coordinate transformation or motor command generation. Thus, the three problems are solved sequentially (Table 15.1). First, the trajectory planning problem is solved to compute the desired trajectory in the extrinsic space (in many cases task-oriented visual coordinates). Then, the coordinate transformation problem is solved to obtain the desired trajectory in the intrinsic space (joint angles, muscle lengths, etc.) from the trajectory in the extrinsic space. Finally, the necessary motor commands for the desired trajectory in the intrinsic space are calculated by a controller.

Bidirectional theories, however, allow both upward and downward information flow. In fact, the former is actually essential for solving the three computational problems in a reasonably short time (Table 15.1). As a result, the higher-level computational problem can be solved while taking into account events that happen at the lower levels. For example, trajectory planning is influenced by the requirement for

Table 15.1 Comparison of the unidirectional and bidirectional theories for goal-directed arm movements.

Theory	Unidirectional	Bidirectional
How to solve three computational problems	Sequential	Simultaneous
Spaces where trajectory is planned	Extrinsic space (task-oriented visual coordinates)	Intrinsic space (body coordinates) and extrinsic space
Optimization principle (Example)	Kinematic (Minimum-jerk)	Dynamic (Minimum-torque-change)
Control	Virtual trajectory control	Inverse dynamics model
Internal models of motor apparatus and environment	Not necessary	Forward dynamics model and inverse dynamics model
Motor learning	—	Acquisition of internal models

smooth motor commands. Thus, the three problems are solved simultaneously rather than sequentially.

One of the most fundamental differences between the two theories concerns the spaces in which the trajectory is first planned. Consequently, at present there is controversy over the coordinate system, extrinsic (kinematic) or intrinsic (dynamic), in which trajectories are planned. The unidirectional theory assumes the trajectory to be planned solely in the extrinsic space (usually task-oriented visual coordinates), while all the kinematic and dynamic factors at the lower levels are neglected. On the other hand, the bidirectional theory assumes that the trajectory is planned in both the intrinsic (body coordinates) and extrinsic spaces. Goals of movement such as the end-point of reaching are given in the extrinsic space while necessary constraints to select a unique trajectory (i.e. to resolve the ill-posedness) are given in the intrinsic space. Thus, the two spaces are used simultaneously for trajectory planning.

The above explanation of the controversy might be too simple and slightly misguided. The difference between the unidirectional and bidirectional theories is not simply whether there is only planning in extrinsic space; somehow, those high-level plans must be passed down to a system that deals with forces and motor commands, in which case there must be a lower-level planner (or controller). As an illustrative example, we can imagine a unidirectional strategy in which first the minimum-jerk model in Cartesian coordinates (Flash and Hogan 1985) specifies the path in extrinsic space, then the minimum-torque-change model (Uno *et al.* 1989) transforms this desired trajectory into joint angle motions, and then finally the minimum-motor-command-change model (Kawato 1992) determines the necessary motor neuron firings from the desired joint angle motions. In this extreme case, motor planning

(or in a wider sense, trajectory planning) is done at all three different levels, but the information flow is unidirectional. The lower-level planner strictly obeys the commands (path constraints or desired joint angle motions) from the higher level, and the higher-level planner ignores the lower-level planner. Thus, the distinction between the unidirectional and bidirectional theories hinges on neither kinematic versus dynamic optimization models nor extrinsic versus intrinsic trajectory planning. The essential difference between the two theories is whether different level motor planners and controllers are arranged in a purely hierarchical manner (unidirectional) or whether they talk to each other (bidirectional) to determine motor behaviour.

However, in most of the biologically plausible models studied, the optimization principles for trajectory planning developed by the two theories are markedly different and are almost inseparably coupled to the spaces for the first trajectory planning. In the unidirectional theory, because the planning process does not take the lower levels into account, the optimization principle has to be kinematic at the highest level and all of the dynamic factors are therefore neglected at the first planning stage. One representative example is the minimum-jerk model defined in Cartesian coordinates (Flash and Hogan 1985). On the other hand, in the bidirectional theory, it is possible to use principles of the optimization of dynamics that take lower levels into account. One representative example is the minimum-torque-change model (Uno *et al.* 1989).

In the bidirectional theory, both the forward dynamics model and the inverse dynamics model are necessary for fast computation in trajectory planning. The inverse and forward models correspond to downward and upward information flows, respectively (Fig. 15.1). These internal models should be learned and stored somewhere in the brain. Acquisition of internal models could form a major part of motor learning. A biologically plausible learning scheme to acquire the inverse dynamics model was proposed earlier (Kawato *et al.* 1987; Kawato and Gomi 1992), and we have already obtained some electrophysiological evidence that internal models reside in the cerebellum (Shidara *et al.* 1993).

In closing this section, I would like to explain intuitively why the unidirectional strategy is not able to solve a large class of optimization problems which appear in vision and motor computations and in which constraints are given in multiple, different spaces.

The general formulation of the problem can be given as follows. Let us assume that there are several spaces $\mathcal{S}_1, \mathcal{S}_2, ..., \mathcal{S}_n$ hierarchically arranged and represented by different areas of the brain. Suppose $\mathcal{S}_1$ is attached to the input interface of the brain (such as vision, audition, somato-sensory system) and $\mathcal{S}_n$ is attached to the output interface of the brain (descending motor commands to motor neurons, muscle tensions, joint torques). $x_1, x_2, ..., x_n$ are states of representations at these different spaces. There exist functional relationships between these representations. If the mapping is one-to-one, then $x_{i+1} = f(x_i)$ and $x_i = f^{-1}(x_{i+1})$ hold. However, the correspondence generally is many-to-many, and thus only the following inclusion relationships hold: $x_{i+1} \in \mathcal{G}(x_i)$ and $x_i \in \mathcal{H}(x_{i+1})$. Let us suppose that different constraints

$\mathscr{C}_1, \mathscr{C}_2, ..., \mathscr{C}_n$ are given at different spaces $\mathscr{S}_1, \mathscr{S}_2, ..., \mathscr{S}_n$, respectively. We assume that there exists a unique optimal solution $(x_1^*, x_2^*, ... x_n^*)$ that satisfies several hard constraints and minimizes (or maximizes) several soft constraints. This optimal solution also satisfies the inclusion relationship given above between different hierarchies.

In the unidirectional theory framework, at each space a unique solution must be calculated. However, this apparently cannot be done. For example, the constraint $\mathscr{C}_1$ at $\mathscr{S}_1$ cannot determine a unique solution if it is a hard constraint (for example a target point in reaching movements, or retinal images in vision computation). On the other hand, if $\mathscr{C}_1$ is a soft constraint it determines the unique solution that does not satisfy other constraints in other spaces (for example, the smoothest possible trajectory in the space is not to move, or the smoothest 2D surface is a fronto-parallel plane).

Consequently, different spaces and different constraints given must talk to each other to find the optimal solution while taking into account the inclusion relationships between different spaces.

The simplest example is the minimum-torque-change trajectory. Here, the trajectory X is represented in the Cartesian space $\mathscr{S}_1$. The torque τ is represented in the torque space $\mathscr{S}_2$. The relationship between X and τ is given by the Lagrangian equation of motion. If there is no kinematic or dynamic redundancy, the mapping is one-to-one, but with this redundancy the mapping is one-to-many. The hard constraint in the Cartesian space is that the trajectory must reach the target at a fixed time $X(t_f) = X_{\text{target}}$. On the contrary, the soft constraint in the torque space is to minimize the rate of change of torque integrated over the entire movement. The hard constraint in $\mathscr{S}_1$ cannot uniquely determine the solution because there is an infinite number of possible trajectories ending at the specified target at the specified time. On the other hand, if we seek the smoothest solution in the torque space $\mathscr{S}_2$, the solution is no movement, which obviously does not succeed in reaching the target. Thus, we should deal with the two spaces simultaneously to find the torque and trajectory that reach the specified target with the smoothest torque time course. Furthermore, any algorithm for calculating this optimal solution either implicitly or explicitly uses both of the two-directional inclusion relationships $x_{i+1} \in \mathscr{G}(x_i)$ and $x_i \in \mathscr{H}(x_{i+1})$ (inverse dynamics and forward dynamics in this example).

Bidirectional theory for several movements

We have developed several neural network models that can generate the dynamic optimal trajectory and control a motor apparatus along it (Kawato *et al.* 1990). Recently, we developed a new neural network model that can generate the trajectory within a small number of iterations (Kawato 1992; Wada and Kawato 1993). This model is called FIRM (Forward–Inverse Relaxation Model) because it contains both the forward dynamics model and the inverse dynamics model of the controlled object.

In reaching movements, the locations of the start- and end-points and the specified movement duration provide the two-point boundary conditions for the optimization problem where the performance index is the time integral of the sum of the squares of the rate of change of torques. The non-linear dynamics of the arm governs the relationship between the control variable (joint torques) and the trajectory. The subject can pass through specified via-points at the optimal times. According to Marr's three-level approach to understanding brain function (Marr 1982), we can summarize our study of reaching movements as follows:

(1) the computational theory of reaching is the minimum-torque-change model;
(2) representation of the task is given as the start-, via- and end-points and the movement duration;
(3) algorithm and hardware are FIRM.

We hypothesized that this computational framework might be extended to other classes of voluntary movements such as handwriting or speech. For this extension of the theory, the above first and third levels are easily transferred, but the representation level needs careful consideration. For speech, we believe that each phoneme determines the via-point target location. For handwriting, we developed an algorithm to extract the minimum number of via-points for a given trajectory X_{data} with some level of error threshold θ. If a fixed number of via-points $\mathscr{S} = \{P_1, P_2, ..., P_N\}$ are given and the arm dynamics is known, we can calculate the optimal trajectory $X_{opt}(\mathscr{S})$ passing through these via-points. The above problem is to find the minimum value of N that gives a trajectory satisfying $\|X_{data} - X_{opt}(\mathscr{S})\| < \theta$. Note that this via-point extraction problem is again a non-linear optimization problem. Our via-point extraction algorithm uses FIRM and suggests a duality between movement pattern formation and movement pattern perception (Wada and Kawato 1995).

We succeeded in reconstructing a cursive handwriting trajectory quite accurately from about 10 via-points for each character (Wada and Kawato 1995). The extracted via-points included not only kinematically definable feature points with maximum curvature and lowest velocity but also other points not easily extracted by any purely kinematic method that does not take account of the dynamics of the arm or the dynamic optimization principle. A simple word recognition system from cursive connected handwriting was constructed based on this via-point representation and it worked without using a word dictionary. When the same algorithm was applied to speech articulator motion during natural speech, the extracted via-points corresponded fairly well to phonemes that were determined from a simultaneously recorded acoustic signal. Natural speech movement was well reconstructed from those phoneme-like via-points (Wada *et al.* 1995).

Thus, we have accumulated evidence that the bidirectional theory approach is a promising computation-model candidate for several types of movements.

Bidirectional theory for vision

In the domain of vision, we have proposed the same bidirectional architecture for fast computation in early vision, and fast and reliable integration of different vision

modules in middle-vision problems, especially integrating surface normal estimation, boundary detection, and light source estimation in shape from shading (Kawato
et al. 1991, 1993*b*; Hayakawa *et al.* 1994).

Recent findings on multiple visual cortical areas that represent distinct visual cues
such as colour, motion, and shape, and their parallel organization all the way through
from the retina to the visual association cortices, pose a difficult computational problem: how are parallel visual modules integrated to allow coherent scene perception
within a short time?

Visual images *I* are generated when light rays reflected from 3D objects in the
visual world hit a 2D image sensor such as the retina, CCD, or film. The imaging
process *R*, which we call 'optics', compresses 3D objects into 2D images and thus
loses information; hence a many-to-one mapping. Consequently, the early vision
problems of estimating different aspects *S* of the geometrical structure in the 3D
world from 2D images cannot be properly solved unless some constraints are given
beforehand (Marr 1982; Poggio *et al.* 1985) because they are one-to-many mappings.
That is, the early vision problems are each computationally characterized as an
inverse process of optics and a priori knowledge about the visual world is introduced
as the constraint required. Accordingly, in many computational vision algorithms,
the following sum *J* of two objective functions is minimized to find the best visual-
world representation *S* that explains the image data *I* as well as satisfies the a priori
knowledge (Poggio *et al.* 1985).

$$J = \|R(S) - I\|^2 + \|Q(S)\|^2 \tag{15.1}$$

where the first term requires that the reconstruction of the image *R(S)* from the
representation *S* using the optics operator *R* be compatible with the real data *I*, and
the second term imposes the a priori knowledge about the visual world, such as
smoothness of the representation. Minimization is especially difficult when *R* or *Q*
is strongly non-linear; it can, however, be done by a kind of steepest descent method
—the stochastic relaxation algorithm or its recurrent neural-network (mean-field
approximation) version. However, a large number of iterations (usually more than
a few hundred) are required, and no explanation exists for the typical visual
information processing time in humans (100–400 ms) (Potter 1976). Thus, recurrent
neural-network models have, in the past, been rejected as fast visual computational
mechanisms (Thorpe and Imbert 1989).

We proposed that the backprojection connections provide a forward model of the
optics process, while the feedforward connections between the two areas provide an
approximated inverse model of that optics process (Fig. 15.2) (Kawato *et al.* 1991,
1993*b*; Hayakawa *et al.* 1994). Although there exists no unique inverse optics operation, by giving some consideration to the two terms in eqn 15.1, it is always possible
to derive approximate inverse optics operations, which compute a rough estimation
of *S* from the image data *I* by one-shot calculation, in the form of feedforward neural
connections. These inverse-optics computations are only approximately valid under
very restricted conditions; thus, if they were solely used the brain would generally

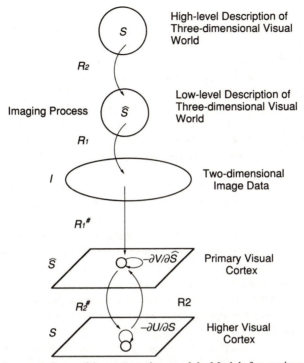

High-level Description of
Three-dimensional Visual
World

Low-level Description of
Three-dimensional Visual
World

Imaging Process

Two-dimensional
Image Data

Primary Visual
Cortex

Higher Visual
Cortex

Fig. 15.2 Fundamental forward-inverse optics model. Model for reciprocal interactions between V1 and the higher visual cortex (HVC). In the upper half of the figure, the optics operation R in the outer world is decomposed into lower and higher parts, R_1 and R_2. A model of this hierarchy in the brain is shown in the lower half of the figure.

not be able to execute correct vision computations. On the other hand, such computations by themselves can solve simple vision tasks.

When new image data impinge on the retina, a rough estimate of the higher representation is first calculated by using only the feedforward connections (Fig. 15.2). This higher representation is then transformed back to an intermediate representation by the backprojection connections and then compared with the current representation in V1 to calculate the error. The error is filtered by the approximated inverse operation and sent again to the higher visual cortex to modify the higher representation. Intrinsic connections within V1 and higher visual cortices make the estimates more compatible with a priori knowledge about the structures in the 3D visual world.

This relaxation computation converges very rapidly (within a few iterations) because it is in some sense a Newton-like method. Its convergence property can be shown mathematically. Thus, the bidirectional theory for vision can explain the very fast human vision computation, although ill-posed vision problems necessitate relaxation computations.

The other computational advantage of the bidirectional theory for vision is its capability to integrate rapidly different vision modules using bidirectional information flows between different hierarchies. This was demonstrated in computer vision experiments of 'shape from shading' (Hayakawa *et al.* 1994). Here, we give a more conceptual yet more intuitive explanation for this advantage using the famous *binding* problem in vision as an example (Fig. 15.3).

Figure 15.3 (see plate section) shows a schematic diagram of the visual system while emphasizing parallel information streams (colour, form, 3D shape (depth), and motion) from V2 to different higher visual cortical areas. At the same time, this figure emphasizes that different parallel visual pathways are specifically used for different kinds of movements.

For simplicity of explanation, let us assume that the thick stripe in the V2–MT–MST pathway deals with object motion as well as observer motion for controlling eye movements such as the smooth-pursuit eye movement. The inter-stripe in V2–V3a–AIP (Anterior Intraparietal Area) is assumed to represent the 3D form information of objects and to send their output for reaching and grasping movements by the arm and the hand. The inter-stripe in V2–V4–IT is assumed to represent the form information of objects and is specialized for pattern recognition and object shape memory. The thin stripe in the V2–V4 pathway is assumed to deal with colour information. Note that we take the task-specific vision view rather than the conventional gigantic central map like the 2½D sketch of Marr (1982).

When there are two objects in front of the eye, the leftward moving red ball and the rightward moving blue cube, each higher visual cortex shows increased activities of two populations of neurons. In the MST, neurons representing rightward motion and leftward motion are activated. In the AIP, neurons representing a ball and a cube are activated. In V4, neurons representing red and blue are activated. In the IT, neurons representing a circle and a square are activated. The brain can tell that there is a leftward moving red ball and a rightward moving blue cube, and not a leftward moving blue cube for example, by somehow observing the neural activities in the four higher cortical areas. This is the 'binding' problem. Von der Malsburg (1988) postulated ingenious coding to solve this binding problem by using temporal encoding and the dynamic link architecture.

The bidirectional theory could provide a complementary and probably orthogonal computational mechanism to solve the binding problem as symbolically designated by two closed loops shown at the level of V1 in Fig. 15.3. By tracing both the forward and backward neural connections between different hierarchies, different objects can be recognized as different because the closed loop can go back to the V2 or V1 level where different objects are discriminated by their spatial location due to high spatial resolution. For example, if a subject is asked to eye track the object with a red colour, the activities of neurons representing red colours in V4 are enhanced by central commands, and then all activities of neurons in the closed loop corresponding to the leftward moving red ball are enhanced by the feedback and feedforward connections. In the MST, neurons representing leftward motion then win against

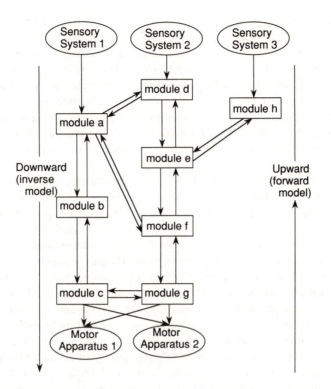

Fig. 15.4 A general bidirectional and hierarchical scheme for module integration in both sensory and motor information processing.

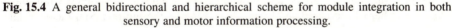

neurons representing rightward motion and send their outputs to the oculomotor control system.

Consciousness in sensory-motor integration

The mathematical structures of the bidirectional models for motor control and vision are almost identical. Thus, although we do not have any strong psychological, anatomical, or physiological data, it is very tempting to propose that the same bidirectional architecture might be applicable to the integration of different modules from sensory information processing through to motor control (Fig. 15.4).

The basic assumption in this proposal is that the brain consists of a number of modules that roughly correspond to different cortical areas, and these modules are organized in a hierarchical yet parallel manner (Colby *et al.* 1993; Graziano and Gross 1993). We do not assume a single gigantic map that plays a central role in integration. Instead, we are proposing a parallel distributed way of integrating different modules. It is well known in neuroanatomy that if one area is connected to the other area by a feedforward connection, there always exists a backward or feedback connection (Pandya and Yeterian 1988). The core of my proposal is that the downward information flow implemented by the feedforward connection constitutes an approximated inverse model of some physical process outside the brain such as kinematics transformation, dynamics transformation, and optics, that is, the image generation process. On the other hand, the upward information flow implemented by the feedback connection provides a forward model of the corresponding physical process.

What are the advantages of this bidirectional architecture? The first advantage is its fast computation. The cascade of inverse models gives a feedforward and one-shot calculation. This can execute reflexes and fixed action patterns triggered by specific stimuli. However, if we do not have forward models, and if we must rely solely on computational machinery provided by the unidirectional theory, the repertoire of our behaviour must be very limited. Equifinality, optimality, or adaptability to different environmental situations can be realized only if the brain uses some kind of internal forward model, in other words an emulator or a predictor of external events. The relaxation calculation circulating the inverse and forward models converges very rapidly, within a few iterations, to a sub-optimal solution. This is the second computational advantage. Third, integration of parallel modules can be done within a short time. Thus, bidirectional theory may give an understanding of how a coherent perception of the visual world is obtained while there exist a number of different visual cortical areas, and how coherent behaviour is adopted while there exist a number of motor-related brain areas. Finally, the bidirectional theory might give a concrete computational algorithm for the motor theory of movement pattern perception (Kawato *et al.* 1994).

Let us summarize the statement relevant to consciousness developed in this and previous sections. The first hypothesis involves the coherent perception and behaviour. We assume that coherent perception and behaviour (I was very much influenced by von der Malsburg (see Chapter 13) for this definition) can be achieved only if parallel and multiple sensory-motor transformation modules talk to each other and settle down into a coherent state. Our proposal is that this coherent state is achieved by fast relaxation computation through bidirectional information flow between different levels of the hierarchy.

Computational advantage for self-consciousness

In the previous sections, I have been developing a bidirectional theory in which integration of many sensory-motor modules can be achieved by fast relaxation computation through inverse and forward models of the external physical world such as optics, kinematics, or dynamics. If the brain has the capability to acquire both forward and inverse models of the external world, it should be easier for some part

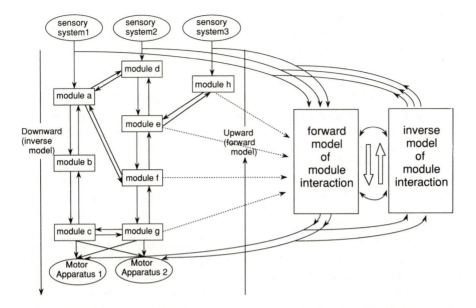

Fig. 15.5 Schematic diagram showing how the self-consciousness is envisioned as the forward and inverse models of interactions between parallel sensory-motor modules.

of the brain to acquire internal models of some other part of the brain. In fact, this was the basic idea behind our feedback-error-learning model of cerebellar motor learning (Kawato *et al.* 1987; Kawato and Gomi 1992), and its origin can be found in Ito (1970).

Let me start by asking, 'What is consciousness for?' or, 'What is the computational advantage of consciousness?' I propose that some portion of self-consciousness and self-awareness can be understood as forward and inverse modelling of interactions between multiple sensory-motor modules. The computational advantage of relaxation computation through these forward and inverse models of the brain itself is to set good approximate initial conditions for the relaxation computation through all the relevant modules for sensory information processing or behaviour selection, and thus accelerate the convergence to the coherent steady state in which interactions between multiple modules settle into a stable equilibrium. In order to obtain a coherent scene perception, or to adopt a consistent behavioural plan, many brain regions or sensory-motor modules should talk to each other and settle into a coherent equilibrium where the state of every module satisfies constraints given by all other modules connected to it. We advocated that this convergence could be quite rapid in the bi-directional architecture even if there is no single gigantic map or central processing unit integrating everything. However, this convergence can be even more accelerated if a model of this dynamics of module interactions could be acquired through frequent observations of this convergence process, which is not difficult because all the necessary variables are available in the brain (Fig. 15.5). The only computational difficulty is the capacity of such internal models of module interaction. If the model itself is the same size as the brain region which is modelled, it does not make any sense with regard to economy of hardware or speed of convergence. Thus the internal model must be a smaller and poorer approximation of the modelled interactions between the sensory-motor modules.

I propose viewing the forward model of module interactions as an approximate model of the other brain regions. Thus, self-consciousness is just a very rough and incorrect model of all the complicated dynamical interactions of many brain modules always working subconsciously to solve the most difficult ill-posed sensory-motor integration problems. Although the forward model is just approximate machinery, it is very useful for setting a reasonable initial condition and accelerating the module integration. Overall, the forward model of the brain itself does transformations from sensory signals to motor outputs. Thus, it is closer to some inverse model of the external world. On the other hand, the inverse model of the brain can be classified as the forward model of the external world. By relaxation computation through these forward and inverse models, emulation of oneself, prediction of one's behaviour in interaction with the environment, and retrospection can be made possible.

It is also tempting to assume that the brain possesses both forward and inverse models of another's brain (Barlow, Chapter 7). Of course, it is much more difficult to model somebody else's brain than one's own brain because the necessary state variables cannot be directly measured. Thus, it is inevitable to use the *a priori* constraint that another's brain should be similar to one's own brain. The forward model of others can be used to predict the behaviour of another person. On the other hand, the inverse model of others can be used to infer intentions from their behaviour. I imagine that these kinds of models are essential for successful communication between humans as well as between animals.

A natural biological question arising from the hypothesis is which brain regions constitute such internal models of other brain modules. It is certainly not a single brain region because we do not know that lesion of some specific part destroys only self-consciousness. At least several brain regions, such as the prefrontal cortex as interfaces to sensory modules, the basal ganglia as interfaces to motor modules, and the lateral part of the cerebellum as some types of memory storage, should constitute the internal models (Fig. 15.5). Inclusion of the cerebellum may sound quite strange, but recent theoretical (Ito 1993; Leiner *et al.* 1993) as well as neuro-imaging studies (Decety *et al.* 1994; Raichle *et al.* 1994) strongly suggest essential involvement of the newest part of the cerebellar cortex in non-motor and cognitive functions.

Let me close this chapter by restating the second hypothesis concerning self-consciousness. By extending our internal model hypothesis, we propose that some network within the brain (possibly including the prefrontal cerebral cortex, the lateral part of the cerebellum, and the caudate part of the basal ganglia) models the interactions between parallel sensory-motor modules. These internal models of the brain itself are acquired by continuous monitoring of activities of the other parts of the brain through learning and synaptic plasticity. This hypothesis is similar to the philosophical theory of Rosenthal (1986, 1993) because the specific network within the brain is above the other part of the brain and monitors and controls its activities.

References

Bennett, D.J. (1993). Torques generated at the human elbow joint in response to constant position errors imposed during voluntary movements. *Experimental Brain Research*, **95**, 488–98.

Bennett, D.J., Hollerbach, J.M., Xu, Y., and Hunter, I.W. (1992). Time-varying stiffness of human elbow joint during cyclic voluntary movement. *Experimental Brain Research*, **88**, 433–42.

Colby, C.L., Duhamel, J.R., and Goldberg, M.E. (1993). The ventral intraparietal area (VIP) of the macaque: anatomical location and visual response properties. *Journal of Neurophysiology*, **69**, 902–14.

Decety, J., Perani, D., Jeannerod, M. *et al.* (1994). Mapping motor representations with positron emission tomography. *Nature*, **371**, 600–2.

Flash, T. and Hogan, N. (1985). The coordination of arm movements: an experimentally confirmed mathematical model. *Journal of Neuroscience*, **5**, 1688–703.

Gomi, H. and Kawato, M. (1996). Equilibrium-point control hypothesis examined by measured arm-stiffness during multi-joint movement. *Science*, **272**, 117–20.

Gomi, H., Koike, Y., and Kawato, M. (1992). Human hand stiffness during discrete point-to-point multi-joint movement. *Proceedings of the IEEE, Engineering in Medicine and Biology Society*, October 29–November 1, Paris, France, pp. 1628–9.

Graziano, M.S.A. and Gross C.G. (1993). A bimodal map of space: somatosensory receptive field in the macaque putamen with corresponding visual receptive field. *Experimental Brain Research*, **97**, 96–109.

Hayakawa, H., Nishida, S., Wada, Y., and Kawato, M. (1994). A computational model for shape estimation by integration of shading and edge information. *Neural Networks*, **7**, 1193–209.

Ito, M. (1970). Neurophysiological aspects of the cerebellar motor control system. *International Journal of Neurology*, **7**, 162–76.

Ito, M. (1993). Movement and thought: identical control mechanism by the cerebellum. *Trends in Neuroscience*, **16**, 448–50.

Katayama, M. and Kawato, M. (1993). Virtual trajectory and stiffness ellipse during multi-joint arm movement predicted by neural inverse models. *Biological Cybernetics*, **69**, 353–62.

Kawato, M. (1992). Optimization and learning in neural networks for formation and control of coordinated movement. In *Attention and performance*, XIV: Synergies in experimental psychology, artificial intelligence, and cognitive neuroscience—a silver jubilee (ed. D. Meyer and S. Kornblum), pp. 821–49. MIT Press, Cambridge, MA.

Kawato, M., Furukawa, K., and Suzuki, R. (1987). A hierarchical neural-network model for control and learning of voluntary movement. *Biological Cybernetics*, **57**, 169–85.

Kawato, M. and Gomi, H. (1992). The cerebellum and VOR/OKR learning models. *Trends in Neuroscience*, **15**, 445–53.

Kawato, M., Maeda, Y., Uno, Y., and Suzuki, R. (1990). Trajectory formation of arm movement by cascade neural network model based on minimum torque-change criterion. *Biological Cybernetics*, **62**, 275–88.

Kawato, M., Inui, T., Hongo, S., and Hayakawa, H. (1991). Computational theory and neural network models of interaction between visual cortical areas. ATR Technical Report, TR-A-0105, ATR, Kyoto.

Kawato, M., Gomi, H., Katayama, M., and Koite, Y. (1993a). Supervised learning of coordinative motor control. In *Computational learning and cognition*, SIAM Frontier Series (ed. E.B. Baum), pp. 126–61. Society for Industrial and Applied Mathematics, Philadelphia.

Kawato, M., Hayakawa, H., and Inui, T. (1993b). A forward-inverse optics model of reciprocal connections between visual areas. *Network: Computation in Neural Systems*, **4**, 415–22.

Kawato, M., Gandolfo, F., Gomi, H., and Wada, Y. (1994). Teaching by showing in Kendama based on optimization principle. In *Proceedings of the international conference on artifical neural networks*, Sorrento, Italy, 26–29 May 1994 (ed. M. Marinara and P.G. Morasso), pp. 601–6.

Leiner, H.C., Leiner, A.C., and Dow, R.S. (1993). Cognitive and language functions of the human cerebellum. *Trends in Neuroscience*, **16**, 444–53.

Marr, D. (1982). *Vision*. Freeman, San Francisco.

Morasso, P. (1981). Spatial control of arm movements. *Experimental Brain Research*, **42**, 223–7.

Pandya, D.N. and Yeterian, E.H. (1988). Architecture and connections of cortical association areas. In *Cerebral cortex*, Vol. 4, *Association and auditory cortices* (ed. A. Peters and E.G. Jones), pp. 3–61. Plenum Press, New York.

Poggio, T., Torre, V., and Koch, C. (1985). Computational vision and regularization theory. *Nature*, **317**, 314–9.

Potter, M.C. (1976). Short-term conceptual memory of pictures. *Journal of Experimental Psychology: Human Learning and Memory*, **2**, 509–22.

Raichle, M.E., Fiez, J.A., Videen, T.O. *et al.* (1994). Practice related changes in human brain functional anatomy during nonmotor learning. *Cerebral Cortex*, **4**, 8–26.

Rosenthall, D.M. (1986). Two concepts of consciousness. *Philosophical Studies*, **49**, 329–59.

Rosenthal, D.M. (1993). Thinking that one thinks. In *Consciousness* (ed. M. Davies and G.W. Humphreys), pp. 197–223. Blackwell, Oxford.

Shidara, M., Kawano, K., Gomi, H., and Kawato, M. (1993). Inverse-dynamics encoding of eye movement by Purkinje cells in the cerebellum. *Nature*, **365**, 50–2.

Thorpe, S.J. and Imbert, M. (1989). Biological constraints on connectionist modelling. In *Connectionism in perspective* (ed. R. Pfeifer, Z. Schreter, F. Fogelman-Soulie, and L. Steels), pp. 63–92. North-Holland, Amsterdam.

Uno, Y., Kawato, M., and Suzuki, R. (1989). Formation and control of optimal trajectory in human multijoint arm movement—minimum torque-change model. *Biological Cybernetics*, **61**, 89–101.

von der Malsburg, C. (1988). Pattern recognition by labeled graph matching. *Neural Networks*, **1**, 141–8.

Wada, Y. and Kawato, M. (1993). A neural network model for arm trajectory formation using forward and inverse dynamics models. *Neural Networks*, **6**, 919–32.

Wada, Y. and Kawato, M. (1995). A theory for cursive handwriting based on the minimization principle. *Biological Cybernetics*, **3**, 3–13.

Wada, Y., Kioke, Y., V-Bateson, E., and Kawato, M. (1995). A computational theory for movement pattern recognition based on optimal movement pattern generation. *Biological Cyberetics*, **73**, 15–25.

16

The computational role of conscious processing in a model of semantic memory

R. LAURO-GROTTO, S. REICH, AND M.A. VIRASORO

Introduction: semantic memory as an attractor neural network

Attractor Neural Network (ANN) models (Amit 1989) constitute the realization of Hebb's project in a context that can be computationally and analytically controlled.

In his classical book *The organisation of behaviour*, Hebb (1949) proposed that every mental state, for instance the one resulting from remembering a particular episode of our life, is represented (codified) in the brain by a specific *assembly* of coactive neurons. In addition, he assumed that the mnemonic trace is encoded in values of the synaptic efficacies that were modified to that end when the episode first took place. This second process is generically called 'learning', while the act of remembering, i.e. the recall of the totality of the information from partial cues, is called 'retrieval'.

The neural network 'learns' and 'retrieves' using essentially the Hebbian mechanism, and can store pieces of information as patterns of activation that complete themselves when only a part is externally excited (attractor states). As such it is called a *Content Addressable Memory* to distinguish it from normal memory units in computers where the address and the content bear no relation.

This aspect of the ANN is probably its most important feature and it is difficult to imagine a radically alternative mechanism that could reproduce it. Other positive features, relevant to biosystems modelling, include:

- tolerance to input error or noise during retrieval
- robustness with respect to slow degradation (graceful decay)

Any alternative system should share at least three properties: it should be distributed—every meaningful representation must be encoded by a large number of neurons; it should be adaptive so as to incorporate learning; and finally memories should correspond to attractors of the retrieval dynamics so that remembering can proceed to a large extent autonomously.

However, to complete the construction of the model one has to include some technical assumptions that are not easily justified and that in some cases are unrealistic. In so doing we are reassured by a long tradition in science in the use of models. In the context of brain studies there is at the moment an explosion of interest in disciplines like psychology, neurobiology, and physics motivated by the common idea that using simple models may aid to understand complex functioning of the brain. In this chapter we follow more specifically the line of research initiated by Hopfield in 1982, under the strong influence of developments that have occurred during the 1960s and 1970s in the modern statistical mechanics of fields concerning the so-called *Universality of Collective Emergent Behaviours*. This expression summarizes general ideas extracted from many examples and embodied in the principle of the renormalization group method according to which large ensembles of interacting units show collective behaviour with little or no similarity with what is observed in small groups of the same units. This was concisely expressed in the proposition 'More is different', the manifesto by P.W. Anderson 1972) where this new attitude towards reductionism was announced.

However, invoking *universality* leads to serious methodological difficulties. In fact, not all aspects of the behaviour of a system are universal. The choice of which one to study or what to confront requires intuition and serendipity. The theory suggests focusing on phase transitions: discontinuous changes of regime occurring at critical values of some parameter. Hence the interest in the limit of capacity (Amit 1989): the critical number of patterns above which the ANN is incapable of retrieving any information. But, in general, the theoretical suggestions are not sufficient and one has to rely on the heavy use of computers to check, a posteriori and partially, whether a certain feature is universal and to what extent.

The computer is the privileged common tool in all lines of research that originate in other disciplines and converge towards brain modelling. There still remain methodological differences that have practical consequences. *Collective behaviours* can be rigorously characterized only in the limit of an infinite number of elements. Therefore, computer simulations should be done with a variable, and in general large, number of neurons so as to control the limit.[1]

At the present level of development, models of the brain are useful to integrate pieces of observation and to suggest new areas of search. The pieces in the puzzle are still insufficient to guess the final form. But locally they do suggest the form of a missing piece. Our work here is an attempt along these lines.

The detailed ingredients of the model will be discussed in the following sections after a review of some facts about semantic memory relevant to our discourse. Here we would like to say that the traditional amorphous, fully interconnected Hopfield architecture is replaced by a *modular* structure for semantic memory. The hierarchical structure that follows translates current ideas about the structure of semantic memory into the neural network domain (Shallice 1985). In the simplest version, to be adopted in this chapter, it consists of several modules, each one being an amorphous ensemble of neurons that are interconnected with a certain probability. Neurons lying in different modules are connected with a smaller probability (thus respecting qualitative anatomical facts (Braitenberg and Schuz 1992)).

Starting from a purely computational analysis of a Hebb–Hopfield-type model for semantic memory, the archetype of associative memory, the explicit construction of the model makes clear that the 'content addressability' property is compromised unless one introduces new mechanisms during both learning and retrieval. Among

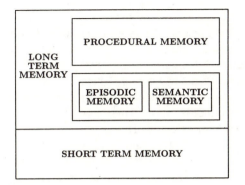

Fig. 16.1 Location of semantic memory in a schematic model of memory.

others, we consider the so-called *unlearning* stage (Crick and Mitchison 1983), as well as a new mechanism (Treves and Rolls 1992) that tends to balance external and internal signals in each module.

However, the nature of the semantic function leads us to a more radical proposal. Although it is computationally advantageous to process most of the information automatically, in parallel, and therefore unconsciously, we will show that for a few degrees of freedom, essentially global module-specific variables, a better, more flexible and efficient alternative is to process them under explicit conscious control.

Semantic memory

What we call memory is a web of different cognitive functions that are presumably implemented by different, more or less independent, brain systems. Semantic memory is one component in this galaxy. Figure 16.1 shows schematically its location. It deals, essentially, with the information about the world and the definitions of words. Patterns of information stored in semantic memory have many components that may be evoked simultaneously. Thus, for instance, when recalling the concept 'car' we may derive a visual component (that may itself be decomposed into colour, shape, size), a motor one (how to drive it), a linguistic one (the word itself, synonyms or associated verbs), etc. Retrieval of these pieces of information will cause associated activity in several cortical areas. It is by now well confirmed both from single cell recordings and brain imaging techniques that the same cortical areas are involved in mnemonic and late perceptual processes (see for instance Damasio and Damasio 1993).

It is therefore reasonable to discuss semantic memory as composed of different, geographically separated but interconnected modules. Each of these may be characterized by its functional role. Thus one will encode visual information, while another may store the motor or verbal information.[2] Each particular pattern will appear distributed among a subgroup of modules depending on its semantic characteristics.

This picture is nowadays shared by many authors (Shallice 1985; Funnell and Allport 1987; Moscovitch and Umiltà 1990; Damasio and Damasio 1993) although there have been a few attempts to transform it into a full neural network model (Farah and McClelland 1991; Lauro-Grotto 1993).

Our proposal builds a model by coupling several ANNs. The connectivity among neurons is diluted according to a statistical distribution that introduces an implicit hierarchy. Two neurons in different modules have a lower probability of being connected than two in the same module. This is obviously in (qualitative) agreement with anatomical information (Braitenberg and Schuz 1992).

This model reproduces some evidence about the function and dysfunction of semantic memory. In particular, it gives a natural explanation of *Category Specificity* that in non-distributed models is almost impossible to incorporate. The explanation realizes in the context of the model some old ideas about the phenomenon (Shallice 1985; Funnell and Allport 1987; Farah and McClelland 1991). However, it enforces some technical constraints in the model that we make explicit in the following sections.

Parenthesis on category-specific impairments

Warrington and Shallice (1984) observed a curious correlation in memory dysfunction. On a series of patients whose memory had been irreversibly damaged as a consequence of a herpes simplex encephalitis they remarked that the frequency of errors in different tests was strongly correlated with the semantic category. In particular there was a striking difference between the categories of the living (plants and animals and body parts) and non-living.[3]

Since then, there have been many reports in the literature of category specificity, sometimes with a different profile of category dependency. Although there are cases where the degree of impairment was complementary (i.e. Y.O.T.), it is fair to say that in the majority of cases inanimate objects and in particular tools (but not musical instruments!) seem to be more robust.

Semantic memory can also be probed in patients suffering from acquired dyslexia if one accepts that reading can proceed through a double route: the phonological route where *rules of pronunciation* are applied, or the semantic route that goes from the visual word form to the phonetic form passing through semantic memory. There are patients who seem to have completely lost the use of the phonological route (so-called deep dyslexia) and rely exclusively on memory. In this case again the frequency of errors depends on the category: in almost all cases abstract words seem less robust than concrete words.

The phenomena represent an important clue to understanding how the brain states (the attractors, the set of coactive neurons) are organized. It was originally pointed out by Funnell and Allport (1987) and later by many others (e.g. Hinton and Shallice 1991) that the natural explanation relies on the fact that a particular neuron will receive more or less inputs according to the number of coactive modules. Thus, for instance, if one is trying to find the name matching a picture there must be activation of the word module arising from activity in visual modules. There will be more paths from one to the other if the object is a tool than if it is an animal.

This explanation is important because there are not many that can replace it. It will be at stake in the rest of the paper. It leads us implicitly to an operational definition of the category of a pattern as the *assembly of coactive modules when the brain is in the corresponding attractor.*

The model

A neural network model is defined in terms of its architecture, its retrieval dynamics, and its learning mechanism. The latter, in general, presupposes certain statistical properties of the patterns to be learned.

The architecture

The model is composed of N neurons in each of M modules. Each neuron will connect forward to $C_{intra} \times N$ neurons in the same module and to $C_{inter} \times N$ neurons in each of the $M - 1$ other modules. We denote $\mathcal{I}(a,i)$ ($\mathcal{O}(a,i)$) the set of neurons that send information to (receive information from) the ith neuron in the ath module. These sets are chosen at random and independently. A first simulation was performed with a single module of 4000 neurons. A second series of simulations involved 5 modules with 1333 neurons each. The values of C_{intra} and C_{inter} were then chosen equal to 0.05 and 0.025 to reflect qualitatively the different long-range and short-range connectivities in the cortex.

Statistical properties of the patterns

Each pattern is represented by an assembly of simultaneously active neurons. The active neurons may belong to a variable number of modules: some patterns may be present in one single module while others activate several modules simultaneously. On the other hand, inside an active module the percentage of active neurons will be independent of the pattern. The number is chosen to be around aN with fluctuations proportional to $\sqrt{aN}$. In the simulations $a = 0.1$, so that there were around 133 ± 11 neurons active in a module. Therefore the total number of active neurons fluctuates from 133 to 665 (in the simulation with a single module the active neurons were 400 ± 20).

The retrieval dynamics

We imagine formal neurons that may fire at only two different rates, and we call these states active and inactive. Only active neurons send downstream signals. At any particular neuron the incoming signals from upstream neurons multiplied by the synaptic efficacies are summed to give the total signal. The same neuron is also subject to an overall inhibition equal to the number of active neurons in all modules multiplied by a constant γ. If the sum of these two terms is larger than a threshold U, the neuron becomes active, otherwise it remains inactive. Both γ and U are parameters that have to be tuned so that the average proportion of active neurons (the activity) is kept of order a (see, however, Amit and Brunel (1995) for analog neurons). In addition, recall must work. The usual hypothesis, that will be found to be false, is that this tuning can be done once and for all and is not dependent on the particular pattern of information that is being recalled.

The hypothesis of a two-state neuron was motivated by purely computational reasons. A large amount of experience has shown that binary and multiple-valued neuron models have similar qualitative behaviour. This is one example of the *universality* previously discussed.

The learning mechanism

To build the model we will have to assume a specific learning rule. This is perhaps the least satisfactory aspect of the neural network framework because there is no proposal that can simultaneously accommodate the animal's capacity for one-shot learning and its ability to reduce and control interference between old and new memories. Probably this means that there is more than one learning mechanism in the brain.

However, the purpose of any learning mechanism is to build new attractors in a way that interferes as little as possible with previous attractors. A measure of this interference is the so-called storage capacity. Buhmann *et al.* (1989) have proposed an explicit, one-step learning mechanism, that in the limit of low activity leads to a very large storage capacity almost reaching the theoretical upper bound (Gardner 1988). We chose this rule and discuss how our conclusions may depend on the choice.

In the cognitive psychology literature the rule of choice is the so-called δ-rule (see Farah and McClelland 1991). It has the property of giving the maximum possible storage capacity and minimum interference. Unfortunately, this rule is unrealistic exactly in those aspects that make it efficient. It assumes that any new incoming information requires a long and costly reshuffling of *all* previous mnemonic traces. Its implementation in our model could only be misleading.

We denote by $\xi_{a,i}^\mu$ that state of activation of the ith neuron in the ath module for pattern μ: $\xi_{a,i}^\mu$ is equal to 1 when active and 0 when inactive. The value of i varies from 1 to N, a from 1 to M, and μ from 1 to P. Any pattern μ will activate a subset C_μ of modules.

Then the learning rule gives an explicit formula for the efficacy of the synapse between neuron a,i and neuron b,j:

$$J_{(a,i)(b,j)} = \sum_{\mu=0}^{P} \frac{(\xi_{a,i}^\mu - a)(\xi_{b,j}^\mu - a)}{a(1-a)N} \quad \text{if } a \text{ and } b \in \mathscr{C}_\mu$$

$$J_{(a,i)(b,j)} = 0 \quad\quad\quad\quad \text{if } a \text{ or } b \notin \mathscr{C}_\mu \quad\quad (16.1)$$

Admittedly this learning rule is not realistic. Real synapses have plastic strengths but with characteristics that do not correspond to what we assume here. According to this equation the synaptic efficacy increases when both neurons are active simultaneously, but decreases when one is active and the other one is inactive independently of whether the active neuron is pre- or postsynaptic. When both neurons are inactive, eqn 16.1 shows an apparent positive contribution equal to $\frac{aP}{(1-a)N}$ but this is less relevant because it can be reabsorbed in the inhibition γ term (see eqn 16.2). There are no reasons to believe that the features we will be discussing do depend on these unrealistic ingredients.

Treves and Rolls (1992) observe that the average synaptic couplings among neurons in the same module may be smaller when compared with those connecting across modules. We therefore multiply $J_{(a,i)(b,j)}$ by a modulating function $R_{a,b}$. Its role will be discussed in the section on modifications of the model.

Putting together the retrieval dynamics and the explicit formula for the synaptic efficacies (eqn 16.1) we derive the total signal on the ith neuron in the ath module:

$$h_{a,i} = \sum_{(b,j) \in \mathscr{I}(a,i)} R_{a,b} \, J_{(a,i)(b,j)} S_{b,j} - \frac{\gamma}{aN} \sum_j S_{a,j} \tag{16.2}$$

Updating is done asynchronously. At each instant of time one neuron is selected, the signal on it is calculated according to eqn 16.2 and if it is larger (smaller) than the threshold U the neuron is turned on (turned off).

Simulations

The simulations were performed on an IBM 550E with 128 Mbytes of RAM. We first discuss numerical experiments done on a single isolated module. They provide a good example of correct functioning of a neural network and help us understand the role of the parameters γ and U.

One isolated module

In addition to the parameters already discussed (a = fraction of active neurons in each pattern = 0.1; $N = 4000$; $C_{\text{intra}} = 0.05$) we chose: P = total number of patterns = 71, a value below but near the theoretical limit of capacity.

We considered different values of γ and U. We observed the following behaviour:

- For γ and U both large (≥ 0.5) the only stable configuration corresponds to the zero state in which all neurons are inactive.
- For γ and U both small all the patterns are stable. But also 'unions' of patterns are stable. These are states in which all the neurons that would be active in one pattern in the union are simultaneously active. We consider this situation unsatisfactory because the module does not discriminate.

- For γ between 0.2 and 0.4 but U too small (≤ 0.1) the unions of patterns become unstable while the patterns themselves are stable. However, if we start the module from an initial condition that is orthogonal to any stored pattern, the system still converges to either one of the patterns themselves or to a spurious attractor that has a large number of active neurons. This situation is also unsatisfactory. The module is 'recognizing' when there is nothing to recognize. Furthermore, if this situation reappears once we couple the M modules, the spurious activity will generate noise that will be difficult to treat.
- Finally for $0.2 < \gamma < 0.3, 0.3 > U > 0.2$ and $\gamma + U = 0.5 \pm 0.05$ the patterns are stable, the zero state is stable, and if the initial state is far from any stored pattern the module converges to the zero state with no active neuron. This is the ideal situation: non-recognition corresponds to a zero state that transmits minimal noise to the other parts of the brain.

Therefore, this preliminary experiment teaches us that both the inhibition parameter and the threshold must be tuned. Theoretical analysis confirm these results: γ prevents the stabilization of states with too many active neurons, while U controls the stability and the basin of attraction of the zero state.

Multimodule model simulations

The numerical experiments involved 5 modules with 1333 neurons each. The intra-module connectivity C_{intra} was equal to 5% while the intermodule one $C_{inter} = 2.5\%$.

How a pattern is represented depends on its semantic content. The semantic category, as defined in the previous section, determines the modules that will be active for the specific pattern. The remaining modules should converge to the zero state. For instance, an abstract concept cannot evoke a visual component; some other concepts may not be associated with information in the motor modules, etc.

The model must therefore guarantee the existence and stability of attractors corresponding to patterns that are distributed over many modules, and of those that are present only in a limited small subset. It is this requirement that will prove difficult to satisfy.

For simplicity, we have confronted only two extreme categories of patterns: a first one in which patterns are distributed in all modules, and a second one composed of patterns that are present in a single module.

It is evident, and we have checked it in the simulations, that the first class is more stable than the second one.

Thus when we increase the number of stored patterns, near the limit of capacity, the distributed patterns will be the last to be destabilized.

Furthermore, the noise produced by a distributed pattern on an isolated one is larger. Therefore, at constant number of stored patterns, the signal to noise ratio will increase if we increase the percentage of distributed patterns. It is then necessary to analyse the behaviour of the model in terms of two parameters: the total number of patterns, and the ratio of distributed to isolated patterns.

We began by considering 17 patterns distributed over 5 modules and 2 isolated ones in each different module (in total, 27 patterns).

The distributed patterns were stable for U around 0.3 and $\gamma = 0.2$. It was enough to start with a signal in one of the modules for the system to reconstruct the whole pattern. The zero state was also stable.

In contrast, the isolated patterns could not be recalled at all. Even starting with the initial state coinciding with an isolated pattern, the system would run away towards meaningless configurations.

We then repeated the experiments reducing the number of distributed patterns. When this number reached 5, while those isolated were more than 14, we entered into a transitional regime in which a larger fraction of isolated patterns became stable. Finally, with 1 and 18 all the representations were stable. Therefore, decreasing the number of more distributed patterns strengthens the isolated patterns.

This scenario is not acceptable. A correct model for semantic memory should not impose limits on the number of distributed patterns that are to be stored. In the next section we discuss possible modifications to improve the performance.

Possible modifications of the model

The strategies that one can follow include modifying the learning mechanism and/or the retrieval dynamics. They are not mutually exclusive.

Modifying the learning mechanism

If the low performance is due to the larger signal and noise of the distributed patterns one may try to depress their trace on the synaptic efficacies. We observe that the noise of M incoherent sources adds to a total value of order $\sqrt{M}$, while the signal adds coherently and therefore is of order M. It would thus be ideal to divide the corresponding term in eqn 16.1 by a factor proportional to M. When the different degrees of connectivity are taken into account, an exact calculation yields a dividing factor equal to $(C_{intra} + (M - 1)C_{inter})$. In this case the signals of distributed patterns and of isolated ones are equal, while the noise produced by the former is smaller.

Unfortunately, it is difficult to imagine how this ideal solution could be realized. Let us consider, for instance, the case where an old pattern is complemented with new information. The synaptic trace left by the original information must be depressed to compensate for the new association that perhaps involves other modules.

The only biologically inspired proposal specifically designed to balance basins of attraction is the so called *unlearning* mechanism. In its original version (Crick and Mitchison 1983) there was an explicit reference to the REM dream phase. In work by Hopfield *et al.* (1983) the mechanism was implemented in a neural network. The net effect was to decrease the interference between patterns and to increase the storage capacity. The idea that such a mechanism exists is attractive because of its automaticity. During the REM phase the system is supposed to be activated spontaneously, starting from a random configuration and evolving into an attractor. Once the latter is reached the synaptic couplings are modified following a rule similar to the one in eqn 16.1 but with the opposite sign. Larger attractors will be reached more often and therefore will be depressed more. Unlearning must stop at a certain moment otherwise all of the traces would disappear. The automatic tuning of this moment is problematic because it cannot depend on checking whether the goal of equal basins of attraction has been reached. A safe conclusion is that the difference between basins of attraction will be reduced but will not disappear.

In fact, there is independent evidence that the basins of attraction of different patterns do not become equal. The differential robustness against damage of certain categories and the existence of factors like *familiarity* (Funnell and Sheridan 1922) and *frequency* on the strength of a representation could not persist if that was not the case.

Modifying the retrieval dynamics

We now discuss the possibility of changing the parameters of the retrieval dynamics.

Redesigning the inhibition

Inhibition is supposed to be mediated by an independent class of neurons. In the model the inhibition term is proportional to the overall activity in the whole network. This could be improved in several ways. The most general case would be to substitute the unique constant γ with a matrix $\gamma(a,b)$ that would generate an inhibition effect in module a proportional to the activity in module b. To implement such a mechanism signals coming from other modules should remain sufficiently segregated so as to be independent inputs to different aggregates of inhibitory neurons. Surprisingly enough, there is partial evidence[4] that in the hippocampus the total external signal and the internal one: 1) project into different parts of the excitatory neurons; 2) are processed independently (in that different classes of inhibitory neurons control different parts of the dendrite). Reassured by this evidence, and in order to obtain the correct functioning of the hippocampus as an associative memory, Treves and Rolls (1994) have suggested a general principle that should govern the competition between signals of different origin: the external signal should be renormalized so that it is of the same order as the internal one. In this way the external system selects but does not deform the internal attractor.

This idea goes in the right direction, but does not solve the problem we face in the multimodular cortex. It treats external signals and external noise in the same way and in some cases it even amplifies the noise (we have observed this effect in the simulations). For instance, if a pattern activates modules A and B and is absent in the $M-2$ remaining modules, the external signal on A will mix the signal (and noise) from B plus the pure noise for the other $M-2$ modules. It is clear that renormalizing the total external signal will not have much effect on the signal to noise ratio. We believe that the mechanism is useful when the origin of the signal is essentially always the same.

Modulating intermodular synapses (or thresholds)

In a content addressable memory, retrieval uses input information to reconstruct the whole pattern. In the section on category-specific impairments we have identified a new type of information: the category to which the pattern belongs, defined as the set of coactive modules. It is natural to expect that such information can be used as input.

For this purpose we propose a mechanism that, on the basis of the category information, modulates the thresholds and/or the intermodule synapses. Its effect will be to depress the activity in the modules where the pattern is supposed to be absent and/or to disconnect them from the rest.

In the simulations we multiplied all the synaptic couplings that connect two given modules by a common factor (the R_{ab} in eqn 16.2) and simply reduced it to zero when needed. This mechanism reduces to zero the noise coming from inactive modules. It improves dramatically the efficiency of retrieval. Acting together with some form of unlearning the system reaches the optimal storage capacity.

As a by-product this mechanism could be useful in another task. It is well known that information stored in semantic memory (and in fact also in episodic memory) is *composite*: it can be decomposed into pieces that retain a meaning. The decomposition can be done in different ways and up to different depth levels and it stops if one reaches the 'atoms' of meaning. This *compositionality* of thinking is hard to implement in amorphous neural networks but acquires an interesting sense of reality with the existence of more or less independent modules. One part of a representation could be that information pertaining to a single module. As with the categorization process, this provides only a very partial implementation. However, to take advantage of it, that is to make it function, it is necessary that recall acts on the parts separately. We are therefore led again to the idea that turning on or off each module should be under control. This time it is clear that the control must be conscious. It is not the input information that triggers the modulation but rather the final goal.

This argument suggests that the modulation controlling centre is conscious and therefore operates serially. An immediate possible objection is that fast computation requires parallel and automatic processing because central processing is presumably slow (although more flexible). But this can be arranged if the fraction of the total information handled automatically is large enough so that the computing times spent by the parallel and the serial processes are the same. It is also reasonable to expect that only global variables, averages over large number of neurons, be under central control. The modulation we are discussing is of this type. The number of variables is very small and the spatial and time resolution large. Even a neuromodulator acting partially through diffusion could do the job.

On the implicit–explicit memory distinction and semantic priming

It is parsimonious to suppose a unique mechanism that both uses the information in the input about the category, and focuses the attention resources on pieces of the pattern to be retrieved.

In this case there is an interesting possibility to investigate experimentally our proposal because there are experimental paradigms that distinguish 'implicit' (synonym of unconscious) memory processes from explicit ones (see Rugg 1995). They have been identified in particular in the study of the 'priming' effect.

The semantic priming effect is the reduction in reaction time or error rate in reading or classifying word targets when preceded by semantically related instead of unrelated words. The effect is generally small (less than 40 ms) when compared with the related *identical word priming* but is clearly observable. It is suggested that current views abstract three possible mechanisms (Neely 1991): automatic spreading activation, an expectancy mechanism, and a postlexical semantic matching mechanism. According to Posner and Snyder (quoted in Neely 1991), spreading activation emanating from the priming word's node (a) can occur without a person's intention or awareness and (b) is fast acting. On the contrary, the expectancy (a) is under a person's strategic control and cannot occur without a person's intention or awareness and (b) is relatively slow. Our model incorporates naturally these two mechanisms. In addition, it predicts that unconscious spreading activation will work efficiently intramodularly while the intentional expectancy mechanism requires modulation.

In experiments it was observed that if the first word (prime) denoted a category (tools, body parts, building parts, birds, etc.), the subject could create an expectancy for individuals belonging to the same category or to a partner category. A category like 'tools' enters into the definition described earlier and our modulation mechanism immediately implements an expectancy component for it. But what about the other categories? We do not claim to implement every categorization process for all kinds of categories. Therefore the question remains open.

On the other hand, it would be extremely important to check whether the *category specificity* effect and the expectancy component are correlated; for instance, if more robust categories lead to larger semantic priming effects.

The manipulation of certain parameters (and also studies made on subjects with extensive damage to semantic memory) have confirmed that *identical word priming* or semantic priming with associate words (table and chair, cottage and cheese), both of which are mediated by the activation spreading mechanism, are present even when conscious recall is not possible (Chertkow *et al.* 1994). In these cases the efficiency of priming decreases significantly if prime and target words appear in different modalities (Schacter *et al.* 1993). This in fact confirms the above-mentioned prediction.

Conclusions

Through a careful analysis of the efficiency of retrieval we have arrived at the conclusion that purely automatic processing is not plausible. At a certain moment this type of processing must be complemented with some conscious, serial elaboration (see Bechtel 1995 for related issues). We would like to speculate that this is so also for other mental processes. Many problems that one has to solve require simultaneous analysis at decreasing levels of detail and at the same time larger contexts. This hierarchical picture lies far from the pure neural network with a single layer of complexity. Perhaps hierarchical trees with modules inside modules could be the answer.

In this first approach we have left aside important aspects of semantic memory. In particular, we have not considered the problem of *binding* which appears whenever the information is supposed to reach independent modules. In essence the problem can be formulated in the following way: in a scene there are both a red cube and a blue sphere. Assuming that the red and blue information is in the colour module while the sphere and cube information is in the shape module; where is the information that binds the sphere and the colour blue on one side and the cube and the colour red on the other? Starting from this question, von der Malsburg (Wang *et al.* 1990) has proposed a radical modification of the information encoding. His proposal requires fast modulation of synapses different for each single neuron. We have preferred not to attack this problem although we understand its relevance. We can imagine new modules that contain relational information but the need to tackle the combinatorial explosion would lead us to invoke external control mechanisms acting on hypothetical new modules.

Finally, we would like to stress that modular structures appear everywhere in the cortex. In all of these cases there will be external signals confronting internal ones. The mechanisms we have discussed in great detail suggest new lines of research. But, obviously, the right solution for semantic memory might not be adequate in other cases.

Acknowledgements

We are glad to acknowledge conversations with T. Shallice, D. Parisi, M.C. Silveri, D. Amit, and C. Burani.

Endnotes

[1] Hopfield obtained the (almost) right limit of capacity with just 100 neurons. One cannot expect to be so lucky in other cases.

[2] It is also possible that there are 'relay' modules that play some auxiliary role in the interconnection of the functionally defined ones. For the limited purposes of our arguments they would amount to a redefinition of the effective intermodule couplings. See, however, in the last section the discussion of the *binding* problem.

[3] To have an idea of the degree of the difference we quote the performance of patient J.B.R. (or S.B.Y.) who would make 94% (100%) errors upon trying to identify or name an object belonging to the category of the *living* and 10% (25%) when the object belonged to the category of the inanimate.

[4] E. Rolls, personal communication (Treves and Rolls 1994; Buhl *et al.* 1994).

References

Amit, D. (1989). *Modeling brain function*. Cambridge University Press.

Amit, D.J. and Brunel, N. (1995). Learning internal representations in an attractor neural network with analog neurons. *Network*, **6**, 359–94.

Anderson, P. (1972). More is different. *Science*, **177**, 393–4.

Bechtel, W. (1995). Consciousness: perspectives from symbolic and connectionist AI. *Neuropsychologia*, **33**, 1075–86.

Braitenberg, V. and Schuz, A. (1992). *Anatomy of the cortex*. Springer Verlag, Berlin.

Buhl, E.H., Halasy, K., and Somogyi, P. (1994). Diverse sources of hippocampal unitary inhibitory postsynaptic potentials and the number of synaptic release sites. *Nature*, **368**, 823–8.

Buhmann, J., Divko, R., and Schulten, K. (1989). Associative memory with high information content. *Physical Review A*, **39**, 2689–94.

Chertkow, H., Bub, D., Bergman, H., Bruemmer, A., Merling, A., and Rothfleisch, J. (1994). Increased semantic priming in patients with dementia of the Alzheimer's type. *Journal of Clinical and Experimental Neuropsychology*, **16**, 608–22.

Crick, F. and Mitchison, G. (1983). More is different. *Nature*, **304**, 111–4.

Damasio, A. and Damasio, H. (1993). Cortical systems underlying knowledge retrieval: evidence from human lesion studies. In *Exploring brain functions: models in neuroscience* (ed. T.A. Poggio and D.A. Glaser). Wiley, New York.

Farah, M.J. and McClelland, J.L. (1991). A computational model of semantic memory impairment: modality specificity and emergent category specificity. *Journal of Experimental Psychology: General*, **120**, 339–57.

Funnell, E. and Allport, A. (1987). Non-linguistic cognition and word meanings: neuropsychological exploration of common mechanisms. In *Language perception and production*, Chapter 17, pp. 367–400. Academic Press, London.

Funnell, E. and Sheridan, J. (1922). Categories of knowledge? Unfamiliar aspects of living and nonliving things. *Cognitive Neuropsychology*, **9**, 135–53.

Gardner, E. (1988). The space of interactions in neural networks. *Journal of Physics A: Mathematical, Nuclear and General*, **21**, 257–79.

Hebb, D.O. (1949). *The organization of behavior*. Wiley, New York.

Hinton, G. and Shallice, T. (1991). Lesioning an attractor network: investigation of acquired dyslexia. *Psychological Review*, **98**, 74–95.

Hopfield, J.J., Feinstein, D.I., and Palmer, R. (1983). Unlearning has a stabilizing effect in collective memories. *Nature*, **304**, 158–9.

Lauro-Grotto, R. (1993). Memoria semantica: funzione e disfunzione in un modello di reti neuronali (tesi di laurea). Technical report, Università di Roma *La Sapienza*, Facoltà di Scienze Matematiche, Fisiche e Naturali, Ple A. Moro 2, I-00185, Roma.

Moscovitch, M. and Umiltà, C. (1990). Modularity and neuropsychology: modules and central processes in attention and memory. In *Modular deficits in Alzheimer-type dementia* (ed. M.F. Schwartz), A Bradford Book. MIT Press, Boston.

Neely, J.H. (1991). Semantic priming effects in visual word recognition: a selective review of current findings and theories. In *Basic processes in reading and visual word recognition* (ed. D. Besner and G. Humphreys), pp. 207–48. Academic Press, New York.

Rugg, M.D. (1995). Memory and consciousness: a selective review of issues and data. *Neuropsychologia*, **33**, 1131–41.

Schacter, D.L., Chiu, C.P., and Ochsner, K. (1993). Implicit memory: a selective review. *Annual Review of Neuroscience*, **16**, 159–82.

Shallice, T. (1985). *From neuropsychology to mental structure*. Cambridge University Press.

Treves, A. and Rolls, E.T. (1992). Computational constraints suggest the need for two distinct input systems to the hippocampal ca3 network. *Hippocampus*, **2**,189–99.

Treves, A. and Rolls, E.T. (1994). A computational analysis of the role of the hippocampus in memory. *Hippocampus*, **4**, 374–91.

Wang, D., Buhmann, J., and von der Malsburg, C. (1990). Pattern segmentation in associative memory. *Neural Computation*, **2**, 94–106.

Warrington, E. and Shallice, T. (1984). Category specific impairments. *Brain*, **107**, 829–54.

Index